CIMA

Paper F1

Financial Operations

Study Text

WORKING TOGETHER FOR YOU

CIMA Publishing is an imprint of Elsevier
The Boulevard, Langford Lane, Kidlington, Oxford, OX5 1GB, UK
225 Wyman Street, Waltham, MA02451, USA
Kaplan Publishing UK, Unit 2 The Business Centre, Molly Millars Lane, Wokingham, Berkshire RG41 2QZ

Notice
No responsibility is assumed by the publisher for any injury and/or damage to persons or property as a matter of products liability, negligence or otherwise, or from any use or operation of any methods, products, instructions or ideas contained in the material herein.

British Library Cataloguing in Publication Data
A catalogue record for this book is available from the British Library

ISBN: 978-0-85732-461-0

Printed and bound in Great Britain

11 12 11 10 9 8 7 6 5 4 3 2 1

Contents

Page

Paper Introduction

How to Use the Materials

These Official CIMA learning materials brought to you by Elsevier/CIMA Publishing and Kaplan Publishing have been carefully designed to make your learning experience as easy as possible and to give you the best chances of success in your *'Financial Operations'* exam.

The product range contains a number of features to help you in the study process. They include:

- a detailed explanation of all syllabus areas;
- extensive 'practical' materials;
- generous question practice, together with full solutions;

This Study Text has been designed with the needs of home-study and distance-learning candidates in mind. Such students require very full coverage of the syllabus topics, and also the facility to undertake extensive question practice. However, the Study Text is also ideal for fully taught courses.

This main body of the text is divided into a number of chapters, each of which is organised on the following pattern:

- *Detailed learning outcomes* expected after your studies of the chapter are complete. You should assimilate these before beginning detailed work on the chapter, so that you can appreciate where your studies are leading.

- *Step-by-step topic coverage*. This is the heart of each chapter, containing detailed explanatory text supported where appropriate by worked examples and exercises. You should work carefully through this section, ensuring that you understand the material being explained and can tackle the examples and exercises successfully. Remember that in many cases knowledge is cumulative: if you fail to digest earlier material thoroughly, you may struggle to understand later chapters.

- *Activities*. Some chapters are illustrated by more practical elements, such as comments and questions designed to stimulate discussion.

- *Question practice*. The test of how well you have learned the material is your ability to tackle exam-standard questions. Make a serious attempt at producing your own answers, but at this stage do not be too concerned about attempting the questions in exam conditions. In particular, it is more important to absorb the material thoroughly by completing a full solution than to observe the time limits that would apply in the actual exam.

- *Solutions*. Avoid the temptation merely to 'audit' the solutions provided. It is an illusion to think that this provides the same benefits as you would gain from a serious attempt of your own. However, if you are struggling to get started on a question you should read the introductory guidance provided at the beginning of the solution, where provided, and then make your own attempt before referring back to the full solution.

If you work conscientiously through the official CIMA Study Text according to the guidelines above you will be giving yourself an excellent chance of success in your exam. Good luck with your studies!

Icon Explanations

 Definition - these sections explain important areas of knowledge which must be understood and reproduced in an exam environment.

 Key Point - identifies topics which are key to success and are often examined.

 Supplementary reading- indentifies a more detailed explanation of key terms, these sections will help to provide a deeper understanding of core areas. Reference to this text is vital when self studying.

 Test Your Understanding - following key points and definitions are exercises which give the opportunity to assess the understanding of these core areas.

 Illustration - to help develop an understanding of particular topics. The illustrative exercises are useful in preparing for the Test your understanding exercises.

 Exclamation Mark - this symbol signifies a topic which can be more difficult to understand, when reviewing these areas care should be taken.

Study technique

Passing exams is partly a matter of intellectual ability, but however accomplished you are in that respect you can improve your chances significantly by the use of appropriate study and revision techniques. In this section we briefly outline some tips for effective study during the earlier stages of your approach to the exam. Later in the text we mention some techniques that you will find useful at the revision stage.

Planning

To begin with, formal planning is essential to get the best return from the time you spend studying. Estimate how much time in total you are going to need for each subject you are studying for the Managerial Level. Remember that you need to allow time for revision as well as for initial study of the material. You may find it helpful to read "Pass First Time!" second edition by David R. Harris ISBN 978-1-85617-798-6. This book will provide you with proven study techniques. Chapter by chapter it covers the building blocks of successful learning and examination techniques. This is the ultimate guide to passing your CIMA exams, written by a past CIMA examiner and shows you how to earn all the marks you deserve, and explains how to avoid the most common pitfalls. You may also find "The E Word: Kaplan's Guide to Passing Exams" by Stuart Pedley-Smith ISBN: 978-0-85732-205-0 helpful. Stuart Pedley-Smith is a senior lecturer at Kaplan Financial and a qualified accountant specialising in financial management. His natural curiosity and wider interests have led him to look beyond the technical content of financial management to the processes and journey that we call education. He has become fascinated by the whole process of learning and the exam skills and techniques that contribute towards success in the classroom. This book is for anyone who has to sit an exam and wants to give themselves a better chance of passing. It is easy to read, written in a common sense style and full of anecdotes, facts, and practical tips. It also contains synopses of interviews with people involved in the learning and examining process.

With your study material before you, decide which chapters you are going to study in each week, and which weeks you will devote to revision and final question practice.

Prepare a written schedule summarising the above and stick to it!

It is essential to know your syllabus. As your studies progress you will become more familiar with how long it takes to cover topics in sufficient depth. Your timetable may need to be adapted to allocate enough time for the whole syllabus.

Students are advised to refer to the notice of examinable legislation published regularly in CIMA's magazine (Financial Management), the students e-newsletter (Velocity) and on the CIMA website, to ensure they are up-to-date.

Tips for effective studying

(1) Aim to find a quiet and undisturbed location for your study, and plan as far as possible to use the same period of time each day. Getting into a routine helps to avoid wasting time. Make sure that you have all the materials you need before you begin so as to minimise interruptions.

(2) Store all your materials in one place, so that you do not waste time searching for items around your accommodation. If you have to pack everything away after each study period, keep them in a box, or even a suitcase, which will not be disturbed until the next time.

(3) Limit distractions. To make the most effective use of your study periods you should be able to apply total concentration, so turn off all entertainment equipment, set your phones to message mode, and put up your 'do not disturb' sign.

(4) Your timetable will tell you which topic to study. However, before diving in and becoming engrossed in the finer points, make sure you have an overall picture of all the areas that need to be covered by the end of that session. After an hour, allow yourself a short break and move away from your Study Text. With experience, you will learn to assess the pace you need to work at.

(5) Work carefully through a chapter, making notes as you go. When you have covered a suitable amount of material, vary the pattern by attempting a practice question. When you have finished your attempt, make notes of any mistakes you made, or any areas that you failed to cover or covered more briefly.

(6) Make notes as you study, and discover the techniques that work best for you. Your notes may be in the form of lists, bullet points, diagrams, summaries, 'mind maps', or the written word, but remember that you will need to refer back to them at a later date, so they must be intelligible. If you are on a taught course, make sure you highlight any issues you would like to follow up with your lecturer.

(7) Organise your notes. Make sure that all your notes, calculations etc can be effectively filed and easily retrieved later.

Structure of subjects and learning outcomes

Each subject within the syllabus is divided into a number of broad syllabus topics. The topics contain one or more lead learning outcomes, related component learning outcomes and indicative knowledge content.

A learning outcome has two main purposes:

(a) To define the skill or ability that a well prepared candidate should be able to exhibit in the examination

(b) To demonstrate the approach likely to be taken in examination questions

The learning outcomes are part of a hierarchy of learning objectives. The verbs used at the beginning of each learning outcome relate to a specific learning objective e.g.

Calculate the break-even point, profit target, margin of safety and profit/volume ratio for a single product or service

The verb **'calculate'** indicates a level three learning objective. The following table lists the learning objectives and the verbs that appear in the syllabus learning outcomes and examination questions.

PAPER F1
FINANCIAL OPERATIONS

Syllabus overview

The core objectives of Paper F1 are the preparation of the full financial statements for a single company and the principal consolidated financial statements for a simple group. Coverage of a wide range of international standards is implicit in these objectives, as specified in the paper's content.

Similarly, understanding the regulatory and ethical context of financial reporting, covered in the paper, is vital to ensuring that financial statements meet users' needs. Principles of taxation are included, not only to support accounting for taxes in financial statements, but also as a basis for examining the role of tax in financial analysis and decision-making within subsequent papers (Paper F2 Financial Management and Paper F3 Financial Strategy).

Syllabus structure

The syllabus comprises the following topics and study weightings:

A	Principles of Business Taxation	25%
B	Regulation and Ethics of Financial Reporting	15%
C	Financial Accounting and Reporting	60%

Assessment strategy

There will be a written examination paper of three hours, plus 20 minutes of pre-examination question paper reading time. The examination paper will have the following sections:

Section A – 20 marks
A variety of compulsory objective test questions, each worth between two and four marks. Mini scenarios may be given, to which a group of questions relate.

Section B – 30 marks
Six compulsory short answer questions, each worth five marks. A short scenario may be given, to which some or all questions relate.

Section C – 50 marks
One or two compulsory questions. Short scenarios may be given, to which questions relate.

F1 – A. PRINCIPLES OF BUSINESS TAXATION (25%)

Learning outcomes
On completion of their studies students should be able to:

Lead	Component	Indicative syllabus content
1. explain the types of tax that can apply to incorporated businesses, their principles and potential administrative requirements.	(a) identify the principal types of taxation likely to be of relevance to an incorporated business in a particular country; (b) describe the features of the principal types of taxation likely to be of relevance to an incorporated business in a particular country; (c) explain key administrative requirements and the possible enquiry and investigation powers of taxing authorities associated with the principal types of taxation likely to be of relevance to an incorporated business; (d) explain the difference in principle between tax avoidance and tax evasion; (e) illustrate numerically the principles of different types of tax based on provided information.	• Concepts of direct versus indirect taxes, taxable person and competent jurisdiction. • Types of taxation, including direct tax on the company's trading profits and capital gains, indirect taxes collected by the company, employee taxation and withholding taxes on international payments, and their features (e.g. in terms of who ultimately bears the tax cost, withholding responsibilities, principles of calculating the tax base). • Sources of tax rules (e.g. domestic primary legislation and court rulings, practice of the relevant taxing authority, supranational bodies, such as the EU in the case of value added/sales tax, and international tax treaties). • Indirect taxes collected by the company: – in the context of indirect taxes, the distinction between unit taxes (e.g. excise duties based on physical measures) and ad valorem taxes (e.g. sales tax based on value); – the mechanism of value added/sales taxes, in which businesses are liable for tax on their outputs less credits for tax paid on their inputs, including the concepts of exemption and variation in tax rates depending on the type of output and disallowance of input credits for exempt outputs. • Employee taxation: – the employee as a separate taxable person subject to a personal income tax regime; – use of employer reporting and withholding to ensure compliance and assist tax collection. • The need for record-keeping and record retention that may be additional to that required for financial accounting purposes. • The need for deadlines for reporting (filing returns) and tax payments.

Learning outcomes
On completion of their studies students should be able to:

Lead	Component	Indicative syllabus content

		• Types of powers of tax authorities to ensure compliance with tax rules:
		  – power to review and query filed returns;
		  – power to request special reports or returns;
		  – power to examine records (generally extending back some years);
		  – powers of entry and search;
		  – exchange of information with tax authorities in other jurisdictions.
		• The distinction between tax avoidance and tax evasion, and how these vary among jurisdictions (including the difference between the use of statutory general anti-avoidance provisions and case law based regimes).

2. explain fundamental concepts in international taxation of incorporated businesses.	(a) identify situations in which foreign tax obligations (reporting and liability) could arise and methods for relieving foreign tax;
	
	(b) explain sources of tax rules and the importance of jurisdiction.
		• International taxation:
		  – the concept of corporate residence and the variation in rules for its determination across jurisdictions (e.g. place of incorporation versus place of management);
		  – types of payments on which withholding tax may be required (especially interest, dividends, royalties and capital gains accruing to non-residents);
		  – means of establishing a taxable presence in another country (local company and branch);
		  – the effect of double tax treaties (based on the OECD Model Convention) on the above (e.g. reduction of withholding tax rates, provisions for defining a permanent establishment).

Lead	Component	Indicative syllabus content
3. prepare corporate income tax calculations.	(a) prepare corporate income tax calculations based on a given simple set of rules.	• Direct taxes on company profits and gains: – the principle of non-deductibility of dividends and systems of taxation defined according to the treatment of dividends in the hands of the shareholder (e.g. classical, partial imputation and imputation); – the distinction between accounting and taxable profits in absolute terms (e.g. disallowable expenditure on revenue account, such as entertaining, and on capital account, such as formation and acquisition costs) and in terms of timing (e.g. deduction on a paid basis); – the concept of tax depreciation replacing book depreciation in the tax computation and its calculation based on the pooling of assets by their classes, including balancing adjustments on the disposal of assets; – the nature of rules recharacterising interest payments as dividends (e.g. where interest is based on profitability); – potential for variation in rules for calculating the tax base dependent on the nature or source of the income (scheduler systems); – the need for rules dealing with the relief of losses; – principles of relief for foreign taxes by exemption, deduction and credit. – the concept of tax consolidation (e.g. for relief of losses and deferral of capital gains on asset transfers within a group).
4. apply the accounting rules for current and deferred taxation.	(a) apply the accounting rules for current and deferred taxation, including calculation of deferred tax based on a given set of rules.	• Accounting treatment of taxation and disclosure requirements under IAS 12.

F1 – B. REGULATION AND ETHICS OF FINANCIAL REPORTING (15%)

Learning outcomes
On completion of their studies students should be able to:

Lead	Component	Indicative syllabus content
1. explain the need for and methods of regulating accounting and financial reporting.	(a) explain the need for regulation of published accounts and the concept that regulatory regimes vary from country to country; (b) explain potential elements that might be expected in a national regulatory framework for published accounts; (c) describe the role and structure of the International Accounting Standards Board (IASB) and the International Organisation of Securities Commissions (IOSCO); (d) explain the meaning of given features or parts of the IASB's Framework for the Presentation and Preparation of Financial Statements; (e) describe the process leading to the promulgation of an IFRS; (f) describe ways in which IFRSs can interact with local regulatory frameworks; (g) explain in general terms, the role of the external auditor, the elements of the audit report and types of qualification of that report.	• The need for regulation of accounts. • Elements in a regulatory framework for published accounts (e.g. company law, local GAAP, review of accounts by public bodies). • GAAP based on prescriptive versus principles-based standards. • The role and structure of the IASB and IOSCO. • The IASB's Framework for the Presentation and Preparation of Financial Statements. • The process leading to the promulgation of a standard practice. • Ways in which IFRSs are used: adoption as local GAAP, model for local GAAP, persuasive influence in formulating local GAAP. • The powers and duties of the external auditors, the audit report and its qualification for accounting statements not in accordance with best practice.
2. apply the provisions of the CIMA Code of Ethics for Professional Accountants.	(a) explain the importance of the exercise of ethical principles in reporting and assessing information; (b) describe the sources of ethical codes for those involved in the reporting or taxation affairs of an organisation, including the external auditors; (c) apply the provisions of the CIMA Code of Ethics for Professional Accountants of particular relevance to the information reporting, assurance and tax-related activities of the accountant.	• Ethical requirements of the professional accountant in reporting and assessing information (the fundamental principles). • Sources of ethical codes (IFAC, professional bodies, employing organisations, social/religious/personal sources). • Provisions of the CIMA Code of Ethics for Professional Accountants of particular relevance to information reporting, assurance and tax-related activities (especially section 220 and Part C).

F1 – C. FINANCIAL ACCOUNTING AND REPORTING (60%)

Learning outcomes
On completion of their studies students should be able to:

Lead	Component	Indicative syllabus content
1. prepare the full financial statements of a single company and the consolidated statements of financial position and comprehensive income for a group (in relatively straightforward circumstances).	(a) prepare a complete set of financial statements, in a form suitable for publication for a single company; (b) apply the conditions required for an undertaking to be a subsidiary or an associate of another company; (c) prepare the consolidated statement of financial position (balance sheet) and statement of comprehensive income for a group of companies in a form suitable for publication for a group of companies comprising directly held interests in one or more fully-controlled subsidiaries and associates (such interests having been acquired at the beginning of an accounting period); (d) apply the concepts of fair value at the point of acquisition, identifiability of assets and liabilities, and recognition of goodwill.	• Preparation of the financial statements of a single company, as specified in IAS 1 (revised), including the statement of changes in equity. • Preparation of the statement of cash flows (IAS 7). • Preparation of the consolidated statement of financial position (balance sheet) and statement of comprehensive income where: interests are directly held by the acquirer (parent company; any subsidiary is fully controlled; and all interests were acquired at the beginning of an accounting period. (IFRS 3 and IAS 27, to the extent that their provisions are relevant to the specified learning outcomes).
2. apply international standards dealing with a range of matters and items.	(a) apply the accounting rules contained in IFRSs and IASs dealing with reporting performance, non-current assets, including their impairment, inventories, disclosure of related parties to a business, construction contracts (and related financing costs), post-balance sheet events, provisions, contingencies, and leases (lessee only); (b) explain the accounting rules contained in IFRSs and IASs governing share capital transactions. .	• Reporting performance: recognition of revenue, measurement of profit or loss, prior period items, discontinuing operations and segment reporting (IAS 1(revised), 8 and 18, IFRS 5 and 8). • Property, Plant and Equipment (IAS 16): the calculation of depreciation and the effect of revaluations, changes to economic useful life, repairs, improvements and disposals. • Research and development costs (IAS 38): criteria for capitalisation. • Intangible Assets (IAS 38) and goodwill: recognition, valuation, amortisation. • Impairment of Assets (IAS 36) and Non-Current Assets Held for Sale (IFRS 5) and their effects on the above. • Inventories (IAS 2). • The disclosure of related parties to a business (IAS 24).

Learning outcomes
On completion of their studies students should be able to:

Lead	Component	Indicative syllabus content
		• Construction contracts and related financing costs (IAS 11 and 23): determination of cost, net realisable value, the inclusion of overheads and the measurement of profit on uncompleted contracts.
		• Post-balance sheet events (IAS 10).
		• Provisions and contingencies (IAS 37).
		• Leases (IAS 17) – distinguishing operating from finance leases and the concept of substance over form (from the Framework); accounting for leases in the books of the lessee.
		• Issue and redemption of shares, including treatment of share issue and redemption costs (IAS 32 and 39), the share premium account, the accounting for maintenance of capital arising from the purchase by a company of its own shares.

MATHS TABLES AND FORMULAE

Present value table

Present value of $1, that is $(1 + r)^{-n}$ where r = interest rate; n = number of periods until payment or receipt.

Periods (n)	Interest rates (r)									
	1%	2%	3%	4%	5%	6%	7%	8%	9%	10%
1	0.990	0.980	0.971	0.962	0.952	0.943	0.935	0.926	0.917	0.909
2	0.980	0.961	0.943	0.925	0.907	0.890	0.873	0.857	0.842	0.826
3	0.971	0.942	0.915	0.889	0.864	0.840	0.816	0.794	0.772	0.751
4	0.961	0.924	0.888	0.855	0.823	0.792	0.763	0.735	0.708	0.683
5	0.951	0.906	0.863	0.822	0.784	0.747	0.713	0.681	0.650	0.621
6	0.942	0.888	0.837	0.790	0.746	0.705	0.666	0.630	0.596	0.564
7	0.933	0.871	0.813	0.760	0.711	0.665	0.623	0.583	0.547	0.513
8	0.923	0.853	0.789	0.731	0.677	0.627	0.582	0.540	0.502	0.467
9	0.914	0.837	0.766	0.703	0.645	0.592	0.544	0.500	0.460	0.424
10	0.905	0.820	0.744	0.676	0.614	0.558	0.508	0.463	0.422	0.386
11	0.896	0.804	0.722	0.650	0.585	0.527	0.475	0.429	0.388	0.350
12	0.887	0.788	0.701	0.625	0.557	0.497	0.444	0.397	0.356	0.319
13	0.879	0.773	0.681	0.601	0.530	0.469	0.415	0.368	0.326	0.290
14	0.870	0.758	0.661	0.577	0.505	0.442	0.388	0.340	0.299	0.263
15	0.861	0.743	0.642	0.555	0.481	0.417	0.362	0.315	0.275	0.239
16	0.853	0.728	0.623	0.534	0.458	0.394	0.339	0.292	0.252	0.218
17	0.844	0.714	0.605	0.513	0.436	0.371	0.317	0.270	0.231	0.198
18	0.836	0.700	0.587	0.494	0.416	0.350	0.296	0.250	0.212	0.180
19	0.828	0.686	0.570	0.475	0.396	0.331	0.277	0.232	0.194	0.164
20	0.820	0.673	0.554	0.456	0.377	0.312	0.258	0.215	0.178	0.149

Periods (n)	Interest rates (r)									
	11%	12%	13%	14%	15%	16%	17%	18%	19%	20%
1	0.901	0.893	0.885	0.877	0.870	0.862	0.855	0.847	0.840	0.833
2	0.812	0.797	0.783	0.769	0.756	0.743	0.731	0.718	0.706	0.694
3	0.731	0.712	0.693	0.675	0.658	0.641	0.624	0.609	0.593	0.579
4	0.659	0.636	0.613	0.592	0.572	0.552	0.534	0.516	0.499	0.482
5	0.593	0.567	0.543	0.519	0.497	0.476	0.456	0.437	0.419	0.402
6	0.535	0.507	0.480	0.456	0.432	0.410	0.390	0.370	0.352	0.335
7	0.482	0.452	0.425	0.400	0.376	0.354	0.333	0.314	0.296	0.279
8	0.434	0.404	0.376	0.351	0.327	0.305	0.285	0.266	0.249	0.233
9	0.391	0.361	0.333	0.308	0.284	0.263	0.243	0.225	0.209	0.194
10	0.352	0.322	0.295	0.270	0.247	0.227	0.208	0.191	0.176	0.162
11	0.317	0.287	0.261	0.237	0.215	0.195	0.178	0.162	0.148	0.135
12	0.286	0.257	0.231	0.208	0.187	0.168	0.152	0.137	0.124	0.112
13	0.258	0.229	0.204	0.182	0.163	0.145	0.130	0.116	0.104	0.093
14	0.232	0.205	0.181	0.160	0.141	0.125	0.111	0.099	0.088	0.078
15	0.209	0.183	0.160	0.140	0.123	0.108	0.095	0.084	0.079	0.065
16	0.188	0.163	0.141	0.123	0.107	0.093	0.081	0.071	0.062	0.054
17	0.170	0.146	0.125	0.108	0.093	0.080	0.069	0.060	0.052	0.045
18	0.153	0.130	0.111	0.095	0.081	0.069	0.059	0.051	0.044	0.038
19	0.138	0.116	0.098	0.083	0.070	0.060	0.051	0.043	0.037	0.031
20	0.124	0.104	0.087	0.073	0.061	0.051	0.043	0.037	0.031	0.026

Cumulative present value of $1 per annum, Receivable or Payable at the end of each year for n years

$$\frac{1-(1+r)^{-n}}{r}$$

Periods (n)	Interest rates (r)									
	1%	2%	3%	4%	5%	6%	7%	8%	9%	10%
1	0.990	0.980	0.971	0.962	0.952	0.943	0.935	0.926	0.917	0.909
2	1.970	1.942	1.913	1.886	1.859	1.833	1.808	1.783	1.759	1.736
3	2.941	2.884	2.829	2.775	2.723	2.673	2.624	2.577	2.531	2.487
4	3.902	3.808	3.717	3.630	3.546	3.465	3.387	3.312	3.240	3.170
5	4.853	4.713	4.580	4.452	4.329	4.212	4.100	3.993	3.890	3.791
6	5.795	5.601	5.417	5.242	5.076	4.917	4.767	4.623	4.486	4.355
7	6.728	6.472	6.230	6.002	5.786	5.582	5.389	5.206	5.033	4.868
8	7.652	7.325	7.020	6.733	6.463	6.210	5.971	5.747	5.535	5.335
9	8.566	8.162	7.786	7.435	7.108	6.802	6.515	6.247	5.995	5.759
10	9.471	8.983	8.530	8.111	7.722	7.360	7.024	6.710	6.418	6.145
11	10.368	9.787	9.253	8.760	8.306	7.887	7.499	7.139	6.805	6.495
12	11.255	10.575	9.954	9.385	8.863	8.384	7.943	7.536	7.161	6.814
13	12.134	11.348	10.635	9.986	9.394	8.853	8.358	7.904	7.487	7.103
14	13.004	12.106	11.296	10.563	9.899	9.295	8.745	8.244	7.786	7.367
15	13.865	12.849	11.938	11.118	10.380	9.712	9.108	8.559	8.061	7.606
16	14.718	13.578	12.561	11.652	10.838	10.106	9.447	8.851	8.313	7.824
17	15.562	14.292	13.166	12.166	11.274	10.477	9.763	9.122	8.544	8.022
18	16.398	14.992	13.754	12.659	11.690	10.828	10.059	9.372	8.756	8.201
19	17.226	15.679	14.324	13.134	12.085	11.158	10.336	9.604	8.950	8.365
20	18.046	16.351	14.878	13.590	12.462	11.470	10.594	9.818	9.129	8.514

Periods (n)	Interest rates (r)									
	11%	12%	13%	14%	15%	16%	17%	18%	19%	20%
1	0.901	0.893	0.885	0.877	0.870	0.862	0.855	0.847	0.840	0.833
2	1.713	1.690	1.668	1.647	1.626	1.605	1.585	1.566	1.547	1.528
3	2.444	2.402	2.361	2.322	2.283	2.246	2.210	2.174	2.140	2.106
4	3.102	3.037	2.974	2.914	2.855	2.798	2.743	2.690	2.639	2.589
5	3.696	3.605	3.517	3.433	3.352	3.274	3.199	3.127	3.058	2.991
6	4.231	4.111	3.998	3.889	3.784	3.685	3.589	3.498	3.410	3.326
7	4.712	4.564	4.423	4.288	4.160	4.039	3.922	3.812	3.706	3.605
8	5.146	4.968	4.799	4.639	4.487	4.344	4.207	4.078	3.954	3.837
9	5.537	5.328	5.132	4.946	4.772	4.607	4.451	4.303	4.163	4.031
10	5.889	5.650	5.426	5.216	5.019	4.833	4.659	4.494	4.339	4.192
11	6.207	5.938	5.687	5.453	5.234	5.029	4.836	4.656	4.486	4.327
12	6.492	6.194	5.918	5.660	5.421	5.197	4.988	7.793	4.611	4.439
13	6.750	6.424	6.122	5.842	5.583	5.342	5.118	4.910	4.715	4.533
14	6.982	6.628	6.302	6.002	5.724	5.468	5.229	5.008	4.802	4.611
15	7.191	6.811	6.462	6.142	5.847	5.575	5.324	5.092	4.876	4.675
16	7.379	6.974	6.604	6.265	5.954	5.668	5.405	5.162	4.938	4.730
17	7.549	7.120	6.729	6.373	6.047	5.749	5.475	5.222	4.990	4.775
18	7.702	7.250	6.840	6.467	6.128	5.818	5.534	5.273	5.033	4.812
19	7.839	7.366	6.938	6.550	6.198	5.877	5.584	5.316	5.070	4.843
20	7.963	7.469	7.025	6.623	6.259	5.929	5.628	5.353	5.101	4.870

FORMULAE

Annuity

Present value of an annuity of $1 per annum, receivable or payable for n years, commencing in one year, discounted at $r\%$ per annum:

$$PV = \frac{1}{r}\left[1 - \frac{1}{[1+r]^n}\right]$$

Perpetuity

Present value of $1 per annum, payable or receivable in perpetuity, commencing in one year, discounted at $r\%$ per annum:

$$PV = \frac{1}{r}$$

CIMA Verb Hierarchy – operational level exams

Chapter learning objectives

CIMA VERB HIERARCHY

CIMA place great importance on the choice of verbs in exam question requirements. It is thus critical that you answer the question according to the definition of the verb used.

1 Operational level verbs

In operational level exams you will meet verbs from levels 1, 2, and 3. These are as follows:

Level 1: KNOWLEDGE

What you are expected to know

VERBS USED	DEFINITION
List	Make a list of
State	Express, fully or clearly, the details of/facts of
Define	Give the exact meaning of

Level 2: COMPREHENSION

What you are expected to understand

VERBS USED	DEFINITION
Describe	Communicate the key features of
Distinguish	Highlight the differences between
Explain	Make clear or intelligible/state the meaning or purpose of
Identify	Recognise, establish, or select after consideration
Illustrate	Use an example to describe or explain something

Level 3: APPLICATION

How you are expected to apply your knowledge

VERBS USED	DEFINITION
Apply	Put to practical use
Calculate	Ascertain or reckon mathematically
Demonstrate	Prove with certainty or exhibit by practical means
Prepare	Make or get ready for use
Reconcile	Make or prove consistent/compatible
Solve	Find an answer to
Tabulate	Arrange in a table

2 Further guidance on operational level verbs that cause confusion

Verbs that cause students confusion at this level are as follows:

Level 2 verbs

- **The difference between "describe" and "explain".**

   An explanation is a set of statements constructed to describe a set of facts which clarifies the **causes**, **context**, and **consequences** of those facts.

   For example, if asked to **describe** the features of activity based costing (ABC) you could talk, amongst other things, about how costs are grouped into cost pools (e.g. quality control), cost drivers identified (e.g. number of inspections) and an absorption rate calculated based on this cost driver (e.g. cost per inspection). This tells us what ABC looks like.

   However if asked to **explain** ABC, then you would have to talk about why firms were dissatisfied with previous traditional costing methods and switched to ABC (causes), what types of firms it is more suitable for (context) and the implications for firms (consequences) in terms of the usefulness of such costs per unit for pricing and costing.

   More simply, to describe something is to answer "what" type questions whereas to explain looks at "what" and "why" aspects.

- **The verb "to illustrate"**

The key thing about illustrating something is that you may have to decide on a relevant example to use. This could involve drawing a diagram, performing supporting calculations or highlighting a feature or person in the scenario given. Most of the time the question will be structured so calculations performed in part (a) can be used to illustrate a concept in part (b).

For example, you could be asked to explain and illustrate what is meant by an "adverse variance".

Level 3 verbs

- **The verb "to apply"**

Given that all level 3 verbs involve application, the verb "apply" is rare in the real exam. Instead one of the other more specific verbs is used instead.

- **The verb "to reconcile"**

This is a numerical requirement and usually involves starting with one of the figures, adjusting it and ending up with the other.

For example, in a bank reconciliation you start with the recorded cash at bank figure, adjust it for unpresented cheques, etc, and (hopefully!) end up with the stated balance in the cash "T account".

- **The verb "to demonstrate"**

The verb "to demonstrate" can be used in two main ways.

Firstly, it could mean to prove that a given statement is true or consistent with circumstances given. For example, the Finance Director may have stated in the question that the company will not exceed its overdraft limit in the next six months. The requirement then asks you to demonstrate that the Director is wrong. You could do this by preparing a cash flow forecast for the next six months.

Secondly, you could be asked to demonstrate **how** a stated model, framework, technique or theory could be used in the particular scenario. Ensure you do not merely describe the model but use it to generate some results.

Principles of Business Taxation

Chapter learning objectives

- Identify the principal types of taxation likely to be of relevance to an incorporated business in a particular country, including direct tax on the company's trading profits and capital gains, indirect taxes collected by the company, employee taxation, withholding taxes on international payments.

- Describe the features of the principal types of taxation likely to be of relevance to an incorporated business in a particular country (e.g. in terms of who ultimately bears the tax cost, withholding responsibilities, principles of calculating the tax base).

- Describe the likely record-keeping, filing and tax payment requirements associated with the principal types of taxation likely to be of relevance to an incorporated business in a particular country.

- The need for deadlines for reporting (filing returns) and tax payments.

- Describe the possible enquiry and investigation powers of taxing authorities to ensure compliance with tax rules.

- Identify situations in which foreign tax obligations (reporting and liability) could arise and methods for relieving foreign tax.

- Explain the difference in principle between tax avoidance and tax evasion.

- Describe sources of tax rules and explain the importance of jurisdiction.

- Prepare corporate income tax calculations based on a given set of rules.

1 Session content

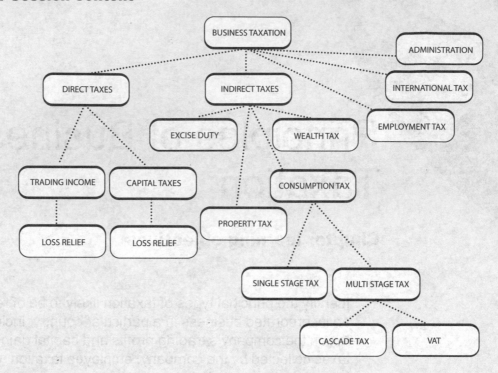

2 Introduction

Principles of business tax are based on a benchmark tax regime (e.g. UK, USA, etc.) The Government needs tax revenues to finance expenditure such as the Health Service, Retirement Pensions, Social Benefits and to finance Government borrowing. The Government will use tax to stimulate one sector of the economy and control another. For example, allowances on capital expenditure may develop the manufacturing sector, while high taxes on tobacco and alcohol may discourage sales.

In *Wealth of Nations*, Adam Smith proposed that a good tax should have the following characteristics:

- fair (reflect person's ability to pay);
- absolute (certain not arbitrary);
- convenient (easy to pay);
- efficient (low collection costs).

The 3 major principles of good tax policy are as follows:

- equity - A good tax should be fairly levied between one taxpayer and another.
- efficiency - A good tax should be cheap and easy to collect, i.e. UK tax system uses the PAYE (pay-as-you-earn) to collect tax at source on salaries and wages.

- economic effects - A good tax should consider the way in which a tax should be collected.

What is a good tax?

The American Institution of Certified Public Accountants lists the following principles that a good tax policy should have:

- equity and fairness
- transparency and visibility
- certainty
- economy in collection
- convenience of payment
- simplicity
- appropriate government revenues (determining the amount of tax revenues and date of collection)
- minimum tax gap (the difference between actual collection and amount due)
- neutrality
- economic growth and efficiency

It is not always possible to incorporate all ten into a tax system.

Definition of terms

A tax is either a direct or indirect tax.

Direct taxes

These are imposed directly on the person or enterprise required to pay the tax, i.e. tax on personal income such as salaries, tax on business profits or tax on disposals of chargeable assets. The person or enterprise must pay the tax directly to the tax authorities on their income. Examples in the UK of direct taxes would be income tax, capital gains tax or corporation tax.

Indirect taxes

This tax is imposed on one part of the economy with the intention that the tax burden is passed on to another. The tax is imposed on the final consumer of the goods or services. The more the consumer consumes the greater the tax paid. An example in the UK of indirect tax would be VAT.

Incidence

The incidence of a tax is the distribution of the tax burden, i.e. who is paying the tax.

What is incidence?

Incidence

This can be split into two elements:

(1) **Formal incidence:** this is the person who has direct contact with the tax authorities, i.e. who is legally obliged to pay the tax.

(2) **Actual Incidence:** this is the person who actually ends up bearing the cost of the tax, i.e. who actually bears the burden of the tax.

If we consider VAT - the formal incidence would be the entity making the sale because they will be responsible for making the payment to the relevant tax authorities. The actual incidence would be the consumer who bears the cost of the tax when they make a purchase from the entity.

Taxable person

The person accountable for the tax payment, e.g. individual or company

Competent jurisdiction

A taxable person normally pays tax in the country of origin. Competent jurisdiction is the tax authority that has the legal power to assess and collect the taxes. This is usually the combined responsibility of the central government and local authorities within a country. The tax law is enforceable by sanction (fines or imprisonment).

Hypothecation

This means that certain taxes are devoted entirely to certain types of expenditure, e.g. road tax is used entirely on maintaining roads, London congestion charge is used to pay for transport in the capital.

Tax gap

This is the gap between the tax theoretically collectable and the amount actually collected. The tax authorities will aim to minimise this gap.

Tax rate structure

There are three types of taxes:

(1) **Progressive taxes:** These take an increasing proportion of income as income rises. (E.g. UK Income tax – 20%, 40%, 50%).

(2) **Proportional taxes:** These take the same proportion of income as income rises.

(3) **Regressive taxes:** These take a decreasing proportion of income as income rises. (E.g. UK National Insurance contributions – 11% then 1%).

Tax rate structure

Progressive tax means the proportion of tax increases as income increases, i.e. salary $10,000 pays tax of $1,000 = 10% but a salary of $20,000 pays tax of $3,000 = 15%.

Proportionate tax means the proportion of tax remains the same, regardless of the level of income, i.e. salary $10,000 pays tax of $1,000 = 10% and a salary of $20,000 pays tax of $2,000 = 10%.

Regressive tax means the proportion of tax reduces as income increases, i.e. salary $10,000 pays tax of $1,000 = 10% but a salary of $20,000 pays tax of $1,800 = 9%.

Source of tax rules

The sources of tax rules are as follows:

- Legislation produced by a national government of the country, e.g. Finance Acts in the UK.

- Precedents based on previous legislation. Tax authorities also issue interpretations, e.g. Tax bulletins in the UK.

- Directives from international bodies such as European Union guidelines on VAT.

- Agreements between different countries such as double tax treaties, e.g. UK/US Double tax treaties.

Income can be taxed twice

Foreign income is often taxed twice, once in the country of origin and once in the country of residency. In order to avoid this "double taxation", countries enter into tax treaties which will decide which country gets to tax the income, e.g. withholding tax.

Tax base

Taxes are classified according to their tax base (what is being taxed).

- Income or profits – e.g. Income and Corporation tax in the UK
- Assets – e.g. Capital gains tax in the UK
- Consumption – e.g. Sales tax in the UK

Most countries separate different types of income into categories and have a set of rules to determine how that income will be taxed. This may be called a "schedular system".

The schedular system

A schedular system puts similar income into categories and then applies a set of rules to each particular type of income, for example:

- Property business income
- Trading profit
- Interest income

This ensures each type of income is taxed correctly when completing the tax return.

3 Direct taxes

There are two types of direct tax you need to consider:

Trading income

Trading income is income from the main business activity.

The tax base is profits.

The accounting profit needs to be adjusted for tax purposes as in many countries there are differences between what the accounting standards allow you to show as an income/expense and what the tax system deems to be the income/expense. These adjusted profits will enable you to calculate the taxable profit.

The standard proforma is as follows:

	$
Accounting profit	X
Less: income exempt from tax or taxed under other rules	(X)
Add: disallowable expenses	X
Add: depreciation	X
Less: tax depreciation	(X)
Taxable profit	X

The taxable profit will then be charged at the appropriate tax rate for that accounting period.

The rules for allowed and disallowed items will vary according to the tax regime of the country in question. This will always be given by the examiner. The tax rules are also released on the CIMA website prior to the exam on:

www.cimaglobal.com/Students/2010-professional-qualification/Operational-level/F1-study-resources/

The tax rules will be given in the following format:

COUNTRY Y - TAX REGIME FOR USE THROUGHOUT THE EXAMINATION PAPER
Relevant Tax Rules for the years ended 31 March 20X0 to 20X1
Corporate Profits

Unless otherwise specified, only the following rules for taxation of corporate profits will be relevant, other taxes can be ignored:

- Accounting rules on recognition and measurement are followed for tax purposes.

- All expenses other than depreciation, amortisation, entertaining, taxes paid to other public bodies and donations to political parties are tax deductable.

- Tax depreciation is deductable as follows: 50% of additions to Property, Plant and Equipment in the accounting period in which they are recorded; 25% per year of the written-down value (i.e. cost minus previous allowances) in subsequent accounting periods except that in which the asset is disposed of. No tax depreciation is allowed on land.

- The corporate tax on profit is at a rate of 25%.

- Tax losses can be carried forward to offset against future taxable profits from the same business.

Value Added Tax

Country Y has a VAT system which allows entities to reclaim input tax paid. In Country Y the VAT rates are:

Zero rated 0%

Standard rated 15%

Calculation of the trading profit

The **accounting profit** is the profit shown in financial statements before taxation.

Income exempt from tax or taxed under other rules is any income included in the accounting profit which does **not** relate to the main trading activity, i.e. rental income, dividend income, interest receivable, etc, that maybe taxed under other rules or income exempt from taxation under that particular countries rules.

Disallowable expenses are expenses that have been deducted from the accounting profit, i.e. they are allowable under the accounting standards, but for tax purposes can't be claimed. These expenses will differ from country to country and the examiner will always tell you the rules for that particular country in the question. Examples of disallowable expenses in the UK are entertaining customers, gift aid payments, political donations.

Depreciation is added back because it is an accounting entry that is not allowed for tax purposes because it is too subjective (i.e. you can choose the way to depreciate your assets). It is replaced with tax depreciation.

Tax depreciation may be called capital allowances in the exam. The rules will be given in the exam to tell you what can be claimed. It is a replacement for depreciation. They are often given on a reducing balance basis. Allowances are given if the asset is owned at the accounting date, i.e. no time apportionment for mid-year acquisitions.

Balancing allowances and charges

When an asset is disposed of, we will calculate, for accounting purposes, the accounting profit or loss on disposal. This will be calculated by:

	$
Proceeds	X
Less: Carrying amount (SOFP)	(X)
Accounting profit/(loss)	X

If the proceeds are greater than the carrying amount = profit
If the proceeds are less than the carrying amount = loss

An accounting profit or loss will be treated as disallowable for tax purposes. A profit will be deducted from the accounting profit (similar to non-trade income) and a loss will be added to the accounting profit (similar to depreciation).

This will then be replaced by either a balancing charge or allowance for tax purposes.

These are calculated in the same way as the accounting profit or loss on disposal:

	$
Proceeds	X
Less: tax written down value (TWDV)	(X)
Balancing charge/(allowance)	X

If the proceeds are greater than the TWDV= balancing charge
If the proceeds are less than the TWDV= balancing allowance

A balancing charge will be added to the accounting profit and a balancing allowance will be deducted from the accounting profit.

Capital allowances (tax depreciation) are not normally given in the year of disposal of the asset - these are replaced by balancing allowances or charges.

Illustration 1 : Trading income

In year ending 31/12/2011 Zippy Ltd made an accounting profit of $50,000. Profit included $3,500 of entertaining expenses which are disallowable for tax purposes and $5,000 of income exempt from taxation.

Zippy Ltd has $70,000 of non-current assets which were acquired on 01/01/2010 and are depreciated at 10% on cost. Tax depreciation rates are 20% reducing balance.

Assuming a tax rate of 30%, what is the tax payable by Zippy Ltd for 2011?

Solution

	$
Accounting profit	50,000
Less: exempt income	(5,000)
Add back: disallowable expenses	3,500
Add back: depreciation ($70,000 x 10%)	7,000
Less: tax depreciation (W1)	(11,200)
Taxable profit	**44,300**
Tax at 30%	13,290

(W1) Tax depreciation

WDV at start of year	$56,000	($70,000 × 80%)
Tax depreciation at 20%	$11,200	

The asset had been purchased in the previous accounting period, therefore tax depreciation has already been claimed for Ye. 31/12/10. This year's tax depreciation must be calculated on the tax WDV at the beginning of the year, i.e. $56,000.

Test your understanding 1 : Trading income

In year ending 31/03/2011, Bungle Ltd made an accounting profit of $60,000. Profit included $4,500 of political donations which are disallowable for tax purposes and $4,000 of income exempt from taxation.

Bungle Ltd has $10,000 of plant and machinery which was acquired on 01/04/2009 and purchased a new machine costing $5,000 on 01/04/2010. This new machine is entitled to FYA's (first year allowances) of 100%. All plant and machinery is depreciated at 10% on cost. Tax depreciation rates on plant and machinery are 20% reducing balance.

Bungle Ltd also has a building that cost $100,000 on 01/04/2000 and is depreciated at 4% on a straight line basis. Tax depreciation is calculated at 3% on a straight line basis.

Assuming a tax rate of 30%, what is the tax payable by Bungle Ltd for the accounting period ending 31/03/2011?

Illustration 2 : Trading income

Using the previous illustration Zippy Ltd, recalculate the tax if the rates were as follows:

01/04/10 – 31//03/11 = 28%

01/04/11 – 31/03/12 =30%

Solution

The taxable profit for Zippy Ltd was $44,300 for accounting period to 31/12/11.

Tax would be:

($44,300 x 3/12 x 28%) + ($44,300 x 9/12 x 30%) = $13,068.50

The taxable profit is pro-rated based on the amount of months that fall into each of the tax rate periods, i.e.

01/01/11 – 31/03/11 = 3 months at the rate of 28%
01/04/11 – 31/12/11 = 9 months at the rate of 30%

Test your understanding 2 : Trading income

Arnold Ltd has an accounting period ending 30/06/11 and a taxable profit of $800,000.

The rates of tax were as follows:

01/04/10 – 31/03/11 = 26%

01/04/11 – 31/03/12 = 28%

Calculate the tax liability for the period ending 30/06/11.

Trading losses

When a company makes a trading loss the assessment for that tax year will be nil.

The company must now claim loss relief based on the rules of the country's tax regime. The examiner will tell you the rules of the country in the question.

Possible ways of relieving a loss are:

- Carry losses forwards against future profits of the **same** trade;
- Carry losses backwards against previous periods;
- Offset losses against group company profits;
- Offset losses against capital gains in the same period.

It is important to read the rules of the tax regime for the country. All countries are different as some allow losses to be carried backwards and forwards, others only allow losses to be carried forwards. Many countries do not allow trading losses to be offset against capital gains in any period.

Illustration 3 : Trading losses

In country X, trading losses in any year can be carried back and set off against trading profits in the previous year, and any unrelieved losses can be carried forward to set against the first available trade profits in future years.

Hall and Co had the following taxable profits and losses in year 1 to 4.

Year	Trading profit/(loss)
1	25,000
2	(45,000)
3	15,000
4	35,000

What are Hall and Co's taxable profits in each year?

Solution

Year	Trading profit/(loss)	Workings
1	–	25,000 - 25,000
2	–	
3	–	15,000 - 15,000
4	30,000	35,000 - 5,000 (balance of the loss)

The trading loss is carried back first against the trading profit in year 1, this must be done to the maximum extent, i.e. you can't use part of the profit for relief if all of it is needed. The balance of the loss must then be carried forward against the **first available trading profit** in year 3, again to the maximum extent required until it has been relieved in full. There is no limit on how many years you are able to carry forward a trading loss.

Test your understanding 3 : Trading losses

In country A, trading losses in any year can be carried back and set off against profits in the previous year, and any unrelieved losses can be carried forward to set against profits in future years.

Looser Ltd had the following taxable profits and losses in year 1 to 4.

Year	Trading profit/(loss)
1	20,000
2	(45,000)
3	19,000
4	25,000

What are Looser Ltd's taxable profits in each year?

Cessation of business

If an enterprise ceases to trade, most countries allow the company to carry back the loss against profits of previous years to generate a tax refund. In the UK, this is called Terminal Loss Relief and enables the loss to be carried back three years. The examiner will tell you the terminal loss rules of that country.

Test your understanding 4 : Cessation losses

In 2011, Dunbadly closed its business having made a trading loss of $60,000. In Dunbadly's country of residence, trading losses may be carried back two years on a LIFO basis.

	2009	2010	2011
	$	$	$
Trading profits/losses	100,000	50,000	(60,000)

What is the impact on taxable profits for each year?

Capital taxes

Capital tax gains are gains made on the disposal of investments and other assets. The most common assets taxed are listed stocks and shares.

The tax base is assets.

At a simple level, the gain is calculated as proceeds from sale less cost of the asset.

In most countries, the computation is based on cost but in a few countries an allowance is made for inflation. In the UK, the cost can be indexed, in certain cases, using the Retail Price Index. Indexation will be calculated on all allowable costs from the date of purchase to the disposal date of the asset. This indexation allowance will **reduce** the gain.

The standard proforma is as follows:

	$
Proceeds	X
Less: costs to sell	(X)
Net proceeds	X
Less: cost of original asset	(X)
Less: costs to buy	(X)
Less: enhancement costs	(X)
Less: indexation allowance	(X)
Chargeable gain	X

The chargeable gain will then be charged at the appropriate tax rate for that accounting period.

Some countries allow an annual exemption from capital gains. This means the taxpayer will only be taxed on gains in excess of the annual exemption. The examiner will give you the annual exemption in the question if it is applicable.

Allowable costs for deduction

Costs that can be deducted from proceeds are:

- original cost of purchasing the asset;

- costs to buy the assets, i.e. legal fees, estate agent fees;

- costs to sell the assets, i.e. legal fees, estate agent fees;

- enhancement/improvement costs, i.e. extensions to an existing asset.

Illustration 4 : Capital taxes

A company bought an asset for $20,000 on 01/02/00. The asset was sold for $50,000 on 21/11/11.

The indexation factor from February 2000 to November 2011 was 30%

Capital gains are taxed at 30%.

What is the capital tax to be paid on the disposal?

Solution

	$
Sale proceeds	50,000
Less: Cost	(20,000)
	_____
	30,000
Less: Compensation for inflation	
20,000 × 30%	(6,000)
	_____
Chargeable gain	**24,000**
	_____

Capital tax = $24,000 x 30% = $7,200

Test your understanding 5 : Capital taxes

Take It Ltd bought a building for $50,000 on 01/02/00. They incurred costs at the date of purchase of $1,500 for legal fees.

The building was extended on 01/04/02 at a cost of $12,000 and repairs to the roof were undertaken on 01/06/03 after a violent storm, costing $5,000.

The building was sold for $150,000 on 21/11/11 and costs to sell were incurred of $2,000.

The indexation factors were as follows:

February 2000 to November 2011 was 30%

April 2002 to November 2011 was 20%

June 2003 to November 2011 was 10%

Capital gains are taxed at 30%.

What is the capital tax to be paid on the disposal?

Items exempt from Capital Gains Tax

Usually, certain types of assets are exempt from Capital Gains Tax. In the UK, exempt assets include:

- Qualifying Corporate Bonds;
- private motor vehicles;
- chattels sold for less than £6,000 (tangible movable property);
- wasting chattels, e.g. boats and animals.

Certain disposals are exempt from Capital Gains Tax and include:

- gifts to charities or certain assets such as works of art;
- gifts to museums or government institutions.

You will not be expected to remember these; the examiner will state in the question if any items are exempt.

Capital losses

Most countries keep capital losses separate from trading activities.

Possible ways of relieving capital gains are:

- Carry forwards against future capital gains;
- Carry back against previous capital gains;
- Offset against trading income in the current period.

Most countries only allow capital gains to be carried forwards against future capital gains but the examiner will explain the rules of the country in the question.

Illustration 5 : Capital losses

In country X, capital losses can be set off against capital gains in the same tax year, but unrelieved capital losses cannot be carried back. Unrelieved capital losses may be carried forward and set against capital gains in future years.

Hall and Co had the following capital gains and losses in year 1 to 4.

Year	Capital gain/(loss)
1	3,000
2	(4,000)
3	2,500
4	3,000

What are Hall and Co's taxable gains in each year?

Solution

Year	Capital gain/(loss)	Workings
1	3,000	
2	–	
3	–	2,500 - 2,500
4	1,500	3,000 - 1,500 (balance of the loss)

The capital loss **can't** be carried back against year 1, only carried forward against the **first available** capital gain. There is no limit to how many years it can be carried forward for.

Test your understanding 6 : Loss relief

In country Y, capital losses can be set off against capital gains in the same tax year, but unrelieved capital losses cannot be carried back. Unrelieved capital losses may be carried forward and set against capital gains in future years.

Trading losses in any year can be carried back and set off against profits in the previous year, and any unrelieved losses can be carried forward to set against profits in future years. They cannot be relieved against capital gains.

Robbie and Co had the following trading profits/losses and capital gains/losses in year 1 to 3.

Calculate the taxable gains and profits for all years.

Year	Capital gain/(loss)	Trading profit/(loss)
1	4,000	27,000
2	(6,000)	(30,000)
3	9,000	16,000

Rollover relief

In some countries, gains may be postponed using rollover relief. Rollover relief enables a business to postpone paying tax on a gain if it reinvests the same proceeds in a replacement asset. The gain is effectively postponed until the replacement asset is sold at some time in the future.

4 Group loss relief

Tax consolidation enables a tax group to be recognised, allowing trading losses to be surrendered between different companies. Some countries enable losses to be surrendered only between resident companies, while others allow overseas companies to be included based on profits within that country. Generally, tax groups are different from groups for accounting purposes. There are various restrictions on the transfer such as in the UK where only losses of the current accounting period can be surrendered.

It is important to appreciate, each company will still produce their own individual accounts and will be taxed individually. However, if they are part of a group for tax purposes it may enable them to transfer losses between group members to save tax for the group as a whole.

Capital losses cannot usually be surrendered between group companies. In the UK, group companies can transfer ownership of an asset to a group company at nil gain/nil loss. A capital gain or loss only arises when an asset is sold outside the group to a third party. In this way, the entire capital loss group is effectively treated as one entity by the authorities for capital gains tax.

Group relief may be used to:

- Save tax (the surrendering company may pay tax at a lower rate that the group company receiving the loss);

- Enable relief to be gained earlier (the surrendering company may only be able to carry losses forwards which result in the company waiting for loss relief).

Interaction of corporate tax system with the personal tax system

Appropriations of profit such as dividends cannot be deducted in arriving at an enterprise's taxable profits and is therefore taxable in the hands of the company.

The dividend is then distributed to the shareholders who may be taxed on the income as part of their personal tax.

As a result, the dividend is often taxed twice. There are four main systems to deal with this situation:

Classical system

The shareholder is treated as an independent entity from the company. The dividend is taxed twice, firstly as part of the company's taxable earnings and secondly when received by the shareholder as part of shareholder's personal income.

Imputation system

The shareholder receives a tax credit equal to the underlying corporate income tax paid by the company. In this way, the company is taxed on the dividend while the shareholder is not as they receive a full credit.

Partial imputation system

A tax credit is offered to the shareholder but only for part of the underlying corporate income tax paid by the company.

Split rate system

These systems distinguish between distributed profits and retained profits and charge a lower rate of corporate income tax on distributed profits to avoid the double taxation of dividends.

Re-characterising debt

As a general rule interest is tax deductible and dividends are not. It is therefore advantageous from a tax perspective for group companies to transfer funds from one company to another in the form of interest on intercompany loans rather than dividends.

Many countries have addressed this issue by limiting the amount of interest that is tax deductible. Interest in excess of this value will be classified as a dividend. Where a company is deemed to exceed this limit, it is known as thin capitalisation.

Illustration 6 : The classical and imputation system

Taxable profits are $100,000 and the company decides to distribute a dividend of $42,500 (net). Profits are taxed at 15% and shareholders are subject to income tax of 20% on all dividends received.

Calculate the total tax paid by the company and the shareholders under the classical system, the imputation system, and the partial imputation system where a tax credit of 10% is allowed.

Solution

Classical System

Tax on profits for the company	$100,000 x 15%	$15,000
Tax on dividends for the shareholders	$42,500 x 20%	$8,500
		___
Total tax paid		$23,500

Full Imputation System

Tax on profits for the company	$100,000 x 15%	$15,000
Tax on dividends for the shareholders:		
Dividend received	$42,500	
Tax credit (42,500/85 x 15)	$ 7,500	
Gross dividend	$50,000	
Tax at 20%	$10,000	
Less: tax credit	$ (7,500)	$2,500
		___
Total tax paid		$17,500

Partial Imputation System

Tax on profits for the company	$100,000 x 15%	$15,000
Tax on dividends for the shareholders:		
Dividend received	$42,500	
Tax credit (42,500/90 x 10)	$ 4,722	
Gross dividend	$47,222	
Tax at 20%	$ 9,444	
Less: tax credit	$ (4,722)	$4,722
		___
Total tax paid		$19,722

5 Indirect taxes and employee taxation

Types of indirect taxes

Unit taxes

This is a tax based on the number or weight of items, e.g. excise duties.

Ad valorem taxes

This is a tax based on the value of items, e.g sales tax.

Excise duties

This is a type of unit tax and it is on certain products such as alcoholic drinks, tobacco, mineral oils and motor vehicles. These duties are imposed to:

- discourage over consumption of harmful products;
- to pay for extra costs, such as increased healthcare or road infrastructure;
- to tax luxuries (in the USA, this would include fishing equipment, firearms and air tickets).

Property taxes

Many countries impose tax on property based on either the capital value or the annual rental value. Most countries tax land and buildings although in the USA, certain states also impose a tax on cars, livestock and boats.

Wealth taxes

Some countries also impose a wealth tax on an individual's or enterprise's total wealth. The wealth can include pension funds, insurance policies and works of art.

Consumption taxes

These are taxes imposed on the consumption of goods and added to the purchase price. There are two types of consumption tax.

- **Single stage taxes**

  Single stage taxes apply to one level of production only, for example at either the manufacturing, wholesale or retail level. The USA is a country which uses a retail sales tax although the tax rate is determined at the local state government level instead of at the central government or federal level.

- **Multi-stage sales tax**

  This is a tax charged each time a component or product is sold. There are two types of multi-stage sales tax:

  Cascade tax, and

  Valued added tax (VAT).

Cascade tax

This is where tax is taken at each stage of production and is a business cost. No refunds are provided by local government.

Illustration 7 : Multi-stage sales tax

A shoe manufacturer sells shoes to a wholesaler who then sells it to a retailer. Finally the retailer sells it to a final consumer.

M sells it to W for $ 50

W sells it to R for $80

R sells it to C for $150

The rate of tax is 10%.

Calculate the total sales tax due.

> ### Solution
>
> Each time a sale is made, sales tax due by each enterprise is computed as follows:
>
> | | |
> |---|---|
> | M's sale to W | $50 x 10% = $5 |
> | W's sale to R | $80 x 10% = $8 |
> | R's sale to C | $150 x 10% = $15 |
> | **Total Tax Due** | **$28** |
>
> Each business has to charge tax and pay it to the tax authorities. Total tax paid is $28 and is not recoverable.

Value added tax (VAT)

VAT is charged each time a component or product is sold but the government allows businesses to claim back all the tax they have paid (input tax). The entire tax burden is passed to the final consumer. The VAT system is used by almost all countries in the world.

Vat payable = output tax – input tax

Output tax – VAT charged on sales to customers

Input tax – VAT paid on purchases

VAT aims to tax most business transactions which are referred to as taxable supplies.

Therefore, supplies could be:

Standard Rated	– Taxed at the standard rate of VAT
Higher Rated	– Taxed at a higher rate
Zero Rated	– Taxed at a rate of 0%
	(Basic food, e.g. bread)
Exempt	– Not subject to VAT

In the UK, supplies such as food, children's clothing and exports are zero rated for the purpose of VAT. Businesses who sell zero rated sales are allowed to claim back input VAT on purchases.

Alternatively, in the UK, supplies such as finance and insurance are exempt for the purpose of VAT. Businesses who sell exempt sales cannot claim back input VAT on purchases.

You will not be required to know the types of goods and services that are zero or exempt rated for the exam; the examiner will make this clear in the question.

It is important to identify the type of supply in order to claim back input tax. Input tax can only be claimed back on taxable supplies, i.e. zero and standard rated goods and services. Exempt supplies are outside the VAT system and VAT cannot be charged to customers but neither can the input tax on purchases be claimed back.

Taxable supplies, therefore, have a selling price exclusive of VAT (net price) and a selling price inclusive of VAT (gross price).

If the exclusive price is given, VAT is calculated by:
exclusive price x tax rate

If the inclusive price is given VAT is calculated by:

inclusive price   **x tax rate**
100 + tax rate

VAT registration

VAT registration is required by a taxable person making a taxable supply.

A taxable person can be an individual or a company.
A taxable supply is zero or standard rated sales.

They will be required to register for VAT once their taxable turnover (zero and standard rated sales) reach a certain limit (this will vary from tax year to tax year).

Once registered they must:

- Issue VAT invoices
- Keep appropriate VAT records
- Charge VAT on taxable supplies to customers
- Be able to claim back VAT from purchases that are used for taxable supplies
- Complete a quarterly VAT return and make payments

For example, in the UK VAT **cannot** be recovered on:

- Cars (unless for resale, i.e. by a car dealer)
- Entertaining (unless for staff entertaining)

Illustration 8 : VAT

A shoe manufacturer sells shoes to a wholesaler who then sells it to a retailer. Finally the retailer sells it to a final consumer.

M sells it to W for $ 50.

W sells it to R for $80.

R sells it to C for $150.

The rate of value added tax is 10% and all figures are exclusive of VAT.

Calculate the amount of VAT that will be payable by each party.

Solution

Enterprise	Output Tax $	Input Tax $	VAT collected and payable to local government $
M			
–Sale to W = 50 x 10%	5		5 paid by M
W			
–Sale to R = 80 x 10%	8		
–Purchase from M = 50 x 10%		5	3 paid by W
R			
–Sale to C = 150 x 10%	15		
–Purchase from W = 80 x 10%		8	7 paid by R
Total suffered by C = 150 x 10%			15

The total tax on the sale of $15 is suffered by C as unable to claim back the input tax.

Test your understanding 7 : VAT

Country Ozz operates a VAT system where VAT is charged on goods and services and registered traders are able to reclaim input VAT on purchases.

VAT is charged at the following rates:

Standard rate	15%
Luxury rate	20%
Zero rate	0%

During the last VAT period Troyster Ltd purchased materials to produce a product called Paws, costing $90,000, excluding VAT and materials to produce a product called Claws, costing $60,000, excluding VAT. All materials were charged at standard rate VAT.

Sales were made of the "Paws" during the year totalling $120,000. These were zero rated supplies.

Sales were made of the "Claws" during the year totalling $240,000, inclusive of VAT. These were luxury rated supplies.

Calculate the amount of VAT to be paid to the tax authorities and the accounting profit Troyster would make during the year.

Employee taxation

Employees are taxed on their earnings under income tax. Earnings can include salaries, bonuses, commissions and benefits in kind.

Benefits in kind are non-cash benefits in lieu of further cash payments such as:

- company cars;
- living accommodation;
- loans;
- private medical insurance.

The basis of assessment is based on the individual country:

- France – amount earned in previous year.
- Switzerland – average of previous two years' earnings.
- UK – amount actually received in the current tax year.

Employees can deduct certain expenses which are **wholly, exclusively and necessary** for employment, such as business travel, contributions to pension plans, donations to charity through a payroll deduction scheme and professional subscriptions.

Both employees and companies have to pay social security taxes based on salaries paid to employees. This tax is used to fund benefits such as the Public Health Service and Retirement Benefits. In the UK, this is called national insurance.

Most governments expect enterprises to withhold tax on employees' salaries and report earnings to the tax authorities. In the UK, this tax system is referred to as Pay-As-You-Earn (PAYE).

The benefits of having a PAYE system are:

• tax is collected at source, hence taxpayers are less likely to default payment;

• tax authorities receive regular payments from employers - helps to budget cash flows for the government;

• the tax authority only has to deal with the employer, rather than a number of individuals;

• most of the administration costs are borne by the employer, instead of the government.

Certain countries, such as the USA, require banks to collect property taxes with the mortgage payments. In addition to this, in the USA there is a separate Unemployment Compensation Tax.

The standard proforma is as follows:

	$
Salary	X
Plus: bonus, commission, benefits	X
Less: subscriptions	(X)
Less: pension contributions	(X)
Less: charity donations	(X)
Less: personal allowances	(X)
Taxable income	X

The taxable income will then be charged at the appropriate tax rate for the tax year.

Illustration 9 : Employee taxation

Barry is a 25-year-old accountant and earns $23,000 per annum.

During the tax year, Barry also earned a 5% bonus and has a taxable benefit of medical insurance worth $500.

As a qualified accountant, Barry must pay a membership subscription of $400 each year.

Required:

Prepare Barry's income tax computation assuming the following:

(a) the personal allowance for the year is $6,500 and

(b) the tax rates are as follows based on taxable earnings:

　　　–　10% on the first $1,900;

　　　–　22% after that.

Solution

	$
Income	23,000
Bonus (23,000 × 5%)	1,150
Benefit in kind – insurance	500
Less subscription	(400)
Less personal allowance	(6,500)
Taxable earnings	**17,750**
Tax	
$1,900 × 10%	190
$17,750 – 1,900 × 22%	3,487
Total	**3,677**

> ### Test your understanding 8 : Employee taxation
>
> Doris is a sales woman and earns $35,000 per annum.
>
> During the tax year, she also earned a 3% bonus and paid 5% of her salary into an occupational pension scheme. Her employer provides her with a company car, the benefit of which is calculated as $2,000 and a gym membership costing the company $500 per year.
>
> **Required:**
>
> Prepare Doris's income tax computation assuming the following:
>
> (a) the personal allowance for the year is $6,500 and
>
> (b) the tax rates are as follows based on taxable earnings:
>
> – 20% on the first $15,000;
>
> – 40% after that.

6 International taxation

Corporate residence

Entities normally pay taxation on their worldwide income in the country they are resident in.

An enterprise is deemed to be resident for tax purposes either in the place of incorporation or place of control/central management.

Generally a company will be treated as being resident in the country of control, i.e. place where the head office is located or board meetings held.

Double taxation

An enterprise may end up being taxed in more than one country, this is called double taxation.

For example, a company may earn income in country X, despite being located in country Y.

Double taxation may arise if that income is taxed in the country where it was earned (X) as well as the country where the company is resident (Y). Double taxation relief is often available in this situation.

Double taxation relief

There are three main methods of giving double taxation relief:

(1) Exemption - The countries agreed on certain types of income which will be exempt or partially exempt in one country or the other.

(2) Tax credit - Tax paid in one country may be allowed as a tax credit in another country. Relief is normally restricted to the lower of the foreign or country of residency tax.

(3) Deduction - Tax relief is gained by deducting the foreign tax from the foreign income so that only the "net" amount will be subject to tax in the country of residency.

Types of overseas operations

An overseas operations can be run as a branch or a subsidiary.

Subsidiary (refer to chapter 3 for more detail)

The features of operating as a subsidiary are:

- The overseas subsidiary is a separate company for tax purposes. The holding company will only pay tax on any dividends received from the subsidiary.

- Loss relief is not available for the group.

- The overseas subsidiary cannot claim tax depreciation on any assets and assets transferred from the parent may result in capital gains tax.

Branch

The features of operating as a branch are:

- The branch is treated as an extension of the UK activity and all profits from it will be subject to UK taxation.

- Loss relief is available for the group.

- Assets can be transferred between the branch and holding company at no gain/no loss.

- The branch can claim tax depreciation on all assets.

Types of foreign tax

Withholding tax

Some countries will deduct tax at source on items such as interest, royalties, rent, dividends and capital gains. The net income (gross payment less tax) is then received by the beneficiary in the foreign country.

Both withholding and underlying tax may be reduced by various methods of double tax relief. Methods of double tax relief include exemption, tax credits for foreign tax suffered, and deduction of foreign tax from tax due in the home country.

Underlying tax

When a company pays out a dividend, it is done so out of post tax profits. Therefore, the amount of profit distributed as a dividend will have already suffered tax on profits.

If a company receives a dividend from an overseas subsidiary, the dividend will have been taxed once in the overseas country as part of normal tax on profits, and then again in the country of receipt, as income on dividends. This tax is known as underlying tax.

This is calculated as follows:

$$\frac{\text{Tax on profits}}{\text{Profit after tax}} \times \text{Gross dividend}$$

Illustration 10 : International taxation

Homely is a UK company and owns 100% of the shares in a foreign company called Faraway.

During the year Faraway earned the following income;

Profit before tax	$200,000
Income tax	$(40,000)
Profit after tax	$160,000

Faraway pays a dividend of $80,000 out of profit after tax to Homely. This dividend is subject to 15% withholding tax.

What is the total foreign tax suffered on the dividend?

Solution

	$
Withholding tax	
$80,000 × 15%	12,000
Underlying tax	
($80,000/$160,000) × $40,000	20,000
	32,000

This means:

The dividend distributed by Faraway was $80,000.

The foreign country deducted withholding tax of $12,000 and, therefore, the shareholder would only receive $68,000 in cash.

The profits in Faraway were taxed before the $80,000 was distributed. Therefore, the underlying tax is the amount of tax the dividend has already suffered prior to distribution when it was taxed as a profit.

Illustration 11 : Double tax relief

Use the information from the previous illustration:

A tax treaty exists between the two countries using the tax credit method, calculate the tax payable in the UK (Homely's country of residence) assuming a tax rate of 40%.

Solution

	$
Net dividend received	68,000
Add back WHT	12,000
	80,000
Add back UT	20,000
Gross dividend	100,000
Total foreign tax ($100,000 – $68,000)	**32,000**
Tax in UK	
Tax at 40%	40,000
Less DTR (lower of foreign and UK tax)	(32,000)
Tax paid in UK	8,000

Test your understanding 9 : International taxation

Britas is a UK company and owns 80% of the shares in a foreign company called Cheers.

During the year, Cheers earned the following income;

Profit before tax	$372,000
Income tax	$(62,000)
Profit after tax	$310,000

Cheers pays a total dividend of $100,000 out of profit after tax to its shareholders. This dividend is subject to 5% withholding tax.

Calculate the total foreign tax suffered on the dividend and show how double tax relief would apply in the UK using the tax credit method, assuming a rate of 40% tax is charged?

OECD model tax convention

The OECD model addresses the issues of double residency.

This model states that business profits of an enterprise will only be taxable in a state if an enterprise has a permanent establishment in that country. A permanent establishment could include the following:

(1) A factory

(2) A workshop

(3) An office

(4) A branch

(5) A place of management

(6) A mine, an oil or gas well, or a place of extraction of natural resources

(7) A construction project or building site if it lasts more than 12 months

If an entity has a permanent establishment in a country, it can be taxed in that country, causing a possible problem of double taxation.

 Where an entity is deemed to have residency in several countries, the OECD model suggests that the entity is resident in the country of its effective management.

7 Administration
Record-keeping

Enterprises need to keep records to satisfy tax requirements for the following taxes.

Corporate income tax

All records required to support their financial statements and also the additional documents required to support the adjustments made to those statements when completing their tax returns.

Sales tax

Adequate records should be maintained of all the sales and purchases records such as:

- Orders and delivery notes

- Purchase and sales invoices

- Credit and debit notes

- Purchase and Sales Books

- Import and Export Documents
- Bank Statements
- Cashbooks and receipts
- VAT account

Overseas subsidiaries

Tax authorities would require documentation about the transfer pricing policy between the subsidiary and the parent. These are the prices charged for goods or services provided from one to the other. Most tax authorities require the price to be the same as it would be if charged to a third party.

Employee tax

Employers have to keep detailed records of employee tax and social security contributions. They will also be required to prepare a number of year end returns to show the total deductions they have made from employees wages, the employer's contributions and an analysis of any other amounts deducted. The employer is also required to provide details to the employee.

Tax authorities set deadlines for the payment of tax and the submission of the tax return. The enterprise will either be required to pay tax following an assessment from the tax authorities or will pay tax via self-assessment. In the UK and the USA, tax is paid via self-assessment. The tax authorities will then check the tax return to confirm if the correct tax has been paid.

Minimum retention of records

There will be a minimum length of time for the retention of records; in the UK this is six years for all records relating to earnings and capital gains. The purpose of this is to enable the tax authorities to question or challenge records up to several years later.

Payment of tax

This will depend on the rules of the tax authority and will depend on the type of tax that is due. The tax is not always paid when the return is filed, it may happen earlier or later. Interest will be charged on late payments of tax.

Powers of tax authorities

The revenue authorities have various powers to impose penalties and interest on late payment of tax. In addition, they have the power to:

- Review and query filed returns.
- Request special reports if they believe inaccurate information has been submitted.

- Examine records of previous years (in the US, tax authorities can go back 20 years).

- Enter and search the enterprise's premises and seize documents.

- Pass on information to foreign tax authorities.

Tax avoidance and tax evasion

Tax avoidance is tax planning to arrange affairs, within the scope of the Law, to minimise the tax liability.

Tax evasion is the illegal manipulation of the tax system to avoid paying tax. Evasion is the intentional disregard of the law to escape tax and can include falsifying tax returns and claiming fictitious enterprises.

The tax authorities use various methods to prevent both tax avoidance and tax evasion:

(1) Reducing opportunity, e.g. by deduction of tax at source and the use of third party reporting.

(2) Simplifying tax structure by minimising the relief, allowances and exemptions.

(3) Increasing perceived risk by auditing tax returns and payments.

(4) Developing good communication between tax authorities and enterprises.

(5) Changing social attitudes towards evasion and avoidance by maintaining an honest and customer friendly tax system. The government should create a fair tax system and should encourage an increasing commitment.

(6) Reducing lost revenue by reviewing the penalty structure.

Test your understanding 10 : Objective Test Questions

(1) Most governments require detailed records to be kept for certain taxes. **List three taxes for which records should be maintained.**

(3 marks)

(2) As a management accountant it is necessary to understand the difference between tax evasion and tax avoidance. **In no more than 45 words, define both tax evasion and tax avoidance.**

(2 marks)

(3) **List five possible powers that a tax authority may have to ensure that enterprises comply with the tax legislation.**

(5 marks)

(4) Many countries impose duties on petrol and diesel to compensate for the damage caused to the environment.

This duty is a:

A   Direct tax

B   Ad valorem tax

C   Single stage tax

D   Cascade tax

(2 marks)

(5) Enterprises reward employees with a remuneration package consisting of a salary and benefits in kind.

Define 'benefits in kind' in less than 30 words.

(2 marks)

(6) Many countries impose duties on alcoholic drinks and cigarettes to discourage excessive consumption.

This duty is a:

A   Excise duty

B   Ad valorem tax

C   Direct tax

D   Cascade tax

(2 marks)

(7) In the UK, the Pay-As-You-Earn system requires enterprises to withhold tax on employees' salaries.

What are the advantages for the government and employees?

(3 marks)

(8) A South American country has a VAT system which allows enterprises to reclaim input tax paid. VAT is at 20% of selling price.

A manufactures mobile phones and sells them to B, a wholesaler. B resells them to C a retailer. C eventually sells them to D for $140 (excluding VAT). The prices at which transactions take place (excluding VAT) are as follows:

– A sells to B for $60;
– B sells to C for $90.

Calculate the VAT due from A, B and C.

(3 marks)

(9) An enterprise imports goods from an overseas enterprise at a cost of $40. The goods are subject to excise duties of $10 per item and VAT at 15%. **If the enterprise imports 100 items, what is the TOTAL tax payable?**

A $1000

B $750

C $1,750

D $1,500

(2 marks)

(10) An enterprise purchases raw materials for $2000 and pays VAT at standard rate on them. The materials are used to produce two products R and S. The enterprise sells 400 units of product R at $20 each and 800 units of product S at $30 each. Product R is zero rated for VAT purposes and product S is standard rated.

Assume that there are no other transactions affecting the VAT payments and that the standard rate of VAT is 17.5%. All figures are exclusive of VAT.

At the end of the accounting period how much VAT is due to the tax authorities?

A $4,200

B $350

C $3,850

D $2,550

(2 marks)

(11) **If a product is zero rated for VAT purposes, it means that an enterprise:**

A   Can charge VAT on sales at standard rate and cannot reclaim input tax on purchases

B   Cannot charge VAT on sales and can reclaim input taxes paid on purchases

C   Cannot charge VAT on sales and cannot reclaim input taxes paid on purchases

D   Can charge VAT on sales and can reclaim input taxes paid on purchases

(2 marks)

(12) **Which of the following could NOT be used to indicate an enterprise is resident in a country?**

A   Country in which directors' meetings are held

B   Country of incorporation

C   Country in which control and management is exercised

D   Country in which goods are sold.

(2 marks)

(13) **In no more than 30 words, define the meaning of a overseas subsidiary.**

(2 marks)

(14) **Which of the following would not be subject to a withholding tax?**

A   Profits of the enterprise

B   Rental profits

C   Equity dividends

D   Interest received from finance companies

(2 marks)

(15) A double taxation treaty between two countries usually allows relief of foreign tax through a number of methods.

Which one of the following is not a method of relieving foreign tax?

A   Deduction based on lower tax

B   Exemption from corporate tax in one country

C   Tax Credits (deduction from tax liability)

D   Loss relief

(2 marks)

(16) Permanent establishment is defined under the OECD model in several ways.

Which of the following would not be classed as a 'permanent establishment'?

A   An office

B   An agent with authority to enter into contracts

C   A workshop

D   A warehouse used for storage

(2 marks)

(17) **Define 'Incidence of Tax' using a maximum of 15 words.**

(2 marks)

(18) **Which of the following is not one of Adam Smith's characteristics of a Good Tax?**

A   Fair

B   Absolute

C   Convenient

D   Simple

(2 marks)

(19) **An indirect tax is a tax which is:**

A   Paid by one person with the intention of passing on

B   Imposed directly on a person

C   Paid indirectly to tax authorities

D   Based on a person's income

(2 marks)

(20) **Define 'hypothecation' using no more than 30 words.**

(2 marks)

Total 46 marks

Test your understanding 11 : Objective Test Questions 2

(1) **Which of the following is not usually a source of tax rules in a country:**

    A   Local legislation

    B   Double tax treaties

    C   Statements of practice of tax authorities

    D   International law

(2 marks)

(2) **What does 'competent jurisdiction' mean in the context of an enterprise being subject to a tax liability?**

    A   Country where enterprise has an office

    B   Country who has enforcement laws that apply to an enterprise

    C   Country where enterprise has business operations

    D   Country where enterprise has employees

(2 marks)

(3) **List the three main tax bases used in developed countries.**

(2 marks)

(4) BM has a taxable profit of $30,000 and receives a tax assessment of $3,000.
BV has a taxable profit of $60,000 and receives a tax assessment of $7,500.
BM and BV are resident in the same tax jurisdiction. This tax could be said to be:

    A   a progressive tax

    B   a regressive tax

    C   a direct tax

    D   a proportional tax

(2 marks)

(5) **A schedular system of corporate tax means:**

A   A method used to calculate the corporate income tax payable

B   A system that has a number of schedules which set out how different types of income should be taxed

C   A system that has a number of schedules which sets out when tax returns and tax payments should be made

D   A system that has a number of schedules which set out the various tax rates.

(2 marks)

(6) **Accounting depreciation is replaced by tax depreciation:**

A   To reduce the amount of depreciation allowed for tax

B   To increase the amount of depreciation allowed for tax

C   To ensure that standard rates of depreciation are used by all organisations for tax purposes

D   So that government can more easily manipulate the amount of tax organisations pay

(2 marks)

(7) **Rollover relief allows:**

A   Deferral of the payment of corporate income tax on gains arising from the disposal of a business asset

B   Stock values to be rolled over, replacing cost of purchases with current values

C   Trading losses to be carried forward or rolled over to future periods

D   Capital losses to be carried forwards or rolled over to future periods

(2 marks)

(8) **An imputation system of corporate income tax means:**

    A   All the underlying corporate income tax on the dividend distribution is passed as a credit to the shareholders

    B   The organisation pays corporate income tax on its profits and the shareholder pays income tax on the dividend received

    C   Withholding tax paid on dividends is passed as a credit to shareholders

    D   A percentage of the underlying tax is passed as credit to shareholders

(2 marks)

(9) Country IDT has a duty that is levied on all drinks of an alcoholic nature where the alcohol is above 20% by volume. This levy is $2 per 1 litre bottle. This duty could be said to be:

    A   Ad valorem tax

    B   Unit tax

    C   Direct tax

    D   VAT

(2 marks)

(10) **Which ONE of the following powers is a tax authority least likely to have granted to them?**

    A   Power of arrest

    B   Power to examine records

    C   Power of entry and search

    D   Power to give information to other countries' tax authorities

(2 marks)

(11) **List THREE possible reasons why governments set deadlines for filing returns and/or paying taxes.**

(2 marks)

(12) **In no more than 15 works define the meaning of a "branch".**

(2 marks)

(13) EB has an investment of 25% of the equity shares of XY, an entity resident in a foreign country. EB receives a dividend of $90,000 from XY, the amount being after the deduction of withholding tax of 10%. XY had profits before tax for the year of $1,200,000 and paid corporate tax of $200,000. **How much underlying tax can EB claim for double taxation relief?**

(2 marks)

(14) The following details relate to EA:

- Incorporated in Country A

- Carries out its main business activities in Country B

- Its senior management operate from Country C and effective control is exercised from Country C

- Assume countries A, B and C have all signed double tax treaties with each other, based on the OECD model tax convention.

Which country will EA be deemed to be resident in for tax purposes?

A   Country A

B   Country B

C   Country C

D   Both countries B and C

(2 marks)

(15) **Explain the meaning of withholding and underlying tax.**

(2 marks)

Total 30 marks

8 Summary diagram

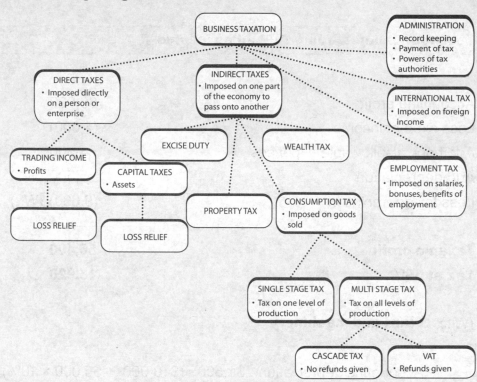

Test your understanding answers

	$
Accounting profit	60,000
Less exempt income	(4,000)
Add back disallowable expenses	4,500
Add depreciation	5,500 (W1)
Less tax depreciation	(9,600) (W2)
Taxable profit	**56,400**
Tax at 30%	**16,920**

(W1)   **Plant and machinery**

Accounting depreciation $1,500 ($10,000 + $5,000 × 10%)

Building

Accounting depreciation $4,000 ($100,000 x 4%)

Total accounting depreciation = ($1,500 + $4,000) = $5,500

(W2)   **Plant and machinery**

Tax depreciation
NBV at start of year $8,000   ($10,000 × 80%)
Tax depreciation at 20% $1,600

The asset had been purchased in the previous accounting period, therefore tax depreciation has already been claimed for Ye. 31/03/10. This year's tax depreciation must be calculated on the tax NBV at the beginning of the year, i.e. $8,000.

The new plant and machinery is given 100% FYA which means relief in given on the total cost in the year of purchase of $5,000.

The building tax depreciation of 3% is based on cost of $100,000 = $3,000

Total tax depreciation = ($1,600 + $5,000 + $3,000) = $9,600

Test your understanding 2 : Trading income

Tax payable is:

($800,000 x 9/12 x 26%) + ($800,000 x 3/12 x 28%) = $212,000

The accounting period runs from 01/07/10 to 30/06/11.

9 months of the accounting period profit (01/07/10 – 31/03/11) is charged at 26% and 3 months of the accounting period profit (01/04/11 – 30/06/11) is charged at 28%.

Test your understanding 3 : Trading losses

Year	Trading profit/(loss)	Workings
1	–	20,000 - 20,000
2	–	
3	–	19,000 -19,000
4	19,000	25,000 - 6,000 (balance of the loss)

The trading loss is carried back first against the trading profit in year 1, this must be done to the maximum extent, i.e. you cannot use part of the profit for relief if all of it is needed. The balance of the loss must then be carried forward against the **first available trading profit** in year 3, again to the maximum extent and this means year 4 will be reduced by the remainder of the loss $6,000, i.e. ($45,000 – $20,000 – $19,000). Year 4 will therefore have trading profits of $19,000 ($25,000 – $6,000).

Test your understanding 4 : Cessation losses

	2009	2010	2011
	$	$	$
Trading profits	100,000	50,000	-
Loss relief	(10,000)	(50,000)	-
Revised trading profits	90,000	–	-

On cessation, trading losses must be carried back on a LIFO basis, i.e. most recent trading profits are used first. When you carry back make sure you relieve the loss against the profit to the maximum possible extent in the year, you can't use part of it.

If the loss had been carried back as far as possible (years dependant on the rule for that country) and was still not fully relieved, then the remainder of the loss would be wasted.

Test your understanding 5 : Capital taxes

	$
Sale proceeds		150,000
Less: cost to sell		(2,000)
		———
Net proceeds		148,000
Cost to purchase	50,000	
Cost to buy	1,500	
Improvements	12,000	(63,500)
	———	———
		84,500
Less: Compensation for inflation		
($50,000 + $1,500) x 30%		(15,450)
12,000 × 20%		(2,400)
		———
Chargeable gain		**66,650**

Capital tax = $66,650 x 30% =$19,995

NB. Roof repairs are not an allowable cost for deduction, i.e. they are not a "new" capital cost or a cost to buy/sell. They are a cost to replace an existing structure.

Test your understanding 6 : Loss relief

Year	Capital gain/(loss)	Trading profit/(loss)
1	4,000	–
2	–	–
3	3,000	13,000

The capital loss **cannot** be carried back against year 1, only carried forward against the **first available** capital gain. It will be used against the gain in year 3 to reduce it to $3,000 ($9,000 – $6,000).

The trading loss is carried back first against year 1 to reduce the profit to nil. The remainder of the loss of $3,000 ($30,000 – $27,000) is carried forward against year 3 to reduce the profit to $13,000 ($16,000 – $3,000).

Test your understanding 7 : VAT

Output VAT		VAT
		$
Sales of Paws – $120,000 x 0%		–
Sales of Claws – $240,000 x 20/120		40,000
		40,000
Input VAT		
Purchases $90,000 x 15%	13,500	
Purchases $60,000 x 15%	9,000	
		22,500
		17,500

Profit is based on **net sales and purchases.**

	$
Sales of Paws (240,000 – 40,000)	120,000
Sales of Claws	200,000
	320,000
Purchases (90,000 + 60,000)	(150,000)
Profit	170,000

Test your understanding 8 : Employee taxation

	$
Income	35,000
Bonus (35,000 × 3%)	1,050
Pension (35,000 x 5%)	(1,750)
Benefit in kind – car	2,000
Benefit in kind – gym membership	500
Less personal allowance	(6,500)
Taxable earnings	**30,300**
Tax	
$15,000 × 20%	3,000
$30,300 – 15,000 × 40%	6,120
Total	**9,120**

Test your understanding 9 : International taxation

	$
Net dividend received	76,000
WHT 5%	4,000
($100,000 x 80%)	80,000
UT – $80,000 x (62/310)	16,000
Gross dividend	96,000
Total foreign tax ($96,000 – $76,000)	**20,000**
Tax in UK	
Tax at 40% on gross dividend $96,000	38,400
Less DTR (lower of foreign and UK tax)	(20,000)
Tax paid in UK	18,400

Test your understanding 10 : Objective Test Questions

(1) (a) VAT

(b) Employee tax deducted from salaries

(c) Corporate income tax (corporation tax)

(2) Tax evasion is the illegal manipulation of the tax system to avoid paying tax.

Tax avoidance is tax planning to arrange the affairs of the enterprise within the scope of the law to minimise the income tax liability.

(3) Tax authorities may have the following powers:

– Power to review and query filed returns.

– Power to request special reports if inadequate information has been submitted.

– Power to examine records of previous periods.

– Powers of entry and search.

– Power to pass on information to foreign tax authorities.

(4) B Ad valorem tax

(5) Benefits in kind are non-cash benefits given by the employer to an employee, often in place of cash payments.

(6) A Excise duty

(7) The advantages for the government are:

– The tax is collected earlier than the usual self-assessment systems which collect tax after the tax year which gives a cash flow benefit.

– The costs of tax collection and administration are passed on to the employer who acts as a tax collector.

The advantage for the employee is:

– The tax is collected gradually over the year thus is easier to bear than a single lump sum payment.

(8)

Enterprise	Input tax $	Output tax $	VAT paid $
A Sale to B		12	12 paid by A
B Purchase from	12		
B Sale to C		18	6 paid by B
C Purchase from B	18		
B Sale to D		28	10 paid by C
Total suffered by D			28

(9) You need to add the excise duty of $1,000 (100 items x $10) and compute VAT on the inclusive price of $5,000 (100 items x $40 plus excise duty of $1,000). The VAT is 15% of $5,000 which results in 750. Total tax payable is $1,000 excise duty and $750 VAT = $1,750.

(10) It is necessary to compute the VAT on sales (output VAT) and the VAT on purchases (input VAT):

Output VAT charged on standard rated sales (800 × $30) × 17.5% = $4,200

Input VAT paid (2,000 x 17.5%) $350
   _____

VAT paid to tax authorities $3,850

The VAT can be claimed back on standard-rated and zero-rated supplies. The correct answer is C.

(11) The correct answer is B.

(12) D   The correct answer is country in which goods are sold.

(13) An overseas subsidiary is an enterprise resident for tax purposes in a foreign country whose share capital is owned by a company resident in another country.

(14) A   Profits of the enterprise.

(15) D   Loss relief.

(16) D   A warehouse used for storage.

(17) Incidence of Tax is the distribution of the tax burden - who actually pays the tax.

(18) D

(19) A   Paid by one person with the intention of passing it on.

(20) Hypothecation is the extent to which a certain type of tax is entirely allocated to a certain type of expenditure.

(1) D   International Law.

(2) B   Country that has enforceable laws that apply to an enterprise.

(3) The three main tax bases are: assets (capital), Income and consumption.

(4) A $3,000 tax on $30,000 = 10% and $7,500 tax on $60,000 = 12.5%. The tax rates increase as the income rises, hence a progressive tax.

(5) B   A system that has a number of schedules which set out how different types of income should be taxed.

(6) C   To ensure that standard rates of depreciation are used by all organisations for tax purposes.

(7) A   Deferral of the payment of corporate income tax on gains arising from the disposal of a business asset.

(8) A   All the underlying corporate income tax on the dividend distribution is passed as a credit to the shareholders .

(9) B   Unit tax - This is a tax based on the number or weight of items, e.g. excise duties.

(10) A   Power of arrest.

(11) Answers could be:

- So that entities know when payment is required;

- It enables the tax authorities to forecast their cash flows more accurately;

- Provides a reference for late payment - useful for applying penalties for not paying;

- To prevent entities spending tax money deducted from employees. If tax is deducted from employees at source and not paid to the tax authorities fairly quickly, there is more chance of an entity spending the amount deducted, instead of paying it to the tax authorities.

(12) A branch of the entity is merely an extension of the entity's business.

(13) Gross dividend = $90,000/90 x 100 = $100,000
Underlying tax = (Tax on profits/profits after tax) x gross dividend
Underlying tax = (200,000/1,000) x 100,000 = $20,000

(14) C   Country C - An entity is considered to be resident in the country of effective management.

(15) Withholding tax is a tax deducted at source from a payment before it is made to the recipient. Underlying tax is the tax on the profits out of which a dividend is paid.

Accounting for Investments in Subsidiaries and Associates

Chapter learning objectives

On completion of their studies students should be able to:

- Explain the relationships between investors and investees and the meaning of control.

1 Introduction

This chapter introduces the appropriate accounting for investments in other entities. The extent of the investment will often determine the appropriate accounting treatment, and this chapter examines the investments that will be accounted for as:

- Basic investments
- Investments in associates
- Investments in subsidiaries

2 Accounting for investments

Entities will often invest in the equity of other businesses. The extent of the equity shareholding will determine how the investment should be accounted for. The accounting treatment applied for investments is intended to reflect the importance of the investment in the financial statements of the investee and how the future performance and financial position might be affected by these investments. It follows then that the greater the level of investment, the more detailed the financial information will be. A significant investment in another entity may require additional financial statements to be produced.

Investment in associates

An investor who has significant influence over an entity would be are treated as an associate and would be accounted for in accordance with IAS 28 Accounting for Associates. If an entity holds, directly or indirectly, 20 per cent of the voting rights of an entity then it is normally considered significant influence and treated as an associated entity. IAS 28 states that there is a presumption that the investor has significant influence over the entity, unless it can be clearly demonstrated that this is not the case.

The key concept in the definition is 'significant influence'. IAS 28 explains that significant influence is the power to participate in the financial and operating policy decisions of the entity but is not control over those policies. The existence of significant influence by an investor is usually evidenced in one or more of the following ways:

- representation on the board of directors;
- participation in policy-making processes;
- material transactions between the investor and the entity;
- interchange of managerial personnel;
- provision of essential technical information.

The impact of this level of investment on the investing entity is likely to be greater than that of a simple investment. There is greater exposure to the results of the associate and a decline in its value will have a greater negative impact on the statement of financial position of the investing entity. The information provided therefore is a step further than that provided for simple investments.

The investment in the associate is equity accounted and the investment shown in the statement of financial position will include the investing entity's share of the gains of the associate from the date the investment was made. The investing entity will show the share of realised and recognised gains it is entitled to by virtue of this investment rather than just the dividend received.

Investment in subsidiaries

It is often the case that businesses conduct part of their operations by making investments in other business entities. For example, a business that aims to expand its market share could opt to purchase one or more of its competitors, rather than taking the slower route of building market share by gradual growth. Another example is where a business purchases an investment in one or more of its suppliers of key goods and services in order to integrate and secure its supply chain.

In order to fulfil the needs of investors and other users, additional information is likely to be required, and therefore the IASB has in issue several accounting standards setting out the principles and practices that must be followed where an investment comprises a significant proportion of the total equity of the investee entity.

An investment in a subsidiary generally occurs when the entity acquires a controlling interest in another entity, i.e. more than 50%. (see later for more detail on control).

3 The principle of control

This chapter will start to examine the accounting required under IFRS for investments in subsidiaries. The accounting standard that sets out the requirements for recognition of an entity as a subsidiary is IAS 27 Consolidated and Separate Financial Statements. This standard was revised in January 2008, but its basic principles have been part of IFRS for many years.

First, some relevant definitions taken from the standard

A **parent** is an entity that has one or more subsidiaries.

A **subsidiary** is an entity, including an unincorporated entity such as a partnership, which is controlled by another entity (known as the parent).

The key concept in determining whether or not an investment constitutes a subsidiary is that of **control.**

Control is the power to govern the financial and operating policies of an entity so as to obtain benefit from its activities.

There is a presumption that control exists where the investor entity owns over half of the voting power of the other entity. If an investor entity, ABC, owns 55% of the voting share capital of entity DEF, in the absence of any special circumstances, ABC is presumed to be in control of DEF. The maximum investment that could be held by another investor is 45%, and so ABC will always have the capacity to win a vote over the other investor(s). The nature of the relationship between ABC and DEF is that of parent and subsidiary.

In most cases, control can be easily determined by looking at the percentage ownership of the ordinary share capital in the investee entity. Provided ownership is greater than 50% a parent/subsidiary relationship can be assumed. However, there are exceptions. A parent/subsidiary relationship can exist even where the parent owns less than 50% of the voting power of the subsidiary since the key to the relationship is control. IAS 27 supplies the following instances:

When there is:

(a) power over more than half of the voting rights by virtue of an agreement with other investors;

(b) power to govern the financial and operating policies of the entity under a statute or agreement;

(c) power to appoint or remove the majority of the members of the board of directors or equivalent governing body, and control of the entity is by that board or body; or

(d) power to cast the majority of votes at meetings of the board of directors or equivalent governing body, and control of the entity is by that board or body.

The reason for describing the nature of control in such detail in IAS 27 is that entities have sometimes created ownership structures designed to evade the requirements for accounting for subsidiaries.

In the Financial Operations examination, you will only be examined on a subsidiary that is fully controlled by the parent (100% control).

4 The requirements to prepare consolidated financial statements

Where a parent/subsidiary relationship exists, IAS 27 requires that the parent should prepare consolidated financial statements. It is important to realise from the outset that this is an additional set of financial statements. The parent and subsidiary continue to prepare their own financial statements. Therefore in a group comprising one parent and one subsidiary, a total of three sets of financial statements are required. Where a group comprises, say, the parent and four subsidiaries, a total of six sets of financial statements are required: one for the parent, one for each of the four subsidiaries and one set of consolidated financial statements.

Exclusion from preparing consolidated accounts

A full set of financial statements in addition to those already prepared is, of course, quite an onerous requirement. IAS 27 includes some exemptions, as follows:

A parent need not present consolidated financial statements if and only if:

(a) the parent is itself a wholly owned subsidiary, or is a partially-owned subsidiary of another entity and its other owners, including those not otherwise entitled to vote, have been informed about, and do not object to, the parent not presenting consolidated financial statements;

(b) the parent's debt or equity instruments are not traded in a public market (a domestic or foreign stock exchange or an over-the-counter market, including local and regional markets);

(c) the parent did not file, nor is it in the process of filing, its financial statements with a securities commission or other regulatory organisation for the purpose of issuing any class of instruments in a public market;

(d) the ultimate or any intermediate parent of the parent produces consolidated financial statements available for public use that comply with IFRS.

These provisions have been spelt out in some detail so as to minimise the risk of entities evading the accounting requirements.

Goodwill

When a controlling investment is made the parent is investing in the net assets of the subsidiary. The value of the assets presented on the statement of financial position is unlikely to be what is paid by the investing entity. Usually, the owners of a profitable business will expect to receive more in exchange for the investment than its net asset value. This additional amount arises for various reasons. It is quite likely that the assets recognised in the statement of financial position do not represent all the assets of the firm but intangibles such as good reputation and customer loyalty may be worth something to the purchaser. The difference between the cost of investment and the fair value of the net assets acquired is known as goodwill on acquisition, and the accounting standard IFRS 3 Business Combinations requires its recognition in consolidated financial statements.

IFRS 3 Business combinations

IFRS 3 was originally issued in March 2004 replacing an earlier standard. However, it was just the first stage in a longer term IASB project on accounting for business combinations. The next stage culminated in the issue, in January 2008, of the revised version of IFRS 3.

IFRS 3 requires that entities should account for business combinations by applying the acquisition method of accounting. This involves recognising and measuring the identifiable assets acquired, the liabilities assumed and any non-controlling interest in the acquiree entity. Measurement should be at fair value on the date of acquisition. Where 100% of the equity of a subsidiary is acquired, goodwill on acquisition is calculated as follows:

Goodwill on acquisition is the aggregate of:
Consideration, measured at fair value
LESS
Net assets acquired (the fair value of identifiable assets acquired less liabilities assumed)

This measures goodwill on acquisition which is recognised in the consolidated financial statement of position within non-current assets. Goodwill on acquisition is an asset of the group (not of the individual entities within the group) and is subject to impairment reviews to ensure its value is not overstated. The goodwill arises at the date of acquisition and will not change unless impairment is identified, whereby it will be held net of impairment losses (which should be recognised in accordance with IAS 36 Impairment of Assets).

Consolidated Statement of Financial Position

Chapter learning objectives

On completion of their studies students should be able to:

- Identify the circumstances in which a subsidiary is excluded from consolidation;

- Prepare consolidated financial statements for a group of companies;

- Explain the treatment in consolidated financial statements for pre and post-acquisition reserves, goodwill (including its impairment), fair value adjustments, unrealised profit in inventory and intra-group transactions.

1 Session content

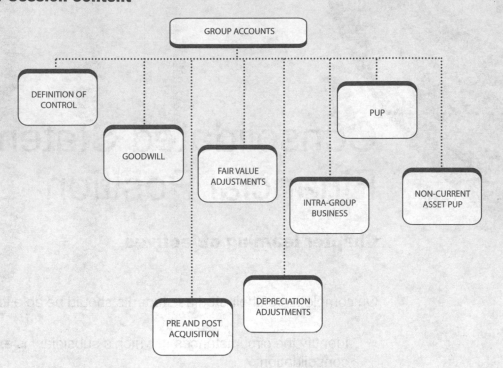

2 What is a Group?

IAS 27 Consolidated and Separate Financial Statements

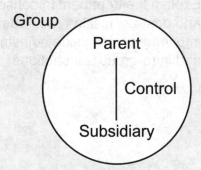

A group will exist where one company **controls** another company.

Control is the power to govern the financial and operating policies so as to obtain benefits from its activities.

Control is normally achieved by the parent company owning 51% or more of the voting rights of the subsidiary.

Legally, the parent and subsidiary are separate entities and separate financial statements must be prepared.

In substance, the parent and subsidiary can be viewed as a single entity, known as the group.

Group financial statements are prepared to reflect the substance of the situation. They are referred to as consolidated accounts and are prepared in addition to single entity financial statements.

> **Further details on what is a group?**
>
> Although from the legal point of view every company is a separate entity, from the economic point of view several companies may not be separate.
>
> In particular, when one company owns enough shares in another company to have a majority of votes at that company's annual general meeting (AGM), the first company may appoint all the directors of, and decide what dividends should be paid by, the second company.
>
> This degree of control enables the first company to manage the trading activities and future plans of the second company as if it were merely a department of the first company.
>
> The first company referred to above is called the parent, and the second is called a subsidiary. For the moment, it is sufficient to note that the essential feature of a group is that one company controls all the others.
>
> International Accounting Standards recognise that this state of affairs often arises, and require a parent company to produce consolidated financial statements showing the position and results of the whole group.

3 Acquisition accounting

IAS 27 requires acquisition accounting (the purchase method) to be used to prepare consolidated financial statements.

This requires the following rules to be followed:

- Add the parent's and subsidiary's assets, liabilities, income and expenses;

- The cost of the investment in the parent's books is eliminated against the share of subsidiary's net assets at acquisition, with any resulting goodwill being treated in accordance with IFRS 3 (revised) *Business Combinations*;

- The share capital of the group is always only the share capital of the parent;

- Adjustments are made to record the subsidiary's net assets at fair value;

- Uniform accounting policies must be used;

- Intra-group balances and transactions must be eliminated in full;

- Profits/losses on intra-group transactions that are recognised in assets should be eliminated in full (the provision for unrealised profit adjustment – PUP adjustment).

Standard consolidated statement of financial position (CSFP) workings

(W1) Group structure

Parent

%

Subsidiary

(W2) Net assets of subsidiary

	Acquisition Date	Reporting Date
Share capital	X	X
Retained earnings	X	X
Other reserves	X	X
	X	X

(W3) Goodwill

Cost of investment	X
Fair value of net assets (NAs) acquired (W2)	(X)
Goodwill at acquisition	X
Impairment	(X)
Goodwill at reporting date	X

(W4) Non-controlling interests

Not relevant to F1

(W5) Retained earnings – group reserves

	Retained earnings	Other reserves
Parent	X	X
Sub (% × post-acq reserves)	X	X
Impairment	(X)	–
	X	X

4 Goodwill

As mentioned in the previous section, goodwill is treated in accordance with IFRS 3 (revised) *Business Combinations*. In this chapter the assumption is that the parent purchases 100% of the shares of another entity. Alternative scenarios will be dealt with in F2.

The parent may pay more than the value of the entity's net assets because of:

- the entity's positive reputation;
- a loyal customer base; or
- staff expertise, etc.

This excess is called goodwill and is capitalised on the consolidated statement of financial position (CSFP). It is subject to an annual impairment review to ensure its value has not fallen below the carrying value.

Occasionally the parent company may pay less than the value of the subsidiary's net assets. This may occur because a quick purchase is necessary. In this rare situation the "negative goodwill", or discount on acquisition, is credited to group retained earnings (to increase group profits).

Illustration 1 : Simple groups

Statements of financial position at 31 December 2010

	P	S
	$000	$000
Non-current assets		
Property, plant and equipment	1,000	600
Investment in S	900	–
Current assets	200	200
	2,100	800
Equity		
Share capital	1,000	500
Retained earnings	800	200
Current liabilities	300	100
	2,100	800

P acquires 100% of S on 31 December 2010.

Required:

Prepare a consolidated statement of financial position (CSFP) at 31 December 2010.

Solution

Firstly, draw up the group structure to understand what the relationship is between the companies. This is a good habit to form as it will be very useful when the group becomes more complex.

(W1) Group structure

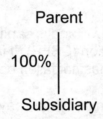

Parent

100%

Subsidiary

The next task is to add across the parent and subsidiary's assets and liabilities in the consolidated statement of financial position on your answer paper.

The share capital and share premium of the group is only ever the share capital and premium of the parent.

Note: Use the statement of financial position in the question as a starting point but insert a row above property, plant and equipment (under non-current assets) for goodwill, and ignore the parent's investment in the subsidiary.

The parent's investment in the subsidiary is ignored in the consolidated statement of financial position because the investment in the subsidiary is cancelled against the share of net assets acquired and the excess is calculated as goodwill.

Consolidated statement of financial position as at 31 December 2010

		$000
Non-current assets		
Goodwill	(W3)	
Property, plant and equipment	(1,000 + 600)	1,600
Current assets	(200 + 200)	400

Equity

Share capital		1,000
Retained earnings	(W5)	
Non-controlling interest	(W4)	0
Current liabilities	(300 + 100)	400

Then we can continue with the standard workings (W2) to (W5) on the workings piece of paper to complete the remainder of the CSFP.

(W2) **Net assets of subsidiary**

	Acquisition date	Reporting date
Share capital	500	500
Retained earnings	200	200
	700	700

In this case the acquisition date was 31 December 2010 which was the same as the reporting date so the columns include the same figures. The share capital and retained earnings are taken from the subsidiary's individual statement of financial position (SFP).

The accounting equation states that net assets = share capital + reserves.

The totals from the two columns are then used in subsequent workings.

(W3) **Goodwill**

Cost of investment	900
Fair value of net assets (NAs) acquired (100% × 700) (W2)	(700)
Goodwill at reporting date	200

The cost of investment is taken directly from the parent's statement of financial position in this case. The amount paid by the parent may alternatively be given to you as a separate figure in the question.

(W4) **Non-controlling interests**

Not applicable because the parent owns 100% of the subsidiary's shares.

(W5) **Retained earnings**

Parent	800
Subsidiary (100% × post acq profits)	–
Impairment	–
	800

Working 5 includes the parent's share of the subsidiary's post acquisition profits. Because S was acquired on the reporting date there are no post acquisition profits to include.

Now we can take the figures for goodwill and group retained earnings onto the CSFP to complete the requirement.

Consolidated statement of financial position as at 31 December 2010

		$000
Non-current assets		
Goodwill	(W3)	200
Property, plant and equipment	(1,000 + 600)	1,600
Current assets	(200 + 200)	400
		2,200
Equity		
Share capital		1,000
Retained earnings	(W5)	800
Non-controlling interest	(W4)	0
Current liabilities	(300 + 100)	400
		2,200

Illustration 2 : Simple groups 2

Statements of financial position at 31 March 2011

	P	S
	$000	$000
Non-current assets		
Property, plant and equipment	1,650	750
Investment in S	1,100	–
Current assets	250	650
	3,000	1,400
Equity		
Share capital	1,500	500
Retained earnings	900	400
Current liabilities	600	500
	3,000	1,400

P acquires 100% of S on 31 March 2011.

Required:

Prepare a consolidated statement of financial position (CSFP) at 31 March 2011.

Solution

Consolidated statement of financial position as at 31 March 2011

		$000
Non-current assets		
Goodwill	(W3)	200
Property, plant and equipment	(1,650 + 750)	2,400
Current assets	(250 + 650)	900
		3,500

Equity

Share capital		1,500
Retained earnings	(W5)	900
Non-controlling interest	(W4)	0
Current liabilities	(600 + 500)	1,100
		3,500

Workings

(W1) Group structure

Parent

100%

Subsidiary

(W2) Net assets of subsidiary

	Acquisition date	Reporting date
Share capital	500	500
Retained earnings	400	400
	900	900

(W3) Goodwill

Cost of investment	1,100
Fair value of net assets (NAs) acquired (100% × 900) (W2)	(900)
Goodwill at reporting date	200

(W4) Non-controlling interests

N/A

(W5) Retained earnings

Parent	900
Subsidiary (100% × post acq profits)	–
Impairment	–
	900

5 Pre and post-acquisition

In Illustrations 1 and 2 the parent acquired its shares in the subsidiary on the reporting date. In the case where the parent made the purchase some months or years prior to the reporting date, the subsidiary's reserves must be split out into pre and post-acquisition.

The parent has influenced any change in reserves since the acquisition date only, e.g. the parent can only share in the change in asset value after acquisition. Any changes before this date would have been due to the influence of the previous parent.

Illustration 3 : Pre and post-acquisition reserves

Statements of financial position at 31 December 2010

	P	S
	$000	$000
Non-current assets		
Property, plant and equipment	3,330	550
Investment in S	1,540	–
Current assets	1,030	660
	5,900	1,210
Equity		
Ordinary share capital	2,500	525
Retained earnings	3,000	585
Current liabilities	400	100
	5,900	1,210

P acquired 100% of S one year ago on 1 January 2010 when the balance on the retained earnings of S stood at $505,000. Goodwill has been impaired by $120,000 since the acquisition.

Required:

Prepare the consolidated statement of financial position (CSFP) at 31 December 2010.

Solution

Firstly, draw up the group structure on a separate piece of paper to your answer to understand what the relationship is between the companies.

(W1) Group structure

Parent

100%

Subsidiary

The next task is to add across the parent's and subsidiary's assets and liabilities in the consolidated statement of financial position on your answer piece of paper. The share capital of the group is always only the share capital of the parent.

Note: Use the statement of financial position in the question as a starting point but insert a row below non-current assets for goodwill and ignore the parent's investment in the subsidiary.

The parent's investment in the subsidiary is ignored in the CSFP because the investment in the subsidiary is cancelled against the share of net assets acquired and the excess is calculated as goodwill.

Consolidated statement of financial position as at 31 December 2010

		$000
Non-current assets		
Goodwill	(W3)	
Property, plant and equipment	(3,330 + 550)	3,880
Current assets	(1,030 + 660)	1,690

Equity

Share capital		2,500
Retained earnings	(W5)	
Non-controlling interest	(W4)	0
Current liabilities	(400 + 100)	500

Then we can continue with the standard workings (W2) to (W5) on the workings piece of paper to complete the remainder of the CSFP.

(W2) **Net assets of subsidiary**

	Acquisition date	Reporting date
Share capital	525	525
Retained earnings	505	585
	1,030	1,110

The subsidiary's retained earnings at the acquisition date will be given to you in the question.

Share capital of the subsidiary will not change from acquisition to reporting date so you can copy the share capital from the subsidiary's SFP to W2 in both columns.

The totals from the two columns are then used in subsequent workings.

(W3) **Goodwill**

Cost of investment	1,540
Fair value of net assets (NAs) acquired (100% × 1,030) (W2)	(1,030)
Goodwill at acquisition	510
Impairment	(120)
Goodwill at reporting date	390

The cost of the investment is taken from the parent's SFP. The fair value of net assets acquired must be taken from the *acquisition date* column of (W2).

The amount of the impairment is given in the question. The double entry is to reduce the value of goodwill (credit) and reduce group retained earnings (debit).

(W4) Non-controlling interests

N/A

(W5) Retained earnings

Parent	3,000
Subsidiary (100% × post acq profits)	
100% x (1,110 – 1,030 (W2))	80
Impairment (W3)	(120)
	2,960

The parent is responsible for its share of the subsidiary's post acquisition profits only. The parent's percentage holding is multiplied by the *change* in net assets from (W2), i.e. the difference between the totals in each column.

Remember that impairments reduce group retained earnings and must be deducted from (W5) in addition to (W3).

Now we can take the figures for goodwill and group retained earnings onto the CSFP to complete the requirement.

Consolidated statement of financial position as at 31 December 2010

		$000
Non-current assets		
Property, plant and equipment	(3,330 + 550)	3,880
Goodwill	(W3)	390
Current assets	(1,030 + 660)	1,690
		5,960

Equity		
Share capital		2,500
Retained earnings	(W5)	2,960
Non-controlling interest	(W4)	0
Current liabilities	(400 + 100)	500
		5,960

Test your understanding 1 : Pre and post-acquisition reserves

Statements of financial position at 31 May 2011

	P	S
	$000	$000
Non-current assets		
Property, plant and equipment	2,300	400
Investment in S	1,000	
Current assets	900	500
	4,200	900
Equity		
Ordinary share capital	1,000	475
Retained earnings	2,750	275
Current liabilities	450	150
	4,200	900

P acquired 100% of S two years ago on 1 June 2009 when the balance on the retained earnings of S stood at $125,000. Goodwill should be written down to 75% of its original value to allow for impairment.

Required:

Prepare the consolidated statement of financial position (CSFP) at 31 May 2011.

6 Fair value adjustment

The group accounts must include the subsidiary's net assets at their fair value at the date of acquisition.

This reflects the "cost" to the group at acquisition and ensures an accurate measurement of goodwill.

The actual value of a company must be reflected in the consolidated accounts, which is not necessarily represented by the individual company in their Statement of Financial Position. For example, land and buildings may be held at historic costs and may actually be worth much more than they are stated at in the accounts.

Therefore an adjustment is required if the subsidiary's book values are not equal to their fair values.

Adjust:

- **W2** Both columns (unless the asset is sold by the reporting date)
- Face of CSFP (NCA)

Illustration 4 : Fair value adjustments

The following summarised statements of financial position are provided for Wensum and Yare as at 31 December 2010

	Wensum	Yare
	$000	$000
Non-current assets		
Property, plant and equipment	1,500	440
Investment in Yare	1,600	–
Current assets	50	860
	3,150	1,300
Equity		
Share capital ($1 ordinary)	2,000	350
Retained earnings	900	850
Current liabilities	250	100
	3,150	1,300

Wensum purchased 350,000 shares in Yare on 31 December 2010 for $1.6m. It is estimated that the non-current assets of Yare had a fair value of $770,000 on the 31 December 2010.

Required:
Prepare the consolidated statement of financial position (CSFP) for the Wensum group as at 31 December 2010.

Solution

Firstly, draw up the group structure to understand what the relationship is between the companies.

(W1) Group Structure

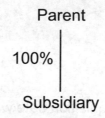

Parent

100%

Subsidiary

The next task is to add across the parent and subsidiary's assets and liabilities in the consolidated statement of financial position.

The share capital of the group is always only the share capital of the parent.

Consolidated statement of financial position as 31 December 2010

		$000
Non-current assets		
Goodwill	(W3)	
Property, plant and equipment	(1,500 + 440	
Current assets	(50 + 860)	910
		———
		———
Equity		
Share capital		2,000
Retained earnings	(W5)	
Non-controlling interest	(W4)	0
Current liabilities	(250 + 100)	350
		——— .
		———

Then we can continue with the standard workings (W2) to (W5) on the workings piece of paper to complete the remainder of the CSFP.

Note: we only do not total the PPE amount until we have considered the fair value adjustments that need to be made, as per (W2). This is because the PPE amounts in the subsidiary books are understated and must be valued at fair value for the consolidation.

(W2) Net assets of subsidiary

	Acquisition/ Reporting date
Share capital	350
Retained earnings	850
Fair value adjustment (770–440)	330
	1,530

In this case the acquisition date was 31 December 2010 which was the same as the reporting date so we have used one column. The share capital and retained earnings are taken from the subsidiary's individual statement of financial position (SFP).

The subsidiary's net assets must be measured at fair value on the acquisition date. The book value for non-current assets of $440,000 must be uplifted to the fair value of $770,000. This increase is recorded in W2 as above and also **on the face of the consolidated statement of financial position**.

If Yare had been purchased some years ago, the fair value adjustment of $330,000 would have been recorded in both the acquisition date **and** the reporting date columns. This is the case unless the question explicitly states that the asset involved has been sold before the reporting date.

(W3) Goodwill

Cost of investment	1,600
Fair value of NAs acquired (100% × 1,530) (W2)	(1,530)
Goodwill at reporting date	70

(W4) Non-controlling interests

N/A

(W5) Retained earnings

Wensum	900
Yare (100% × post acq profits)	–
Impairment	–
	900

Working 5 includes the parent's share of the subsidiary's post acquisition profits. Because Yare was acquired on the reporting date there are no post acquisition profits to include.

Now we can take the figures for goodwill and group retained earnings onto the CSFP to complete the requirement.

Remember also to record the fair value adjustment to non-current assets.

Consolidated statement of financial position as at 31 December 2010

		$000
Non-current assets		
Goodwill	(W3)	70
Property, plant and equipment	(1,500 + 440 + 330)	2,270
Current assets	(50 + 860)	910
		3,250
Equity		
Share capital		2,000
Retained earnings	(W5)	900
Non-controlling interest	(W4)	0
Current liabilities	(250 + 100)	350
		3,250

7 Depreciation adjustment

Fair value adjustments may involve adjusting non-current asset values which will consequently involve an adjustment to the depreciation figure. Depreciation must be based upon the carrying value of the non-current assets concerned, so if non-current asset values are changed at acquisition, then so depreciation values must be changed in the post-acquisition period.

Adjust:

- **W2** NAs @ reporting date column
- Face of CSFP (NCA)

Illustration 5 : Depreciation adjustment

P acquired 100% of the ordinary share capital of S on 1 October 2009 when S's retained earnings stood at $150,000. S's statement of financial position at 30 September 2011 is as follows:

Statement of financial position

	$000
Non-current assets	
Property, plant and equipment	900
Current assets	500
	1,400
Equity	
Share capital	800
Retained earnings	250
Current liabilities	350
	1,400

On 1 October 2009 the fair value of S's non-current assets was $1.2m compared to the book value at the time of $1m. The difference was due to a building which had a remaining useful life of 10 years on 1 October 2009.

Required:

Prepare (W2) Net assets of the subsidiary for S for use by your colleague in preparing the consolidated statement of financial position for the P group at 30 September 2011.

Solution

(W2) Net assets of subsidiary

	Acquisition Date	Reporting Date
Share capital	800	800
Retained earnings	150	250
Fair value adjustment (1,200 – 1,000)	200	200
Depreciation on fair value adjustment 200/10 x 2 yrs	–	(40)
	1,150	1,210

The fair value adjustment is made to both columns because the question does not state that the subsidiary has sold the building prior to the reporting date.

The depreciation on the fair value uplift is deducted from the reporting date column only, as the depreciation adjustment is required only *after* the acquisition date. We are calculating depreciation for 2 years because the fair value adjustment happened 2 years ago (acquisition 1 October 2009, reporting date 30 September 2011).

Both adjustments must also be made to the face of the consolidated statement of financial position, i.e.

Non-current assets for the group (P + 900 + 200 – 40)

Test your understanding 2 : Fair value adjustments

The following summarised statements of financial position are provided for Kemp and Solent as at 31 December 2010

	Kemp $000	Solent $000
Non-current assets		
Property, plant and equipment	2,000	500
Investment in Solent	1,900	
Current assets	200	800
	4,100	1,300
Equity		
Share capital ($1 ordinary)	3,000	300
Retained earnings	1,000	900
Current liabilities	100	100
	4,100	1,300

Kemp purchased 300,000 shares in Solent on 1 January 2009 for $1.9m when Solent's retained earnings were $750,000. It is estimated that the non-current assets of Solent possessed a fair value $200,000 more than book value at that date. The difference was due to a building which had a remaining useful life of 10 years on 1 January 2009. Goodwill should be impaired by 20% at 31 December 2010.

Required:

The consolidated statement of financial position (CSFP) at 31 December 2010.

8 Intra-group balances

Intra-group balances must be eliminated in full. The group as a single entity, cannot owe or be owed balances to itself, i.e the parent may have a receivable due from the subsidiary and the subsidiary may have a payable owed to the parent. This is fine in the individual accounts but must be eliminated on consolidation.

Intra-group balances may arise in the following situations:

- P and S trading with each other, resulting in current account balances, i.e. receivables and payables
- Intra-group loans, resulting in an investment and loan balance

These are amounts owing within the group rather than outside the group and, therefore, must not appear in the consolidated statement of financial position.

They are, therefore, cancelled off against each other on consolidation:

- Reduce receivables
- Reduce payables

Current account balances may disagree. This is most likely to be due to cash in transit or goods in transit.

Cash in transit

Cash has been sent by one group company, but has not been received and so is not recorded in the books of the other group company. The following journal entry will be required:

Dr   Bank

Cr   Receivables current account

You will not be required to prepare the journal entries in the examination, hence you may find it easier to remember the following:

Increase   Bank (cash in transit)

Reduce   Receivables (amount in the seller's books)

Goods in transit

Goods have been sent by one company, but have not been received and so are not recorded in the books of the other group company. The following journal entry will be required:

Dr   Inventory

Cr   Payables current account

You will not be required to prepare the journal entries in the examination, hence you may find it easier to remember the following:

      Increase   Inventory (goods in transit)

      Increase   Payables (amount in the buyer's books)

These adjustments are for the purpose of consolidation only.

Once these adjustments have been made, the current account balances should agree and can be removed from both the receivables and payables in the consolidated statement of financial position.

Illustration 6 : Intra-group balances

The following extracts are provided from the statements of financial position of P and S at the year-end:

	P	S
	$000	$000
Current assets		
Inventory	100	50
Receivables	270	80
Cash	120	40
Current liabilities		
Payables	160	90

P's statement of financial position includes a receivable of $40,000 being due from S. S has a payables balance of $30,000 due to P.

Shortly before the year-end, S sent a cheque for $4,000 to P. P did not receive this cheque until after the year-end.

Also, P had dispatched goods to S with a value of $6,000 but S had not received them by the year-end.

Required:

What balances will be shown in the consolidated statement of financial position (CSFP) of the P group for the above items?

Solution

Consolidated statement of financial position (extract)

		$000
Current assets		
Inventory	100 + 50 + 6	156
Receivables	270 + 80 - 40 -4	310
Cash	120 + 40 + 4	164
Current liabilities		
Payables	160 + 90 - 30	220

Start by adding across P and S's assets and liabilities for the consolidated statement of financial position.

For the cash in transit, neither entity is recording the cash so this needs to be amended, i.e. add $4,000 to cash.

			$000
Cr	Receivables	↓	4
Dr	Bank	↑	4

The goods in transit have also not been recorded in the receiving entity's books. The $6,000 must be added to inventory and recorded in payables.

			$000
Dr	Inventory	↑	6
Cr	Payables	↑	6

The inter-company balance will now agree, i.e. receivable $36,000 and payables $36,000. We do not need to show all of the entries just the increase in cash and inventory and the removal of the inter-company balance.

Test your understanding 3 : Intra-group balances

The following statements of financial position exist at the 31 December 2010.

	P	S
	$000	$000
Non-current assets		
Property, plant and equipment	5,400	2,000
Investment in S	3,700	
Current assets		
Inventory	750	140
Receivables	650	95
Cash	400	85
	10,900	2,320
Equity		
Ordinary share capital	7,000	1,400
Share premium	1,950	280
Retained earnings	1,050	440
Current liabilities	900	200
	10,900	2,320

P acquired 100% of S five years ago when the balance on the retained earnings of S was $300,000. Any goodwill arising is now thought to be worth 2/3 of its original value. The share premium in S arose on the issue of their ordinary shares many years ago.

Some of the non-current assets of S had a fair value of $1.2m at the date of acquisition by P. Their book value recorded at this time was $1m. These non-current assets will be depreciated on a straight line basis over 20 years from the date of acquisition.

P and S traded with each other and at the reporting date P owed S an amount of $25,000. On 30 December 2010 P sent a cheque for $5,000 to S which S had not received by year end.

Required:

A consolidated statement of financial position (CSFP) as at 31 December 2010.

9 Provisions for Unrealised Profits (PUPs)

P and S may sell goods to each other, resulting in a profit being recorded in the selling company's financial statements. If these goods are still held by the purchasing company at the year-end, the goods have not been sold outside of the group. The profit is therefore unrealised from the group's perspective and should be removed.

The adjustment is also required to ensure that inventory is stated at the cost to the group.

Adjust

- **W2** NAs @ reporting date column **if S sells** the goods or **W5 if P sells** the goods

- Inventory on the face of the CSFP

Illustration 7 : PUPs

Parent sells to subsidiary

P sells goods to S for $100 at cost plus 25%. All goods remain in the inventory of S at the end of the year.

$$\text{Profit made on the sale} \qquad \frac{25}{125} \times 400 \quad = 80.$$

Individual FS

P records profit	80
S records inventory	400

Group financial statements should show the cost to the group

Profit	0
Inventory	320

PUP adjustment

Dr Group profit reserves (W5)	↓	80
Cr Group inventory (CSFP)	↓	80

The group profit figure for the parent will be reduced as it is the parent that recorded the profit in this case.

It is important to note that the adjustment takes place in the group accounts only. The individual accounts are correct as they stand and will not be adjusted as a result.

Subsidiary sells to parent

Individual FS

S records profit	80
P records inventory	400

PUP adjustment

Dr Net assets at reporting date (W2)	↓	80
Cr Group inventory (CSFP)	↓	80

The subsidiary's profit will be reduced as it is the subsidiary that recorded the profit in this case. It is important that the adjustment is made in W2 as the amended figures then flow through to the remaining standard workings.

The distinction between making the adjustment in W2 or W5 is important for when the parent does not own 100% of the subsidiary and non-controlling interests are introduced in F2.

Cost structures

The cost structure of the intra-group sale may be given to you in one of two ways.

Mark up on cost

This occurs most frequently in questions. If, for example, goods are sold for $440 and there is a 25% mark up on cost, you need to calculate the profit included within the $440.

	%	$	
Revenue	125	440	
Cost of sales	100		
Gross profit	25	88	= 440 x 25/125

The PUP is $88.

Gross profit margin

The gross profit margin gives the profit as a percentage of revenue.
Using the same figures as above but with a gross profit margin of 25%.

	%	$	
Revenue	100	440	
Cost of sales	75		
Gross profit	25	110	= 440 x 25/100

The PUP is $110.

Test your understanding 4 : PUPs

P sells goods to S for $522 at a mark-up of 20%. 40% of these goods were sold on by S to external parties by the year end.

Required:

What is the PUP adjustment in the group accounts?

Test your understanding 5 : PUPs

S sells goods to P at a mark-up of 33 1/3%. The selling price is $360. All goods remained unsold at the year end.

Required:

What is the PUP adjustment in this case?

Illustration 8 : PUPs

The following statements of financial position exist at 30 June 2011:

	P	S
	$000	$000
Non-current assets		
Property, plant and equipment	4,000	2,000
Investment in S	3,400	
Current assets		
Inventory	500	100
Other current assets	100	300
	8,000	2,400
Equity		
Ordinary share capital	6,000	1,500
Retained earnings	1,600	700
Current liabilities	400	200
	8,000	2,400

P acquired 100% of S when the balance on S's retained earnings stood at $250,000.

During the year, P sold goods to S for $120,000 at a mark-up of 20%. Half of these goods remain in inventory at the year end.

Required:

Prepare the consolidated statement of financial position (CSFP) of the P group.

Solution

Consolidated statement of financial position as at 30 June 2011

		$000
Non-current assets		
Goodwill	(W3)	1,650
Property, plant and equipment	(4,000 + 2,000)	6,000
Current assets		
Inventory	(500 + 100 − 10 (W6))	590
Other current assets	(100 + 300)	400
		8,640
Equity		
Share capital		6,000
Retained earnings	(W5)	2,040
Non-controlling interest	(W4)	0
Current liabilities	(400 + 200)	600
		8,640

Workings

(W1) Group structure

Parent

100%

Subsidiary

(W2) Net assets of subsidiary

	Acquisition date	Reporting date
Share capital	1,500	1,500
Retained earnings	250	700
	1,750	2,200

Because P sells the goods to S there is no adjustment required in (W2).

(W3) Goodwill

Cost of investment	3,400
NAs acquired	
100% × 1,750 (W2)	(1,750)
Goodwill at reporting date	1,650

(W4) Non-controlling interests

N/A

(W5) Retained earnings

Parent (1,600 − 10 (W6))	1,590
Subsidiary (100% × (2,200 − 1,750)(W2))	450
	2,040

(W6) PUP

Profit on sale $\quad$ 20/120 × 120 = 20

Profit in inventory = PUP = ½ × 20 = 10

Since P sold to S, adjust W5 and inventory on CSFP.

When answering the question using exam technique you would be well advised to follow these steps:

(1) Draw up the group structure including all group companies and when the shares were purchased.

(2) Draw up an outline consolidated statement of financial position (CSFP) and add across assets and liabilities and insert the parent's share capital figure.

(3) Start on (W2) net assets of the subsidiary working. Ensure you read all the information in the question before proceeding in case item will effect (W2).

(4) If calculations are required, e.g. for a PUP, add an extra working and call it (W6).

(5) Then proceed to (W3) through to (W5).

(6) Complete the CSFP with goodwill and retained earnings figures.

(7) Don't forget any changes necessary to the face of the CSFP, e.g. inventory PUP or fair value uplift to non-current assets.

Test your understanding 6 : PUPs

The following statements of financial position exist at 30 June 2011

	P	S
	$000	$000
Non-current assets		
Property, plant and equipment	4,000	2,000
Investment in S	3,400	
Current assets		
Inventory	500	100
Other current assets	100	300
	8,000	2,400
Equity		
Ordinary share capital	6,000	1,500
Retained earnings	1,600	700
Current liabilities	400	200
	8,000	2,400

P acquired 100% of S when the balance on S's retained earnings stood at $250,000.

During the year, S sold goods to P for $120,000 at a mark-up of 20%. Half of these goods remain in inventory at the year end.

Required:

Prepare the consolidated statement of financial position (CSFP) of the P group.

Note: This TYU uses the same figures as Illustration 8 in expandable text above but in Illustration 8, P sells the goods to S.

10 Non-current assets PUPs

P and S may sell non-current assets to each other, resulting in a profit being recorded in the selling company's financial statements. If these non-current assets are still held by the purchasing company at the year-end, the profit is unrealised from the group's perspective and should be removed.

The profit on disposal should be removed from the seller's books.

In addition to the profit based on the excess of the transfer price over the carrying value in the selling company's books, there is depreciation to deal with.

Prior to the transfer, the asset is depreciated based on the original cost. After the transfer depreciation is calculated on the transfer price, i.e. a higher value. Therefore depreciation charged is higher after the transfer and this extra cost must be eliminated in the consolidated accounts, i.e. profits increased.

The extra depreciation should be removed from the purchaser's books.

The easiest way to calculate the adjustment required is to compare the carrying value (CV) of the asset now with the carrying value that it would have been held at had the transfer never occurred:

CV at reporting date with transfer	X
CV at reporting date without transfer	(X)
Adjustment required	X

The calculated amount should be:

- Deducted from the retained earnings of the seller (**W2** net assets @ reporting date column **if S sells** the asset or reduce **W5 if P sells** the asset)
- Deducted when adding across P and S's non-current asset in CSFP

Illustration 9 : Non-current assets PUPs

If P transfers a non-current asset to its subsidiary

P acquired 100% of the share capital of S some years ago. P's reporting date is 31 August. P transfers an asset on 1 March 2009 for $75,000 when its carrying value is $60,000. The remaining useful life at the date of sale is 2.5 years. The group depreciation policy is the straight line basis with a proportionate charge in the years of acquisition and disposal.

What adjustment is required in the consolidated financial statements of P for the year ended 31 August 2010?

CV at reporting date with transfer	75,000
CV at reporting date without transfer	60,000
Adjustment required	15,000

Adjustment (parent sells)

Dr	Group retained earnings (W5)	↓	15,000
Cr	NCA (CSFP)	↓	15,000

We must now consider the effect on depreciation. The extra depreciation charged since transfer = (75,000 – 60,000) x 1.5/2.5 = 9,000 (we transferred the asset one and half years ago before the reporting date). This extra depreciation charge must be removed from the books.

Adjustment (parent sells)

Dr	NCA (CSFP)	↑	9,000
Cr	Group retained earnings (W5)	↑	9,000

We could have accounted for this by just looking at the net change in the carrying value as follows:

	CV before transfer	CV after transfer	Difference
Carrying value	60,000	75,000	
Additional depreciation (1.5/2.5)	36,000	45,000	
Carrying value	24,000	30,000	6,000

Adjustment (parent sells)

Dr	Group retained earnings (W5)	↓	6,000
Cr	NCA (CSFP)	↓	6,000

If S transfers a non-current asset to the parent

Using the same example as above, but S has sold the asset to P.

Adjustment (sub sells)

Dr	Group retained earnings (W2)	↓	6,000
Cr	NCA (CSFP)	↓	6,000

Alternative approach

The approach we have taken is the most common way of dealing with non-current asset PUP's. However, there is an alternative view that states the seller should record the profit on the transfer but the buyer should record the depreciation expense. This would result in the following adjustments:

If the parent transfers a non-current asset to the subsidiary

If the parent sells:

- Difference in non-current asset CV at acquisition reduces W5

- Difference in depreciation charge increases W2

If we applied this view in the previous illustration it would give us the following results:

Adjustment (parent sells)

Dr	Group retained earnings (W5)	↓	15,000
Cr	Net assets of subsidiary at reporting date (W2)	↑	9,000
Cr	NCA (CSFP)	↓	6,000

If the subsidiary transfers a non-current asset to the parent

If the subsidiary sells:

- Difference in non-current asset CV at acquisition reduces W2

- Difference in depreciation charge increases W5

Using the same example as above, but S has sold the asset to P.

Adjustment (sub sells)

Dr	Net assets of subsidiary at reporting date (W2)	↓	15,000
Cr	Group retained earnings (W5)	↑	9,000
Cr	NCA (CSFP)	↓	6,000

Test your understanding 7 : Non-current assets PUPs

Rio purchased 100% of Salvador on 1 January 2009. On 30 June 2010 Salvador sold a lorry to Rio for $25,000. Its carrying value in Salvador's books was $20,000 and the remaining useful economic life at the date of transfer was 3 years.

Required:

What adjustment is required to the financial statements of the Rio group for the year ended 31 December 2010?

Aston and Martin

Aston acquired 100% of the share capital of Martin for $40,000 on 1 January 2007 when the balance on the retained earnings of Martin stood at $9,000. The statements of financial position of the two companies are as follows at the 31 December 2010:

	Aston $000	Martin $000
Non-current assets		
Property, plant and equipment	88	39
Investment in Martin	40	
	128	39
Current assets		
Inventory	80	26
Receivables	24	32
Bank and cash		15
	104	73
	232	112
Equity		
Called-up share capital	100	24
Retained earnings	46	48
Current liabilities		
Overdraft	14	10
Payables	72	30
	86	40
	232	112

At the date of acquisition, the fair value of Martin's property, plant and equipment was $5,000 higher than the carrying value. These assets were estimated to have a remaining useful economic life of ten years at this date. A full year's depreciation charge is to be made in the year of acquisition. The fair value of all other net assets was equal to the carrying values.

Aston's payables balance includes $6,000 payable to Martin, and Martin's receivables balance includes $20,000 owing from Aston. At the year end, it was established that Martin had despatched goods to Aston with a selling price of $9,000 and that Aston did not receive delivery of these items until after the year end. At the same time, Aston had put a cheque in the post to Martin for $5,000 which also did not arrive until after the year end.

In addition to the goods in transit of $9,000, there were also some items included in Aston's inventory which had been purchased by Aston at the price of $21,000 from Martin. Martin had priced these goods at a mark-up of 20%.

The group policy toward goodwill arising on consolidation is to subject it to an annual impairment review. It was felt that the goodwill should be carried at 60% of its original value.

Required:

A consolidated statement of financial position (CSFP) as at 31 December 2010 for the Aston Group.

Mid year acquisitions

Mid year acquisitions are only relevant to the statement of financial position when completing (W2) Net assets of the subsidiary. Reserves at acquisition are required and this figure may not be readily available if the acquisition took place part way through an accounting period at which point financial statements of the subsidiary are not prepared.

It is assumed that profits accrue evenly over the year and therefore profits for the year can by time apportioned and added to the reserves brought forward at the beginning of the year to calculate pre acquisition reserves.

For example, an entity is acquired on 1 March 2010, its profits for the year ended 31 December 2010 are $12,000 and retained earnings carried forward are $55,000. Retained earnings at acquisition will be 55,000 − (10/12 x 12,000) = $45,000.

This is not relevant to F1 and will be studied in more detail in F2.

Test your understanding 9 : Exam standard question

On 1 December 2010 K bought 100% of S paying $140,000 cash.

The summarised statements of financial position for the two companies as at 30 November 2011 are:

	K $		S $
Non-current assets			
Property, plant and equipment	138,000		115,000
Investments	162,000		
	300,000		115,000
Current assets			
Inventory	15,000	17,000	
Receivables	19,000	20,000	
Bank and cash	2,000	–	
	36,000		37,000
	336,000		152,000
Equity			
Called-up share capital	114,000		40,000
Retained earnings	189,000		69,000
	303,000		109,000
Non-current liabilities			
8% Debentures	–		20,000
Current liabilities			
Payables	33,000		23,000
	336,000		152,000

The following information is relevant:

(1) The inventory of S includes $8,000 of goods purchased from K at cost plus 25%.

(2) On 1 December 2010 a piece of plant with a carrying value of $30,000 had a fair value of $48,000. It had a remaining life of 10 years as at this date.

(3) Impairments to date total $5,100.

(4) S earned a profit after tax of $5,250 in the year ended 30 November 2011 and did not pay any dividends during the year.

(5) The debenture in S's books represents monies borrowed from K on 1 December 2010. All of the debenture interest has been accounted for.

(6) Included in K's receivables is $4,000 relating to inventory sold to S since acquisition. S raised a cheque for $2,500 and sent it to K on 29 November 2011. K did not receive this cheque until 4 December 2011.

Required:

Prepare the consolidated statement of financial position (CSFP) of the K group as at 30 November 2011.

You will need this information to attempt the next test your understanding.

Test your understanding 10 : Objective test questions

(1) **Using the information you have prepared in TYU 9, what is the correct figure for goodwill?**

   A $13,150

   B $31,150

   C $25,900

   D $18,250

(2) **Using the information you have prepared in TYU 9, what is the correct figure for inventory?**

   A $32,000

   B $24,000

   C $30,000

   D $30,400

(3) **Using the information you have prepared in TYU 9, what is the correct figure for retained earnings?**

   A $185,750

   B $189,000

   C $192,450

   D $187,350

(4) **Using the information you have prepared in TYU 9, what is the correct figure for property, plant and equipment?**

A $253,000

B $271,000

C $269,200

D $264,100

(5) **Using the information you have prepared in TYU 9, what is the correct figure for receivables?**

A $39,000

B $35,000

C $43,000

D $36,500

Test your understanding 11 : Objective test questions 2

(1) LPD buys goods from its 100% owned subsidiary QPR. QPR earns a mark-up of 25% on such transactions. At the group's year end, 30 June 2011 LPD had not yet taken delivery of goods, at a sales value of $100,000, which were despatched by QPR on 29 June 2011. At what amount would the goods in transit appear in the consolidated statement of financial position of the LPD group at 30 June 2011?

A $60,000

B $75,000

C $80,000

D $100,000

(2 marks)

(2) STV owns 100% of the ordinary share capital of its subsidiary TUW. At the group's year end, 28 February 2011, STV's payables include $3,600 in respect of inventories sold by TUW.

TUW's receivables include $6,700 in respect of inventories sold to STV. Two days before the year end STV sent a payment of $3,100 to TUW that was not recorded by the latter until two days after the year end.

The in-transit item should be dealt with as follows in the consolidated statement of financial position at 28 February 2011:

A $2,325 to be included as cash in transit

B $3,100 to be added to consolidated payables

C $3,100 to be included as inventories in transit

D $3,100 to be included as cash in transit

(2 marks)

(3) **Where the purchase price of an acquisition is less than the aggregate fair value of the net assets acquired, which ONE of the following accounting treatments of the difference is required by IFRS 3 Business Combinations?**

A Deduction from goodwill in the consolidated statement of financial position?

B Immediate recognition as a gain in the statement of changes in equity?

C Recognition in the statement of comprehensive income over its useful life

D Immediate recognition as a gain in profit or loss.

(2 marks)

(4) On 30 September 2011 GHI purchased 100% of the ordinary share capital of JKL for $1.80 million. The book value of JKL's net assets at the date of acquisition was $1.35 million. A valuation exercise showed that the fair value of JKL's property, plant and equipment at that date was $100,000 greater than book value, and JKL immediately incorporated this revaluation into its own books.

Calculate goodwill on acquisition in accordance with IFRS 3 Business Combinations.

(2 marks)

11 Summary diagram

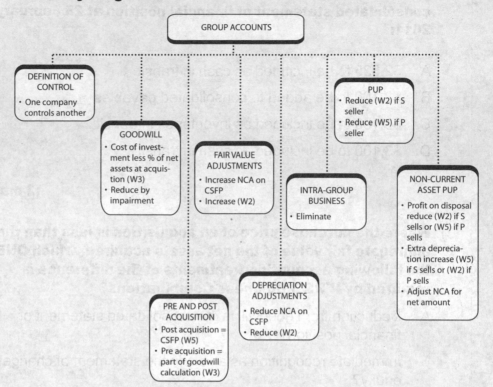

Test your understanding answers

Test your understanding 1 : Pre and post-acquisition reserves

Consolidated statement of financial position as at 31 May 2011

		$000
Non-current assets		
Goodwill	(W3)	300
Property, plant and equipment	(2,300 + 400)	2,700
Current assets	(900 + 500)	1,400
		4,400
Equity		
Share capital		1,000
Retained earnings	(W5)	2,800
Non-controlling interest	(W4)	0
Current liabilities	(450 + 150)	600
		4,400

Workings

(W1) Group structure

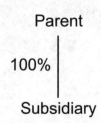

Parent

100%

Subsidiary

(W2) Net assets of subsidiary

	Acquisition date	Reporting date
Share capital	475	475
Retained earnings	125	275
	600	750

(W3) Goodwill

Cost of investment	1,000
Fair value of net assets (NAs) acquired (100% × 600) (W2)	(600)
Goodwill at acquisition	400
Impairment (25% x 400)	(100)
Goodwill at reporting date	300

(W4) Non-controlling interests

N/A

(W5) Retained earnings

Parent	2,750
Subsidiary (100% × post acq profits) 100% x (750 − 600) (W2)	150
Impairment	(100)
	2,800

Test your understanding 2 : Fair value adjustments

Kemp Group consolidated statement of financial position as at 31 December 2010

		$000
Non-current assets		
Goodwill	(W3)	520
Property, plant and equipment	(2000 + 500 + 200 - 40)	2,660
Current assets	(200 + 800)	1,000
		4,180
Equity		
Share capital		3,000
Retained earnings	(W5)	980
Non-controlling interest	(W4)	0
Current liabilities	(100 + 100)	200
		4,180

Workings

(W1) Group structure

Parent

100%

Subsidiary

(W2) Net assets of subsidiary

	Acquisition Date	Reporting Date
Share capital	300	300
Retained earnings	750	900
Fair value adjustment	200	200
Depreciation on fair value adjustment 200/10 x 2 yrs	–	(40)
	1,250	1,360

(W3) Goodwill

Cost of investment	1,900
Fair value of net assets (NAs) acquired	(1,250)
(100% × 1,250) (W2)	
Goodwill at acquisition	650
Impairment 20%	(130)
Goodwill at reporting date	520

(W4) Non-controlling interests

N/A

(W5) Retained earnings

Parent	1,000
Subsidiary (100% × post acq profits)	
100% x (1,360 – 1,250 (W2))	110
Impairment (W3)	(130)
	980

Test your understanding 3 : Intra-group balances

Consolidated statement of financial position as at 31 December 2010

		$000
Non-current assets		
Goodwill	(W3)	1,013
Property, plant and equipment	(5400 + 2000 + 200 – 50)	7,550
Current assets		
Inventory	(750 + 140)	890
Receivables	(650 + 95 – 30)	715
Cash	(400 + 85 + 5)	490
		10,658
Equity		
Share capital		7,000
Share premium		1,950
Retained earnings	(W5)	633
Non-controlling interest	(W4)	0
Current liabilities	(900 + 200 – 25)	1,075
		10,658

Workings

(W1) Group structure

Parent

100%

Subsidiary

(W2) Net assets of subsidiary

	Acquisition date	Reporting date
Share capital	1,400	1,400
Share premium	280	280
Retained earnings	300	440
Fair value adj (1,200 – 1,000)	200	200
Depreciation adj (200 x 5/20)		(50)
	2,180	2,270

(W3) Goodwill

Cost of investment	3,700
Net assets acquired (100% × 2,180)	(2,180)
Goodwill on acquisition	1,520
Impairment (1/3 x 1,520)	(507)
Goodwill at reporting date	1,013

(W4) Non-controlling interests

N/A

(W5) Retained earnings

Parent retained earnings	1,050
Subsidiary (100% × (2,270 – 2,180) (W2))	90
Impairment	(507)
	633

(W6) Intra-group balances

Cash (increase)	$5,000
Receivables (decrease)	$30,000
Payables (decrease)	$25,000

Test your understanding 4 : PUPs

The PUP will be:

$$(522 \times \frac{20}{120}) \times 60\% \qquad = 52.2$$

The value of the goods sold intra-group is $522 and included within the selling price is the profit mark up of 20% on cost. Multiply 522 by 20/120 to extract the unrealised profit.

40% of the goods were sold on to external parties so only 60% is still unrealised.

PUP = 52.2

Reduce W5 because P is the seller and inventory on the CSFP.

Test your understanding 5 : PUPs

The PUP will be:

$$(360 \times \frac{33\frac{1}{3}}{133\frac{1}{3}}) \qquad = 90$$

Reduce W2 (as S is the seller) & inventory on CSFP.

Test your understanding 6 : PUPs

P Group consolidated statement of financial position as at 30 June 2011

		$000
Non-current assets		
Goodwill	(W3)	1,650
Property, plant and equipment	(4,000 + 2,000)	6,000
Current assets		
Inventory	(500 + 100 − 10 (W6))	590
Other current assets	(100 + 300)	400
		8,640
Equity		
Share capital		6,000
Retained earnings	(W5)	2,040
Non-controlling interest	(W4)	
Current liabilities	(400 + 200)	600
		8,640

Workings

(W1) Group structure

Parent

100%

Subsidiary

(W2) Net assets of subsidiary

	Acquisition date	Reporting date
Share capital	1,500	1,500
Retained earnings	250	700
PUP (W6)	–	(10)
	1,750	2,190

(W3) Goodwill

Cost of investment	3,400
NAs acquired	
100% × 1,750 (W2)	(1,750)
	___
Goodwill at reporting date	1,650
	___

(W4) Non-controlling interests

N/A

(W5) Retained earnings

Parent	1,600
Subsidiary (100% × (2,190 – 1,750)(W2))	440
	___
	2,040
	___

(W6) PUP

Profit on sale   20/120 × 120 = 20

Profit in inventory = PUP = ½ × 20 = 10

Since S sold to P, adjust W2 and inventory on CSFP.

Test your understanding 7 : Non-current assets PUPs

The most common approach would be:

CV at reporting date with transfer	25,000
CV at reporting date without transfer	20,000
	_____
Adjustment required	5,000

Adjustment (sub sells)

Dr Net assets of subsidiary at reporting date (W2)	↓	5,000
Cr NCA (CSFP)	↓	5,000

We must now consider the effect on depreciation. The extra depreciation charged since transfer = (25,000 – 20,000) x 0.5/3 = 833 (we transferred the asset half a year ago before the reporting date). This extra depreciation charge must be removed from the books.

Adjustment (sub sells)

Dr NCA (CSFP)	↑	833
Cr Net assets of subsidiary at reporting date (W2)	↑	833

We could have accounted for this by just looking at the net change in the carrying value as follows:

	CV before transfer	CV after transfer	Difference
Carrying value	20,000	25,000	
Additional depreciation (0.5/3)	3,333	4,167	
Carrying value	16,667	20,833	4,167

Adjustment (sub sells)

Dr Net assets of subsidiary at reporting date (W2)	↓	4,167
Cr NCA (CSFP)	↓	4,167

The alternative approach could have been:

Adjustment (sub sells)

Dr Net assets of subsidiary at reporting date (W2)	↓	5,000
Cr Group retained earnings (W5)	↑	833
Cr NCA (CSFP)	↓	4,167

Test your understanding 8 : Exam standard question

Consolidated statement of financial position – Aston Group as at 31 December 2010

		$000
Non-current assets		
Goodwill	(W3)	1.2
Property, plant and equipment	(88 + 39 + 5 FV adj – 2 depn on FV adj)	130.0

Current assets

Inventory	(80 + 26 + 9 goods in transit – 5 pup)	110.0
Receivables	(24 + 32 – 20 inter company)	36.0
Bank & cash	(15 + 5 cash in transit)	20.0
		297.2

Equity

Share capital		100.0
Retained earnings	(W5)	77.2
Non-controlling interest	(W4)	0.0

Current liabilities

Overdraft	(14 + 10)	24.0
Payables	(72 + 30 – 6 inter company)	96.0
		297.2

Workings

(W1) Group structure

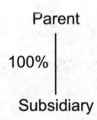

Parent

100%

Subsidiary

(W2) Net assets of subsidiary

	Acquisition date	Reporting date
Share capital	24	24
Retained earnings	9	48
Fair value adjustment	5	5
Depreciation adj (5 x 4/10)	–	(2)
PUP (W6)	–	(5)
	38	70

(W3) Goodwill

Cost of investment	40
FV of NAs acquired (100% × 38 (W2))	(38)
Goodwill at acquisition	2
Impairment (40%)	(0.8)
Goodwill at reporting date	1.2

(W4) Non-controlling interests

N/A

(W5) Retained earnings

Aston	46
Martin (100% × (70 – 38)(W2))	32
Impairment (W3)	(0.8)
	77.2

(W6) PUP

Goods in Aston inventory	21
Goods in transit	9
	30

PUP = 20/120 x 30 = 5

Martin (sub) sold the goods – adjust W2 and inventory on CSFP.

(W7) Intra-group balances

Cash (increase)	$5,000
Inventory (increase)	$9,000
Receivables (decrease)	$20,000
Payables (decrease)	$6,000

Test your understanding 9 : Exam standard question

Consolidated statement of financial position – K Group as at 30 November 2011

		$
Non-current assets		
Goodwill	(W3)	13,150
Property, plant and equipment	(138,000 + 115,000 + 18,000 – 1,800)	269,200
Investments	(162,000 – 140,000 – 20,000)	2,000
		_____
		284,350
Current Assets		
Inventory	(15,000 + 17,000 – 1,600 (W6))	30,400
Receivables	(19,000 + 20,000 – 4,000 inter co)	35,000
Bank & cash	(2,000 + 0 + 2,500 cash in transit)	4,500
		_____
		354,250
		_____
Equity		
Share capital		114,000
Retained earnings	(W5)	185,750
Non-controlling interest	(W4)	0
Non-current liabilities		
8% Debentures	(0 + 20,000 – 20,000)	–
Current liabilities		
Payables	(33,000 + 23,000 – 1,500 inter co)	54,500
		_____
		354,250
		_____

Workings

(W1) Group structure

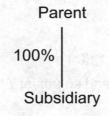

Parent

100%

Subsidiary

(W2) Net assets of subsidiary

	Acquisition date	Reporting date
Share capital	40,000	40,000
Retained earnings (69,000 – 5,250)	63,750	69,000
FV adj (48,000 – 30,000)	18,000	18,000
Depreciation adj (18,000 × 1/10)	–	(1,800)
	121,750	125,200

(W3) Goodwill

Cost of investment	140,000
Fair value of net assets acquired (100% × 121,750)	(121,750)
Goodwill @ acquisition	18,250
Impairment	(5,100)
Goodwill @ reporting date	13,150

(W4) Non-controlling interests

N/A

(W5) Retained earnings

K	189,000
PUP (W6)	(1,600)
S (100% × (125,200 – 121,750)(W2))	3,450
Impairment (W3)	(5,100)
	185,750

(W6) PUP

25/125 × 8,000 = 1,600

K sold the goods and so adjust W5 and inventory on the CSFP.

Note: All investments have not been eliminated in this question because the investments are not just from subsidiary and associate investments.

Don't forget we can have investments with companies outside of the group. In this case we had a total investment by the parent of $162,000 but only $140,000 and $20,000 related to the group. Hence, investments will not be eliminated in full and balance of £2,000 will remain in the consolidated accounts.

Test your understanding 10 : Objective test questions

(1) A

(2) D

(3) A

(4) C

(5) B

Test your understanding 11 : Objective test questions 2

(1) C Inventory in transit is valued at $100,000 but we must remove PUP.
PUP is calculated as $100,000/125 x 25 = $20,000. Hence we increase inventory by $100,000 but remove the PUP of $20,000.
The value of goods in transit to the group is $80,000.

(2) D $3,100 to be included in cash in transit.

(3) D

(4) Goodwill:

Cost of investment	1,800,000
Fair value of net assets acquired (100% × 1,350,000 + 100,000)	(1,450,000)
Goodwill @ acquisition	350,000

Consolidated Statement of Comprehensive Income

Chapter learning objectives

On completion of their studies students should be able to:

- Prepare consolidated financial statements (including the statement of changes in equity) for a group of companies.

- Explain the treatment in consolidated financial statements of pre and post-acquisition reserves, goodwill (including its impairment), fair value adjustments, PUPs, intra-group transactions and dividends.

1 Session content

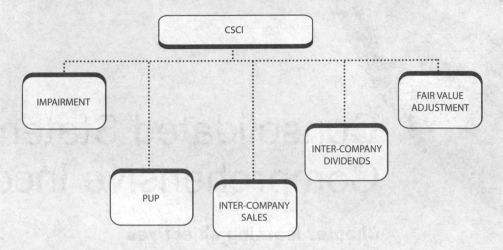

2 Consolidated statement of comprehensive income

The principles of consolidation are continued to the statement of comprehensive income (CSCI).

A statement of comprehensive income reflects the income and expenses generated by the net assets reflected on the statement of financial position.

Since the group controls the net assets of the subsidiary, the income and expenses of the subsidiary should be fully included in the consolidated statement of comprehensive income, i.e. add across 100% parent plus 100% subsidiary.

This chapter deals with 100% owned subsidiaries. Where the parent controls the subsidiary and does not own 100% of the shares, there will be non-controlling interests which own some of the subsidiary's profit and this is dealt with in paper F2.

3 Consolidated statement of comprehensive income adjustments

Adjustments will be necessary to the parent and subsidiary's own accounts to reflect that the group is one economic unit.

The consolidated figures will be calculated as:

Parent + subsidiary +/– adjustments

Consolidation adjustments should be dealt with as follows:

Impairments

Impairments of goodwill relating to the current year will be charged as an expense in the consolidated statement of comprehensive income.

Fair value adjustments

Fair value adjustments may be required as seen in chapter 4 *Consolidated statement of financial position* in order to reflect the fair value of the subsidiary's net assets at acquisition. This may result in a change to the profits of the subsidiary for consolidation purposes. For example, an adjustment is required to increase depreciation if a fair value uplift is made to a depreciating asset.

Intra-group transactions

The group as a single economic entity cannot generate profit with itself and so intra-group transactions will need eliminating, e.g. sales between group companies, dividends from subsidiary to parent and interest paid by one company and received in another.

Provision for unrealised profit (PUP)

An adjustment is required to increase the cost of sales of the selling company to remove the unrealised profit included in inventories at the reporting date.

Mid-year acquisitions

Time apportion the income and expenses of the subsidiary to reflect the period of ownership, i.e. if a subsidiary is acquired on 1 September and the reporting date is 31 December, 4/12 of the subsidiary's income and expenses should be consolidated. **Note this is not examinable for F1 but will be relevant when you study F2.**

Further explanation of adjustments

Impairments

Once the impairment of goodwill is calculated for the current year, it will be charged as an expense in the consolidated statement of comprehensive income. Goodwill is reflected in the consolidated financial statements only and so any impairment in the goodwill must be recorded as a consolidation adjustment as it will not be reflected in the individual company's financial statements.

The entry required to adjust for the impairment is as follows:

Dr   Profits   ↓
Cr   Goodwill on CSFP   ↓

Impairments may be charged as an increase to administrative expenses (reduction in profits) and they do not adjust the subsidiary's profit attributable to non-controlling interest in the case of fully owned subsidiaries, i.e. adjust in the parent's column when using a columnar approach.

Fair value adjustments

Fair value adjustments, for example an increase in the fair value of a property held by the subsidiary on acquisition, are reflected in the statement of financial position. However, if the fair value adjustment related to a depreciable asset, there will need to be a depreciation adjustment which will affect the consolidated statement of comprehensive income.

This is because the fair value adjustment is made in the CSFP only and not to the subsidiary's individual financial statements and so depreciation in the subsidiary's books will be charged on the original book value, not the fair value.

Depreciation may be charged to cost of sales or administrative costs, depending on the nature of the asset and it *will* affect the subsidiary's profit attributable to non-controlling interest, i.e. adjustment in the subsidiary's column when using a columnar approach.

The entry required to adjust for the depreciation is as follows:

Dr Profits   ↓
Cr Non-current asset on CSFP   ↓

Fair value uplifts on inventory are included in the consolidated statement of comprehensive income when the goods are sold and the increased cost of sales must be reflected, again in the subsidiary column.

Intra-group transactions and PUPs

With the case of intra-group trading between the parent and subsidiary there are two effects to bear in mind when preparing the consolidated statement of comprehensive income.

- The intra-group trading must be eliminated from revenue and cost of sales. It is irrelevant who sold the goods; the revenue of one company is the cost to the other. Therefore adjust both revenue and cost of sales by the same amount which is the amount of the sale.

- If the goods are still held by the buying company at the reporting date, there needs to be a provision for unrealised profits (PUP).

Chapter 4 looked at PUPs with respect to the CSFP and stated that the adjustment required is:

Dr Profits of selling company   ↓
Cr Inventory on CSFP   ↓

When this adjustment is applied to the CSCI it is necessary to identify where the reduction to profits will take place. The PUP is adjusted for as an increase to cost of sales (a reduction in profits) in the column of the selling company. So if the subsidiary sold the goods, adjust the cost of sales in the subsidiary's column and if the parent sold the goods, adjust the cost of sales in the parent's column.

Dividends that are paid by the subsidiary will be received in part or in full by the parent depending on the percentage of shares held. These intra-group dividends are eliminated on consolidation, i.e. deduct the dividend received from the subsidiary from the parent's investment income.

Any other intra-group transactions, for example interest paid by one company in the group and received by another, are cancelled out against each other as a consolidation adjustment in the adjustment column. The amount is deducted from investment income and deducted from finance cost.

Mid-year acquisitions

The parent controls the subsidiary's assets and liabilities from the acquisition date and so should include only the subsidiary's income and expenses from the acquisition date.

Time apportion the subsidiary's results on a line by line basis.

This is not examinable in F1 but will be relevant when studying F2.

Illustration 1 : Proforma

	Parent	Subsidiary	Adjustments	Consolidated
	$	$	$	$
Revenue	X	X		X
– Intra-group trading			(X)	
Cost of sales	(X)	(X)		(X)
– Intra-group trading			X	
– Depreciation on fair value adjustment		(X)		
– Inventory adjustment		(X)		
– PUP (if P selling)	(X)			
– PUP (if S selling)		(X)		
Gross profit				X
Distribution costs	(X)	(X)		(X)
Administrative expenses	(X)	(X)		(X)
– Impairment			(X)	(X)
Operating profit				X
Dividend income	X		(X)	–
Finance cost	(X)	(X)	X	(X)
Profit before tax				X
Tax	(X)	(X)		(X)
Net profit		X		X
Other comprehensive income (e.g. property revaluation)	X	X		X
Total comprehensive income		X		X*
Attributable to:				
Non-controlling interests **(relevant to F2)**				–
Parent shareholders				X*
				X*

For the purposes of this chapter, subsidiaries are 100% owned and therefore non-controlling interest are not applicable. The profit marked (*) above that the group has generated will be the same as the profit attributable to the parent shareholders. F2 will consider CSCI rules where subsidiaries are not 100% owned.

Alternative presentation:

	$000
Revenue (P + S - inter-company sales)	X
Cost of sales (P + S - inter-company sales + PUP + depn adj)	(X)
Gross profit	X
Distribution costs (P + S)	(X)
Administrative expenses (P + S + impairment adj)	(X)
Profit from operations	X
Investment income (P + S - inter-company interest/dividends)	X
Finance cost (P + S - inter-company interest)	(X)
Profit before taxation	X
Taxation (P + S)	(X)
Profit for the year	X
Other comprehensive income	–
Total comprehensive income	X
Amount attributable to:	
Non-controlling interests (N/A) **(relevant to F2)**	–
Parent shareholders	X
	X

Illustration 2 : Consolidated statement of comprehensive income

On 1 January 2010 Zebedee acquired all of the ordinary shares of Xavier.

The following statements of comprehensive income have been produced by Zebedee and Xavier for the year ended 31 December 2010.

	Zebedee	Xavier
	$000	$000
Revenue	1,260	520
Cost of sales	(420)	(210)
Gross profit	840	310
Distribution costs	(180)	(60)
Administration expenses	(120)	(90)
Profit from operations	540	160
Investment income from Xavier	36	–
Profit before taxation	576	160
Taxation	(130)	(26)
Profit for the year	446	134
Other comprehensive income	–	–
Total comprehensive income	446	134

During the year ended 31 December 2010 Zebedee had sold $84,000 worth of goods to Xavier. These goods were sold at a mark up of 50% on cost. On 31 December 2010 Xavier still had $36,000 worth of these goods in inventories.

Required:

Prepare the consolidated statement of comprehensive income for the Zebedee group for the year ended 31 December 2010.

Solution

Follow these steps to answer a CSCI question:

(1) Prepare the CSCI proforma with a column for the parent, each subsidiary, adjustments and a final column for the consolidated figures.

(2) Prepare W1 Group structure to determine the subsidiary status of each company and add dates to highlight any mid-year acquisitions and the number of months since control was acquired.

(3) Complete the proforma with the parent and subsidiary's figures from the question. Take care to note any mid-year acquisitions from W1 and to time apportion the subsidiary's income and expenses.

(4) Review the extra information in the question to determine any adjustments required. Calculate the adjustment needed in a separate working to ensure your workings are clear for a marker to understand.

(5) Look out for dividend income from the subsidiary in the parent's books as this must be eliminated.

Zebedee consolidated statement of comprehensive income for the year ended 31 December 2010

	Zebedee	Xavier	Adjustments	Consolidated
	$000	$000	$000	$000
Revenue	1,260	520	(84)	1,696
Cost of sales	(420)	(210)	84	(558)
– PUP (W2)	(12)			
Gross profit				1,138
Distribution costs	(180)	(60)		(240)
Administrative expenses	(120)	(90)		(210)
Profit from operations				688
Investment income from Xavier	36		(36)	–
Taxation	(130)	(26)		(156)
Profit for the year				532
Other comprehensive income	–	–		–
Total comprehensive income				532
Amount attributable to:				
Non-controlling interests (N/A)				–
Parent shareholders				532
				532

Workings

(W1) Group structure

Zebedee

100% | 1 January 2010

Xavier   i.e. 1 year

(W2) PUP

The goods were sold at a mark up of 50% on cost so the unrealised profit is stripped out by multiplying by 50/150. The profit is unrealised on only the inventory remaining in Xavier at the reporting date.

$36,000 x 50/150 = $12,000

Zebedee sold the goods so the adjustment should be made in Zebedee's column, i.e. the column of the seller.

Alternative presentation

As an alternative to the columnar approach used earlier in this example, brackets may be used to add across the parent, subsidiary and adjustments. This is illustrated below.

Zebedee consolidated statement of comprehensive income for the year ended 31 December 2010

	Consolidated
	$000
Revenue (1,260 + 520 - 84)	1,696
Cost of sales (420 + 210 - 84 + 12 (W2))	(558)
Gross profit	1,138
Distribution costs (180 + 60)	(240)
Administrative expenses (120 + 90)	(210)
Profit from operations	688
Investment income (36 – 36)	–
Taxation (130 + 26)	(156)
Profit for the year	532
Other comprehensive income	–
Total comprehensive income	532
Amount attributable to:	
Non-controlling interests (N/A)	–
Parent shareholders	532
	532

Test your understanding 1 - Simple CSCI

Given below are the income statements for Paris and its subsidiary London for the year ended 31 December 2010.

	Paris	London
	$000	$000
Revenue	3,200	2,560
Cost of sales	(2,200)	(1,480)
Gross profit	1,000	1,080
Distribution costs	(160)	(120)
Administrative expenses	(400)	(80)
	440	880
Investment income	160	–
	600	880
Taxation	(400)	(480)
Profit for the year	200	400

Additional information:

- Paris acquired 100% of London's share capital on 31 December 2006.

- A goodwill impairment of $38,000 was found to be necessary at the year end. Impairments are included within administrative expenses.

- Paris made sales to London, at a selling price of $600,000 during the year. Not all of the goods had been sold externally by the year end. The profit element included in London's closing inventory was $30,000.

- The figure for investment income in Paris's income statement represents the dividend received from London for the year.

Required:

Prepare a consolidated statement of comprehensive income for the year ended 31 December 2010 for the Paris group.

Test your understanding 2 : Exam standard question

On 1 April 2010 Tudor purchased all of the shares in Windsor. The summarised draft statement of comprehensive income for each company for the year ended 31 March 2011 was as follows:

	Tudor	Windsor
	$000	$000
Revenue	60,000	24,000
Cost of sales	(42,000)	(20,000)
Gross profit	18,000	4,000
Distribution costs	(2,500)	(50)
Administration expenses	(3,500)	(150)
Profit from operations	12,000	3,800
Investment income	75	–
Finance cost	–	(200)
Profit before tax	12,075	3,600
Tax	(3,000)	(600)
Profit for the year	9,075	3,000
Other comprehensive income	–	–
Total comprehensive income	9,075	3,000

The following information is relevant:

(1) The fair values of Windsor's assets at the date of acquisition were mostly equal to their book values with the exception of plant, which was stated in the books at $2,000,000 but had a fair value of $5,200,000. The remaining useful life of the plant in question was four years at the date of acquisition. Depreciation is charged to cost of sales and is time apportioned on a monthly basis.

(2) During the year Tudor sold Windsor some goods for $12 million. The goods had originally cost $9 million. During the remaining months of the year Windsor sold $10 million (at cost to Windsor) of these goods to third parties for $13 million.

(3) Tudor purchased 1,000,000 of Windsor's 7.5% $1 loan notes on 1 April 2010.

(4) Revenues and expenses should be deemed to accrue evenly throughout the year.

(5) Goodwill impairment of $300,000 needs to be recorded for the current year.

Required:

Prepare a consolidated statement of comprehensive income for the Tudor group for the year to 31 March 2011.

Illustration 3 : CSCI

Kew bought 100% of Richmond on 1 April 2009. The following are the statements of comprehensive income for Kew and Richmond for the year ended 31 March 2011:

	Kew	Richmond
	$	$
Revenue	44,500	15,900
Cost of sales	(32,300)	(10,500)
Gross profit	12,200	5,400
Operating expenses	(8,000)	(2,300)
Profit from operations	4,200	3,100
Investment income	1,100	–
Profit before tax	5,300	3,100
Tax	(1,600)	(1,000)
Profit for the year	3,700	2,100
Other comprehensive income		
Gain on available for sale investments	600	–
Total comprehensive income	4,300	2,100

The following are the statements of changes in equity for Kew and Richmond for the year ended 31 March 2011:

	Kew	Richmond
	$	$
Equity b/f	20,300	11,000
Comprehensive income	4,300	2,100
Dividends paid	(2,000)	(1,100)
Equity c/f	22,600	12,000

The following information is available:

(1) On 1 April 2009, an item of plant in the books of Richmond had a fair value of $2,000 in excess of its carrying value. At this time, the plant had a remaining life of 4 years. Depreciation is charged to cost of sales.

(2) During the year Richmond sold goods to Kew for $2,200. Of this amount, $500 was included in the inventory of Kew at the year-end. Richmond earns a 20% profit margin on its sales.

(3) Richmond's retained earnings were $6,000 on 1 April 2009 and Richmond has 2,000 $1 equity shares in issue.

Required:

Prepare the consolidated statement of comprehensive income for the year ended 31 March 2011.

Solution

Follow these steps to answer the question:

(1) Prepare the CSCI proforma with a column for the parent, subsidiary, adjustments and a final column for the consolidated figures.

(2) Prepare W1 Group structure to determine the subsidiary status of each company and add dates to highlight any mid-year acquisitions and the number of months or years since control was acquired.

(3) Complete the proforma with the parent and subsidiary's figures from the question.

(4) Review the extra information in the question to determine any adjustments required. In this case there is depreciation on the fair value adjustment and intragroup trading plus a PUP.

(5) Look out for dividend income from the subsidiary in the parent's books as this must be eliminated. In this question the dividend income is not given explicitly in a note but is provided in the subsidiary's individual statement of changes in equity.

(i) **Kew Group consolidated statement of comprehensive income for the year ended 31 March 2011**

	Kew	Richmond	Adjustment	Consolidated
	$	$	$	$
Revenue	44,500	15,900	(2,200)	58,200
Cost of sales	(32,300)	(10,500)	2,200	(41,200)
– Depreciation on fair value adj (W2)		(500)		
– PUP (W3)		(100)		
Gross profit				17,000
Operating expenses	(8,000)	(2,300)		(10,300)
Profit from operations				6,700
Investment income	1,100	–	(1,100)	–
Profit before tax				6,700
Tax	(1,600)	(1,000)		(2,600)
Profit for the year				4,100
Other comprehensive income				
Gain on available for sale investments	600	–		600
Total comprehensive income				4,700
Attributable to:				
Non-controlling interests (N/A)				–
Parent shareholders				4,700
				4,700

Workings

(W1) Group structure

```
                Kew
100%             |        1 April 2009
              Richmond    i.e. 2 years
```

(W2) Depreciation on fair value adjustment

Fair value adjustment = $2,000

Depreciation per year = $2,000 / 4 = $500

(W3) PUP

Inventory remaining at reporting date = $500

Unrealised profit within inventory = $500 x 20% = $100

Test your understanding 3 : CSCI

P bought 100% of S on 1 April 2008 when S's retained earnings were $5,000. The following are the statements of comprehensive income of P and S for the year ended 31 March 2011:

	P	S
	$	$
Revenue	31,200	10,400
Cost of sales	(17,800)	(5,600)
Gross profit	13,400	4,800
Operating expenses	(8,500)	(1,200)
Profit from operations	4,900	3,600
Investment income	2,000	–
Profit before tax	6,900	3,600
Tax	(2,100)	(500)
Profit for the year	4,800	3,100
Other comprehensive income	–	–
Total comprehensive income	4,800	3,100

The following are the statements of changes in equity for P and S for the year ended 31 March 2011:

	P	S
	$	$
Equity b/f	50,600	22,670
Comprehensive income	4,800	3,100
Dividends paid	(2,500)	(500)
Equity c/f	52,900	25,270

The following information is available:

(1) On 1 April 2008, a property in the books of S had a fair value of $24,000 in excess of its carrying value. At this time, the plant had a remaining life of 10 years. Depreciation is charged to operating expenses.

(2) During the year S sold goods to P for $4,400. Of this amount, $500 was included in the inventory of P at the year-end. S earns a 35% margin on its sales.

(3) Goodwill amounting to $800 arose on the acquisition of S. Goodwill was impaired by 10% in the year ended 31 March 2010 and is to be impaired by another 10% on the book value at 31 March 2010 for the current year. Impairment losses should be charged to operating expenses.

(4) S has total share capital of 1,000 $1 shares.

Required:

Prepare the consolidated statement of comprehensive income for the year ended 31 March 2011.

Test your understanding 4 : Exam standard question

Wolf acquired a 100% holding of the ordinary share capital of Hawk on 1 January 2009. The share capital of Wolf and Hawk is $350,000 and $200,000 respectively. The retained earnings at that date for Hawk were $10,000. The goodwill impairment charges for this year are $6,000 ($2,000 last year).

During the year Wolf sold goods to Hawk at an invoice value of $20,000. Wolf has a pricing policy based upon a mark-up of 25%. A quarter of these goods remain in inventory at the year end.

Non-current assets in the books of Hawk are carried at a value which gives rise to a depreciation expense of $60,000 per annum. At acquisition an adjustment of $100,000 was recorded to increase these non-current assets to their fair value. The remaining useful economic life of these assets was 10 years as at acquisition. Depreciation is charged to cost of sales.

The individual statements of comprehensive income for the year ended 31 December 2010 are as follows:

	Wolf	Hawk
	$000	$000
Revenue	1,000	2,000
Cost of sales	(600)	(1,200)
Gross profit	400	800
Distribution costs	(300)	(50)
Administration expenses	(18)	(500)
Profit from operations	82	250
Investment income	8	
Profits before tax	90	250
Tax	(40)	(100)
Profit for the year	50	150
Other comprehensive income	–	–
Total comprehensive income	50	150

The individual statement of changes in equity for the year ended 31 December 2010 is as follows:

	Wolf	Hawk
	$000	$000
Equity b/f	450	310
Comprehensive income	50	150
Dividends paid	(15)	(8)
Equity c/f	485	452

Required:

A consolidated statement of comprehensive income for the period ending 31 December 2010.

You will need this information to attempt the next test your understanding.

Test your understanding 5 : Objective test questions

(1) **Using the information you have prepared in TYU 4, what is the correct figure for PUP?**

    A $5,000

    B $1,000

    C $1,250

    D $4,000

(2) **Using the information you have prepared in TYU 4, what is the correct figure for the depreciation adjustment in the CSCI?**

    A $10,000

    B $20,000

    C $4,000

    D $nil

(3) **Using the information you have prepared in TYU 4, what is the correct figure for COS?**

    A $1,800,000

    B $1,791,000

    C $1,780,000

    D $1,770,000

(4) GPT regularly sells goods to its subsidiary in which it owns 100% of the ordinary share capital. During the group's financial year ended 31 August 2011 GPT sold goods to its subsidiary valued at $100,000 (selling price) upon which it makes a margin of 20%. By the group's year end all of the goods had been sold to parties outside the group.

What is the correct consolidation adjustment in respect of these sales for the year ended 31 August 2011?

    A   No adjustment required.

    B   DR Revenue $60,000; CR Cost of sales $60,000

    C   DR Revenue $80,000; CR Cost of sales $80,000.

    D   DR Revenue $100,000; CR Cost of sales $100,000.

(2 marks)

The following information should be used to answer questions 5 to 7:

The individual statements of comprehensive income of Hope and Despair for the year ended 30 June 2011 are as follows:

	Hope	Despair
	$	$
Revenue	159,800	108,400
Cost of sales	(79,200)	(61,600)
Gross profit	80,600	46,800
Administration expenses	(27,000)	(16,000)
Profit from operations	53,600	30,800
Investment income	10,000	1,500
Finance cost	(6,000)	(4,000)
Profits before tax	57,600	28,300
Tax	(29,400)	(14,800)
Profit for the year	28,200	13,500
Other comprehensive income	–	–
Total comprehensive income	28,200	13,500

The following information is available:

(1) Hope acquired 100% of Despair on 30 June 2007 A dividend was paid by Despair during the year amounting to $9,000.

(2) During the year Hope sold good to Despair at a selling price of $19,000. The goods yielded a profit margin of 20%. $8,000 of these goods were still held in inventory at the end of the year by Despair.

(5) **What would be the revenue figure to be included on the group consolidated statement of comprehensive income?**

A $268,200

B $249,200

C $260,200

D $253,000

(2 marks)

(6) **What would be the cost of sales figure to be included on the group consolidated statement of comprehensive income?**

$140,800

$121,800

$123,400

$120,200

(2 marks)

(7) **What would be the profit for the period to be included on the group consolidated statement of comprehensive income?**

$31,100

$40,100

$32,700

$29,500

(2 marks)

4 Summary diagram

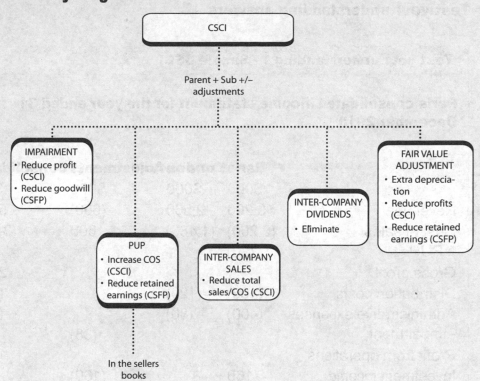

Test your understanding answers

Test your understanding 1 - Simple CSCI

Paris consolidated income statement for the year ended 31 December 2010

	Paris	London	Adjustments	Consolidated
	$000	$000	$000	$000
Revenue	3,200	2,560	(600)	5,160
Cost of sales	(2,200)	(1,480)	600	(3,110)
– PUP	(30)			
Gross profit				2,050
Distribution costs	(160)	(120)		(280)
Administrative expenses	(400)	(80)		(518)
- Impairment			(38)	
Profit from operations				1,252
Investment income	160		(160)	–
Profit before tax				1,252
Taxation	(400)	(480)		(880)
Profit for the year				372
Other comprehensive income				–
Total comprehensive income				372
Attributable to:				
Non-controlling interests (N/A)				–
Parent shareholders				372
				372

Workings

(W1) **Group structure**

Paris
100% | 31 December 2006
London   i.e. 4 years

Alternative presentation:

Paris consolidated income statement for the year ended 31 December 2010

	Consolidated
	$000
Revenue (3,200 + 2,560 – 600)	5,160
Cost of sales (2,200 + 1,480 – 600 + 30)	(3,110)
Gross profit	2,050
Investment income (160 – 160)	–
Distribution costs (160 + 120)	(280)
Administrative expenses (400 + 80 + 38)	(518)
Profit before tax	1,252
Taxation (400 + 480)	(880)
Profit for the year	372
Other comprehensive income	–
Total comprehensive income	372
Attributable to:	
Non-controlling interests (N/A)	–
Parent shareholders	372
	372

Test your understanding 2 : Exam standard question

Consolidated statement of comprehensive income for period ended 31 March 2011

	Tudor	Windsor	Adjustments	Consolidated
	$000	$000	$000	$000
Revenue	60,000	24,000		72,000
– Intra-group trading			(12,000)	
Cost of sales	(42,000)	(20,000)		(51,300)
– Depreciation of fair value adj (W2)		(800)		
– Intra-group trading			12,000	
– PUP (W3)	(500)			
				———
Gross profit				20,700
Distribution costs	(2,500)	(50)		(2,550)
Administration expenses	(3,500)	(150)		(3,950)
– Impairment			(300)	
				———
Profit from operations				14,200
Investment income	75	–		–
– Intra-group interest (W4)			(75)	
Finance cost	–	(200)		(125)
– Intra-group interest (W4)			75	
				———
Profit before tax				14,075
Tax	(3,000)	(600)		(3,600)
				———
Profit for the year				10,475
Other comprehensive income				–
				———
Total comprehensive income				10,475
				———
Attributable to:				
Non-controlling interests (N/A)				–
Parent shareholders				10,475
				———
				10,475
				———

Workings

(W1) Group structure

Tudor

100% | 1 April 2010

Windsor   i.e 1 year

(W2) Depreciation on fair value adjustment

Fair value adjustment = 5,200,000 – 2,000,000 = 3,200,000

Depreciation = 3,200,000 / 4 years = 800,000

(W3) PUP

	$000	Gross profit margin cost structure	Mark up cost structure
Selling price	12,000	100%	133 ⅓%
Cost of sales	(9,000)	75%	100%
Gross profit	3,000	25%	33 ⅓ %

The goods were sold at a gross profit margin of 25% or a mark-up of one third.

Of the inventory sold to Windsor for $2,000,000 and remaining at the reporting date, there is unrealised profit to be eliminated of:

- $2,000,000 x 25% = $500,000; or
- $2,000,000 x 33 ⅓ / 133 ⅓ = $500,000

(W4) Loan interest

Interest = 7.5% x 1,000,000 = 75,000

Consolidated statement of comprehensive income for the year ended 31 March 2011

	P $	S $	Adjustments $	Consolidated $
Revenue	31,200	10,400	(4,400)	37,200
Cost of sales	(17,800)	(5,600)	4,400	(19,175)
– PUP (W3)		(175)		
Gross profit				18,025
Operating expenses	(8,500)	(1,200)		(12,172)
– Depreciation on fair value adjustment (W2)		(2,400)		
– Impairment (W4)			(72)	
Profit from operations				5,853
Investment income	2,000		(500)	1,500
Profit before tax				7,353
Tax	(2,100)	(500)		(2,600)
Profit for the year				4,753
Other comprehensive income	–	–		–
Total comprehensive income				4,753
Attributable to:				
Non-controlling interests (N/A)				–
Parent shareholders				4,753
				4,753

Workings

(W1) **Group Structure**

$$
\begin{array}{c}
\text{P} \\
100\% \quad \bigg| \quad \text{1 April 2008} \\
\text{S} \quad \text{i.e. 3 years}
\end{array}
$$

(W2) **Fair value depreciation**

Fair value adjustment = $24,000

Depreciation adjustment per year = $24,000/10 years = $2,400

(W3) **Intra-group sales and PUP**

Intra-group sales of $4,400 need eliminating from revenue and cost of sales.

PUP in inventory = 35% × $500 = $175

The PUP will increase cost of sales in the subsidiary's column as the subsidiary is the seller.

(W4) **Impairment**

		$
Goodwill on acquisition		800
Impairment year ended 31 March 2010	(10% x 800)	(80)
Goodwill at 31 March 2010		720
Impairment year ended 31 March 2011	(10% x 720)	(72)
Goodwill at 31 March 2011		648

Test your understanding 4 : Exam standard question

Consolidated statement of comprehensive income for the year ended 31 December 2010

	Wolf	Hawk	Adj	Total
	$000	$000	$000	$000
Revenue	1,000	2,000	(20)	2,980
Cost of sales	(600)	(1,200)	20	
– Depreciation adjustment (W3)		(10)		
– PUP (W2)	(1)			(1,791)
Gross profit				1,189
Distribution costs	(300)	(50)		(350)
Administrative expenses	(18)	(500)		
– Impairment			(6)	
				(524)
Operating profit				315
Investment income	8		(8)	–
Profit before tax				315
Tax	(40)	(100)		(140)
Profit for the year				175
Other comprehensive income				–
Total comprehensive income				175
Attributable to:				
Non-controlling interests (N/A)				–
Parent shareholders				175
				175

Workings

(W1)

$$\begin{array}{c} \text{Wolf} \\ 100\% \quad | \quad \text{1 January 2009} \\ \text{Hawk} \quad \text{i.e. 2 years} \end{array}$$

(W2) **PUP**

Inventory remaining = 20 x 1/4 = 5

Unrealised profit in inventory = 5 x 25/125 = 1

(W3) **Depreciation adjustment**

Depreciation adjustment = 100/10 yrs = 10

Test your understanding 5 : Objective test questions

(1) B

(2) A

(3) B

(4) D   The sales of $100,000 must be removed from the revenue and cost of sales for the group.

(5) B

(6) C

(7) A

The consolidated statement of income would be as follows:

	$
Revenue (159,800 + 108,400 - 19,000)	249,200
Cost of sales (79,200 + 61,600 - 19,000 + 1,600 (W2))	(123,400)
Gross profit	125,800
Administrative expenses (27,000 + 16,000)	(43,000)
Profit from operations	82,800
Investment income (10,000 + 1,500 - 9,000)	2,500
Finance cost (6,000 + 4,000)	(10,000)
Profit before taxation	75,300
Taxation (29,400 + 14,800)	(44,200)
Profit for the year	31,100
Other comprehensive income	–
Total comprehensive income	31,100
Amount attributable to:	
Non-controlling interests (N/A)	–
Parent shareholders	31,100
	31,100

Associates

Chapter learning objectives

On completion of their studies students should be able to:

- Explain the conditions required for an undertaking to be a subsidiary or an associate of another company;

- Explain and apply the accounting treatment of associates (IAS 28).

1 Session content

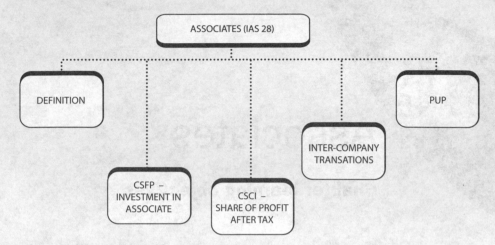

2 Associates (IAS 28)

Definition:

* An **associate** is an entity over which the investor has **significant influence** and which is neither a subsidiary nor a joint venture of the investor.

* **Significant influence** is the power to participate in, but not control, the financial and operating policy decisions of an entity. A holding of 20% or more of the voting power is presumed to give significant influence unless it can be clearly demonstrated that this is not the case. At the same time a holding of less than 20% is assumed not to give significant influence unless such influence can be clearly demonstrated.

IAS 28 explains that an investor probably has significant influence if:

* It is represented on the board of directors.
* It participates in policy-making processes, including decisions about dividends or other distributions.
* There are material transactions between the investor and investee.
* There is interchange of managerial personnel.
* There is provision of essential technical information.

3 Accounting for associates

Associates are not consolidated as the parent does not have control. Instead they are **equity accounted.**

Consolidated statement of financial position

The CSFP will continue to consolidate 100% of the assets and liabilities of the parent and subsidiary on a line by line basis.

There will be a line within non-current assets representing the associate called 'Investment in associate'.

It is possible to calculate the investment in associate in two ways as follows:

Investment in associate (preferred by the examiner)

	$000
Cost of investment	X
Add: share of increase in net assets, i.e. share of post acquisition reserves	X
Less: impairment losses	(X)
Less: PUP (where P is selling – see later)	(X)
	X

Investment in associate (alternative)

	$000
Share of net assets at reporting date	X
Add: carrying value of goodwill	X
Less: PUP (where P is selling – see later)	(X)
	X

You will need to produce W2 (net assets) for the associate to calculate the share of the increase in net assets (post-acquisition profits).

You will need to include in W5 (group retained earnings) the **group's share of A's post acquisition profits** less any impairments in both the subsidiary and the associate.

Consolidated statement of comprehensive income

The CSCI will continue to consolidate 100% of the income and expenses of the parent and subsidiary on a line by line basis.

There will also be a line before profit before tax representing the group's share of the associate's (**profit after tax** less any impairment losses) called "share of profit of associate".

Dividends received by the parent from the associate are excluded as the share of associate's profit is calculated in its place as above.

Note: Non-controlling interests are not applicable for associates as the group only reflects its share in the associates net assets and profit for the year.

Note: In order to equity account, the parent must already be producing consolidated financial statements i.e. it already controls at least one subsidiary.

4 Trading with the associate

Inter-company transactions

Remember that you do **not** eliminate inter-company sales and purchases, receivables or payables between the group and the associate as the associate is outside of the group. The only exception to this is any unrealised profit on transactions, of which the **group's share** must be eliminated.

Provisions for unrealised profit (PUP)

IAS 28 requires that only the group share of unrealised profit is removed:

$$PUP = \textbf{A\%} \times \text{unrealised profit in inventory}$$

Parent sells to associate

In CSFP the following adjustment is necessary for the group share of the PUP:

- Reduce W5 retained earnings (group reserves)
- Reduce investment in associate (CSFP)

In the CSCI, the reduction in profit for the current year is adjusted for as follows:

- Reduce revenue and reduce cost of sales of the parent by the parent's share of the sale resulting in unrealised profit. This results in the required reduction in gross profit by the parent's share of the PUP.

- The *exam alternative* is to increase the cost of sales of the parent company by the parent's share of the PUP.

Illustration 1 - Parent sells to associate

The parent (P) has an associate (A). P owns 40% of A.

P has sold $200,000 of goods to A at a price which represents cost plus 25%.

At the reporting date 60% of these items remain in inventory.

There is no intra-group trading to be eliminated between a group and associate as the associate is not a group member. The only adjustment will be for the PUP on closing inventory.

Profit on sale	200,000 x 25/125 = 40,000
Profit in inventory	60% × 40,000 = 24,000
PUP (group share of profit)	40% × 24,000 = 9,600

CSFP treatment

Dr Retained earnings (W5)	↓	9,600
Cr Investment In associate	↓	9,600

CSCI treatment

The $9,600 represents the fall in the parent's gross profit.

Since the value of the sales have not been eliminated in the consolidated statement of comprehensive income, it is necessary to adjust both sales and cost of sales to achieve the fall in gross profit of $9,600. This is achieved by recording the following double entry:

Dr Revenue	↓	48,000	(9,600 × 125/25)
Cr Cost of sales	↓	38,400	(9,600 × 100/25)

and so Gross profit	↓	9,600

Exam Alternative:

Dr Cost of sales	↑	9,600

And so Gross profit	↓	9,600

Associate sells to the parent

In CSFP the following adjustment is necessary for the group share of the PUP:

- Reduce retained earnings (W5)
- Reduce inventory (CSFP)

In the CSCI, the reduction in profit for the current year is adjusted for as follows:

- Reduce share of associate's profits

Illustration 2 - Associate sells to parent

Using the same scenario as illustration 1 above, the parent's share of the PUP is $9,600.

CSFP treatment

Dr Retained earnings	↓	9,600 (W5)
Cr Inventory	↓	9,600 (CSFP)

The reduction in retained earnings is achieved by reducing the share of associates post acquisition profit.

CSCI treatment

Dr Share of associates profits	↓	9,600

No adjustment is required to sales and cost of sales.

Test your understanding 1 : PUP

A parent company owns 25% of its associate. The parent made sales to the associate during the year amount to $450,000. The sales have been made at cost plus 20%. At the reporting date 30% of these items remain in inventory.

Required:

Identify the relevant adjustments required to be made to the group accounts – statement of financial position and statement of comprehensive income.

Illustration 3 : CSFP

Below are the statements of financial position of three companies as at 31 December 2010.

	Tom $000	James $000	Emily $000
Non-current assets			
Property, plant & equipment	959	980	840
Investments			
840,000 shares in James	805	–	–
168,000 shares in Emily	224	–	–
	1,988	980	840
Current assets			
Inventory	380	640	190
Receivables	190	310	100
Bank	35	58	46
	605	1,008	336
	2,593	1,988	1,176
Equity			
$1 ordinary shares	1,120	840	560
Retained earnings	1,232	602	448
	2,352	1,442	1,008
Current liabilities			
Trade payables	150	480	136
Taxation	91	66	32
	241	546	168
	2,593	1,988	1,176

You are also given the following information:

(1) Tom acquired its shares in James on 1 January 2010 when James had retained losses of $56,000.

(2) Tom acquired its shares in Emily on 1 January 2010 when Emily had retained earnings of $140,000.

(3) An impairment test at the year end shows that goodwill for James remains unimpaired but the goodwill arising on the acquisition of Emily has impaired by $2,800.

Required:

Prepare the consolidated statement of financial position for the year ended 31 December 2010.

Solution

Tom consolidated statement of financial position as at 31 December 2010

	$000	$000
Non-current assets		
Goodwill (W3)		21.0
Property, plant & equipment (959 + 980)		1,939.0
Investment in associate (W6)		313.6
		2,273.6
Current assets		
Inventory (380 + 640)	1,020.0	
Receivables (190 + 310)	500.0	
Cash (35 + 58)	93.0	
		1,613.0
		3,886.6

Equity

$1 ordinary shares	1,120.0
Retained earnings (W5)	1,979.6
	3,099.6
Non-controlling interest (W4)	–

Current liabilities

Trade payables (150 + 480)	630.0	
Taxation (91 + 66)	157.0	
		787.0
		3,886.6

Workings

(W1) Group structure

```
            Tom
   100%      |      1 January 2010
          James   i.e. 1 year


            Tom
  168/560    |      1 January 2010
   = 30%      
          Emily   i.e. 1 year
```

(W2) Net assets – James

	Acquisition date	Reporting date
	$000	$000
Share capital	840.0	840.0
Retained earnings	(56.0)	602.0
	784.0	1,442.0

Note that James has retained losses at the date of acquisition rather than the more usual retained earnings or profits.

Net assets – Emily

	Acquisition date	Reporting date
	$000	$000
Share capital	560.0	560. 0
Retained earnings	140.0	448.0
	700.0	1,008.0

Goodwill – James

	$000	$000
Cost of investment		805.0
Fair value of net asset acquired		
100% × 784 (W2)		(784.0)
Goodwill		21.0

(W4) NCI – N/A

(W5) Retained earnings (group reserves)

	$000
Tom	1,232.0
James – share of post-acquisition reserves 100% × (1,442 – 784) (W2)	658.0
Emily – share of post-acquisition reserves 30% × (1,008 – 700) (W2)	92.4
Less: impairments to date	(2.8)
	1,979.6

(W6) Investment in associate

	$000
Cost of investment	224.0
Share of post-acquisition profits (W5)	92.4
Less: impairment	(2.8)
	313.6

The associate calculation above is preferred by the examiner so this is the working that should be used. The cost of investment is taken from the parent's CSFP.

> W2 must be prepared for all subsidiaries and all associates to give you the figures needed for the other workings. This enables you to provide clear workings in the real exam and to gain credit for them.

Alternative solution

Alternative calculation for investment in associate

(W6) Investment in associate

	$000
Share of net assets at reporting date (30% × 1,008 (W2))	302.4
Carrying value of goodwill (W7)	11.2
	313.6

(W7) Goodwill – Emily

Cost of investment	224
Fair value of net assets acquired (30% x 700 (W2))	(210)
Goodwill on acquisition	14
Less: Impairment	(2.8)
Carrying value of goodwill at reporting date	11.2

This alternative calculation is shown for illustrative purposes only to prove the correct alternative methods of calculation.

Test your understanding 2 : Exam standard CSFP

P acquired 100% of S on 1 December 2008 paying $2,675,000. At this date the balance on S's retained earnings was $870,000. On 1 December 2010 P acquired 30% of A's ordinary shares paying $500,000.

The statements of financial position of the three companies as at 30 November 2011 are as follows:

	P	S	A
	$000	$000	$000
Non-current assets			
Property	890	850	900
Plant and equipment	450	210	150
Investments	3,175	–	–
Current assets			
Inventory	270	230	200
Receivables	100	340	400
Cash	160	50	140
	5,045	1,680	1,790
Equity			
Share capital $1	1,900	500	250
Share premium	650	80	–
Retained earnings	1,145	400	1,200
	3,695	980	1,450
Non-current liabilities			
10% Loan notes	500	300	–
Current liabilities			
Trade payables	520	330	250
Income tax	330	70	90
	5,045	1,680	1,790

The following information is relevant:

- As at 1 December 2008, plant in the books of S was determined to have a fair value of $50,000 in excess of its carrying value. The plant had a remaining life of 5 years at this time.

- During the year, S sold goods to P for $400,000 at a mark-up of 25%. P had a quarter of these goods still in inventory at the year-end.

- In September A sold goods to P for $150,000. These goods had cost A $100,000. P had $90,000 (at cost to P) in inventory at the year-end.

- As a result of the above inter-company sales, P's books showed $50,000 and $20,000 as owing to S and A respectively at the year-end. These balances agreed with the amounts recorded in S's and A's books.

- Goodwill in the subsidiary is to be impaired by 40% at the reporting date. An impairment review found the investment in the associate was to be impaired by $15,000 at the year-end.

- A's profit after tax for the year is $450,000.

Required:

Prepare the consolidated statement of financial position as at 30 November 2011.

Test your understanding 3 : Exam standard CSCI

Below are the statements of comprehensive income the Barbie group and its associated companies, as at 31 December 2010.

	Barbie	Ken	Shelly
	$000	$000	$000
Revenue	385	100	60
Cost of sales	(185)	(60)	(20)
Gross profit	200	40	40
Operating expenses	(50)	(15)	(10)
Profit before tax	150	25	30
Tax	(50)	(12)	(10)
Profit for the year	100	13	20
Other comprehensive income	–	–	–
Total comprehensive income	100	13	20

You are also given the following information:

(1) Barbie acquired 60,000 ordinary shares in Shelly for $80,000 when that company had a credit balance on its retained earnings of $50,000 a number of years ago. Shelly has 200,000 $1 ordinary shares.

(2) Barbie acquired all of the ordinary shares in Ken , a number of years ago, for $70,000 when retained earnings were $20,000.

(3) During the year Shelly sold goods to Barbie for $28,000. Barbie still holds some of these goods in inventory at the year end. The profit element included in these remaining goods is $2,000.

(4) Goodwill and the investment in the associate were impaired for the first time during the year as follows:

Shelly $2,000
Ken $3,000

Impairment of the subsidiary's goodwill should be charged to operating expenses.

Required:

Prepare the consolidated statement of comprehensive income for Barbie for the year ended 31 December 2010.

Test your understanding 4 : Exam standard question

The following are the summarised accounts of H, S, and A for the year ended 30 June 2011.

Statements of financial position as at 30 June 2011

	H	S	A
	$	$	$
Non-current assets			
Property, plant and equipment	87,000	88,000	62,000
Investments			
S (100%)	115,000		
A (30%)	15,000		
Current assets	74,000	40,000	9,000
	291,000	128,000	71,000

Share capital ($1 shares)	200,000	75,000	35,000
Retained earnings	89,000	51,000	34,000
Liabilities	2,000	2,000	2,000
	291,000	128,000	71,000

Statements of comprehensive income for the year ended 30 June 2011

	H $	S $	A $
Revenue	500,000	200,000	100,000
Operating costs	(400,000)	(140,000)	(60,000)
Profit from operations	100,000	60,000	40,000
Tax	(23,000)	(21,000)	(14,000)
Profit after tax	77,000	39,000	26,000
Other comprehensive income	–	–	–
Total comprehensive income	77,000	39,000	26,000

The shares in S and A were acquired on 1 July 2008 when the retained profits of S were $15,000 and the retained profits of A were $10,000.

At the date of acquisition, the fair value of S's non-current assets, which at that time had a remaining useful life of ten years, exceeded the book value by $10,000.

During the year S sold goods to H for $10,000 at a margin of 50%. At the year-end H had sold 80% of the goods.

At 30 June 2011 the goodwill in respect of S had been impaired by 30% of its original amount, of which the current year loss was $1,200. At 30 June 2009 the investment in A had been impaired by $450, of which the current year loss was $150.

Required:

Prepare the consolidated statement of comprehensive income for the year ended 30 June 2011 and consolidated statement of financial position as at 30 June 2011.

Test your understanding 5 : Objective test questions

(1) **Using the information you have prepared in TYU 4, what is the correct figure for revenue?**

   A $700,000

   B $800,000

   C $690,000

   D $790,000

(2) **Using the information you have prepared in TYU 4, what is the correct figure for investment in associate?**

   A $22,200

   B $21,750

   C $14,550

   D $nil

(3) **Using the information you have prepared in TYU 4, what is the correct figure for retained earnings?**

   A $123,250

   B $123,700

   C $285,050

   D $116,050

(4) **Using the information you have prepared in TYU 4, what is the correct figure for property, plant and equipment?**

   A $182,000

   B $244,000

   C $184,000

   D $246,000

(5) **Using the information you have prepared in TYU 4, what is the correct figure for profit in associate?**

   A $7,800

   B $7,650

   C $7,350

   D $7,950

5 Summary diagram

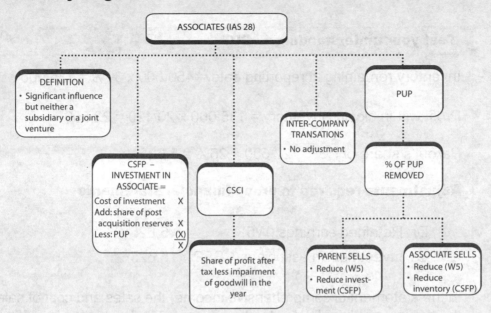

Test your understanding answers

Test your understanding 1 : PUP

Inventory remaining at reporting date = 450,000 x 30% = 135,000

Profit within closing inventory = 135,000 x 20/120 = 22,500

Parent's share of PUP = 22,500 × 25% = 5,625

Adjustments required to group financial statements

Dr	Retained earnings (W5)	5,625
Cr	Investment in associate (CSFP)	5,625

In the statement of comprehensive income, the sales and cost of sales of the group must be adjusted to allow for an overall reduction in profits of $5,625.

Reduce sales by (5,625 x 120/20) = 33,750.

Reduce cost of sales by (5,625 x 100/20) = 28,125

Net impact: gross profit falls by 33,750 – 28,125 = 5,625.

Or: exam alternative is to increase cost of sales by 5,625

Test your understanding 2 : Exam standard CSFP

P Group consolidated statement of financial position as at 30 November 2011

	$000
Non-current assets	
Goodwill (W3)	705
Property (890 + 850)	1,740
Plant & equipment (450 + 210 + 50 – 30)	680
Investment in associate (W6)	620
Current assets	
Inventory (270 + 230 – 20 – 9)	471
Receivables (100 + 340 – 50)	390
Cash (160 + 50)	210
	4,816
Equity	
Share capital	1,900
Share premium	650
Retained earnings (W5)	266
	2,816
Non-controlling interests	–
Non-current liabilities	
10% Loan notes (500 + 300)	800
Current liabilities	
Trade payables (520 + 330 – 50)	800
Tax (330 + 70)	400
	4,816

Workings

(W1) Group structure

P

100% | 1 December 2008
S   i.e. 3 years

P

| 1 December 2010

30% |

A   i.e. 1 year

(W2) Net assets of subsidiary

	Acquisition date	Reporting date
Share capital	500	500
Share premium	80	80
Retained earnings	870	400
Fair value adjustment – plant	50	50
Depreciation on FV adjustment (50/5 × 3)		(30)
PUP (W7)	–	(20)
	1,500	980

Net assets of associate

	Acquisition date	Reporting date
Share capital	250	250
Retained earnings (see below)	750	1,200
	1,000	1,450

Retained earnings at acquisition (balance)	750
Post acquisition profit	450
Retained earnings at reporting date	1,200

(W3) **Goodwill**

Cost of investment	2,675
Fair value of net assets acquired	
100% × 1,500 (W2)	(1,500)
	——
Goodwill on acquisition	1,175
Impairment (40% × 1,175)	(470)
	——
Goodwill at reporting date	705
	——

(W4) **Non-controlling interest**

N/A

(W5) **Group retained earnings**

Parent	1,145
PUP (W8)	(9)
Subsidiary (100% × (980 – 1,500))	(520)
Associate (30% × (1,450 – 1,000))	135
Impairment (15 + 470 (W3))	(485)
	——
	266
	——

(W6) Investment in associate

Cost of investment	500
Share of post-acquisition profits	135
30% x (1,450 – 1,000) (W2)	
Less: impairment	(15)
	620

(W7) PUP – Subsidiary

Profit on sale (25/125 × 400)	80
Profit in inventory (1/4 × 80)	20

(W8) PUP – Associate

Profit on sale (150 – 100)	50
Profit in inventory (90/150 × 50)	30
Group share (30% × 30)	9

Barbie consolidated income statement for the year ended 31 December 2010

	Barbie	Ken	Adjustments	Consolidated
	$000	$000	$000	$000
Revenue	385	100		485.0
Cost of sales	(185)	(60)		(245.0)
				————
Gross profit				240.0
Operating expenses	(50)	(15)		(68.0)
Impairment in subsidiary			(3)	
				————
Profit from operations				172.0
Share of profits of associate company (W2)				3.4
				————
Profit before tax				175.4
Taxation	(50)	(12)		(62.0)
				————
Profit for the year				113.4
Other comprehensive income				–
				————
Total comprehensive income				113.4
				————
Amount attributable to:				
Non-controlling interests (N/A)				–
Parent shareholders				113.4
				————
				113.4
				————

Workings

(W1) Group structure

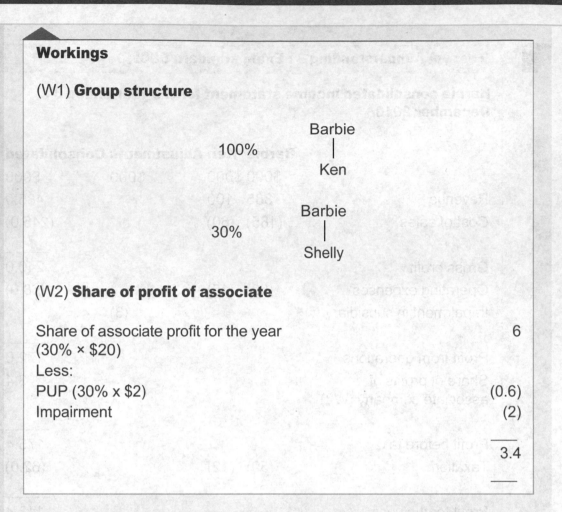

(W2) Share of profit of associate

Share of associate profit for the year (30% × $20)	6
Less:	
PUP (30% x $2)	(0.6)
Impairment	(2)
	3.4

Test your understanding 4 : Exam standard question

H Group statement of comprehensive income for the year ended 30 June 2011

	H	S	Adjustments	Consolidated
	$	$	$	$
Revenue	500,000	200,000	(10,000)	690,000
Operating costs	(400,000)	(140,000)	10,000	(533,200)
Impairment in S			(1,200)	
Depreciation on fair value adjustment		(1,000)		
PUP (10,000 x 20% x 50%)		(1,000)		
Profit from operations				156,800
Share of profit of associate ((30% × 26,000) − goodwill impairment 150)				7,650
Profit before tax				164,450
Tax	(23,000)	(21,000)		(44,000)
Profit for the period				120,450
Other comprehensive income				–
Total comprehensive income				120,450
Attributable to:				
Non-controlling interests				–
Parent shareholders				120,450
				120,450

Consolidated statement of financial position as at 30 June 2011

	$
Non-current assets	
Goodwill (W3)	10,500
Investment in associate (W6)	21,750
Property, plant and equipment	
(87,000 + 88,000 + 10,000 FV − 3,000 FV	
depreciation (W2))	182,000
Current assets (74,000 + 40,000 − 1,000 PUP (W2))	113,000
	327,250
Equity	
Share capital	200,000
Retained earnings (W5)	123,250
Non-controlling interest (W4)	−
Liabilities (2,000 + 2,000)	4,000
	327,250

Workings

(W1) **Group structure**

100%/30%   H   1 July 2008
         S and A   i.e. 3 years

(W2) **Net assets**

	S		A	
	Acq Date	**Rep Date**	**Acq Date**	**Rep Date**
	$	$	$	$
Share capital	75,000	75,000	35,000	35,000
Retained earnings	15,000	51,000	10,000	34,000
Fair value adj	10,000	10,000		
Depreciation (3/10 × 10,000)	−	(3,000)		
PUP		(1,000)		
	100,000	132,000	45,000	69,000

(W3) **Goodwill**

	S $
Cost of investment	115,000
Fair value of net assets at acquisition (100% 100,000)	(100,000)
	15,000
Less: impairment loss (30% x 15,000)	(4,500)
	10,500

(W4) **Non-controlling interest**

N/A

(W5) **Retained earnings**

	$
Parent	89,000
Less: Impairments (4,500 (W3) + 450)	(4,950)
Share of post acquisition profits	
S: 100% × (132,000 – 100,000) (W2)	32,000
A: 30% × (69,000 – 45,000) (W2)	7,200
	123,250

(W6) **Investment in associate**

	$
Cost	15,000
Share of increase in net assets (30% × (69,000 – 45,000) (W2))	7,200
	22,200
Less: impairment	(450)
	21,750

Test your understanding 5 : Objective test questions

(1) C

(2) B

(3) A

(4) A

(5) B

7

Introduction to Published Accounts

Chapter learning objectives

- Prepare financial statements in a form suitable for publication, with appropriate notes;

- Identify the concepts affecting financial statements;

- Prepare the statement of financial position with appropriate notes;

- Prepare the statement of changes in equity;

- Prepare the income statement with appropriate notes;

- Identify the alternative layouts for the statement of comprehensive income and the income statement with a statement of comprehensive income;

- Distinguish between current and non-current assets and liabilities.

1 Session content

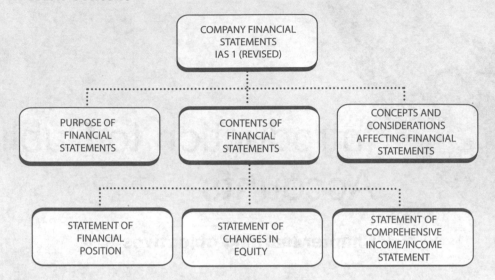

```
                    COMPANY FINANCIAL
                    STATEMENTS
                    IAS 1 (REVISED)

  PURPOSE OF          CONTENTS OF        CONCEPTS AND
  FINANCIAL           FINANCIAL          CONSIDERATIONS
  STATEMENTS          STATEMENTS         AFFECTING FINANCIAL
                                         STATEMENTS

  STATEMENT OF        STATEMENT OF       STATEMENT OF
  FINANCIAL           CHANGES IN         COMPREHENSIVE
  POSITION            EQUITY             INCOME/INCOME
                                         STATEMENT
```

2 IAS 1 (revised) Presentation of Financial Statements

All entities preparing their financial statements in accordance with International Accounting Standards should follow the requirements of IAS 1, revised 2007. IAS 1 (revised) prescribes what a set of financial statements should contain and how they should be presented.

Purpose of financial statements

IAS 1 (revised) states that the objective of financial statements is to provide information about the financial position, performance and cash flows of an enterprise that is useful in making economic decisions. The financial statements will also show how effectively management have looked after the resources of the entity, i.e. it will help users assess the stewardship of management.

Contents of financial statements

A complete set of financial statements includes:

* a statement of financial position;
* either:
  - a statement of comprehensive income, or
  - an income statement plus a statement showing other comprehensive income;
* a statement of changes in equity;
* a statement of cash flows;
* accounting policies note and other explanatory notes.

IAS 1 (revised) does not require the above titles to be used by companies. It is likely that many companies in practice will continue to use the previous terms of balance sheet rather than statement of financial position and cash flow statement rather than statement of cash flows. However, when preparing an answer to an exam question you should always use the revised terms.

Entities are also encouraged to present a financial review by management which describes and explains the main features of the entities financial performance and financial position. This report would be outside of the financial statements.

This chapter looks at the formats of the statement of comprehensive income, statement of financial position and statement of changes in equity. The statement of cash flow is considered in a later chapter. Notes to the financial statements are considered with their relevant standards.

Responsibility for financial statements

The board of directors (and/or other governing body) of an entity is responsible for the preparation and presentation of its financial statements.

3 Concepts and other considerations affecting financial statements

Fair presentation

IAS 1 (revised) states that 'Financial statements should present fairly the financial position, financial performance and cash flows of an enterprise'. Enterprises that comply with all relevant IAS's will virtually always achieve this objective.

A fair presentation requires that entities:

- show a faithful representation of the effects of transactions;

- select and apply accounting policies in accordance with IAS 8 (see later);

- present information in a manner which provides relevant, reliable, comparable and understandable information;

- provide additional disclosures if the requirements of an IFRS are insufficient to enable users to understand the impact of the transaction on the financial position and performance.

If, however, an entity feels that compliance with an IFRS would be misleading and that it is necessary to depart from the requirements of an IFRS in order to show a fair presentation, the entity should make the following disclosures:

- that management have concluded that the financial statements do present fairly the financial position, financial performance and cash flows;

- that the entity has complied with IFRSs except that it has departed from an IFRS in order to show a fair presentation;

- the IFRS that has been departed from, the nature of the departure i.e. the treatment that the IFRS would require and the reason why such treatment would be misleading and the treatment adopted instead;

- the financial impact of the departure on net profit/loss, assets, liabilities, equity and cash flows.

However, departing from the provisions of the standards in the interests of fair presentation, would be very rare .

Going concern

IAS 1 (revised) states that financial statements should be prepared on the going concern basis unless management intend to liquidate the business or to cease trading.

Preparing financial statements on the going concern basis means preparing them on the assumption that the entity will continue to trade for the foreseeable future.

Accruals basis

IAS 1 (revised) requires entities to prepare their financial statements (except for cash flow information) on the accruals basis of accounting.

This means that transactions should be recorded in the accounting period to which they relate regardless of whether or not cash has been received or paid.

This concept also means that expenses should be recognised in the income statement so as to match against directly related income.

Consistency

Presentation and classification of items should be consistent from one period to the next.

Changes are allowed, if required by an IFRS or if it is deemed more appropriate to change the presentation of information.

Materiality and aggregation

Each material class of similar items should be presented separately in the financial statements. Immaterial amounts should be aggregated with amounts of a similar nature and need not be disclosed separately.

Omissions or misstatements of items are material if they could influence the economic decisions of users. Materiality depends on the size and nature of the omission or misstatement.

Off-setting

Assets and liabilities, and income and expenses, should not be offset except when offsetting is required or allowed by an IFRS.

Comparative information

Comparative information should be disclosed in respect of the previous period for all amounts reported in the financial statements unless an IFRS requires or allows otherwise.

Other requirements

Other requirements affecting the preparation of financial statements.

IAS 1 also outlines the following requirements for the preparation of financial statements. (Most of these you will be already familiar with, but are included for completeness.)

- Accounting policies should be selected so that financial statements will comply with IFRSs.

- Management should make an assessment of the entity's ability to continue as a going concern. Financial statements should then be prepared on a going concern basis, unless there are plans to liquidate or cease trading.

- The financial statements should be prepared under the accruals basis of accounting, with the exception of the cash flow information.

- The financial statements should retain a consistent approach to presentation and classification of items year-on-year.

- Material amounts should be presented separately in the financial statements. Immaterial amounts should be aggregated with other like items.

- Assets and liabilities should not be offset, except where required or permitted by another IFRS.

- Income and expenses should not be offset except where it is required or permitted by another IFRS.

- Comparative information should be disclosed for the previous period for all numerical information. Where presentation or classification of an item has changed, the comparative figures should be restated using the new treatment, if possible.

- Financial statements should be presented at least annually and should be issued on a timely basis (within 6 months of the end of the reporting period) to be useful to users.

IAS 1 does not specify the format of financial statements, but it does provide an appendix which sets out illustrative formats for the statements to be included in financial statements. In addition, it provides guidance on the items that should be disclosed in these statements and those that can be relegated to the notes that accompany the statements.

4 The statement of financial position

The suggested format (showing minimum requirements) for the statement of financial position (SOFP) is as follows:

XYZ Ltd Statement of Financial Position as at 31 December 2010

	$000	$000
Assets		
Non-current assets		
Property, plant and equipment	X	
Intangible assets	X	
Available for sale investments	X	
	—	
		X
Current assets		
Inventories	X	
Trade and other receivables	X	
Other current assets	X	
Cash and cash equivalents	X	
	—	
		X
		—
Total assets		X
		—

Equity and liabilities

Capital and reserves

Issued share capital	X
Share premium	X
Revaluation reserve	X
Retained earnings	X
	—
	X

Non-current liabilities

Long-term borrowings	X
Deferred tax	X
Long-term provisions	X
	—
	X

Current liabilities

Trade and other payables	X
Short-term borrowings	X
Current tax payable	X
Short-term provisions	X
	—
	X
	—
Total equity and liabilities	X
	—

The format requires comparative figures for the previous year, these have been omitted as you will not need to prepare comparatives in questions.

Information to be presented in the statement of financial position

IAS 1 requires that, as a minimum, the following line items appear in the statement of financial position (where there are amounts to be classified within these categories):

(a) property, plant and equipment;

(b) investment property;

(c) intangible assets;

(d) financial assets (excluding amounts shown under (e), (h) and (i));

(e) investments accounted for using the equity method;**

(f) biological assets;

(g) inventories;

(h) trade and other receivables;

(i) cash and cash equivalents;

(j) the total of assets classified as held for sale in accordance with IFRS 5 Non-current assets held for sale and discontinued operations;

(k) trade and other payables;

(l) provisions;

(m) financial liabilities (excluding amounts shown under (k) or (l));

(n) liabilities and assets for current tax as defined in IAS 12, Income Taxes;

(o) deferred tax liabilities and deferred tax assets, as defined in IAS 12, Income Taxes;

(p) liabilities included in disposal groups classified as held for sale in accordance with IFRS 5;

(q) minority interest, presented within equity;**

(r) issued capital and reserves attributable to owners of the parent.

** These items relate to group accounts and are beyond the scope of this syllabus.

The above list includes items that the IASB believes are so different in nature or function that they should be separately disclosed, but does not require them to appear in a fixed order or format.

Additional line items, headings and subtotals should be shown in the statement of financial position if another IFRS requires it or where it is necessary to show a fair presentation of the financial position.

In deciding whether additional items should be separately presented, management should consider:

• The nature and liquidity of assets and their materiality (e.g. the separate disclosure of monetary and non-monetary amounts and current and non-current assets);

• Their function within the entity (e.g. the separate disclosure of operating assets and financial assets, inventories and cash); and

• the amounts, nature and timing of liabilities (e.g. the separate disclosure of interest-bearing and non-interest-bearing liabilities and provisions and current and non-current liabilities).

Assets and liabilities that have a different nature or function within an entity are sometimes subject to different measurement bases, for example, plant and equipment may be carried at cost or held at a revalued amount (in accordance with IAS 16). The use of these different measurement bases for different classes of items suggests separate presentation is necessary for users to fully understand the accounts.

Information to be presented in either the SOFP of in the notes

Further subclassifications of the line items should be presented either in the statement of financial position or in the notes. The size, nature and function of the amounts involved, or the requirements of another IFRS will normally determine whether the disclosure is in the statement of financial position or in the notes.

The disclosures will vary for each item, but IAS 1 gives the following examples:

(a) tangible assets are analysed (IAS 16) by class: property, plant and equipment;

(b) receivables are analysed between:

- amounts receivable from trade customers

- receivables from related parties

- prepayments

- other amounts;

(c) inventories are classified (IAS 2) into merchandise, production supplies, materials, work in progress and finished goods;

(d) provisions are analysed showing provisions for employee benefits separate from any other provisions;

(e) equity capital and reserves are analysed showing separately the various classes of paid-in capital, share premium and reserves.

Share capital and reserves disclosures

IAS 1 also requires that the following information on share capital and reserves be made either in the statement of financial position or in the notes:

(a) for each class of share capital:

- the number of shares authorised,

- the number of shares issued and fully paid, and issued but not fully paid,

- par value per share, or that the shares have no par value,

- a reconciliation of the number of shares outstanding at the beginning and at the end of the year, the rights, preferences and restrictions attaching to that class, including restrictions on the distribution of dividends and the repayment of capital,

- shares in the entity held by the entity itself or by subsidiaries or associates of the entity, and

- shares reserved for issuance under options and sales contracts, including the terms and amounts;

(b) a description of the nature and purpose of each reserve within owners' equity;

IAS 1 requires the following to be disclosed in the notes:

- the amount of dividends that were proposed or declared after the reporting period but before the financial statements were authorised for issue;

- the amount of any cumulative preference dividends not recognised.

Note: IAS 1 and IAS 10 do not allow proposed dividends to be included as a liability in the statement of financial position, unless the dividend was declared before the end of the reporting period.

Current/Non-current distinction

An entity shall present current and non-current assets and current and non-current liabilities as separate classifications in the statement of financial position except when a presentation based on liquidity provides information that is reliable and more relevant.

Where an entity chooses not to classify by current and non-current, assets and liabilities should be presented broadly in order of their liquidity.

Whichever method of presentation is adopted, an entity should disclose, for each asset and liability, the amount that is expected to be recovered or settled after more than 12 months.

Most entities will show both current and non-current liabilities in the statement of financial position. However, say, for example, an entity does not normally have non-current trade liabilities but as a result of one particular transaction has a payable due 20 months from the end of the reporting period. The entity may, in this case, classify the entire amount as a trade payable under current liabilities and then show separately a one-off amount that is due in 20 months' time (i.e. in more than 12 months from the end of the reporting period).

In judging the most suitable presentation, management should consider the usefulness of the information they are providing. Information about the financial position of an entity is often used to predict the expected future cash flows and the timing of those cash flows. Information about the expected date of recovery and settlement of items is likely to be useful and therefore worth disclosing.

Current assets

An asset should be classified as a current asset when it is any of the following:

- is expected to be realised in, or is intended for sale or consumption in the entity's normal operating cycle;
- is held primarily for trading purposes;
- is expected to be realised within 12 months of the end of the reporting period; or
- is cash or cash equivalent.

All other assets should be classified as non-current assets.

Current liabilities

A liability should be classified as a current liability when it:

- is expected to be settled in the entity's normal operating cycle;
- is due to be settled within 12 months of the end of the reporting period;
- is held primarily for the purpose of being traded; or
- the entity does not have an unconditional right to defer settlement of the liability for at least 12 months after the end of the reporting period;

All other liabilities should be classified as non-current liabilities.

5 Statement of changes in equity

The statement of changes in equity (SOCIE) provides a summary of all changes in equity arising from transactions with owners in their capacity of owners.

This includes the effect of share issues and dividends.

This statement is useful since the total change in equity reflects the increase or decreases in the net assets of the enterprise in the period and so reflects the change in the wealth of the enterprise in the period.

XYZ Ltd Statement of changes in equity for the year ended 31 December 2010

	Share capital	Share premium	Revaluation reserve	Retained earnings	Total
	$000	$000	$000	$000	$000
Balance at 31 December 2009	X	X	X	X	X
Change in accounting policy				X/(X)	X/(X)
	—	—	—	—	—
Restated balance				X	X
Revaluation gain/loss			X(X)		X/(X)
Transfer to retained earnings			(X)	X	–
Total comprehensive income for the period			X	X	X
Dividends				(X)	(X)
Issue of share capital	X	X			X
	—	—	—	—	—
Balance at 31 December 2010	X	X	X	X/(X)	X
	—	—	—	—	—

Illustration 1 : SOFP and SOCIE

Bernie plc is a quoted company with an authorised share capital of $500,000, consisting of ordinary shares of $1 each. The company prepares its accounts as on 31 March each year and the trial balance before adjustments, extracted on 31 March 2011 is as follows:

	Dr	Cr
	$	$
Ordinary share capital, issued and fully paid		400,000
Share premium		15,000
Retained earnings at 1 April 2010		122,000
6% Loan		100,000
Leasehold factory		
Cost at 1 April 2010	400,000	
Accumulated depreciation at 1 April 2010		152,000
Plant and machinery		
Cost at 1 April 2010	150,000	
Additions in year	20,000	
Accumulated depreciation at 1 April 2010		60,000
Trade payables		280,000
Accrued expenses		60,000
Inventory as at 31 March 2011	320,000	
Trade receivables	200,000	
Prepayments	160,000	
Cash and cash equivalents	180,000	
Profit for year (subject to items in the following notes)		222,000
Interim dividend paid	5,000	
Sale proceeds of plant		24,000
	1,435,000	1,435,000

You ascertain that:

(1) The loan is repayable at par by five equal annual instalments starting on 31 December 2011.

(2) The plant disposed of originally cost $32,000 and depreciation of $6,400 had been charged by the date of disposal.

(3) Annual depreciation is calculated at the year end as:
   – leasehold factory 2% on cost;
   – plant and machinery 20% reducing balance.

(4) A final dividend of 20 cents per share is declared on 5 April 2011.

(5) Tax for the year is estimated to be $20,000.

(6) During the year 100,000 shares had been issued at $1.10 each. This share issue has been accounted for.

Required:

Prepare, in a form suitable for publication, the statement of financial position and statement of changes in equity as at 31 March 2011.

Solution

Bernic Plc Statement of financial position as at 31 March 2011

	$	$
Non-current assets		
Property, plant and equipment (W1)		307,520
Current assets		
Inventories	320,000	
Trade receivables	200,000	
Prepayments	160,000	
Cash and cash equivalents	180,000	
		860,000
Total assets		1,167,520
Equity and liabilities		
Capital and reserves		
Issued capital	400,000	
Share premium	15,000	
Retained earnings	292,520	
		707,520
Non-current liabilities		
6% Loan (W5)		80,000
Current liabilities		
6% Loan (W5)	20,000	
Trade payables	280,000	
Accrued expenses	60,000	
Income tax	20,000	
		380,000
		1,167,520

Bernie Plc Statement of changes in equity for the year ended 31 March 2011

	Share capital	Share premium	Retained earnings	Total
	$	$	$	$
Balance at 1 April 2010	300,000	5,000	122,000	427,000
Net profit for the year (W2)			175,520	175,520
Dividends paid TB			(5,000)	(5,000)
Issue of share capital (W7)	100,000	10,000	–	110,000
Balance at 31 March 2011	400,000	15,000	292,520	707,520

Workings

(W1) Property, plant and equipment

	Leasehold factory	Plant and machinery	Total
	$	$	$
Cost			
At 1 April 2010	400,000	150,000	550,000
Additions	–	20,000	20,000
Disposals	–	(32,000)	(32,000)
At 31 March 2011	400,000	138,000	538,000
Acc dep'n			
At 1 April 2010	152,000	60,000	212,000
Disposals	–	(6,400)	(6,400)
Charge for year (W4)	8,000	16,880	24,880
At 31 March 2011	160,000	70,480	230,480
Carrying value at 31 March 2011	240,000	67,520	307,520
Carrying value at 1 April 2010	248,000	90,000	338,000

(W2) **Profit for the year**

	$
Per TB	222,000
Loss on disposal (W3)	(1,600)
Depreciation – factory (W4)	(8,000)
Depreciation – P&M (W4)	(16,880)
Income tax expense	(20,000)
	175,520

(W3) **Loss on disposal**

	$
Proceeds (TB)	24,000
Carrying value (32,000 – 6,400)	25,600
Loss on disposal	1,600

(W4) **Depreciation**

Factory 2% x $400,000 = $8,000

P & M 20% x (cost $138,000 – depn ($60,000 – $6,400)) = 20% x $84,400 = $16,880

(W5) **Loan**

This is repaid in 5 equal instalments. The first payment is due within 12 months of the reporting date and therefore must be shown as a current liability. Total liability = $100,000 split $20,000 current (1/5) and $80,000 non-current (4/5).

(W6) **Dividends**

No adjustments are made for dividends as declared after the reporting date.

(W7) **Share issue**

Total proceeds = 100,000 x $1.10 = $110,000

Nominal value = 100,000 x $1 = $100,000 (share capital account)

Premium = 100,000 x $0.10 = $10,000 (share premium account)

6 Statement of comprehensive income

IAS 1 (revised) allows a choice of two presentations of comprehensive income:

- A statement of comprehensive income; or
- An income statement showing the realised profit or loss for the period PLUS other comprehensive income, i.e. total comprehensive income.

Total comprehensive income is the realised profit or loss for the period, plus other comprehensive income.

Other comprehensive income is income and expenses that are not recognised in profit or loss (i.e. they are recorded in reserves rather than as an element of the realised profit for the period). For the purpose of F1, other comprehensive income includes any change in the revaluation surplus.

A recommended format to present one statement would be as follows:

XYZ Ltd Statement of total comprehensive Income for the year ended 31 December 2010

	$000
Revenue	X
Cost of sales	(X)
Gross profit/(loss)	X/(X)
Distribution costs	(X)
Administrative expenses	(X)
Profit/(loss) from operations	X/(X)
Income from investments	X
Finance cost	(X)
Profit/(loss) before tax	X/(X)
Income tax expense	(X)
Profit/(loss) for the period	X/(X)
Other comprehensive income	
Gain/loss on revaluation	X
Gain/loss on available for sale investments	X
Total comprehensive income for the year	X

This analysis of expenses is based on the function method. This presentation method is the format most likely to appear in the exam.

Material items

- When items of income and expenses are material, their nature and amount shall be disclosed separately.

- This may either be done on the face of the income statement or in the notes.

- Examples:
    - inventory write-offs;
    - impairment losses (see later notes);
    - restructuring costs;
    - disposals of property, plant and equipment;
    - litigation settlements.

- The revised IAS I has prohibited any income or expenses from being classified as extraordinary items.

Alternative presentation

An entity may present two statements instead of one: a seperate income statement and a statement of comprehensive income.

Income statement plus statement of comprehensive income - function method

A recommended format for the income statement would be as follows:

XYZ Ltd Income statement for the year ended 31 December 2010

	$000
Revenue	X
Cost of sales	(X)
Gross profit/(loss)	X/(X)
Distribution costs	(X)
Administrative expenses	(X)

Profit/(loss) from operations	X/(X)
Income from investments	X
Finance cost	(X)
Profit/(loss) before tax	X/(X)
Income tax expense	(X)
Profit/(loss) for the period	X/(X)

A recommended format for the presentation of other comprehensive income would be:

XYZ Ltd Other comprehensive income for the year ended 31 December 2010

Profit/(loss) for the period	X/(X)
Other comprehensive income	
Gain/loss on revaluation	X/(X)
Gain/loss on available for sale investments	X/(X)
Total comprehensive income for the year	X

Information to be presented in the statement of comprehensive

IAS 1 requires that certain information (as a minimum) is presented in the statement of comprehensive income, including:

(a) revenue;

(b) finance costs;

(c) share of profits and losses of associates (examined) and joint ventures (beyond the scope of this syllabus), accounted for using the equity method;

(d) tax expense;

(e) the total of the post tax profit or loss of discontinued operations and the post tax gain or loss recognised on the remeasurement to fair value less cost to sell, or on the disposal of the assets or disposal group constituting the discontinued operation;

(f) profit or loss;

(g) each component of other comprehensive income classified by nature (excluding amounts in (h));

(h) share of other comprehensive income of associates and joint ventures;

(i) total comprehensive income.

Additional line items, headings and subtotals should be shown in the statement of comprehensive income if another IFRS requires it or where it is necessary to show a fair presentation of the financial position.

Materiality, the nature and function of the item are likely to be the main considerations when deciding whether to include an additional line item in the statement of comprehensive income.

Nature of expenses method

In this method expenses are presented according to their nature rather than their function as follows:

XYZ Ltd Statement of comprehensive Income for the year ended 31 December 2010

	$000
Revenue	X
Other operating income	X
Changes in inventory of WIP and finished goods	(X)
Work performed by the entity and capitalised	X
Raw material and consumables used	(X)
Employee benefits expense	(X)
Depreciation and amortisation expense	(X)
Impairment of property, pland and equipment	(X)
Other expenses	**(X)**
Finance costs	(X)
Profit/(loss) before tax	X/(X)
Income tax expense	(X)
Profit/(loss) for the period	X/(X)
Other comprehensive income	
Gain/loss on revaluation	X
Gain/loss on available for sale investments	X
Total comprehensive income for the year	X

Illustration 2 : Statement of comprehensive income

The following is an extract from the trial balance of Lafford Limited, at 30 September 2011.

	Dr	Cr
	$000	$000
Sales		41,600
Purchases	22,600	
Inventory at 1 October 2010	13,000	
Distribution costs	6,000	
Administration expenses	5,000	
Irrecoverable debts written off	600	
Hire of machinery	500	
Production wages	400	
Loan interest (loan repayable 2020)	1,050	
Dividends received		900
Warehouse machinery:		
Cost	3,000	
Accumulated depreciation at 1 October 2010		1,700
Motor vehicles:		
Cost	1,000	
Accumulated depreciation at 1 October 2010		500

The following information should also be taken into account:

(1) Closing inventory at 30 September 2011 was $15.6 million.

(2) Irrecoverable debts written off are to be included in administrative expenses.

(3) Depreciation is to be provided for on the straight line basis as follows:

  – Warehouse machinery   10 per cent
  – Motor vehicles   25 per cent

(4) Depreciation of motor vehicles is to be divided equally between distribution costs and administrative expenses, and depreciation of warehouse machinery is to be charged wholly to cost of sales.

(5) The estimated income tax expense for the year ended 30 September 2011 is $3 million.

Required:

Prepare Lafford Ltd's statement of comprehensive income for the year ended 30 September 2011 in a form suitable for publication.

Solution

Lafford Statement of comprehensive income for the year ended 30 September 2011

	$000
Revenue	41,600
Cost of sales (W1)	(21,200)
Gross profit	20,400
Distribution costs (W1)	(6,125)
Administration expenses (W1)	(5,725)
Profit from operations	8,550
Income from investments	900
Finance cost	(1,050)
Profit before tax	8,400
Income tax expense	(3,000)
Profit for the period	5,400
Other comprehensive income:	-
Total comprehensive income for the year	5,400

Workings

(W1)

	COS	Distribution	Administration
	$000	$000	$000
Purchases	22,600		
Opening inventory	13,000		
Distribution costs		6,000	
Administration costs			5,000
Bad debts written off			600
Hire of machinery	500		
Production wages	400		
Closing inventory	(15,600)		
Dep'n – WM (10% × 3,000)	300		
Dep'n – MV (25% × 1,000)		125	125
	21,200	6,125	5,725

Notes to financial statements

Notes to the financial statements normally include narrative descriptions or more detailed analysis of items in the financial statements, as well as additional information such as contingent liabilities and commitments.

IAS 1 also provides guidance on the structure of the accompanying notes to financial statements, the accounting policies and other required disclosures.

The notes to the financial statements of an entity should:

(a) present information about the basis of preparation of the financial statements and the specific accounting policies adopted for significant transactions;

(b) disclose the information required by other IFRSs that is not presented elsewhere in the financial statements;

(c) provide additional information which is not presented elsewhere in financial statements but is relevant to an understanding of any of them.

Notes to the financial statements should be presented in a systematic manner and any item in the financial statements should be cross-referenced to any related information in the notes.

Notes are normally provided in the following order, which assists users in understanding the financial statements and comparing them with those of other entities:

(a) statement of compliance with IFRSs;

(b) summary of the significant accounting policies applied;

(c) supporting information for items presented in each financial statement in the order in which each line item and each financial statement is presented;

(d) other disclosures, including:

- contingent liabilities, commitments and unrecognised contractual commitments other financial disclosures;

- non-financial disclosures.

Accounting policies

The summary of significant accounting policies in the notes to the financial statements should describe the following:

- the measurement basis (or bases) used in preparing the financial statements; and

- each specific accounting policy that is necessary for a proper understanding of the financial statements.

Test your understanding 1 : P Ltd

The following information has been extracted from the accounting reports of P:

P - trial balance as at 31 March 2011

	Dr	Cr
	$'000	$'000
Sales revenue		5,300
Cost of sales	1,350	
Dividends received		210
Administration expenses	490	
Distribution costs	370	
Interest payable	190	
Prepayments	25	
Dividends paid	390	
Property, plant and equipment	4,250	
Short-term investments	2,700	
Inventory at 31 March 2011	114	
Trade receivables	418	
Cash and cash equivalents	12	
Trade payables		136
Long-term loans (repayable 2021)		1,200
Share capital		1,500
Share premium		800
Retained earnings at 31 March 2010		1,163
	10,309	10,309

The following information should also be taken into account:

(1) During the year, P paid a final dividend of $240,000 in respect of the year ended 31 March 2010. This was in addition to the interim dividend paid on 1 September 2010 in respect of the year ended 31 March 2011.

(2) The tax charge for the year has been estimated at $470,000.

(3) The directors declared a final dividend of $270,000 on 3 April 2011.

Required:

Prepare, in a form suitable for publication, the statement of financial position and statement of changes in equity for the year ended 31 March 2011.

Test your understanding 2 : Picklette Ltd

The following information has been extracted from the books of Picklette Ltd for the year ended 31 March 2011:

	Dr	Cr
	$000	$000
Administration expenses	170	
Interest paid	5	
Distribution costs	240	
Called up share capital (ordinary $1 shares)		200
Dividends paid	6	
Cash and cash equivalents	9	
Land and Buildings		
Cost at 1 April 2010 (land $110, buildings $100)	210	
Accumulated depreciation at 1 April 2010		48
Plant and machinery		
Cost at 1 April 2010	125	
Accumulated depreciation at 1 April 2010		75
Accruals		90
Retained earnings at 1 April 2010		270
Trade receivables and payables	738	60
Inventory as at 1 April 2010	150	
Purchases	470	
10% Loan		80
Revenue		1,300
	2,123	2,123

Additional information:

(1) Inventory at 31 March 2011 was valued at $250,000.

(2) Buildings and plant and machinery are depreciated on a straight-line basis (assuming no residual value) at the following rate:

On cost:	Buildings	5%
	Plant and machinery	20%

(3) There was no purchases or sales of non-current assets for the year to 31 March 2011.

(4) The depreciation charges for the year to 31 March 2011 are to be apportioned as follows:

Cost of sales	60%
Distribution costs	20%
Administration expenses	20%

(5) Income tax for the year to 31 March 2011 is estimated at $135,000.

(6) The loan is repayable in five years.

Required:

Prepare a statement of comprehensive income, a statement of financial position and a statement of changes in equity for the year to 31 March 2011 for Picklette Ltd. Show all workings clearly.

Test your understanding 3 : Thistle Ltd

Thistle Ltd is a company with authorised share capital of 500,000 $1 5% preference shares and 1,400,000 50c ordinary shares. At the year-end the company has in issue 300,000 preference shares and 1,000,000 ordinary shares, all of which are fully paid.

The company prepares its accounts annually to 30 June and its trial balance for the year ended 30 June 2011, before final adjustments, is as follows:

	Dr	Cr
	$	$
Ordinary share capital, issued and fully paid		500,000
5% Preference share capital, issued and fully paid		300,000
Share premium		100,000
Retained earnings at 1 July 2010		540,000
10% Loan		80,000
Land and Buildings		
Cost at 1 July 2010	1,400,000	
Accumulated depreciation at 1 July 2010		58,000
Motor Vehicles		
Cost at 1 July 2010	67,500	
Accumulated depreciation at 1 July 2010		30,250
Fixtures & Fittings		
Cost at 1 July 2010	19,800	
Accumulated depreciation at 1 July 2010		8,400

Trade receivables and payables	71,500	60,820
Prepayments and accruals	970	1,360
Inventory as at 30 June 2011		
Raw materials	32,500	
Finished goods	29,700	
Cash and cash equivalents	217,360	
Profit for year (subject to items in the following notes)		160,500
	1,839,330	1,839,330

The following information should also be taken into account:

(1) The following transactions have happened during the year in relation to non-current assets, **none** of which have yet been recorded in the books:

–   Land is included in the trial balance at its original cost of $800,000.

–   A building was purchased which cost $100,000.

–   Motor vehicles which had originally cost $24,000 were sold during the year for $12,000. Accumulated depreciation of $14,000 had been charged on these motor vehicles at 1 July 2010.

(2) Depreciation for the year is to be provided using the following policies:

Land	nil depreciation
Buildings	2% per annum, straight line
Motor vehicles	20% per annum, reducing balance
Fixtures & fittings	10% per annum, straight line

A full year's charge is made in the year of acquisition and none in the year of disposal.

(3) The directors have estimated that the company's tax liability for the year will be $18,500.

(4) The directors would like to declare a final ordinary dividend of 7 cents per share. The company has not yet paid the preference dividends in respect of the year.

(5) Interest on the loan is paid annually in arrears on 1 July. The debentures are repayable in 2023.

(6) During the year 100,000 ordinary shares were issued at a premium of 40 cents per share. This share issue is reflected in the trial balance.

Required:

Prepare, in a form suitable for publication, the statement of financial position and statement of changes in equity for the year ended 30 June 2011.

Test your understanding 4 : Objective test questions

(1) **Which of the following best describes the purpose of financial statements according to IAS 1 (revised)***Presentation of Financial Statements***?**

   A   To provide information that enables users to assess the stewardship of management

   B   To provide information about the financial position, financial performance and cash flows of an enterprise

   C   To provide a summary of all financial transactions entered into in the accounting period

   D   To provide an income statement and a statement of financial position

(2) **Which of the following are concepts that should be applied when preparing financial statements according to IAS 1 (revised)** *Presentation of Financial Statements***?**

   (i)   Going concern

   (ii) Accruals

   (iii) Consistency

   (iv) Off-setting

   A   i and ii

   B   i and iii

   C   i, ii and iv

   D   All of them

(3) **Which of the following items must be shown on the face of the statement of comprehensive income according to IAS 1 (revised)** *Presentation of Financial Statements*?

(i) Revenue

(ii) Cost of sales

(iii) Gross profit

(iv) Net profit/loss

(v) Income tax expense

A   All of them

B   i, ii, iii and iv

C   i, iv and v

D   i, ii and iii

(4) **Which of the following items would be shown in the statement of changes in equity?**

(i) Net profit for period

(ii) Dividends paid

(iii) Dividends proposed after the reporting period

(iv) Issue of shares

(v) Revaluation surplus

A   i, ii, iv and v

B   i, ii, iii and iv

C   i, iii, iv and v

D   All of them

(5) **Which of the following items would be shown as other comprehensive income on the statement of comprehensive income?**

(i) Net profit for period

(ii) Dividends paid

(iii) Dividends proposed

(iv) Issue of shares

(v) Revaluation surplus

A   i, ii, iv and v

B   i, ii, and iv

C   v

D   All of them

Data for questions 6 and 7:

Trade receivables as at 31 December 2010 were $18,000.

The bad debt provision as at 1 January 2010 was $900.

During the year, irrecoverable debts of $12,000 have been written off to administrative expenses.

After the year-end, but before the accounts had been completed, the entity discovered that a major customer had gone into liquidation and that their outstanding balance of $2,000 was unlikely to be paid.

Furthermore, as a result of the recent bad debt experience, the directors have decided to increase the irrecoverable debt provision at 31 December 2010 to 10 per cent of outstanding trade receivables.

(6) What is the correct balance for trade receivables, net of irrecoverable debt provision, as at 31 December 2010?

    A $3,600

    B $5,400

    C $14,400

    D $16,200

(7) What is the correct charge to the statement of comprehensive income for irrecoverable debts and provisions for the year to 31 December 2010?

    A $14,000

    B $14,400

    C $14,700

    D $15,600

7 Summary diagram

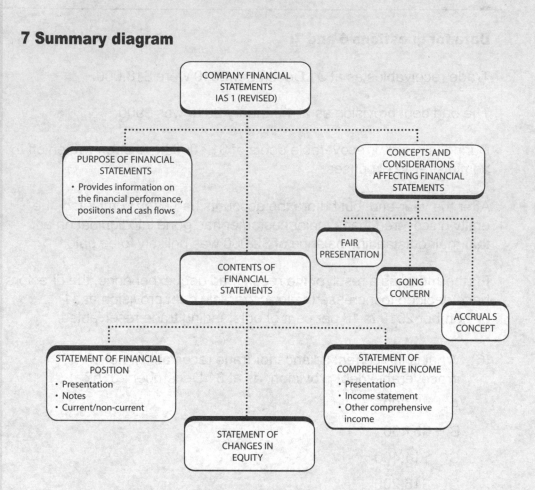

Test your understanding answers

Test your understanding 1 : P Ltd

P Ltd Statement of comprehensive income for the year ended 31 March 2011

	$000
Revenue	5,300
Cost of Sales (W1)	(1350)
Gross profit	3,950
Distribution costs	(370)
Administration expenses	(490)
Profit from operations	3,090
Income from investments	210
Finance cost	(190)
Profit before tax	3,110
Income tax expense	(470)
Profit for period	2,640
Other comprehensive income:	-
Total comprehensive income for the period	2,640

P Ltd Statement of changes in equity for the year ended 31 March 2011

	Share capital	Share premium	Retained earnings	Total
	$	$	$	$
Balance at 1 April 2010	1,500	800	1,163	3,463
Total comprehensive income			2,640	2,640
Dividends			(390)	(390)
Balance at 31 March 2011	1,500	800	3,413	5,713

Note: Dividends declared after the year end will not be adjusted for.

P Ltd Statement of financial position as at 31 March 2011

	$'000	$'000
Non-current assets		
Property, plant and equipment		4,250
Current assets		
Inventories	114	
Trade and other receivables	418	
Prepayments	25	
Investments	2,700	
Cash and cash equivalents	12	
		3,269
Total assets		7,519
Equity and liabilities		
Capital and reserves		
Issued ordinary share capital	1,500	
Share premium	800	
Retained earnings	3,413	
		5,713
Non-current liabilities		
Long-term loans		1,200
Current liabilities		
Trade payables	136	
Income tax	470	
		606
Total equity and liabilities		7,519

Test your understanding 2 : Picklette Ltd

Picklette Ltd Statement of comprehensive income for the year ended 31 March 2011

	$000
Revenue	1,300
Cost of Sales (W1)	(388)
Gross profit	912
Distribution costs (W1)	(246)
Administration expenses (W1)	(176)
Profit from operations	490
Income from investments	–
Finance cost (W2)	(8)
Profit before tax	482
Income tax expense (W3)	(135)
Profit for the period	347
Other comprehensive income:	-
Total comprehensive income for the year	347

Picklette Ltd Statement of financial position as at 31 March 2011

	$000	$000
Non-current assets		
Property, plant and equipment (W4)		182
Current assets		
Inventories	250	
Trade receivables	738	
Cash and cash equivalents	9	
		997
Total assets		1,179

Equity and liabilities

Capital and reserves

Issued capital	200	
Retained earnings (W6)	611	
		811

Non-current liabilities

10% Loan		80

Current liabilities

Trade payables	60	
Accrued expenses (W7)	93	
Income tax	135	
		288
		1,179

Picklette Ltd Statement of changes in equity for the year ended 31 March 2011

	Share capital	Retained earnings	Total
	$000	$000	$000
Balance at 1 April 2010	200	270	470
Total comprehensive income		347	347
Dividends (W2)		(6)	(6)
Balance at 31 March 2011	200	611	611

Workings

(W1)

	COS	Distribution	Administration
	$000	$000	$000
Purchases	470		
Opening inventory	150		
Distribution costs		240	
Administration costs			170
Closing inventory	(250)		
Dep'n – Land and buildings (60:20:20)	3	1	1
Dep'n – Plant and machinery (60:20:20)	15	5	5
	388	246	176

(W2) Loan interest due (10% x $80) = $8 (IS)

Amount paid (TB) $5, therefore accrual required for $3

(W3) **Tax charge**

	$
Estimated charge for the year	135

(W4) **Property, plant and equipment**

	Land and buildings	Plant and machinery	Total
	$	$	$
Cost			
At 1 April 2010	210	125	335
At 31 March 2011	210	125	335
Acc dep'n			
At 1 April 2010	48	75	123
Charge for year (W5)	5	25	30
At 31 March 2011	53	100	153
Carrying value at 31 March 2011	157	25	182
Carrying value at 1 April 2010	162	50	212

(W5) **Depreciation**

Land and buildings 5% x $100 = $5

P & M 20% x $125 = $25

(W6) **Retained earnings**

	$
As at 1 April 2010	270
Profit for the year (IS)	347
Dividends paid	(6)
As at 31 March 2011	611

(W7) Accrued expenses

	$
As per TB	90
Interest accrual (W2)	3
As at 31 March 2011	93

Test your understanding 3 : Thistle Ltd

Thistle Ltd Statement of financial position as at 30 June 2011

	$	$
Non-current assets		
Property, plant and equipment (W1)		1,459,220
Current assets		
Inventories (W4)	62,200	
Trade and other receivables (W3)	72,470	
Cash and cash equivalents (W9)	129,360	
		264,030
Total assets		1,723,250
Equity and liabilities		
Capital and reserves		
Issued ordinary share capital	500,000	
5% Preference share capital	300,000	
Share premium	100,000	
Retained earnings	639,570	
		1,539,570
Non-current liabilities		
10% Loan		80,000
Current liabilities		
Trade payables	60,820	
Accruals	1,360	
Preference dividends (W2)	15,000	
Debenture interest owing (W5)	8,000	
Income tax	18,500	
		103,680
Total equity and liabilities		1,723,250

Thistle Ltd Statement of changes in equity for the year ended 30 June 2011

	Share capital	Share premium	Pref share capital	Retained earnings	Total
	$	$	$	$	$
Balance at 30 June 2010	450,000	60,000	300,000	540,000	1,350,000
Total comprehensive income (W8)				114,570	114,570
Dividends (W2)				(15,000)	(15,000)
Issue of share capital (W2)	50,000	40,000		–	90,000
Balance at 30 June 2011	500,000	100,000	300,000	639,570	1,539,570

Workings

(W1) Property, plant and equipment

	Land and buildings	Motor vehicles	Fixtures & fittings	Total
	$	$	$	$
Cost/Valuation				
At 1 July 2010	1,400,000	67,500	19,800	1,487,300
Additions	100,000			100,000
Disposals		(24,000)		(24,000)
At 30 June 2011	1,500,000	43,500	19,800	1,563,300

Accumulated depreciation:

At 1 July 2010	58,000	30,250	8,400	96,650
Charged during the year (W7)	14,000	5,450	1,980	21,430
Disposals		(14,000)		(14,000)
At 30 June 2011	72,000	21,700	10,380	104,080

Carrying value

At 30 June 2011	1,428,000	21,800	9,420	1,459,220
At 1 July 2010	1,342,000	37,250	11,400	1,390,650

(W2) **Share capital**

	No.
$1 5% Preference shares	
Authorised shares	500,000
Issued and fully paid	300,000

	No.
50c ordinary shares	
Authorised shares	1,400,000
Issued and fully paid	1,000,000

	No.
Number of issued shares at 1 July 2010	900,000
Number Issued in the year	100,000
Number of issued shares at 30 June 2011	1,000,000

Total proceeds = 100,000 x $0.90 = $90,000

Nominal value = 100,000 x $0.50 = $50,000 (share capital account)

Premium = 100,000 x $0.40 = $40,000 (share premium account)

An ordinary dividend of $70,000 (1,000,000 × 0.07) is declared but no adjustment as not done at year end.

A preference dividend for the year is $15,000 (300,000 x 5%). This has not yet been paid (no entry in the TB) and therefore an accrual must be made.

(W3) **Trade and other receivables**

	$
Trade receivables	71,500
Prepayments	970
	72,470

(W4) **Inventory**

	$
Raw materials	32,500
Finished goods	29,700
	62,200

(W5) **Loan interest**

Interest due for the year $8,000 ($80,000 x 10%) payable 1 July 2011

(W6) **Gain on disposal**

	$
Proceeds	12,000
Carrying value (24,000 – 14,000)	10,000
Profit on disposal	2,000

(W7) **Depreciation**

Building 2% x $700,000 (1,400,000 – land $800,000 + additions $100,000) = $14,000

Motor vehicles 20% x (cost $43,500 – depn ($30,250 – $14,000)) = 20% x $27,250 = $5,450

Fixtures and fittings 10% x $19,800 = $1,980

(W8) Net profit for year

	$
Per TB	160,500
Gain on disposal (W6)	2,000
Depreciation(W7)	
– buildings	(14,000)
– motor vehicles	(5,450)
– fixtures & fittings	(1,980)
Income tax expense	(18,500)
Finance cost (W5)	(8,000)
Net profit	114,570

(W9) Cash and cash equivalents

	$
TB	217,360
Proceeds from sale of NCAs	12,000
Purchase of NCAs	(100,000)
Cash and cash equivalents	129,360

Test your understanding 4 : Objective test questions

(1) B

(2) D

(3) C

(4) A

(5) C

(6) C

The irrecoverable debt must be written off against receivables before the provision is calculated for the year, i.e. $18,000 - 2,000 = $16,000

The provision for the year is calculated as 10% x $16,000 = $1,600

The balance on receivables to be shown on the SOFP will be $14,400 (16,000 - 1,600)

(7) C

The total for irrecoverable debts for the year will be $14,000 (12,000 + 2,000)

The provision charged to the statement of comprehensive income will be $700 (the movement 1,600 - 900)

The Regulatory Framework

Chapter learning objectives

- Explain the need for regulation of published accounts and the concept that regulatory regimes vary from country to country;

- Explain potential elements that might be expected in a regulatory framework for published accounts;

- Describe the role and structure of the IASB and IOSCO;

- Describe the process leading to the promulgation of an International Financial Reporting Standard (IFRS);

- Describe ways in which IFRSs can interact with local regulatory frameworks.

1 Session content

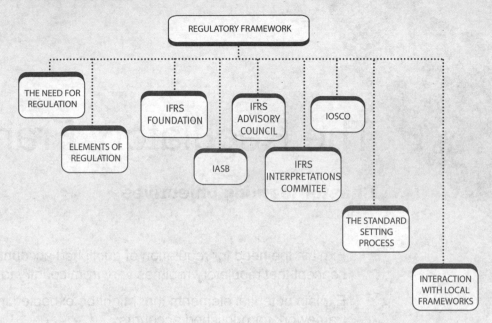

2 Regulatory bodies

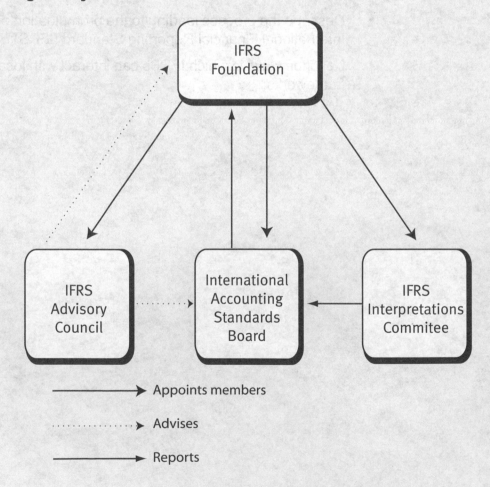

Need for regulation

Financial statements will be used by shareholders and many other types of users to make decisions. In order that they can be relied upon by users, published accounts should be subject to regulation.

Regulation can also promote consistency and so helps users when interpreting financial statements.

Different countries will be subject to a variety of economic, social and political factors. As a result, the way in which published accounts are regulated will vary from country to country.

The need for regulation

Financial statements and reports for shareholders and other users are prepared using principles and rules that can be interpreted in different ways. To provide guidance and try and ensure that they are interpreted in the same way, each time some form of regulation is required.

We have identified that taxable profits are based on accounting profit and that the number and type of adjustments required to compute taxable profits varies from country to country. Part of this variation was due to the differences in the tax regulations, but a part of it was due to the different approaches to the calculation of accounting profit. We have identified that in some countries taxable income is closely linked to the accounting profit and that accounting rules are largely driven by taxation laws. These countries are usually known as code law countries, countries where the legal system originated in Roman law. These countries tend to have detailed laws relating to trading entities and accounting standards are usually embodied within the law. Accounting regulation in these countries is usually in the hands of the government and financial reporting is a matter of complying with a set of legal rules.

In other countries the common law system is used, common law is based on case law and tends to have less detailed regulations. In countries with common law systems, the accounting regulation within the legal system is usually kept to a minimum, with detailed accounting regulations produced by professional organisations or other private sector accounting standard-setting bodies.

Whichever system is adopted, there is a need for every country to have a system for regulating the preparation of financial statements and reports.

Variation from country to country

Accounting and information disclosure practices around the world are influenced by a variety of economic, social and political factors. In addition to the legal system and tax legislation, a range of other factors that contribute to variations between the accounting regulations of countries are discussed below. The wide range of factors influencing the development of accounting regulations have resulted in a wide range of different systems, this has made it difficult and time consuming to try and harmonise accounting practices around the world. With the growth in international investing, there is a growing need for harmonisation of financial statements between countries.

Sources of finance and capital markets

There is more demand for financial information and disclosure where a higher proportion of capital is raised from external shareholders, rather than from banks or family members. Stock markets rely on published financial information by entities. Banks and family members are usually in a position to demand information directly from the entity, whereas shareholders have to rely on publicly available information.

The political system

The nature of regulation and control exerted on accounting will reflect political philosophies and objectives of the ruling party, for example, environmental concerns.

Entity ownership

The need for public accountability and disclosure will be greater where there is a broad ownership of shares as opposed to family ownership or government ownership.

Cultural differences

The culture within a country can influence societal and national values which can influence accounting regulations.

Harmonisation versus standardisation

Harmonisation tends to mean the process of increasing the compatibility of accounting practices by setting bounds to their degree of variation.

Standardisation tends to imply the imposition of a rigid and narrower set of rules. Standardisation also implies that one technically correct method can be identified for every aspect of accounting and then this can be imposed on all preparers of accounts.

Due to the variations between countries discussed above, full standardisation of accounting practices is unlikely. Harmonisation is more likely, as the agreement of a common conceptual framework of accounting may enable a closer harmonisation of accounting practices.

The need for harmonisation of accounting standards

Each country has its own accounting regulation, financial statements and reports prepared for shareholders and other uses are based on principles and rules that can vary widely from country to country. Multinational entities may have to prepare reports on activities on several bases for use in different countries, and this can cause unnecessary financial costs. Furthermore, preparation of accounts based on different principles makes it difficult for investors and analysts to interpret financial information. This lack of comparability in financial reporting can affect the credibility of the entity's reporting and the analysts' reports and can have a detrimental effect on financial investment.

The increasing levels of cross-border financing transactions, securities trading and direct foreign investment has resulted in the need for a single set of rules by which assets, liabilities and income are recognised and measured.

The number of foreign listings on major exchanges around the world is continually increasing and many worldwide entities may find that they are preparing accounts using a number of different rules and regulations in order to be listed on various markets.

Elements of a regulatory framework

A regulatory framework may consist of any of the following elements:

- local law;
- local accounting standards;
- international accounting standards;
- conceptual frameworks e.g. Statement of Principles in the UK;
- requirements of international bodies e.g. EU, IOSCO.

GAAP (Generally accepted accounting practice) encompasses the conventions, the rules and procedures necessary to define accepted accounting practice at a particular time. It includes not only broad guidelines of general application but also detailed practices and procedures. It includes local legislation requirements, accounting standards and any other local regulations. This will therefore vary from country to country as different countries have different regulations, i.e. UK GAAP, US GAAP, etc.

3 Interaction with local frameworks

The IASB invite comments from national standard-setters on exposure drafts and in the past have worked together with both the FASB (Financial Accounting Standards Board – US) and IASB (International Accounting Standards Board – UK) to develop accounting standards.

The IFRS advisory council will also consult national standard-setters and co-ordinate the agendas and priorities of the IASB and national standard-setters.

Some countries will adopt International Accounting Standards as their local accounting standards, or will be heavily influenced by IASs when preparing local standards. This may particularly be the case in countries without a strong accountancy profession.

A country choosing to adopt international standards can apply them in a number of ways:

- Adoption of international standards as local GAAP - This is usually countries where the accounting profession isn't well developed and they adopt the international standards with little or no amendments. This is quick to implement but does not take into account any specific requirements of that country.

- International standards used as a model to create local GAAP - This involves countries taking the international standards and then amending them to reflect the countries needs.

- International standards used as persuasive influence in preparing local GAAP - This is where a country already has their own standards but they may differ to the international ones. They will use the international standards to update their local ones to ensure that they comply with IFRSs in all material aspects.

Alternatively a country may choose to prepare local GAAP with no reference to international standards!

IFRS Foundation

In 1997 it was decided to restructure the IASC into two main bodies – the Trustees and the International Accounting Standards Board (IASB). As a result the IASC Foundation was established in March 2001 as a non-profit making corporation with 22 Trustees. The trustees are responsible for:

- appointing the members of the IASB, the International Financial Reporting Interpretations Committee and IFRS Advisory Council;

- reviewing annually the strategy of the IASB and its effectiveness;

- approving annually the budget and determining the funding of the IASB;

- reviewing broad strategic issues affecting accounting standards;

- promoting the IASB and its work and the rigorous application of IASs;

- establishing and amending operating procedures for the IASB, IFRS Interpretations Committee and IFRS Advisory Council.

International Accounting Standards Board (IASB)

The IASB consists of 15 members and is currently chaired by Sir David Tweedie. The IASB are responsible for developing international accounting standards, now called International Financial Reporting Standards (IFRSs).

All members are appointed for a term of 5 years, renewable once.

The IASB has complete responsibility for all IASB technical matters, including the preparation and publication of IFRS, Exposure Draft, withdrawal of IFRSs and final interpretations by the IFRS Interpretations Committee.

The IASB have also adopted all IASs that were previously issued by the IASC.

IFRS Advisory Council

The IFRS Advisory Council has approximately 30 members and provides a forum for organisations and individuals to participate in the standard setting process. The members are appointed by the trustees from various backgrounds, for a renewable term of 3 years and meet three times a year.

The objectives of the IFRS Advisory Council are:

- to give advice to the IASB on agenda decisions and priorities in its work;

- to inform the IASB of the views of organisations and individuals on the Council on major standard setting projects;

- to give other advice to the Board or to the Trustees.

IFRS Interpretations Committee

The IFRS Interpreations Committee (formaly known as IFRIC), assist the IASB by reviewing accounting issues that are likely to receive divergent or unacceptable treatment in the absence of authoritative guidance, with a view to reaching an appropriate accounting treatment. It was established in 2002 by the IASC Foundation to replace the Standing Interpretations Committee (SIC). Previously SIC Interpretations were issued, now IFRS Interpretation Committee Interpretations are issued.

The IFRIC has two main responsibilities:

- Review, on a timely basis, new financial reporting issues not specifically addressed in IFRS's.

- Clarify issues where unsatisfactory or conflicting interpretations have developed, with a view to reaching a consensus on the most appropriate treatment.

International Organisation of Securities Commissions (IOSCO)

IOSCO is the representative body of the world's securities markets regulators.

Financial information is vital to the operation of markets and differences in the financial information from entities in different countries can reduce the efficiency of markets.

IOSCO has been working with the IASB since 1987 in promoting the improvement of International Standards. Since the mid-1990s IOSCO and IASB have been working on a programme of 'core standards' which could be used by listed companies who offer securities abroad. This project was completed in 1999.

In May 2000, IOSCO issued a report to its members recommending that they use International Accounting Standards when preparing their financial statements.

IOSCO representatives also sit as observers on the IFRS Interpretations Committee.

4 Standard-setting process

There is therefore no strict procedure for the development of a Standard. However, the process may involve the following steps:

- Establishment of an advisory committee to give advice on the issues arising on the project. The IASB will consult with this committee and IFRS Advisory Committee throughout the process.

- On major projects, the IASB develops and publishes a Discussion Paper for public comment. This will give an overview of the issue, possible approaches to address the issue, views of the authors or the IASB and an invitation to comment.

- Following the receipt and review of comments, an Exposure Draft is produced for public comment. The Exposure Draft is based upon the earlier Discussion Paper, together with the IASB review of feedback received from the public - i.e. mainly firms of accountants and companies who are likely to be affected by the introduction of a new or changed reporting standard.

  The Exposure Draft is then the draft standard made available for final review, which can still be amended before final approval as a reporting standard.

- Following the receipt and review of comments, the final Standard will be issued.

Test your understanding 1 : Setting standards

Yozz is a small developing country which currently has no accounting standards and recently a new professional accounting body was created.

Yozz's government has asked the new professional accounting body to prepare a report setting out the country's options for developing and implementing a set of high quality standards.

Required:

As an advisor to the professional accounting body, outline THREE options open to Yozz for the development of accounting standards. Identify any advantages or disadvantages for each option.

Test your understanding 2 : Roles

The existing procedures for setting international accounting standards are now well established.

Required:

Explain the roles of the following in relation to International Accounting Standards:

- The IFRS Foundation;
- The International Accounting Standards Board (IASB);
- The IFRS Interpretations Committee.

Test your understanding 3 : The development of a standard

Explain how the standard-setting authority approaches the task of producing a standard, with particular reference to the ways in which comment or feedback from interested parties is obtained.

Test your understanding 4 : Objective test questions

(1) **Under the current structure of regulatory bodies, which of the bodies listed below acts as the overall supervisory body?**

A   IFRS Interpretations Committee

B   International Accounting Standards Board

C   IFRS Advisory Council

D   IFRS Foundation

(2) **Which of the bodies listed below is responsible for reviewing International Accounting Standards and issuing guidance on their application?**

A   IFRS Interpretations Committee

B   International Accounting Standards Board

C   IFRS Advisory Council

D   IFRS Foundation

(3) **Which of the bodies listed below is responsible for issuing International Financial Reporting Standards?**

A   IFRS Interpretations Committee

B   International Accounting Standards Board

C   IFRS Advisory Council

D   IFRS Foundation

(4) **Which of the bodies listed below is responsible for the approval of Draft Interpretations?**

A   IFRS Interpretations Committee

B   International Accounting Standards Board

C   IFRS Advisory Council

D   IFRS Foundation

(5) **Which of the following best describes the role of the IFRS Advisory Council?**

A To prepare interpretations of International Accounting Standards

B To provide the IASB with the views of its' members on standard setting projects

C To promote the use of International Accounting Standards amongst its members

D To select the members of the IASB

5 Summary diagram

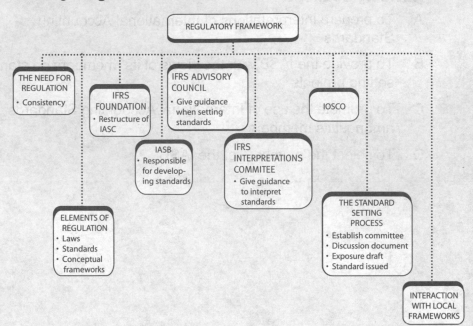

Test your understanding answers

Test your understanding 1 : Setting standards

The options are as follows:

(1) Adopting International Financial Reporting Standards (IFRS) as its local standards. The advantage of this would be is that this approach is quick and cheap to implement but has a disadvantage that it may not take into account any specific local traditions or variations.

(2) Modelling local standards on the IASB's IFRSs, but amending them to reflect local needs and conditions. The advantage of this would be that the standards would be more relevant to the countries needs but still be compliant with international standards. The disadvantages would be that it would take longer to create and implement and would require someone with expertise to exist within the local country to help create these standards.

(3) Yozz could develop its own accounting standards with little or no reference to IFRS's. The advantage would be that the standards would be specific to the needs of the country but have the disadvantage that they could be lengthy and costly to create. The standards may not be compliant with international standards and also require a person in Yozz with the appropriate expertise to help create these standards.

Test your understanding 2 : Roles

The IFRS Foundation

The IASC Foundation is an independent organisation having two main bodies: the Trustees and the IASB. The Trustees hold the responsibility for governance and fundraising and will publish an annual report on IASB's activities, including audited financial statements and priorities for the coming year. They will review annually the strategy of the IASB and its effectiveness and approve the annual budget and determine the basis of funding.

The Trustees also appoint the members of the IASB, the IFRS Advisory Council and the IFRS Interpretations Committee. Although the Trustees will decide on the operating procedures of the committees in the IASB family, they will be excluded from involvement in technical matters relating to accounting standards.

The IASB

The Board has complete responsibility for all IASB technical matters, including the preparation and issuing of International Financial Reporting Standards and Exposure Drafts, and final approval of Interpretations by the International Financial Reporting Interpretations Committee. Some of the full-time members of staff are responsible for liaising with national standard-setters in order to promote the convergence of accounting standards.

IASB publishes its standards in a series of pronouncements called International Financial Reporting Standards (IFRSs). It has also adopted the standards issued by the board of the International Accounting Standards Committee.

The Board may form advisory committees or other specialist technical groups to advise on major projects and outsource detailed research or other work to national standard-setters.

IFRS Interpretations Committee

The IFRS Interpretations Committee provides timely guidance on the application and interpretation of IFRSs, normally dealing with complex accounting issues that could, in the absence of guidance, produce wide-ranging or unacceptable accounting treatments.

Test your understanding 3 : The development of a standard

The process for the development of a standard involves the following steps:

- During the early stages of a project, the IASB may establish an Advisory Committee to advise on the issues arising in the project. Consultation with this committee and the IFRS Advisory Council occurs throughout the project.

- The IASB may develop and publish Discussion Papers for public comment.

- Following receipt and review of comments, the IASB develops and publishes an Exposure Draft for public comment.

- Following the receipt and review of comments, the IASB issues a final International Financial Reporting Standard.

When the IASB publishes a standard, it also publishes a Basis of Conclusions to explain publicly how it reached its conclusions and to provide background information that may help users apply the standard in practice.

Each IASB member has one vote on technical matters and the publication of a Standard, Exposure Draft, or final IFRS Interpretation requires approval by eight of the Board's 15 members. Other decisions including agenda decisions and the issue of a Discussion Paper, require a simple majority of the Board members present at a meeting, provided that the meeting is attended by at least 50 per cent of the members.

Meetings of the IASB, IFRS Advisory Council and IFRS Interpretations Committee are open to public observation. Where the IASB issues Exposure Drafts, Discussion Papers and other documents for public comment, the usual comment period is 90 days. Draft IFRS Interpretations Committee Interpretations are exposed for a 60-day comment period.

Test your understanding 4 : Objective test questions

(1) D

(2) B

(3) B

(4) A

(5) B

The Conceptual Framework

Chapter learning objectives

- Explain the IASB's *Framework for the Preparation and Presentation of Financial Statements*.

1 Session content

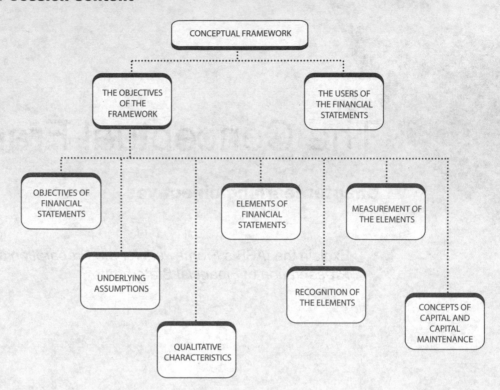

2 Introduction

Over time, transactions that entity's enter into have become increasingly complex. Although the detail of the transactions may vary from situation to situation the basic accounting issues are often the same. As a result, the IASB have developed a conceptual framework, which lays out the broad principles that should be applied when developing accounting standards and when determining an appropriate accounting treatment. This conceptual framework is called the *Framework for the Preparation and Presentation of Financial Statements*.

3 Purpose and status of the framework

According to the Framework, its purpose is to:

- assist the IASB in the development of future IASs and in its review of existing IASs;

- assist the IASB in promoting harmonisation of regulations, accounting standards and procedures by reducing the number of alternative treatments permitted by IASs;

- assist national standard-setting bodies in developing national standards;

- assist preparers of financial statements in applying IASs and in dealing with topics that are not subject to an IAS;

- assist auditors in forming an opinion as to whether financial statements comply with IASs;

- assist users of financial statements in interpreting the information contained in a set of financial statements;

- provide those who are interested in the work of the IASB information about its approach to the formulation of IASs.

The Framework is not an Accounting Standard and does not override the requirements of any IAS.

4 Users and their information needs

The Framework identifies several different user groups of financial statements and discusses their information needs. The Framework states that although it is not possible for a set of financial statements to meet the needs of all users, financial statements that meet the needs of investors will generally meet the needs of other users.

The framework identifies user groups as:

- Investors (existing and potential);

- Lenders (existing and potential);

- Employees;

- Business contacts, i.e. customers, suppliers, competitors;

- The general public;

- The Government, i.e. tax authorities;

5 What does the framework cover?

The framework covers the following topics:

- The objective of financial statements;

- Underlying assumptions of financial statements;

- Qualitative characteristics of financial statements;

- The elements of financial statements;

- Recognition of the elements of financial statements;

- Measurement of the elements of financial statements;

- Concepts of capital and capital maintenance.

6 Objectives of financial statements

The objective of financial statements is to provide information about the:

- financial position
- financial performance
- changes in the financial position

of an enterprise that is useful to a wide range of users in making economic decisions.

Objectives of financial statements

Information about the financial position is primarily found in the Statement of Financial Position (SOFP). The financial position is affected by the resources that it controls, its financial structure, its liquidity and its solvency.

Information about the financial performance is primarily found in the Statement of Comprehensive Income (SOCI). The financial performance is affected by the profitability and is needed to make decisions about resources the enterprise is likely to control and its ability to generate future cash flows.

Information about the changes in financial positions is primarily found in the Statement of Cash Flows.

7 Underlying assumptions

The Framework states that there are two underlying assumptions:

- Accruals;
- Going concern.

The accruals concept means that financial statements should be prepared on the basis of when transactions occur, not when they are paid, e.g. a sale is recognised when it is made, not when the customer pays for the goods.

The going concern concept means the financial statements are prepared on the basis that the enterprise will continue trading for the foreseeable future. It is assumed that the enterprise neither has an intention nor the need to liquidate or significantly reduce the scale of its operations. If this was to be the case the financial statements would be prepared on a different basis, e.g. valuation of assets on the statement of financial position.

8 Qualitative characteristics of financial statements

The Framework discusses four characteristics that make financial information useful to users:

- Understandability;
- Relevance;
- Reliability;
- Comparability.

Understandability

Information needs to be readily understandable by users. Information that may be relevant to decision making should not be excluded on the grounds that it may be too difficult for certain users to understand.

Understandability depends on:

- the way in which information is presented; and
- the capabilities of users.

It is assumed that users:

- have a reasonable knowledge of business and economic activities; and
- are willing to study the information provided with reasonable diligence.

Relevance

Information is relevant when it influences the economic decisions of users by helping them evaluate past, present or future events or confirming or correcting their past evaluations.

The relevance of information can be affected by its nature and materiality. Some items may be relevant to users simply because of their nature whereas some items may only become relevant once they are material. Hence, materiality is a threshold quality of information rather than a primary characteristic.

According to the Framework, information is material if its omission or misstatement could influence the decisions of users.

Reliability

Users must be able to rely on information if it is going to be useful in making economic decisions.

Information is reliable if:

- it is free from material error;
- it is free from deliberate or systematic error (i.e. it is neutral);
- it is complete within the bounds of materiality
- it is a faithful representation;
- in conditions of uncertainty, a degree of caution (i.e. prudence) has been applied in exercising judgement and making the necessary estimates.

To summarise, reliable information should be **free of material error, neutral, complete, have faithful representation; and be prudent.**

Comparability

Users must be able to compare financial statements over a period of time in order to identify trends in financial position and performance. Users must also be able to compare financial statements of different entities to be able to assess their relative financial position and performance.

In order to achieve comparability, similar items should be treated in a consistent manner from one period to the next and from one entity to another. However, it is not appropriate for an entity to continue accounting for transactions in a certain manner if alternative treatments exist that would be more relevant and reliable.

Disclosure of accounting policies should also be made so that users can identify any changes in these policies or differences between the policies of different entities.

Qualities of reliability

Faithful representation

If information is to represent faithfully the transactions and other events that it purports to represent, they must be accounted for and presented in accordance with their substance and economic reality and not just their legal form.

Neutrality

Information must be neutral, i.e. free from bias. Financial statements are not neutral if, by the selection or presentation of information, they influence the making of a decision or judgement in order to achieve a predetermined result or outcome.

Completeness

Information must be complete and free from error within the bounds of materiality. A material error or an omission can cause the financial statements to be false or misleading and thus unreliable and deficient in terms of relevance.

Prudence

Prudence involves using a degree of caution in the use of judgement to make estimates in the financial statements in conditions of uncertainty, i.e. gains and assets are not overstated and losses and liabilities are not understated.

9 The elements of financial statements

Financial statements show the effect of financial transactions by grouping them into broad classes, i.e. the elements of financial statements. The elements of financial statements are:

- Assets;
- Liabilities;
- Equity;
- Income;
- Expenses.

Assets

An asset is a resource controlled by the enterprise as a result of a past event and from which future economic benefits are expected to flow to the enterprise.

Liabilities

A liability is a present obligation arising from past events, the settlement of which is expected to result in an outflow of resources from the enterprise.

Equity

Equity is the residual interest in the assets of the enterprise after deducting all its liabilities.

Income

Income is increases in economic benefits during the accounting period in the form of inflows or enhancements of assets or decreases of liabilities that result in increases in equity, other than those relating to contributions from equity participants.

The definition of income includes revenue and gains.

Revenue is income that arises in the course of ordinary activities, i.e. sales.

Gains represent other items that meet the definition of income, e.g. gains on disposal of non-current assets and unrealised gains, e.g. on revaluation

Expenses

Expenses are decreases in economic benefits during the accounting period in the form of outflows or depletions of assets or incurrence's of liabilities that result in decreases in equity, other than those relating to distributions to equity participants.

The definition of expenses includes losses as well as expenses that arise in the course of ordinary activities.

Expenses that arise in the ordinary course of activities are items such as wages, purchases and depreciation.

Losses include items such as losses on disposal of non-current assets and unrealised losses, e.g. losses on revaluation.

Assets, liabilities and equity interest

Assets

An asset is a resource controlled by the entity as a result of past events and from which future economic benefits are expected to flow to the entity.

To explain further the parts of the definition of an asset:

- Controlled by the entity – control is the ability to obtain the economic benefits and to restrict the access to others (e.g. by a company being the sole user of its plant and machinery, or by selling surplus plant and machinery). An asset does not have to be legally owned, the key factor is whether the entity has control over the future economic benefits that the item will provide. A leased vehicle could therefore be an asset.

- Past events – the event must be past before an asset can arise, e.g. equipment will only become an asset when there is a right to demand delivery or access to the asset. Dependant on the terms of a contract this could be on acceptance of an order or on delivery.

- Future economic benefits – these are evidenced by the prospective receipt of cash. This could be the cash itself, a debt receivable or any item which may be sold, e.g. a factory may not be sold if it houses the materials for manufacturing. When the goods are sold the economic benefit resulting from the use of the factory will be realised in cash.

Liabilities

Liabilities are an entity's obligations to transfer economic benefits as a result of past transactions or events.

To explain further the parts of the definition of a liability:

- Obligations – these may be legal or constructive. A constructive obligation is an obligation which is the result of expected practice rather than required by law or legal contract.

- Transfer of economic benefits – this could be a transfer of cash, or other property, the provision of a service, or the refraining from activities which would otherwise be profitable.

- Past transactions or events – similar points are made here to those under assets.

Equity

Equity is the residual amount after deducting all liabilities of the entity from all of the entity's assets.

Equity may be sub-classified in the financial statements into share capital, retained earnings and other reserves.

10 Recognition of the elements of financial statements

In order to recognise items in the statement of financial position or income statement, the following criteria should be satisfied:

- It meets the definition of an element of financial statements.

- It is probable that any future economic benefit associated with the item will flow to or from the enterprise.

- The item has a cost or value that can be measured with reliability.

Recognition of assets, liabilities, income and expenses

An asset is recognised if:

- it gives rights or other access to future economic benefits controlled by an entity as a result of past events;

- it can be measured with reliability;

- there is sufficient evidence of its existence.

A liability is recognised if:

- there is an obligation to transfer economic benefits as a result of past transactions or events;

- it can be measured with reliability;

- there is sufficient evidence of its existence.

Income is recognised if:

- an increase in future economic benefits arises from an increase in an asset (or a reduction in a liability); and

- the increase can be measured reliably.

> **Expenses are recognised if:**
>
> - a decrease in future economic benefit arises from a decrease in an asset (or an increase in a liability); and
> - the decrease can be measured reliably.

11 Measurement of the elements of financial statements

Measurement is the process of determining the monetary amounts at which the elements of financial statements are to be recognised and carried in the balance sheet and income statement.

There are a number of different ways of measuring the elements including:

Historical cost

Assets are recorded at the amount of cash paid or the fair value of the consideration given to acquire them at the time of their acquisition. Liabilities are recorded at the amount of proceeds received in exchange for the obligation or at the amounts of cash expected to be paid to satisfy the liabilities.

Current cost

Assets are carried at the amount of cash that would have to be paid if the same or an equivalent asset was acquired currently. Liabilities are carried at the amount of cash that would be required to settle the obligation currently.

Realisable (settlement) value

Assets are carried at the amount of cash that could currently be obtained by selling the asset in an orderly disposal. Liabilities are carried at their settlement values, i.e. the undiscounted amount of cash expected to be paid to satisfy the liabilities.

Present value

Assets are carried at the present discounted value of the future net cash inflows that the item is expected to generate. Liabilities are carried at the present discounted value of the future net cash outflows that are expected to be required to settle the liabilities.

The Framework does not state which measurement basis should be used by entities but highlights that the historical cost basis is the most commonly used, often combined with other bases, e.g. inventories being valued at the lower of cost and net realisable value.

12 Concepts of capital and capital maintenance

There are two concepts of capital:

- **A financial concept of capital**. With this method capital = net assets or equity of the entity. This concept should be used if the main concern of the user of the financial statements is the maintenance of the nominal value invested capital. This is used by most entities to prepare financial statements.

- **A physical concept of capital.** With this method capital = productive capacity of the entity (measured as units of output per day). This method should be used if the main concern of the user of the financial statements is the operating capacity of the entity.

Capital maintenance means preserving the value of the capital of the entity, and reporting profit only if the capital of the entity has been increased by activities and events in the accounting period.

13 The Framework and the standard-setting process

The Framework provides a point of reference to the IASB when developing individual standards. Since the standards will then be developed with reference to a common set of concepts the standards themselves will become more consistent.

The IFRS Interpretations Committee) issue guidance where issues have arisen which are not specifically covered by a standard. The IFRS Interpretations Committee can therefore ensure its guidance is consistent with agreed underlying principles by referring to the Framework.

Currently many IASs allow alternative treatments. The development of the Framework is expected to result in these alternatives being removed and the preferred treatment will be the one that is consistent with the Framework.

Test your understanding 1 : Qualitative characteristics

The International Accounting Standards Board's (IASB's) *Framework for the Preparation and Presentation of Financial Statements* identifies four principal qualitative characteristics of financial information.

Required:

Identify and explain EACH of the FOUR principal qualitative characteristics of financial information listed in the IASB's Framework.

Test your understanding 2 : IASB objectives

The Framework for the Preparation and Presentation of Financial Statements has a number of purposes, including:

- assisting the Board in the development of future IFRSs and in its review of existing IFRSs;

- assisting the Board in promoting harmonisation of regulations, accounting standards and procedures relating to the presentation of financial statements by providing a basis for reducing the number of alternative treatments permitted by IFRSs;

- assisting preparers of financial statements in applying IFRSs and in dealing with topics that are yet to be covered in an IFRS.

Required:

Discuss how a conceptual Framework could help IASB achieve these objectives.

Test your understanding 3 : Purpose of the framework

The Framework for the Preparation and Presentation of Financial Statements (Framework) was first published in 1989 and was adopted by The International Accounting Standards Board (IASB).

Required:

Explain the purposes of the Framework.

Test your understanding 4 : Objective test questions

(5) **Under the *Framework for the Preparation and Presentation of Financial Statements*, which of the following is the 'threshold quality' of useful information?**

A   Relevance

B   Reliability

C   Materiality

D   Understandability

(6) **According to the *Framework for the Preparation and Presentation of Financial Statements*, which of the following are the underlying assumptions of a set of financial statements?**

A   Going Concern and Prudence

B   Going Concern and Accruals

C   Accruals and Prudence

D   Prudence and Comparability

(7) **Which of the following best defines information that is relevant to the users of financial information?**

A   Information that is free from material error, bias and is a faithful representation

B   Information that has been prudently prepared

C   Information that is comparable from one period to the next

D   Information that influences the decisions of users

(8) **Which of the following criteria need to be satisfied in order for an item to be recognised in the financial statements?**

(i)   It meets the definition of an element of the financial statements

(ii) It is probable that future economic benefits will flow to or from the enterprise

(iii) It is certain that future economic benefits will flow to or from the enterprise

(iv) The item has a cost or value

(v)   The item has a cost or value that can be reliably measured

A   i, ii and v

B   i, iii and v

C   i, ii and iv

D   i, iii and iv

(9) **Which of the following measurement bases should be used by enterprises according to the *Framework for the Preparation and Presentation of Financial Statements*?**

   A   Historical cost

   B   Current cost

   C   Present value

   D   Any of the above

(10) The IASB's Framework includes reliability as one of the characteristics that make financial information useful.

   A   Complete

   B   Predictive value

   C   Confirmatory value

   D   Neutrality

   E   Faithful representation.

   Which of the characteristics above are listed in the Framework as making financial information reliable?

   A   (i), (iv) and (v)

   B   (ii), (iii) and (iv)

   C   (ii) and (iii)

   D   (ii) and (v)

(11) The IASB Framework for the Preparation and Presentation of Financial Statements (Framework) provides definitions of the elements of financial statement. One of the elements defined by the framework is 'expenses'.
   Required: In no more than 35 words, give the IASB Framework's definition of expenses.

(12) The International Accounting Standards Board's (IASB) Framework for the Preparation and Presentation of Financial Statements (Framework), sets out four qualitative characteristics of financial information.

   Two of the characteristics are relevance and comparability. **List the other TWO characteristics.**

(13) **According to the International Accounting Standards Board's Framework for the Preparation and Presentation of Financial Statements, what is the objective of financial statements?**

(14) The IASB's Framework for the Preparation and Presentation of Financial Statements (Framework) lists the qualitative characteristics of financial statements.

(i) Comparability,

(ii) Relevance,

(iii) Prudence,

(iv) Reliability,

(v) Understandability,

(vi) Matching,

(vii) Consistency.

Which THREE of the above are NOT included in the principal qualitative characteristics listed by the Framework?

A   (i), (iii) and (vii)

B   (i), (ii) and (v)

C   (iii), (vi) and (vii)

D   (iii), (iv) and (vi)

14 Summary diagram

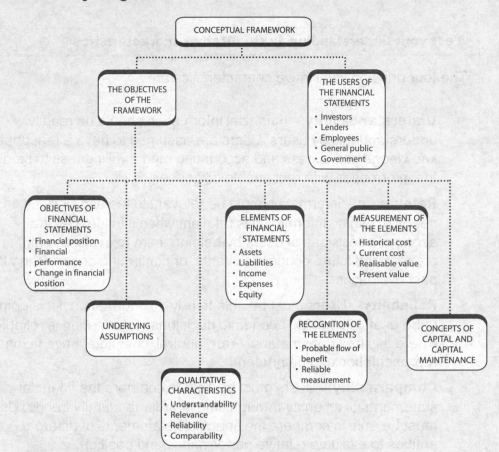

Test your understanding answers

Test your understanding 1 : Qualitative characteristics

The four principal qualitative characteristics are:

- **Understandability** – Financial information should be readily understandable by users. Users are assumed to have a reasonable knowledge of business and accounting, and a willingness to study the information with reasonable diligence.

- **Relevance** – Information must be relevant to the decision-making needs of users. Information is relevant when it influences the economic decisions of users by helping them to evaluate past, present and future economic events, or confirming or correcting their past evaluations.

- **Reliability** – Users must be able to rely on information if it is going to be useful in making economic decisions. Information is reliable where it is free from material error, neutral, complete, have faithful representation and be prudent.

- **Comparability** – Users must be able to compare the financial statements of an entity through time in order to identify trends. Users must be able to compare the financials statements of different entities to evaluate relative performance and position.

Test your understanding 2 : IASB objectives

A conceptual Framework provides guidance on the broad principles of financial reporting. It highlights how items should be recorded, on how they should be measured and presented. The setting of broad principles could assist in the development of accounting standards, ensuring that the principles are followed consistently as standards and rules are developed.

A conceptual Framework can provide guidance on how similar items are treated. By providing definitions and criteria that can be used in deciding the recognition and measurement of items, conceptual Frameworks can act as a point of reference for those setting standards, those preparing and those using financial information.

The existence of a conceptual Framework can remove the need to address the underlying issues over and over again. Where underlying principles have been established and the accounting standards are based on these principles, there is no need to deal with them fully in each of the standards. This will save the standard-setters time in developing standards and will again ensure consistent treatment of items.

Where a technical issue is raised but is not specifically addressed in an accounting standard, a conceptual Framework can help provide guidance on how such items should be treated. Where a short-term technical solution is provided by the standard-setters, the existence of a conceptual Framework will ensure that the treatment is consistent with the broad set of agreed principles

Test your understanding 3 : Purpose of the framework

According to the Framework, its purposes are to:

- assist the Board in the development of future IFRSs and in its review of existing IFRSs;

- assist the Board in promoting harmonisation of regulations, accounting standards and procedures relating to the presentation of financial statements by providing a basis for reducing the number of alternative treatments permitted by IFRSs;

- assist national standard-setting bodies in developing national standards;

- assist preparers of financial statements in applying IFRSs and in dealing with topics that have yet to be covered in an IFRS;

- assist auditors in forming an opinion as to whether financial statements conform with IFRSs;

- assist users of financial statements that are prepared using IFRSs;

- provide information about how the IASB has formulated its approach to the development of IFRSs.

Test your understanding 4 : Objective test questions

(1) C

(2) B

(3) D

(4) A

(5) D

(6) A

(7) Expenses are decreases in economic benefits during the accounting period in the form of outflows or depletions of assets that result in decreases in equity, other than those relating to distributions to equity participants.

(8) Reliability and understandability

(9) The objective of financial statements is to provide information about the financial position, performance, and changes in that position, of an entity that is useful to a wide range of users in making economic decisions.

(10) C

10

External Audit

Chapter learning objectives

- Explain in general terms the role of the external auditor, the elements of the audit report and types of qualification of that report.

1 Session content

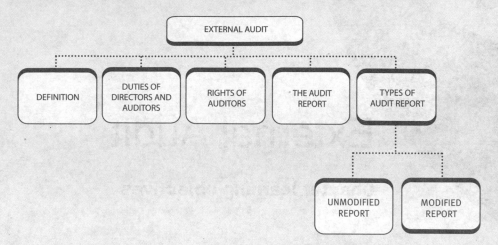

2 External audit

An external audit is when an independent person examines and checks the financial statements. The auditor will then prepare a report to present to the shareholders.

The objective of an audit is for the auditor to express an opinion as to whether the financial statements are fairly presented, i.e that they

- show a true (accurate) and fair (unbiased) view;
- have been prepared in accordance with 'specific legislation' (this will vary internationally).

(This implies that either accounting standards have been complied with or that non-compliance with the accounting standards was necessary in order to show a true and fair view.)

The purpose of an audit is to give users confidence in the financial statements. This is not 100% guarantee, but reasonable assurance.

Duties of directors

Duties of directors can vary from country to country. Typically the legal duties of the directors will include a requirement to:

- safeguard the company's assets and to prevent fraud and errors in the company;
- ensure that the company keeps proper accounting records;
- prepare annual financial statements showing the financial position, financial performance and changes in the financial position during the reporting period;

- deliver to the relevant national regulatory authority a copy of the company's audited financial statements within a defined time limit;

- set up an internal control system in the company to ensure that all of the above requirements are met.

Duties of auditors

The primary duty of the auditor is to report to the shareholders of the entity on whether or not the financial statements show a true and fair view and have been prepared in accordance with the applicable reporting framework.

Auditors also have a duty to report by exception, which means they have a duty to report any problems to shareholders. Again, their duties will vary from country to country but typically they would report on the following matters:

R returns from branches have been received

A accounts are in agreement with underlying accounting records

P proper accounting records have been kept

I information and explanations has been received

D Directors report is consistent with the financial statements, e.g. director's emoluments, related party transactions.

Rights of auditors

In order to carry out their duties, auditors are given certain rights:

- access to accounting records;

- require information and explanations as necessary;

- receive notice of, attend and speak at general meetings of shareholders;

- rights relating to their removal, resignation and retirement.

Benefits and disadvantages of an audit

Benefits

- Disputes between management may be more easily settled.

- Helps with valuation on sale or merger of a business.

- Applications to third parties for finance may be enhanced.

- Auditor may be able to give constructive advice to management.

- Fraud deterrent.

Disadvantages

- Cost – the audit fee.

- Disruption caused – time management must devote to consulting with the auditors.

- In a small company the shareholders may also be the directors, hence no real benefit from the audit.

The audit process

You will not be required to conduct a detailed audit in your exam but should be aware of the main steps of an audit to appreciate the audit process and how to form an audit opinion.

- Step 1 - The auditor is usually appointed by the shareholders at the annual general meeting (AGM).

- Step 2 - The auditor will agree terms with the client, identify the client's business and external factors and identify the risks of material misstatements in the financial statements.

- Step 3 - The auditor will plan the audit, i.e. decide upon their sample sizes and who is to perform the various tests.

- Step 4 - The auditor will begin to gather evidence to support an opinion about the financial statements. This will involve checking the bookkeeping entries to ensure a sample of transactions have been recorded correctly and then a review of the accounting policies adopted by the company.

- Step 5 - The auditor and senior management will review all work files.

- Step 6 - An audit opinion will be formed.

- Step 7 - An audit report is published.

- Step 8 - The auditor will attend the AGM and report their opinion to the shareholders.

3 The audit report

The auditors' work culminates in the audit report. The audit report is usually the only channel of communication between the auditor and the shareholders of the company.

The contents of the audit report are:

- Title and addressee – 'Independent' audit report – This should specify that the auditors are independent, that the report is for the shareholders of the company and the name of the company.

- Introductory paragraph:
  - identifies the name of the company audited, the year end and the statements that have been audited (alternatively, the pages of the financial statements that have been audited);
  - identifies the responsibilities of directors to prepare financial statements, auditors to express opinion on financial statements.

- Scope paragraph – audit carried out in accordance with International standards of auditing, reasonable assurance that financial statements are free from material misstatement.

- Opinion – Basis of opinion and the auditor's opinion of the financial statements. The name and address of the auditors and the date of the audit report should be shown.

- Signature of the auditor or in the name of the audit firm.

A closer look at the audit report

A typical report is analysed in the following sections, to show what the various elements of it mean and why they are required:

Title

The auditor's report should have an appropriate title. It may be appropriate to use the term 'independent auditor' in the title to distinguish the auditor's report from reports that might be issued by others, such as by officers of the entity, the board of directors, or from the reports of other auditors who may not have to abide by the same ethical requirements as the independent auditor.

Addressee

The auditor's report should be appropriately addressed as required by the circumstances of the engagement and local regulations. The report is ordinarily addressed either to the shareholders or the board of directors of the entity whose financial statements are being audited.

Opening or introductory paragraph

The auditor's report should identify the entity whose financial statements have been audited and state that the financial statements have been audited. It should identify the title of each of the financial statements that comprise the complete set of financial statements. It should specify the date of and period covered by the financial statements.

Management's responsibility for the financial statements

The auditor's report should state that management is responsible for the preparation and the fair presentation of financial statements in accordance with the applicable financial reporting framework and that this responsibility includes:

(a) Designing, implementing and maintaining internal control relevant to the preparation and fair presentation of financial statements that are free from material misstatement, whether due to fraud or error;

(b) Selecting and applying appropriate accounting policies; and

(c) Making accounting estimates that are reasonable in the circumstances.

The preparation of such statements requires management to make significant accounting estimates and judgements, as well as to determine the appropriate accounting principles and methods used in preparation of the financial statements. In contrast, the auditor's responsibility is to audit these financial statements in order to express an opinion thereon.

Auditor's responsibility

The auditor's report should state that the responsibility of the auditor is to express an opinion on the financial statements based on the audit.

The auditor's report should state that the audit was conducted in accordance with International Standards on Auditing (these are standards that give guidance to the auditor to enable them to prepare the audit report). The auditor's report should also explain that those standards require that the auditor comply with ethical requirements and that the auditor plan and perform the audit to obtain reasonable assurance whether the financial statements are free from material misstatement.

The auditor's report should describe an audit by stating that:

(a) An audit involves performing procedures to obtain audit evidence about the amounts and disclosures in the financial statements;

(b) The procedures selected depend on the auditor's judgement, including the assessment of the risks of material misstatement of the financial statements, whether due to fraud or error. In making those risk assessments, the auditor considers internal control relevant to the entity's preparation and fair presentation of the financial statements in order to design audit procedures that are appropriate in the circumstances, but not for the purpose of expressing an opinion on the effectiveness of the entity's internal control. In circumstances when the auditor also has a responsibility to express an opinion on the effectiveness of internal control in conjunction with the audit of the financial statements, the auditor should omit the phrase that the auditor's consideration of internal control is not for the purpose of expressing an opinion on the effectiveness of internal control; and

(c) An audit also includes evaluating the appropriateness of the accounting policies used, the reasonableness of accounting estimates made by management, as well as the overall presentation of the financial statements.

The auditor's report should state that the auditor believes that the audit evidence the auditor has obtained is sufficient and appropriate to provide a basis for the auditor's opinion.

Auditor's opinion

An unqualified opinion should be expressed when the auditor concludes that the financial statements give a true and fair view or are presented fairly, in all material respects, in accordance with the applicable financial reporting framework. When expressing an unqualified opinion, the opinion paragraph of the auditor's report should state the auditor's opinion that the financial statements give a true and fair view or present fairly, in all material respects, in accordance with the applicable financial reporting framework (unless the auditor is required by law or regulation to use different wording for the opinion, in which case the prescribed wording should be used).

The terms used to express the auditor's opinion are 'give a true and fair view' or 'present fairly, in all material respects,' and are equivalent. Both terms indicate, among other things, that the auditor considers only those matters that are material to the financial statements.

Date of report

The auditor should date the report as of the completion date of the audit. This informs the reader that the auditor has considered the effect on the financial statements and on the report of events and transactions of which the auditor became aware and that occurred up to that date.

Since the auditor's responsibility is to report on the financial statements as prepared and presented by management, the auditor should not date the report earlier than the date on which the financial statements are signed or approved by management.

Auditor's address

The report should name a specific location, which is ordinarily the city where the auditor maintains the office that has responsibility for the audit.

Auditor's signature

The report should be signed in the name of the audit firm, the personal name of the auditor, or both, as appropriate. The auditor's report is ordinarily signed in the name of the firm because the firm assumes responsibility for the audit.

An example of an audit report is given below.

Extract from the consolidated accounts of the Nestlé Group for the year ended 31 December 2005

Report of the group auditors

To: The General Meeting of Nestlé SA

As Group auditors we have audited the consolidated accounts (statement of financial position, a statement of comprehensive income, statement of cash flows, statement of changes in equity and annex) of the Nestlé Group for the year ended 31 December 2005.

These Consolidated Financial Statements are the responsibility of the Board of Directors. Our responsibility is to express an opinion on these Consolidated Financial Statements based on our audit. We confirm that we meet the legal requirements concerning professional qualification and independence.

Our audit was conducted in accordance with Swiss auditing standards and International Standards on Auditing, which require that an audit be planned and performed to obtain reasonable assurance about whether the Consolidated

> Financial Statements are free from material misstatement. We have examined on a test basis evidence supporting the amounts and disclosures in the Consolidated Financial Statements. We have also assessed the accounting principles used, significant estimates made and the overall Consolidated Financial Statements presentation. We believe that our audit provides a reasonable basis for our opinion.
>
> In our opinion, the Consolidated Financial Statements give a true and fair view of the financial position, the net profit and cash flows in accordance with International Financial Reporting Standards (IFRS) and comply with Swiss law.
>
> We recommend that the consolidated accounts submitted to you be approved.

4 Types of audit report

An audit report will result in one of the following:

Unmodified opinion

When an auditor is able to conclude that the financial statements are free from material misstatement they express an unmodified opinion. To express this they typically use one of the following phrases:

- "The financial statements present fairly, in all material respects..........."; or
- "The financial statements give a true and fair view of...............".

Modified opinion

There are two circumstances when the auditor may choose to not issue an unmodified opinion:

- When the financial statements are not free from material misstatement; or
- When they have been unable to gather sufficient appropriate evidence.

In these circumstances the auditor has to issue a modified version of their opinion. There are three types of modification. Their use depends upon the nature and severity of the matter under consideration. They are:

- The qualified opinion is an "except for" opinion and will be given when there are material issues.
- The adverse opinion is given when there is a material and pervasive misstatement.

- The disclaimer of opinion is given when there is material and pervasive inability to obtain sufficient, appropriate evidence.

Their usage has been summarised in the table below:

Nature of the Matter	Auditor's Judgement about the Pervasiveness of the Matter	
	Material but NOT Pervasive	Material AND Pervasive
Financial statements are materially misstated	Qualified opinion ("...except for...")	Adverse opinion ("...do not present fairly...")
Unable to obtain sufficient appropriate audit evidence	Qualified opinion ("...except for...")	Disclaimer of opinion ("...we do not express an opinion...")

Pervasiveness is a matter of professional judgement regarding whether the matter is isolated to specific components of the financial statements or whether the matter pervades many elements of the financial statements, rendering them unreliable as a whole.

To summarise, if the auditor believes that the financial statements may be relied upon in some part for decision making then the matter is material and not pervasive. If, however, they believe the financial statements should not be relied upon at all for making decisions then the matter is pervasive.

Emphasis of Matter (EOM)

Emphasis of matter and modified opinions are totally separate matters and must not be considered as related. The purpose of an EOM paragraph is to draw the users attention to a matter already disclosed in the financial statements because the auditor believes it is fundamental to their understanding. It is a way of saying to the users; "you know that note in the financial statements, the one about the uncertainty surrounding the legal dispute? Well us auditors think it's really important, so make sure you've read it!"

There are three circumstances when the usage of EOM is appropriate:

- When there is uncertainty about exceptional future events;

- Early adoption of new accounting standards; and

- When a major catastrophe has had a major effect on the financial position.

Of course, in all of these examples the auditor can only refer back to disclosures already made in the financial statements. If the directors haven't disclosed these matters then the auditor may perceive that the financial statements are materially misstated and modify the opinion instead.

5 Summary of audit reports

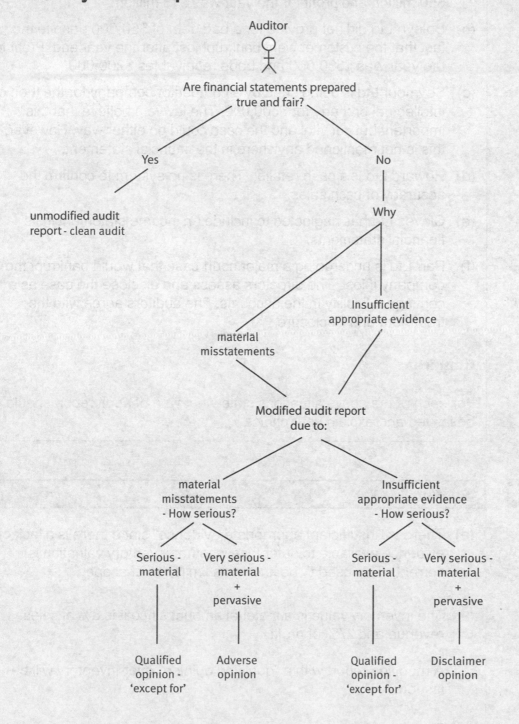

Illustration 1 : Audit reports

(a) Aragon Ltd made a very poor attempt to conduct their inventory count. You attended, however there was insufficient evidence that the inventory valuation at $4 million is accurate. Sales revenue was $50 million and profit for the year was $15 million.

(b) Boleyn Ltd did not provide for a bad debt of $50,000 despite the fact that the customer went bankrupt just after the year end. Profit for the year was $500,000 and trade receivables $200,000.

(c) Seymour Ltd is being sued by a competitor company for the theft of intellectual property for $500,000. The lawyers believe that this important but not vital and the case could go either way. However, this is not mentioned anywhere in the financial statements.

(d) Howard Ltd is a cash retailer. There is no system to confirm the accuracy of cash sales.

(e) Cleves Ltd has neglected to include an income statement in its financial statements.

(f) Parr Ltd is undergoing a major court case that would bankrupt the company if lost. The directors assess and disclose the case as a contingent liability in the accounts. The auditors agree with the treatment and disclosure.

Required:

For each of the above situations state what type of audit report should be issued and explain your choice.

Solution

(a) There is "insufficient appropriate evidence" since there is a lack of evidence available to determine whether inventory valuation is correct. This used to be known as limitation of scope.

The inventory value is a material amount since it is 8% of sales revenue and 27% of profit.

A modified report with a "qualified opinion" over inventory will be issued.

(b) There is a "material misstatement" as the event after the reporting date is an adjusting event in accordance with IAS 10 and therefore the debt should be written off. This used to be known as a disagreement.

The debt of $50,000 is material since it is 10% of profit and 25% of the total debtors.

A modified report with a "qualified" opinion over receivables will be issued.

(c) There is a "material misstatement" since this is a contingent liability in accordance with IAS 37 and so should be disclosed by note. This used to be known as a disagreement.

The matter is material.

A modified report with a "qualified" opinion will be issued.

(d) There is "insufficient appropriate evidence" since if there is no method available to confirm cash sales. This used to be known as limitation of scope.

It can be considered "so material and pervasive" since if cash sales cannot be confirmed, other figures in the financial statements may also be incorrect.

A modified report with a "disclaimer opinion" will be issued.

(e) There is a "material misstatement" since legislation requires companies to publish an income statement. This used to be known as a disagreement.

This can be considered "so material and pervasive".

A modified report with an "adverse opinion" will be issued.

(f) An unqualified opinion since the auditors agree with the treatment and disclosure of the contingent liability.

However, there is a material inherent uncertainty (the outcome of the court case will be determined in the future).

An unmodified report with a 'fundamental uncertainty' emphasis of matter paragraph.

Test your understanding 1 : Objective test questions

(1) **What is the purpose of an audit?**

   A   To prepare the financial statements and ensure that they provide a true and fair view

   B   To detect fraud

   C   To issue an opinion as to whether the financial statements provide a true and fair view

   D   To detect any misstatements in the financial statements

(2) An external audit of a company's financial statements has discovered that a material amount of depreciation has not been recorded.

What type of audit report should be issued in this situation?

   A   An unmodified report with a qualified opinion

   B   A modified report, based on a insufficient appropriate evidence, with a qualified opinion

   C   A modified report, based on material misstatements, with a qualified opinion

   D   A modified report, based on material misstatements, with an adverse opinion

(3) At its year-end a company is being sued for breaching health and safety legislation. If found liable, it is likely that the company will be forced into liquidation. However, the situation will not be resolved until after the financial statements have been approved. The external audit has discovered that this matter has been adequately disclosed in the financial statements.

What type of audit report will be issued in this situation?

   A   An unmodified report with an emphasis of matter paragraph

   B   A modified report with an emphasis of matter paragraph

   C   An unmodified report

   D   A modified report, based on material misstatements, with an 'adverse' opinion

(4) At its year-end a company is being sued for breaching health and safety legislation. If found liable, it is likely that the company will be forced into liquidation. However, the situation will not be resolved until after the financial statements have been approved. The external audit has discovered that this matter has not been adequately disclosed in the financial statements.

What type of audit report will be issued in this situation?

A   An unmodified report with an emphasis of matter paragraph

B   A modified report with an emphasis of matter paragraph

C   A modified report, based on material misstatements, with an 'adverse' opinion

D   An unmodified report

(5) **Which of the following statements are true?**

(i)   External audits are carried out by employees of the company

(ii) External auditors are appointed by the shareholders of the company

(iii) External auditors report to the directors of the company

(iv) The audit report gives assurance that the financial statements are free from all errors

A   ii only

B   i, iii and iv

C   ii and iv

D   i and iii

6 Summary diagram

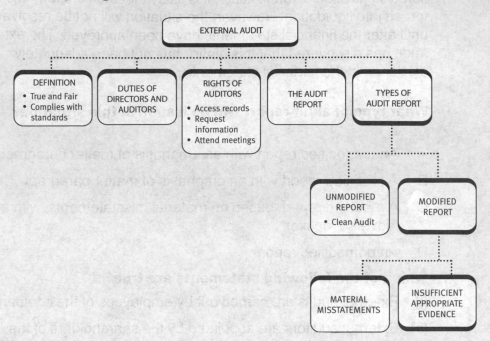

Test your understanding answers

Test your understanding 1 : Objective test questions

(1) C

(2) C

(3) A

(4) C

(5) A

11

Code of Ethics

Chapter learning objectives

- Explain the importance of the exercise of ethical principles in reporting and assessing information;

- Describe the sources of ethical codes for those involved in the reporting or taxation affairs of an organisation, including the external auditors;

- Apply the provisions of the CIMA Code of Ethics for Professional Accountants of particular relevance to the information reporting, assurance and tax related activities of the accountant.

1 Session content

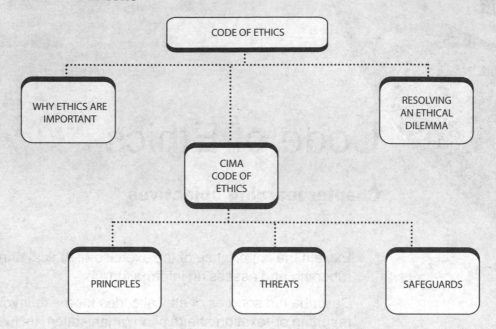

2 Introduction

Chartered Management Accountants (and registered students) have a duty to observe the highest standards of conduct and integrity and, to uphold the good standing and reputation of the profession. They must also refrain from any conduct which might discredit the profession. Members and registered students must have regard for these guidelines irrespective of their field of activity, of their contract of employment, or of any other professional memberships they may hold.

CIMA upholds the aims and principles of equal opportunities and fundamental human rights worldwide, including the handling of personal information. CIMA promotes the highest ethical and business standards, and encourages members to be responsible professionals.

Good ethical behaviour may be above that required by the law. In a highly competitive, complex business world, it is essential that CIMA members sustain their integrity and remember the trust and confidence which is placed in them by whoever relies on their objectivity and professionalism. Members must avoid actions or situations which are inconsistent with their professional obligations. They should also be guided not merely by the terms but by the spirit of this code.

CIMA members should conduct themselves with courtesy and consideration towards all with whom they have professional dealings and should not behave in a manner which could be considered offensive or discriminatory.

To ensure that CIMA members protect the good standing and reputation of the profession, members must inform the institute if they are convicted or disqualified from acting as an officer of a company, or if they are subject to any sanction resulting from disciplinary action taken by another professional body.

CIMA has adopted the following code of ethics. This code is based on the IFAC (International Federation of Accountants) code of ethics. It was developed with input from CIMA and the global accountancy profession. If a member cannot resolve an ethical issue by following this code or by consulting the ethics support information on CIMA's website, he or she should seek legal advice as to both his or her legal rights and any obligations he or she may have. The CIMA charter, bylaws and regulations should also be referred to for definitive rules on many matters. For further information see www.cimaglobal.com/ethics

NB: All references to 'professional accountants' in this code should be taken to refer, as appropriate, to CIMA members or registered students.

3 Why are ethics important?

Ethics relate to fairness, honesty and responsibility. Ethics are a set of moral principles to guide behaviour.

They are important because:

- Accountants should perform their work properly. Ethics describe "how" an entity does its business not what it does. If an accountant carried out work in bad faith this can affect the accountant (who may be disciplined by CIMA), it may have an effect on the business, e.g. financial viability, and in the public sector tax payers money could be wasted.

4 CIMA's code at a glance
Principles

Whether you are employed in business or the public sector or work in practice, CIMA's code of ethics can help you to identify and deal with situations where your professional integrity may be at risk. The code describes the high ethical standards every CIMA member and student must demonstrate, and gives guidance on how to uphold these.

Five fundamental principles form the basis of the code: integrity, objectivity, professional competence and due care and professional behaviour. These are summarised below, but a full explanation, along with guidance on applying the principles, is available in the complete code of ethics.

- **Objectivity** means not allowing bias, conflict of interest, or the influence of other people to override your professional judgement. To protect your objectivity, you should avoid relationships that could bias or overly influence your professional opinion.

- **Professional competence and due care** is an ongoing commitment to maintain your level of professional knowledge and skill so that your client or employer receives a competent professional service. This should be based on current developments in practice, legislation and techniques, and you must also make sure that those working under your authority have the appropriate training and supervision. Work should be completed carefully, thoroughly and diligently, in accordance with relevant technical and professional standards, e.g. accountants will use judgement and estimation when preparing financial statements such as identifying accruals/prepayments, making provisions, counting and valuing inventory, and choosing depreciation methods.

- **Professional behaviour** requires you to comply with relevant laws and regulations. You must also avoid any action that could negatively affect the reputation of the profession.

- **Integrity** means being straightforward, honest and truthful in all professional and business relationships. You should not be associated with any information that you believe contains a materially false or misleading statement, or which is misleading because it omits or obscures the facts.

- **Confidentiality** means respecting the confidential nature of information you acquire through professional relationships such as past or current employment. You should not disclose such information unless you have specific permission or a legal or professional duty to do so. You should also never use confidential information for your or another person's advantage.

The code itself contains further explanation of these principles, and examples of how they can be applied for both Professional Accountants in Business (Part B) and Professional Accountants in Practice (Part C). It is impossible to define every situation that could create a threat to the principles, and it is equally impossible to set out specific safeguards for each case, so instead the code sets out common examples of when these principles might be threatened and guidance as to what action should be taken to reduce or remove the threats.

A principles-based code such as CIMA's is widely considered to be more effective than a set of rules. Whereas there can be a tendency to try and circumvent rules, principles are more flexible and can be applied in a wider variety of situations. Principles also encourage users to think about the underlying intent of the code rather than simply adopting a check-box approach to compliance with rules.

Threats

To apply the fundamental principles of the code (integrity, objectivity, professional competence and due care, confidentiality, and professional behaviour), you first need to be able to identify and evaluate existing or potential threats to them. If a threat exists that is anything other than trivial, you will need to take action to remove the threat or reduce it to an acceptable level.

Although it is impossible to define all the situations that could create a threat to the fundamental principles, the code does identify five categories of common threat:

- **Self-interest threats** can occur as a result of your own or your close family's interests – financial or otherwise. These threats often result in what is commonly called a 'conflict of interest' situation. Working in business, a self-interest threat could result from concern over job security, or from incentive remuneration arrangements. For those in practice it might be the possibility of losing a client or holding a financial interest in a client.

- **Self-review threats** occur when you are required to re-evaluate your own previous judgement, for example if you have been asked to review and justify a business decision you made, or if you are reporting on the operation of financial systems that you were involved in designing or implementing.

- **Familiarity threats** can be present when you become so sympathetic to the interests of others as a result of a close relationship that your professional judgement becomes compromised. Sometimes this can result from long association with business contacts who influence business decisions, long association with colleagues, or from accepting gifts or preferential treatment from a client.

- **Intimidation threats** occur when you are deterred from acting objectively by actual or perceived threats. It could be the threat of dismissal over a disagreement about applying an accounting principle or reporting financial information, or it could be a dominant personality attempting to influence the decision making process.

- **Advocacy threats** can be a problem when you are promoting a position or opinion to the point that your subsequent objectivity is compromised. It could include acting as an advocate on behalf of an assurance client in litigation or disputes with third parties. In general, promoting the legitimate goals of your employer does not create an advocacy threat, provided that any statements you make are not misleading.

Safeguards

So what should you do if there is a threat (or potential threat), to the principles of the code?

CIMA's code of ethics has a 'threats and safeguards' approach to resolving ethical issues. This means that if you are in a situation where there might be a threat to any of the code's fundamental principles you should first assess whether the threat is significant. If it is, you should to take action to remove or mitigate it.

Safeguards can be found in employing organisations, such as whistle blowing or grievance procedures, or can be embedded within the profession in the form of standards or legislation. Safeguards are also the actions that a professional accountant takes to resolve an ethical conflict or dilemma.

If a colleague, employer or client has done something that you think is unethical, if you are under pressure to do something you think goes against the principles of the code of ethics or if you are facing a conflict of interest, then you will need to think about what safeguards or actions to take to resolve it. These safeguards could take a number of forms. The code does not describe all the safeguards that could be implemented, but instead gives general guidance for handling ethical issues, both for accountants working in business and for those in practice.

5 Resolving an ethical dilemma?

What should you do if you think you might be facing an ethical dilemma? How can you decide whether to take action?

All CIMA students should be able to identify, explain, resolve or address ethical problems.

If you think something might be unethical, you will need to think about the relevant facts, the ethical issues involved, the fundamental principles of CIMA's code of ethics that apply and internal company procedures. You can then identify and weigh up alternative courses of action, thinking about the consequences for those affected. What would be the outcome of going down a particular route? How would this compare with the alternatives?

An ethical dilemma exists when one or more principles of the code are threatened. You may have discovered something unethical, illegal or fraudulent going on where you work, or perhaps you feel that you have been asked to do something that compromises your professional integrity. Maybe someone is putting pressure on you to mislead, or to report in a way that is inconsistent, or goes against accepted accounting standards.

Conflicts of interest and confidentiality issues are also ethical problems. In general, ethical issues should be dealt with by taking actions (called safeguards) to reduce them to a level where they are no longer significant or of any consequence.

If you are not sure whether something is significant, it can help to think about what a reasonable third party might think if they had the facts of the situation. How would you feel if someone you know discovered how you had acted? Would you feel proud or embarrassed by your actions?

Whether you work in business, the public sector, or in practice, the following is a process for addressing situations where you have discovered possible fraud or malpractice or where you feel your professional integrity is at risk. If, having read this guidance, you are still unsure what to do or would like to talk the matter through, contact CIMA's ethics helpline for more help.

(1) Start by gathering all the relevant information so you can be sure of the facts and decide whether there really is an ethical problem.

(2) Raise your concern internally. Your manager could be an appropriate person to approach, or you could speak to a trusted colleague. If these are not options, consider escalating the issue, such as to your manager's boss, to the Board, or perhaps to a non-executive director. There might also be an internal grievance or whistle blowing procedure you can follow. If you are in practice, you could raise your concern with the client, unless you suspect money laundering.

(3) If you have raised the issue within the company, your concerns have not been addressed, and you feel that it is a significant or persistent problem, you should think about reporting it externally. You could speak to your company's auditors (if you have them) or contact the relevant trade, industry or regulatory authority. Remember that confidentiality still applies, and get legal advice to be sure of your obligations and rights.

(4) Finally, if you have exhausted these avenues and you are still unable to resolve the ethical conflict, you should consider how you could remove yourself from the situation. Sometimes it might be enough to stop working with a particular team or client or to refuse to be associated with a misleading report. In the most extreme cases of significant unethical behaviour, however, where this is likely to continue despite your best efforts to resolve it, you may need to consider resigning. Again, legal advice will help to clarify your rights and obligations and should be sought before you take the step of resigning.

Throughout the process, document the steps you take to resolve the issue. For example, raise your concern in writing and keep copies of relevant correspondence. This will allow you to demonstrate how you dealt with the problem should you ever need to do so.

Examples of ethical issues

Managers face ethical issues all of the time. Examples include:

- dealing with direct and indirect demands for bribes and attempts at extortion;

- dealing with attempts at unfair competition;

- expectations of social responsibility in relation to society and the environment;

- demand for safety and compliance with legislative standards in relation to products and production;

- honesty in advertising jobs and products;

- management of closures and redundancies;

- non-exploitation of countries and people;

- effects on customer of consuming products;

- dealing with oppressive governments;

- fairness in settling pay and work conditions.

Illustration 1 : Ethical dilemma

You work for a large company as the assistant financial controller. One of your duties is to reconcile the sales ledger each month. Every month it does not agree and you feel sure it is associated with bad debts being written off in the individual customer accounts but not included in the nominal ledger. You consider the differences to be material and have bought this to the attention of the financial controller but he seems unwilling to act.

Required:

What action would you take in this situation?

Solution

The main ethical issue is integrity. It would not be appropriate for an accountant to assist someone with a potentially fraudulent act, or to allow misleading information to be presented to others.

There is also a potential issue of objectivity if you are placed under pressure by the financial controller, as this would mean you have a conflict of interest between your personal prospects and the requirement to behave with integrity.

The possible actions could be:

- informing the financial controller of your concern and also formally asking the financial controller to address it;

- informing the financial controller that you are going to bring the matter to the attention of the financial director or the audit committee;

It would not be advisable to report externally until legal advice has been taken. Hopefully, this situation can be resolved with one of the above actions.

Test your understanding 1 : Ethical dilemma

You manage a number of trainee accountants whom the company sponsors through training at their first attempt at each paper. In June 2011 you employed a final level student who told you during her interview that she did not sit her final exams in May 2011 but was going to sit them for the first time in November of that year. She had actually sat them in May 2011 but worried that she would fail, tarnishing her record with the company, and also she would not get financial support for her re-sit. She passed her exams in May 2011.

Required:

What action would you take in this matter?

Test your understanding 2 : Objective test questions

(1) **Which of the following would be unacceptable in a company's code of conduct for employees?**

A   Maximum number of days off for sickness each year

B   No smoking of cigarettes inside the building

C   Employees who meet the public must be smartly dressed

D   No personal use of company photocopying machines without prior permission from a manager

(2) **Which of the following conditions would be unacceptable in a job advertisement?**

A   Must be a qualified accountant

B   Must be a non-smoker

C   Must be at least 5' 6" tall

D   Must be punctual and self-motivated

(3) **Which of the following is not a fundamental ethical principle identified by CIMA?**

A   Integrity

B   Objectivity

C   Confidentiality

D   Independence

(4) **CIMA's code of ethics requires members to comply with five fundamental principles. Which of the following contains three of these principles?**

A   Integrity, objectivity, honesty

B   Professional competence and due care, professional behaviour, confidentiality

C   Social responsibility, independence, scepticism

D   Courtesy, reliability, responsibility

(5) **In which of the following situations would the company be viewed as having behaved unethically?**

A   Delaying payments to its suppliers despite repeated requests to pay

B   Printing warning signs on its potentially dangerous plastic packaging

C   Informing investors that the profit forecast may not materialise

D   Stating that it will aim to recruit more people from ethnic minority groups

6 Summary diagram

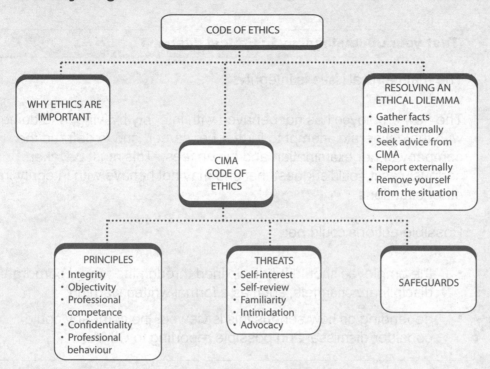

Test your understanding answers

Test your understanding 1 : Ethical dilemma

The main ethical issue is integrity.

The new employee has not behaved with integrity by lying, and doing so with the deliberate attempt to further her career, and to defraud the company of her examination and tuition fees. This must be taken seriously as it could suggest that she may not behave with integrity in other situations.

Possible actions could be:

- the employee should be disciplined through the formal corporate disciplinary channels, such as a formal written warning;

- depending on how serious this is viewed, the company could consider dismissal and possible reporting to CIMA.

Test your understanding 2 : Objective test questions

(1) A – It would be unacceptable to state a fixed number of days for sickness for employees. As long as the employee has a doctors certificate to prove their sickness is genuine.

(2) C – As men are generally taller than women, this would be considered discriminatory.

(3) D

(4) B

(5) A – In situations B and C it is rectifying the results of previous doubtful actions. Option D is an example of a company's ethical aspirations.

12

IAS 2, 8, 18, 24 and IFRS 8

Chapter learning objectives

- Explain and apply the accounting rules contained in IASs dealing with:
    - inventories;
    - accounting policies, changes in estimates and errors;
    - revenue recognition;
    - disclosure of related parties to a business;
    - operating segments.

1 Session content

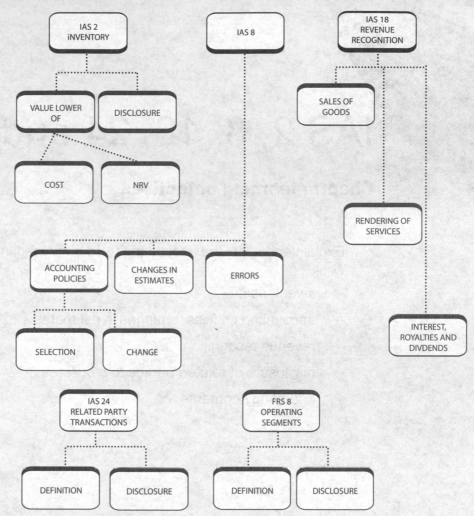

2 IAS 2 Inventories

Inventories are assets that are:

- held for sale;
- in the process of production;
- materials that will be used in the production process.

Measurement of inventories

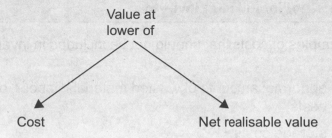

Value at
lower of

Cost

Net realisable value

Cost of purchase, costs of
conversion and costs to bring
inventory to present location
and condition.

Estimated selling prices
less costs to completion
less costs to sell.

Costs of conversion may
include production overheads.
These should be allocated
based on normal production
levels.

Determining cost

Costs of purchase include the purchase price, import duties, handling
costs and other costs directly connected with the acquisition of the
goods.

Costs of conversion include costs directly related to the units being
produced, e.g. direct labour costs, allocation of fixed and variable
overhead costs incurred in production.

Variable production overheads are those indirect costs of production
that vary directly with the volume produced, e.g. heat, light and power.

Fixed production overheads are those indirect costs of production
that do not vary directly with the volume produced and remain constant
regardless of the number of units produced, e.g. depreciation of
machinery, factory administration costs.

Finance costs can be included if the requirements of IAS 23 *Borrowing
Costs* are satisfied.

Costs not included in inventory

Examples of costs that should not be included in inventory are:

- abnormal amounts of wasted materials, labour, or other production costs;
- storage costs;
- administration costs that do not contribute to bringing the inventories to their present location and condition;
- selling and distribution costs.

These costs should be treated as expenses against profit in the period that they arise.

Allocation of overheads

The allocation of fixed production overheads should be based on the normal capacity of the business. Any excess overheads due to inefficiencies or production problems should be treated as an expense in the period that they occur.

3 Calculation of costs

Inventory should be valued at cost – either the actual cost of an item (unit cost), or, if there are a large number of items in inventory which makes this impractical, a reasonable approximation to actual cost should be used. The most common approximations are:

(1) First in first out (FIFO). The closing inventory is assumed to consist of the latest purchases, i.e. oldest inventory is sold first. This means the closing inventory will be valued at the most recent purchase prices.

(2) Average cost. The weighted average cost is calculated by taking the total purchase price of all units purchased in the period divided by the total number of units purchased in the period. This can be calculated using periodic or a continuous method.

Illustration 1 : Calculation of the cost of inventory

The following costs relate to a unit of inventory:

Cost of raw materials	$1.00
Direct labour	$0.50

During the year $60,000 of production overheads were incurred.

8,000 units were produced during the year which is lower than the normal level of 10,000 units. This was as a result of a fault with some machinery which resulted in 2,000 units having to be scrapped.

At the year-end, 700 units are in closing inventory.

Required:

What is the cost of closing inventory?

Solution

Production overheads should be allocated based on the normal level of production, i.e. 10,000 units.

$60,000/10,000 units = $6.00 per unit.

Cost per unit:

	$
Raw materials	1.00
Direct labour	0.50
Production overheads	6.00
	——
Total cost per unit	7.50

Cost of 700 units in closing inventory = 700 × $7.50 = $5,250.

Illustration 2 : Calculation of the cost of inventory using FIFO and

The following purchases and sales took place in Tyrone Ltd during the first four days of June:

Day 1   Opening inventory nil
Day 1   Purchase 200 units at $15 per unit
Day 2   Purchase 100 units at $18 per unit
Day 3   Sales of 250 units at $30 per unit
Day 4   Purchase 150 units at $20 per unit

Required:

Calculate the cost of inventory at the end of day 4 for Tyrone Ltd using:

(a)   the FIFO method;

(b)   the average cost method.

Solution

(a)   **FIFO method**

Total purchases = 200 + 100 + 150 = 450 units

Sales = 250 units

Closing inventory = 450 – 250 = 200 units

FIFO method assumes the oldest inventory is sold first, therefore the 200 units remaining must be from the most recent purchases on day 4 (150 units) and the balance from the day 2 purchases (50 units).

Cost:

50 x $18 =	$900
150 x $20 =	$3,000
	$3,900

Total cost of closing inventory = $3,900

(b) Average cost method

Total purchases = 200 + 100 + 150 = 450 units

Total cost of purchases =

200 x $15 =	$3,000
100 x $18 =	$1,800
150 x $20 =	$3,000
	$7,800

Weighted average cost = $7,800/450 units = $17.33 per unit

Total cost of closing inventory = 200 units x $17.33 = $3,466

NB: An alternative approach could be to calculate the average cost after each transaction, i.e. after day 2 total purchases $4,800/total 300 units = cost of $16. After the sale has taken place this would leave 50 units in inventory valued at $16 per unit = $800. This would then be added to additional purchases to calculate future average costs. Therefore, on day 4, purchases of $3,000 would be added to $800 – $3,800/total units of 200 = cost of $19. This would result in a slightly higher closing inventory value of $3,800.

Illustration 3 : Inventory valuation

Value the following items of inventory.

(a) Materials costing $12,000 bought for processing and assembly for a profitable special order. Since buying these items, the cost price has fallen to $10,000.

(b) Equipment constructed for a customer for an agreed price of $18,000. This has recently been completed at a cost of $16,800. It has now been discovered that, in order to meet certain regulations, further work with an extra cost of $4,200 will be required. The customer has accepted partial responsibility and agreed to meet half of the extra cost.

> ### Solution
>
> (a) Value at $12,000. $10,000 is irrelevant as this is the replacement cost. IAS 2 states value at lower of cost and NRV. The order is profitable and therefore NRV must be higher than cost.
>
> (b) Value at NRV, i.e. $15,900 as below cost,
>
> NRV = contract price of $18,000 – company share of costs to complete $2,100 = $15,900.
>
> Original cost = $16,800.

4 Disclosure

The main disclosure requirements of IAS 2 are:

- accounting policy adopted, including the cost formula used;
- total carrying amount, classified as follows:

	$
Raw materials	X
Work in progress	X
Finished goods	X
	X

This would be disclosed in a note to the financial statements. The total amount of closing inventory will be shown as a current asset on the statement of financial position and a reduction to the cost of sales in the statement of comprehensive income.

- amount of inventories carried at NRV;
- amount of inventories recognised as an expense during the period;
- details of circumstances that have led to the write-down of inventories to their NRV.

5 IAS 8 Accounting Policies, Changes In Accounting Estimates And Errors

IAS 8 governs the following topics:

- selection of accounting policies;
- changes in accounting policies;
- changes in accounting estimates;
- correction of prior period errors.

Accounting policies

Accounting policies are the principles, bases, conventions, rules and practices applied by an entity which specify how the effects of transactions and other events are reflected in the financial statements.

Accounting policies should be selected and applied so as to comply with the requirements of IASs.

If however, there are no specific policies for a particular transaction, the accounting policy should be developed so as to meet the following objectives:

- Relevant to the decision-making needs of users.
- Reliable, i.e.
    - report a faithful representation;
    - report the substance of transactions in preference to legal form;
    - neutral;
    - prudent;
    - complete.
- Entities should consider IASs that deal with similar and related issues. They should also consider the definitions, recognition criteria and measurement concepts contained in the framework.

Changes in accounting policies

Selected policies should be applied consistently as far as possible.

Changes should only be made if:

- **required by an IAS**

    e.g. New accounting standard

For many years proposed dividends were treated as liabilities in the statement of financial position as adjusting events after the reporting date. IAS 10 now treats these as non-adjusting events and they are no longer liabilities but instead appear in the notes. In the year that the change was introduced, all companies had a "change in accounting policy".

- **the change improves the relevance and reliability of financial statements**

   e.g. Provision of more relevant and reliable information

   When a company is using a manual accounting system for valuing year end inventory they often do this on a FIFO basis. However, when they invest in a computerised system they often switch to the weighted average cost method. This is because the software chosen, tailor made for their industry, is only capable of valuing inventory under the weighted average cost method, as this is the standard industry method. In this case a change in accounting policy is justified because it results in financial statements providing reliable and more relevant information, which is actually more comparable to other entities within the industries to which the entity belongs.

A change in accounting policy should be applied retrospectively, i.e. as if the new policy had always applied. Any resulting adjustment should be reported as an adjustment to the opening balance of retained earnings. Comparative information should be restated.

Changes in accounting policies

A change in accounting policy could occur because there has been a change in:

- recognition, e.g. an expense is now recognised as an asset;

- presentation, e.g. depreciation is now classified as cost of sales rather than an administration expense;

- measurement basis, e.g. stating assets should be valued as replacement cost rather than historical cost.

Illustration 4 : Change in accounting policy

During 2010 Bowie Ltd changed its accounting policy with respect to the treatment of borrowing costs that are directly attributable to the construction of a hydro-electric power station, which is in the course of construction for use by Bowie.

In previous periods, Bowie had expensed such costs, in accordance with the allowed benchmark treatment in IAS 23 Borrowing Costs. IAS 23 now states Bowie must now capitalise these costs.

Bowie had borrowing costs in 2010 amounting to $3,000 and $5,200 in periods prior to 2009.

Bowie's accounting records for 2010 and 2009 show:

	2010	2009
	$	$
Profit from operations	30,000	18,000
Finance cost	-	(2,600)
Profit before tax	30,000	15,400
Income tax	(9,000)	(4,620)
Profit for the period	21,000	10,780

In 2009 opening retained earnings were $20,000 and closing retained earnings were $30,780. The income tax rate is 30%.

Required:

Show how the change in accounting policy will be recorded in the financial statements for the year ended 31 December 2010. Comparatives should also be prepared.

Solution

Income statement (extract)

	2010	2009
	$	$
Operating profit	30,000	18,000
Finance cost	-	-
PBT	30,000	18,000
Income tax	(9,000)	(5,400)
Profit for the period	21,000	12,600

Statement of changes in equity (extract)

	2010	2009
	$	$
Retained earnings b/d	30,780	20,000
Restatement due to change in accounting policy on interest costs	5,460	3,640
	36,240	23,640
Profit for the period	21,000	12,600
Retained earnings c/d	57,240	36,240

Extracts from notes to accounts

During 2010 the company changed its accounting policy for the treatment of interest costs. Previously the costs were written off as expenses as they are incurred and the costs are now capitalised where they related to qualifying assets. The change in accounting policy has been accounted for retrospectively via a prior period adjustment. The new accounting policy is consistent with generally accepted accounting practice and increases the relevance and reliability of reported figures.

Explanatory note:

The adjustment in respect of costs capitalised prior to 2009 is dealt with as a restatement to opening retained earnings in the 2009 Statement of Changes in Equity. The $5,200 net of 30% tax is shown as an adjustment.

The adjustment of costs expensed during 2009 is dealt with in the restated 2009 comparative accounts.

The adjustment to 2010 opening retained earnings comprises the overall effect of the 2009 and prior adjustments, net of tax ($2,600 + $5,200) x 70%.

We must remember to consider whether the change in policy will effect profit for the year - if this is the case it will also effect the tax charge. Remember to read the exam question, as sometimes the examiner will tell you to ignore the tax effect.

Test your understanding 1 : Change in accounting policy

Wimbledon Ltd has always valued its inventories on the FIFO basis using a manual system. During 2010 the company purchased a computerised system and discovered that most industry equivalent companies use a weighted average cost method.

The incomes statements prior to the adjustments are:

	2010	2009
	$000	$000
Revenue	500	400
Cost of sales	(200)	(160)
Gross profit	300	240
Administration expenses	(120)	(100)
Distribution costs	(50)	(30)
Profit from operations	130	110

The retained earnings balance as at the beginning of 2009 was $600,000.

The impact on inventory due to the change in policy was determined as:

Inventory as at 31 December 2008: an increase of $20,000.
Inventory as at 31 December 2009: an increase of $30,000.
Inventory as at 31 December 2010: an increase of $40,000.

Required:

Show how the change in accounting policy will be recorded in the financial statements for the year 2010. Comparatives should also be prepared. Assume that the adjustments have no effect on taxation charges.

Changes in accounting estimates

When preparing financial statements, inherent uncertainties result in estimates having to be made and subsequently, these estimates may need to be revised.

Distinguishing between changes in accounting policies and accounting estimates may be difficult. In these circumstances, the change is to be treated as a change in an accounting estimate.

Changes in accounting estimates should be accounted for prospectively. This means that the revised estimate should be included in the calculation of net profit or loss for the current period and future periods if appropriate.

Illustration 5 : Change in accounting estimate

An asset was purchased three years ago for $100,000 at which time it was thought that the asset had no residual value and a useful economic life of ten years. The directors have decided that as a result of using the asset more than was originally planned the remaining useful economic life is only five years as at 1 July 2010. The asset is depreciated on the straight line basis. **Required:**

Show how the change in accounting estimate will be recorded in the financial statements for the year ended 31 June 2011.

Solution

The original depreciation was:

$$\frac{\text{Cost} - \text{residual value}}{\text{Useful economic life}} = \frac{\$100,000 - \text{Nil}}{10} = \$10,000 \text{ pa}$$

The asset has been depreciated for 3 years when the change of useful economic life occurs and therefore the carrying value would be:

Cost $100,000 – (3 x $10,000) = $70,000

The carrying value at the date of the change is the carrying value on the statement of financial position for the asset and must therefore be used to recalculate the new depreciation charge.

$$\frac{\text{Carrying value} - \text{residual value}}{\text{Useful economic life}} = \frac{\$70,000 - \text{Nil}}{5} = \$14,000 \text{pa}$$

Statement of changes in equity (extract)

	2011
	$
Cost	70,000
Accumulative depreciation	44,000
Carrying value	26,000

Extracts from notes to accounts

During 20110 the company changed its accounting estimate for economic useful life of an asset. Previously the asset was had a useful economic life of ten years but due to the asset being used more than originally planned, the life has reduced to five years as at 1 July 2010. This resulted in the annual depreciation charge increases from $10,000 pa to $14,000 pa.

Explanatory note:

The adjustments are only required for future depreciation charges as at the date of the change, i.e. 1 July 2010. We do not need to change the depreciation charged already, hence profits will not be restated. Therefore, the SOFP reflects the historical depreciation of $30,000 charged upto the date of the change plus the new charge for the current year of $14,000.

Changes in accounting estimates

Examples of changes in accounting estimates are changes in:

- the useful lives of non-current assets;
- the residual values of non-current assets;
- the method of depreciating non-current assets.

Errors

Prior period errors are omissions from, and misstatements in, the entity's financial statements for one or more periods arising from a failure to use, or misuse of, reliable information that:

- was available when financial statements for these periods were authorised for issue; and

- could reasonably be expected to have been obtained and taken into account in the preparation and presentation of those financial statements.

Prior period errors should be corrected retrospectively. This means that, similarly to a change in accounting policy, any adjustment resulting from correction of the error should be reported as an adjustment to the opening balance of retained earnings. Comparative information should be restated.

Illustration 6 : Correction of prior period error

During 2010 Beta Co. discovered that certain products that had been sold during 2009 were incorrectly included in inventory at 31 December 2009 at $6,500.

Beta's accounting records show the following results for 2010 and 2009:

	2010	2009
	$	$
Revenue	104,000	73,500
Cost of sales	(86,500)	(53,500)
Profit before tax	17,500	20,000
Income tax expense	(5,250)	(6,000)
Profit for the period	12,250	14,000

In 2009 opening retained earnings was $20,000 and closing retained earnings was $34,000. The income tax rate is 30%.

Required:

Show how the correction of the prior period error will be recorded in the financial statements for the year ended 31 December 2010. Comparatives should also be prepared.

Solution

Extract from the comprehensive income statement

	2010	2009
	$	$
Revenue	104,000	73,500
Cost of sales	(80,000)	(60,000)
PBT	24,000	13,500
Income taxes	(7,200)	(4,050)
Profit for the period	16,800	9,450

Extracts from statement of changes in equity

	2010	2009
	$	$
Retained earnings b/d	34,000	20,000
Correction of error	(4,550)	–
Retained earnings b/d	29,450	20,000
Profit for the period (as above)	16,800	9,450
Retained earnings c/d	46,250	29,450

Extracts from notes to accounts

Some products that had been sold during 2009 had been incorrectly included in inventory at the year end 31 December 2009. The financial statements for the year ending 31 December 2009 have been restated to correct this error.

Explanatory note:

The correction is made as follows:

Dr cost of sales (closing inventory)	$6,500
Cr inventory	$6,500

This happens in the 2009 accounts and has a knock-on effect on the opening inventory of 2010.

The adjustment to 2010 opening retained earnings is net of tax.

Test your understanding 2 : Error

During 2010 Howie Ltd discovered that certain products that had been sold during 2009 were incorrectly included in inventory at 31 December 2009 at $2,500.

Howie's accounting records show the following results for 2010 and 2009:

	2010	2009
	$	$
Revenue	52,100	48,300
Cost of sales	(33,500)	(30,200)
Profit before tax	18,600	18,100
Income tax expense	(4,600)	(4,300)
Profit for the year	14,000	13,800

In 2009 opening retained earnings was $11,200 and closing retained earnings was $25,000. Assume the adjustment has no effect on the tax charge.

Required:

Show how the correction of the error will be recorded in the financial statements for the year ended 31 December 2010. Comparatives should also be prepared.

6 IAS 18 Revenue Recognition

Revenue is income that arises in the course of ordinary activities. The objective of IAS 18 is to prescribe the accounting treatment of revenue arising from certain types of transactions.

The main issue with revenue is determining when it should be recognised in the financial statements. The basic principles that should be applied are that revenue should be recognised when:

- it is probable that future economic benefits will flow to the enterprise; &
- these benefits can be measured reliably.

We must aim to match the revenue earned at the year-end to the related expense at the year-end.

IAS 18 covers when revenue should be recognised in the specific situations of:

- the sale of goods;
- the rendering of services;
- interest, royalties and dividends.

Sale of goods

Revenue from the sale of goods should be recognised when all of the following criteria have been met:

- the significant risks and rewards of ownership have been transferred to the buyer;
- the seller does not retain any influence or control over the goods;
- revenue can be measured reliably;
- it is reasonably certain that the buyer will pay for the goods;
- the costs to the seller can be measured reliably.

Rendering of services

Revenue from services should be recognised when all of the following criteria have been met:

- revenue can be measured reliably;
- it is reasonably certain that the buyer will pay for the services;
- the stage of completion of the transaction can be measured reliably;
- the costs to the seller can be measured reliably.

Interest, royalties and dividends

These items should be recognised when:

- revenue can be measured reliably;
- receipt is reasonably certain.

They should be recognised on an accruals basis, i.e. when earned rather than received. For dividends this is when the right to receive them is established.

Measurement of revenue

Revenue should be measured at the fair value of the consideration received or receivable.

Disclosure

IAS 18 requires disclosure of the accounting policies adopted for recognising revenue, and disclosure of each significant category of revenue in the period, including revenue from:

- the sale of goods;
- providing services;
- interest;
- royalties;
- dividends.

Illustration 7 : Revenue recognition

Should revenue from the sale of goods be recognised in the following circumstances?

(a) **Case 1**. Goods are sold by a manufacturer to a retailer, who has the right to return the goods if it is unable to sell them.

(b) **Case 2**. The goods are shipped to the customer for installation, but they have not yet been installed and the installation cost will be significant part of the contract.

(c) **Case 3**. Goods have been sold on credit to a customer in a country where there has been a political change, and the incoming government has banned domestic companies from making any payments to other countries.

(d) **Case 4**. A company receives $10,000 as an advance payment for the delivery of goods that have not yet been manufactured.

Solution

Case 1

Revenue should not be recognised by the manufacturer as "significant risks have not yet been transferred to the buyer" because the retailer can return the goods. Revenue should be recognised when the customer sells the goods to the customer.

Case 2

Revenue should not be recognised at this stage because "significant risks have not yet been transferred to the buyer" because the installation is not yet complete. Revenue should be recognised when the installation is complete.

Case 3

Revenue should not be recognised because it is not yet "reasonably certain that the customer will pay for the goods", due to the political problems in that country.

Case 4

Payment in advance is not revenue. The money received will be included a current liability in the statement of financial position.

7 IAS 24 Related party transactions

Related party relationships are a normal feature of business.

The existence of a related party relationship and transactions with related parties may affect the profit or loss of an entity. It is therefore important for users to be aware of related parties and any transactions that have occurred in the period.

Definition

Related parties

A party is related to an entity if:

(i) the party controls or is controlled by the entity;

(ii) is under common control with the entity;

(iii) the party is a member of the key management personnel;

(iv) the party is a close member of the family of an individual in (i) or (iii).

Control

Control is the power to govern the financial and operating policies of an entity so as to obtain benefits.

Related party transaction

A transfer of services or resources between related parties, irrespective of whether a price is charged.

Disclosures

If there have been transactions between related parties, the reporting entity should disclose the following:

- The nature of the related party relationship;

- The nature of the transaction;

- The amount of the transaction;

- The amount of any outstanding balances.

Related parties - further detail

In the context of this standard, the following are not necessarily related parties:

(a) two entities simply because they have a director or other member of key management personnel in common, notwithstanding the above definition of 'related party';

(b) two venturers simply because they share joint control over a joint venture;

(c) providers of finance;

(d) trade unions;

(e) public utilities; and

(f) government departments and agencies.
Simply by virtue of their normal dealings with an entity (even though they may affect the freedom of action of an entity or participate in its decision-making process); and

(g) a customer, supplier, franchisor, distributor or general agent with whom an entity transacts a significant volume of business, merely by virtue of the resulting economic dependence.

Disclosure

The standard concerns the disclosure of related party transactions in order to make readers of financial statements aware of the position and to ensure that the financial statements show a true and fair view.

If there have been transactions between related parties, an entity shall disclose the nature of the related party relationship as well as information about the transactions and outstanding balances necessary for an understanding of the potential effect of the relationship on the financial statements.

Disclosures that related party transactions were made on terms equivalent to those that prevail in arm's length transactions are made only if such terms can be substantiated.

At a minimum, disclosures shall include:

- the amount of the transactions;

- the amount of outstanding balances: their terms and conditions, including whether they are secured, and the nature of the consideration to be provided in settlement and details of any guarantees given or received;

- provisions for doubtful debts related to the amount of outstanding balances;

- the expense recognised during the period in respect of bad or doubtful debts due from related parties.

In addition, IAS 24 requires an entity to disclose key management personnel compensation in total and for each of the following categories:

- short-term employee benefits;
- post-employment benefits;
- other long-term benefits;
- termination benefits;
- equity compensation benefits.

Examples of related party transactions

Examples of related party transactions would be:

- Purchases/sales of goods (even if no price is charged);
- Purchases/sales of property or other assets;

- Rendering/receipt of services;
- Leasing arrangements;
- Management contracts;
- Finance arrangements, eg, loan guarantee.

Illustration 8 : Related party transaction

You decide to set up a business in an office block offering training facilities. Your brother is the owner of the building and in order to help you start your business, he agrees to give you your office with no charge for a four year period.

After three successful years of business your student numbers have doubled and you decide to take early retirement and sell your business.

Your business is put up for sale.

Explain what information should be disclosed in the accounts regarding this transaction and why it is important to do this.

Solution

You must disclose:

- the nature of the related party transaction, i.e. you have received the building rent-free during the last three years;
- the related party, i.e. your brother owns the building;
- the amount of the transaction, i.e. how much rent are you saving (what would be the "market rate" for the rental of these premises).

This information is important for a prospective buyer of the business because they will need to be aware of these facts when they look at the profits for the business. If you did not disclose this matter, the prospective buyer would think they could make similar profits if they purchased the business. Although the profit figures are correct, they are distorted by the fact that the new owners would incur a rent charge for that building, hence the profits would reduce, assuming all things remain the same.

Test your understanding 3 : Related party transactions

CB is an entity specialising in importing a wide range of non-food items and selling them to retailers. George is CB's president and founder and owns 40% of CB's equity shares:

- CB's largest customer, XC accounts for 35% of CB's revenue. XC has just completed negotiations with CB for a special 5% discount on all sales.

- During the accounting period, George purchased a property from CB for $500,000. CB had previously declared the property surplus to its requirements and had valued it at $750,000.

- George's son, Arnold is a director in a financial institution, FC. During the accounting period, FC advanced $2 million to CB as an unsecured loan at a favourable rate of interest.

Required:

Explain, with reasons, the extent to which each of the above transactions should be classified and disclosed in accordance with IAS 24 Related Party Disclosures in CB's financial statements for the period.

8 IFRS 8 Operating Segments

IFRS 8 requires an entity to disclose segment information to enable users of the financial statements to evaluate the nature and financial effect of business activities in which it engages and the economic environments in which it operates. Many entities produce a wide range of products and services, often in different countries. Further information on how the overall results of entities are made up from each of these operating segments will help the users of the financial statements.

The requirements of IFRS 8 must be applied by quoted entities. If non-quoted entities choose to report by segment they must comply with the requirements of IFRS 8.

Definitions

IFRS 8 defines an operating segment as a component of an entity:

(a) that engages in business activities from which it earns revenues and incurs expenses;

(b) whose operating results are regularly reviewed by the entity's chief operating decision maker to make decisions about resources to be allocated to the segment and assess its performance;

and

(c) for which discrete financial information is available.

Identification of segments

A segment should be classified as a reportable segment if it contributes more than 10% of the total of any of the following:

- revenue (internal and external);
- profits;
- losses;
- assets.

If, after allocating segments according to the 10% rule, the external revenue of reportable segments is less than 75% of the total revenue of the entity, additional segments will be classified as reportable segments even though they do not meet the 10% rule.

Disclosure

IFRS 8 requires the disclosure of the following:

- factors used to identify the entity's reportable segments, including the basis of segmentation (for example, whether operating segments are based on products or services or geographical areas);
- types of products and services from which each segment derives its revenue.

For each reportable segment an entity should report:

- profit or loss;
- revenues;
- total assets;
- total liabilities.

Illustration 9 : Operating segments

Jimbo Plc, has five business segments which are currently reported in its financial statements. Jimbo is an international hotel group which reports to management on the basis of region. It does not currently report segmental information under IFRS 8 *Operating Segments*. The results of the regional segments for the year ended 31 May 2009 are as follows:

	European $m	Asia $m	Africa $m	Middle East $m	Others $m	Total $m
Revenue						
Internal	10	20	10	50	10	100
External	100	300	100	500	100	1100
Total	110	320	110	550	110	1200
Segmental profits	5	60	5	100	10	180
Segmental assets	150	800	50	1600	600	3200
Segmental liabilities	120	400	30	950	300	1800

Required:

Determine the company's reportable operating segments using the information above.

Solution

The information can be analysed as follows:

	European	Asia	African	Middle East	Others	Total
	$m	$m	$m	$m	$m	$m
Revenue						
Internal	10	20	10	50	10	100
External	100	300	100	500	100	1100
Total	110	320	110	550	110	1200
% to total sales	**9.2%**	**26.7%**	**9.2%**	**45.7%**	**9.2%**	
Segmental profits	5	60	5	100	10	180
% to total profit	**2.8%**	**33.3%**	**2.8%**	**55.6%**	**5.5%**	
Segmental assets	150	800	50	1600	600	3200
% to total assets	**4.7%**	**25%**	**1.7%**	**50%**	**18.6%**	
Segmental liabilities	120	400	30	950	300	1800
% to total liabilities	**6.6%**	**22.2%**	**1.7%**	**52.8%**	**16.7%**	

Explanation:

The only segments that meet the 10% criteria are Asia and Middle East.

However, collectively external revenue is only 66.7% of the total revenue (Asia = 25% (300/1200) and Middle East = 41.7% (500/1200)).

Therefore, additional segments must also be reported to meet the 75% of revenue criteria, i.e. European segment.

Test your understanding 4 : Objective test questions

(1) Tracey's business sells three products – A, B and C. The following information was available at the year end:

	A	B	C
	$ per unit	$ per unit	$ per unit
Original cost	7	10	19
Estimated selling price	15	13	20
Selling and distribution costs	2	5	6
Units of inventory	20	25	15

The value of inventory at the year-end should be:

A $675

B $670

C $795

D $550

(2) Item XYZ has 150 items in inventory as at 31 March 2011. The original cost of the inventory was $5,500. The following alternative valuations have been found .

Which value should be used in the accounts at 31 March 2011?

A   Net realisable value $4,750

B   Original cost $5,500

C   Selling price $7,000

D   Replacement cost $6,500

(3) **Which ONE of the following would be regarded as a change of accounting estimate according to IAS 8** *Accounting Policies, Changes in estimates and errors***?**

A   An entity started capitalising borrowing costs for assets as required by IAS 23 *Borrowing costs*. Borrowing costs had previously been charged to the income statement.

B   An entity started revaluing its properties, as allowed by IAS 16 *Property, plant and equipment*. Previously all property, plant and equipment had been carried at cost less accumulated depreciation.

C   A material error in the inventory valuation methods caused closing inventory at 31 March 2009 to be overstated by $900,000.

D   An entity created a provision for bad debts of 2% of closing receivables but has decided that it should be increase to 5% to be more prudent .

(4) An entity has three segments A, B and C which account for 40%, 30% and 9% of total revenue respectively.

   Which of the segments will be classified as reportable segments in accordance with IFRS 8 *Operating Segments***?**

A   A only

B   C only

C   A and B

D   A, B and C

(5) **When disclosing a related party transaction, which of the following items must be disclosed?**

(i)   A description of the relationship with the related party

(ii)   A description of the transaction

(iii)   Details of the amounts involved

(iv)   Details of any balances outstanding at the year-end

A   i, ii and iv

B   i, iii and iv

C   i and iv

D   i, ii, iii and iv

(6) Revenue from the sale of goods should be recognised when certain conditions are met.

   (i)   the entity selling does not retain any continuing influence or control over the goods;

   (ii) when the goods are dispatched to the buyer;

   (iii) revenue can be measured reliably;

   (iv) the supplier has paid for the goods;

   (v) it is reasonably certain that the buyer will pay for the goods;

   (vi) the buyer has paid for the goods.

Which of the above are included in IAS 18 *Revenue recognition's* conditions for recognition of revenue?

  A   i, ii and v

  B   ii, iii and iv

  C   i, iii and v

  D   i, iv and vi

(7) Which **ONE** of the following would be regarded as a related party of BS:

  A   BX, a customer of BS.

  B   The president of the BS Board, who is also the chief executive officer of another entity, BU, that supplies goods to BS.

  C   BQ, a supplier of BS.

  D   BY, BS's main banker.

9 Summary diagram

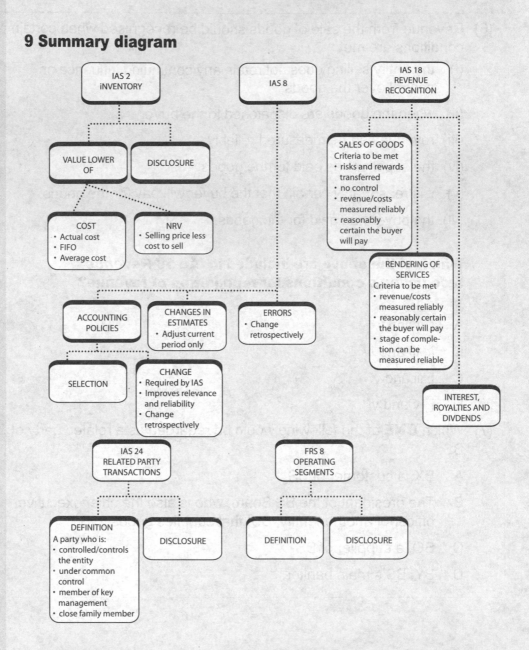

Test your understanding answers

Test your understanding 1 : Change in accounting policy

Income statement

	2010	2009
	$000	$000
Revenue	500	400
Cost of sales (W1)	(190)	(150)
Gross profit	310	250
Administration expenses	(120)	(100)
Distribution costs	(50)	(30)
Profit from operations	140	120

Statement of changes in equity (extract)

	2010	2009
	$000	$000
Retained earnings b/f	710	600
Restatement due to change in policy (note below) accounting policy	30	20
	740	620
Profit for the period	140	120
Retained earnings c/f	880	740

Extracts from notes to accounts

During 2010 the company changed its accounting policy for the treatment of valuing inventory. Previously the inventory was valued using the FIFO method but due to the purchase of a new computer system is now valued using the weighted average cost method. The change in accounting policy has been accounted for retrospectively via a prior period adjustment. The new accounting policy is consistent with generally accepted accounting practice and increases the relevance and reliability of reported figures.

Explanatory note:

The adjustment in change in accounting policy prior to 2009 is dealt with as a reserve movement in the 2009 Statement of Changes in Equity.

The adjustment in change in accounting policy during 2009 is dealt with in the 2009 comparative accounts.

2009 adjustment = prior to 2009 = closing inventory increases by $20,000. This will decrease cost of sales and increase profit.

2010 b/f = prior to 2010 = opening inventory increases by $20,000 and closing inventory increases by $30,000 during 2009. The net effect is profit will increase by $10,000 during 2009. Therefore cumulatively the adjustment is now $20,000 (above) + $10,000 = $30,000

(W1) Cost of sales adjustment

	2010	2009
	$000	$000
Per original accounts	200	160
Opening inventory adjustment	30	20
Closing inventory adjustment	(40)	(30)
Per adjusted accounts	190	150

Test your understanding 2 : Error

Income statement

	2010	2009
	$	$
Revenue	52,100	48,300
Cost of sales	(31,000)	(32,700)
Profit before tax	21,100	15,600
Income taxes	(4,600)	(4,300)
Profit for the period	16,500	11,300

Statement of changes in equity (extract)

	2010	2009
	$	$
Retained earnings b/d (as previously reported)	25,000	11,200
Correction of error	(2,500)	–
Retained earnings b/d	22,500	11,200
Profit for the period (as above)	16,500	11,300
Retained earnings c/d	39,000	22,500

Extracts from notes to accounts

Some products that had been sold during 2009 had been incorrectly included in inventory at the year end 31 December 2009. The financial statements for the year ending 31 December 2009 have been restated to correct this error.

Explanatory note:

The correction is made as follows:

Dr cost of sales (closing inventory)	$2,500
Cr inventory	$2,500

This happens in the 2009 accounts and has a knock-on effect on the opening inventory of 2010.

Test your understanding 3 : Related party transactions

According to IAS 24 Related Party Disclosures, a customer with whom an entity transacts a significant volume of business is not a related party merely by virtue of the resulting economic dependence. XC is not a related party and the negotiated discount does not need to be disclosed.

A party is related to an entity if it has an interest in the entity that gives it significant influence over the entity. The party is related to an entity if they are a member of the key management personnel of the entity.

As founder member and major shareholder holding 40% of the equity, George is able to exert significant influence and is a related party of CB.

George is also a related party as he is CB's president. He is a member of the key management personnel of CB.

The sale of the property for $500,000 will need to be disclosed, along with its valuation as a related party transaction.

Providers of finance are not related parties simply because of their normal dealings with the entity. However, if a party is a close member of the family of any individual categorised as a related party, they are also a related party. As Arnold is George's son and George is a related party, Arnold is also a related party. The loan from FC will need to be disclosed along with the details of Arnold and his involvement in the arrangements.

Test your understanding 4 : Objective test questions

(1) D

	A	B	C
Cost	7	10	19
NRV	13	8	14
Valuation	20 × 7 = 140	25 × 8 = 200	15 × 14 = 210

Total Valuation = 140 + 200 + 210 = 550

(2) A

IAS 2 states that inventory should be valued at the lower of cost or net realisable value.

(3) D

(4) D

Segments A and B only account for 70% of total revenues and therefore IFRS 8 would require C to be classified as a reportable segment even though it does not meet the 10% rule.

(5) D

(6) C

(7) B

Recording S.

Non-Current Assets

Chapter learning objectives

- Explain and apply the accounting rules contained in IASs dealing with:
    - tangible non-current assets;
    - research and development expenditure;
    - intangible non-current assets (other than goodwill on consolidation);
    - impairment of assets.

1 Session content

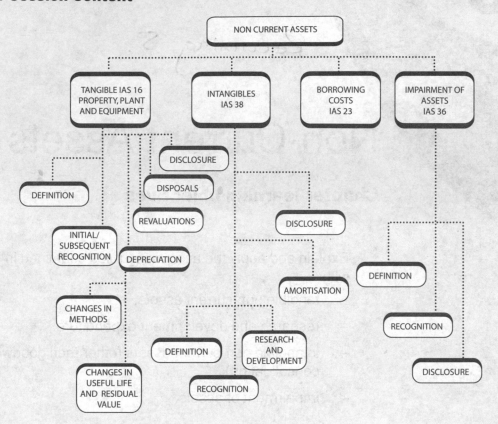

2 IAS 16 Property, Plant And Equipment
Definition

Property, plant and equipment are tangible assets that:

- are held by an enterprise for use in the production or supply of goods or services, for rental to others, or for administrative purposes; and

- are expected to be used during more than one period.

You should know these definitions from your earlier studies. You need to ensure that you know all of the following definitions for your examination.

Property, plant and equipment

Property, plant and equipment are tangible items that are held for use in the production or supply of goods or services, for rental to others, or for administrative purposes.

Carrying amount

The amount at which an asset is recognised, after deducting any accumulated depreciation and impairment losses. Also referred to as book value.

Cost

The amount paid and the fair value of other consideration given to acquire an asset at the time of its acquisition or construction.

Depreciable amount

The cost or valuation of an asset less its residual value.

Depreciation

The systematic allocation of the depreciable amount of an asset over its useful life.

Fair value

The amount for which an asset can be exchanged between knowledgeable, willing parties in an arm's length transaction.

Impairment loss

The amount by which the carrying amount exceeds its recoverable amount.

Recoverable amount

The higher of an asset's net realisable value and its value in use.

Residual value

The residual value of an asset is the amount that the entity would currently obtain from disposal of the asset, after deducting the estimated costs of disposal, assuming that the asset was already at the point where it would be disposed of (using the age and condition that would be assumed to apply at the time of disposal).

Useful life

IAS 16 defines useful life as the period over which the asset is expected to be available for use by the entity or the volume of output expected from the asset.

Initial recognition

Property, plant and equipment should be recognised as an asset when:

- it is probable that future economic benefits will flow to the entity;
- the cost of the asset can be measured reliably.

The asset should initially be measured at its cost. This should include:

- its purchase price;
- directly attributable costs to bring the asset to the location and condition necessary for it to be capable of operating for its intended use, i.e. site preparation, initial delivery costs, installation costs, testing costs, professional fees;
- the initial estimate of the cost of dismantling and removing the item and restoring the site, where there is an obligation to incur such costs.

The cost of a self-constructed asset is determined using the same principles.

Subsequent expenditure

Subsequent expenditure should be capitalised when:

- the expenditure improves the future economic benefits that the asset will generate;
- replaces a component of an asset and the carrying amount of the component replaced is derecognised;
- it is the cost of a major inspection for faults and the carrying amount of the previous inspection is derecognised.

The costs of day-to-day servicing should be recognised in the income statement as incurred.

Measurement after initial recognition

IAS 16 requires that entities either apply to cost model or the revaluation model

Cost Model	Revaluation Model
Book value = Cost	Book value = Fair Value
Less: Accumulated depreciation	Less: Accumulated depreciation
Less: Accumulated impairment losses	Less: Accumulated impairment losses
	• Revaluation shall be carried out with 'sufficient regularity'
	• Where an item is revalued, all items in the same class should be revalued

Depreciation

Depreciation is the systematic allocation of the depreciable amount of an asset over its useful life.

Depreciable amount is the cost/valuation less residual value.

The depreciation charge should be recognised in the income statement unless it is included in the carrying amount of an asset, e.g. depreciation on equipment used for development activities.

Land will not be depreciated since it has an unlimited life. Buildings, however, do have a limited life and so should be depreciated. Therefore, if we are given a total for land and buildings we must remember to remove the land element from the total **before** we calculate the depreciation on the building. For example, total for land and buildings amounts to $100,000.

This includes land at cost of $20,000. Buildings should be depreciated at 10% on a straight line basis. The depreciation would be calculated as ($100,000 - $20,000) x 10% = $8,000 pa.

Repair and maintenance does not negate the need to depreciate the asset.

If the residual value is greater than the carrying value, the depreciation charge is zero.

How do we calculate depreciation?

Depreciation can be calculated using the straight line or the reducing balance method.

The straight line method is based on cost and will be calculated as a % of cost. Each year the depreciation charge will be the same. However, if the % is not given in the examination it can be calculated as:

Cost – residual value
useful economic life

Residual value is the amount the entity would expect to receive from disposal of the asset.

The reducing balance method is based on the carrying value of the asset (NBV). This is usually expressed as a %.

Once the depreciation is calculated the double entry will be:

Dr Depreciation expense (IS)
Cr Accumulative depreciation (SOFP)

Changes in depreciation method

Depreciation methods should be reviewed periodically. If it is decided that there has been a change in the pattern of consumption of benefits, the depreciation method should be changed to reflect this, e.g. a change from the straight line method to the reducing balance method.

Any change in the depreciation method should be treated as a change in accounting estimate and so the new method should be applied in the current and future accounting periods. Changes in depreciation methods do not represent a change in accounting policy and so depreciation charges of earlier periods should not be altered.

Illustration 1 : Changes in depreciation method

An asset was purchased two years ago for $100,000. At this time the directors estimated that the useful life was ten years and that the residual value was $10,700. The directors chose to depreciate the asset using the reducing balance method and so used a rate of 20% per annum. The directors have decided that a fairer presentation would be given if the depreciation method was changed to the straight line basis and will implement the new depreciation method in the year ended 30 June 2011.

> Calculate the depreciation charge for the year ended 30 June 2011 in respect of this asset.

Solution

The original depreciation was:

Year 1 = Cost $100,000 x 20% = $20,000

Year 2 = CV $80,000($100,000 – $20,000) x 20% = $16,000

The asset has been depreciated for 2 years when the change of depreciation method occurs and therefore CV would be:

Cost $100,000 – ($20,000 + $16,000) = $64,000

The CV at the date of the change is the carrying value on the statement of financial position for the asset and must therefore be used to recalculate the new depreciation charge.

$$\frac{CV - \text{residual value}}{\text{Remaining useful economic life}} = \frac{\$64,000 - \$10,700}{8} = \$6,663 \text{ pa}$$

Test your understanding 1 : Changes in depreciation methods

An asset was purchased two years ago for $150,000. At this time the directors estimated that the useful life was ten years and that the residual value was $8,500. The directors chose to depreciate the asset using the reducing balance method and so used a rate of 25% per annum. The carrying value of the asset at 30 June 2010 was therefore $84,375. The directors have decided that a fairer presentation would be given if the depreciation method was changed to the straight line basis and will implement the new depreciation method in the year ended 30 June 2011.

Calculate the depreciation charge for the year ended 30 June 2011 in respect of this asset.

Changes in useful life and residual value

On acquiring an asset, its useful life and residual value will be estimated. Subsequently, it may be appropriate to revise these estimates.

Again, any change in the useful life or residual value will result in adjustments to the depreciation charge for current and future periods but no changes should be made to past accounting periods, i.e. it is a change in accounting estimate.

Illustration 2 : Changes in useful life

An asset was purchased three years ago for $50,000 at which time it was thought that the asset had a residual value of $5,000 and a useful economic life of ten years. The directors have decided that as a result of using the asset more than was originally planned the remaining useful economic life is only five years as at 1 July 2010. Their estimate of residual value has remained unchanged. The asset is depreciated on the straight line basis.

Calculate the depreciation charge for the year ended 30 June 2011 in respect of this asset.

Solution

The original depreciation was:

$$\frac{\text{Cost} - \text{residual value}}{\text{Useful economic life}} = \frac{\$50,000 - \$5,000}{10} = \$4,500 \text{ pa}$$

The asset has been depreciated for 3 years when the change of UEL life occurs and therefore CV would be:

Cost $50,000 – (3 x $4,500) = $36,500

The CV at the date of the change is the carrying value on the statement of financial position for the asset and must therefore be used to recalculate the new depreciation charge.

$$\frac{\text{CV} - \text{residual value}}{\text{Useful economic life}} = \frac{\$36,500 - \$5,000}{5} = \$6,300 \text{ pa}$$

Test your understanding 2 : Changes in useful life of an asset

An asset was purchased on 1 July 2006 for $75,000 at which time it was thought that the asset had a residual value of $5,000 and a useful economic life of seven years. The directors have decided that as a result of not using the asset as much as was originally planned the remaining useful economic life is ten years as at 1 July 2010. Their estimate of residual value has remained unchanged. The asset is depreciated on the straight line basis.

Calculate the depreciation charge for the year ended 30 June 2011 in respect of this asset.

3 Revaluations

IAS 16 allows the treatment of assets to be shown at their revalued amount less accumulated depreciation and accumulated impairment losses.

The revalued amount of an asset is the asset's fair value at the date of revaluation.

Fair value of assets is usually the market value.

If an asset is revalued, any accumulated depreciation at the date of the revaluation should be written off to the revaluation reserve.

Depreciation will then be calculated based on the revalued amount.

Revaluations must be made for the whole of the class of assets, i.e. if we revalue one building we must revalue the whole of the class of buildings at the same time.

The frequency of revaluations will depend upon the volatitlity of the fair values, the more volatile, the more frequent the revaluation.

Revaluations must be carried out by a professionally qualified valuer.

Steps to account for a revaluation:

(1) Restate asset cost to the revalued amount.

(2) Remove any existing accumulated depreciation provision.

(3) Transfer the increase in the cost account and the depreciation provision to the revaluation reserve.

(4) Recalculate current years depreciation on the revalued amount if applicable.

Accounting entries:

Dr Asset Cost (revalued amount – original cost)

Dr Accumulated depreciation (depreciation up to the revaluation date)

Cr Revaluation Reserve (revalued amount – previous CV)

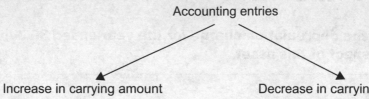

Accounting entries

Increase in carrying amount	Decrease in carrying amount
Dr Asset	Dr Revaluation reserve
Cr Revaluation reserve	Dr Expense
	Cr Asset
The revaluation reserve may be transferred to retained earnings as the asset is used	The revaluation reserve must exist in relation to the same asset, in order to Dr Revaluation reserve
Dr Revaluation reserve	
Cr Retained earnings	
Any remaining surplus when the asset is disposed, may be transferred to retained earnings	

e.g

Illustration 3 : Revaluations

An asset has a carrying value of $30,000. It is subsequently revalued to:

Year 1	$40,000
Year 2	$33,000
Year 3	$24,000

Show how each of the gains or losses will be recorded against the revaluation surplus or the income statement.

Solution

Year 1

The asset has increased in value from $30,000 to $40,000

Dr Asset	$10,000
Cr Revaluation Reserve	$10,000

Year 2

The asset has decreased in value from $40,000 to $33,000. This decrease can charged against the revaluation reserve because the reserve already has $10,000 in it from year 1 for that particular asset.

Dr Revaluation Reserve	$7,000
Cr Asset	$7,000

Year 3

The asset has decreased in value from $33,000 to $24,000. The decrease cannot all be charged against the revaluation reserve because there is only $3,000 left after year 2 for that particular asset. The reserve is reduced to nil and then the balance of the decrease is charged against profits in the IS.

Dr Revaluation Reserve	$3,000
Dr Income statement	$6,000
Cr Asset	$9,000

Illustration 4 : Revaluations

Asset A has a carrying value of $20,000 and is revalued to $25,000.

Asset B has a carrying value of $20,000 and is revalued to $17,000.

Show how each of the gains or losses will be recorded against the revaluation surplus or the income statement.

Solution

Asset A

This asset increases in value from $20,000 to $25,000. The increase is credited to the revaluation reserve.

Dr Asset	$5,000
Cr Revaluation Reserve	$5,000

Asset B

The asset decreases in value from $20,000 to $17,000. The decrease is charged against profits in IS. This asset is has not been revalued in the past and therefore does not have a revaluation reserve you can use. You cannot use the reserve from Asset A.

Dr Income statement	$3,000
Cr Asset	$3,000

Note: The revaluation reserve relates to asset A. Therefore, only future downward valuations of asset A can be set against the revaluation reserve.

Test your understanding 3 : Revaluations

Building A was purchased on 01/01/03 costing $50,000. It has a useful economic life of 50 years and no residual value.

Building B was purchased on 01/01/03 costing $100,000. It has a useful economic life of 40 years and no residual value.

The company has a policy to revalue its assets every four years and has done so as follows:

Building A

Valuation at 31/12/06 $69,000

Valuation at 31/12/10 $84,000

> ### Building B
>
> Valuation at 31/12/06 $108,000
>
> Valuation at 31/12/10 $64,000
>
> **Show how the revaluations will be recorded, clearly showing the carrying value of the assets at 31/12/11.**

Retirement and disposals

An item of property, plant and equipment should be eliminated from the statement of financial position on disposal or when the asset is permanently withdrawn from use.

Gain/(loss) on retirement/disposal = Net disposal proceeds − Carrying value

Gains or losses on retirement/disposal should be recorded in the income statement.

Disposals of revalued assets

When a previously revalued asset is disposed of the gain on disposal is measured as the difference between the carrying value on the SOFP and the proceeds received.

However, if the asset has been revalued in the past it was have an unrealised gain in the revaluation reserve that must now be removed.

The amount should be transferred from the revaluation reserve to retained earnings. This movement will be seen in the SOCIE and will not effect this years profit.

Release of the revaluation reserve

When an asset is revalued the amount will be credited to the revaluation reserve.

An annual release of the reserve may be made (revaluation reserve to retained earnings) which represents the extra depreciation on the revalued amount compared to cost.

Accounting entries:

Dr Revaluation reserve (depreciation on revaluation - depreciation on original cost)

Cr Retained earnings

This would mean the **unrealised gain** on revaluation would gradually be released into profits over the assets life.

You would **not** be required to do this in this examination unless the examiner specifies.

Illustration 5 : Disposal of a revalued asset

Taker's Ltd originally purchased a piece of land on 01/01/07 for $100,000. On the 31/12/08 the land was revalued to $150,000.

The land was sold for $180,000 on 31/12/11.

Calculate the profit or loss on disposal to be shown in the income statement and any revaluation adjustments that need to be made.

Solution

When the land was revalued the entries would be made as follows:

This asset increases in value from $100,000 to $150,000. The increase is credited to the revaluation reserve.

Dr Asset	$50,000
Cr Revaluation reserve	$50,000

When the asset was sold the carrying value was $150,000.

The gain on disposal to the statement of comprehensive income would be $30,000 ($180,000 - $150,000)

The revaluation reserve for the land would now be released into profits as the gain is now realised.

Dr Revaluation reserve	$50,000
Cr Retained earnings	$50,000

This would be shown on the SOCIE.

Disclosure

IAS 16 requires the following disclosure requirements:

For each class of property, plant and equipment

- measurement bases, i.e. cost or valuation;
- depreciation methods with useful life or depreciation rate;
- gross carrying value and accumulated depreciation at the beginning and end of the period;
- reconciliation of additions, disposals, revaluations, impairments and depreciation;
- when assets have been revalued:
    - basis of valuation;
    - date of valuation;
    - whether an independent valuer was used;
    - carrying value if no revaluation had taken place;
    - revaluation surplus.

Property, plant and equipment (PPE)

The property, plant and equipment note (IAS 16) shows the movements in the year for each category of asset.

	Land and buildings	Plant and equipment	Vehicles	Total
	$000	$000	$000	$000
Cost/Valuation				
At 1 January 2010	X	X	X	X
Additions	X	X	X	X
Surplus on revaluations	X			
Disposals	(X)	(X)	(X)	(X)
At 31 December 2010	X	X	X	X

Accumulated Depreciation:

At 1 January 2010	X	X	X	X
Charged during the year	X	X	X	X
Revaluations	(X)	-	-	(X)
Disposals	(X)	(X)	(X)	(X)
At 31 December 2010	X	X	X	X

Carrying value

At 1 January 2010	X	X	X	X
At 31 December 2010	X	X	X	X

Test your understanding 4 : Revaluations

A building was purchased many years ago for $200,000. It has been depreciated at 2% per annum (50 year life)on the straight line basis and the carrying value of the asset at 1 July 2010 is $132,000. The directors have had the asset valued at $750,000 and would like to incorporate this valuation into the financial statements for the year ended 30 June 2011.

Prepare a non-current asset note for the year ended 30 June 2011 and calculate the revaluation surplus assuming that:

(a) **the valuation is as at 1 July 2010;**

(b) **the valuation is as at 30 June 2011.**

4 IAS 23 Borrowing Costs

Definition

Borrowing costs are interest and other costs incurred by an enterprise in connection with the borrowing of funds.

Treatment

Borrowing costs that are directly attributable to the acquisition or construction of a qualifying asset should be capitalised as part of the cost of that asset. All other borrowing costs should be recognised as an expense in the period in which they are incurred, ie. finance cost.

Dr Asset (SOFP)

Cr Bank (SOFP)

A qualifying asset is defined as being an asset that necessarily takes a substantial period of time to get ready for its intended use.

Under this treatment, capitalisation of the borrowing costs will commence when expenditure on the asset and the borrowing costs are being incurred. Capitalisation must cease when substantially all the activities necessary to prepare the asset for use are complete.

Disclosure

IAS 23 requires the following disclosure requirements:

- The borrowing costs capitalised in the period;
- The capitalisation rate used.

IAS 23 states borrowing costs must be **capitalised** as part of the cost of the asset, provided the asset is a qualifying asset.

Illustration 6 : Borrowing costs

On 01/01/10 Aseco began to construct a supermarket which has an estimated useful life of 40 years. They constructed a building at a cost of $25 million and fixtures and fittings at a cost of $9 million. In addition they had to pay legal costs amounting to $1 million. The construction of the supermarket was completed on 30/09/10 and brought into use on 01/01/11.

In order to complete this project Aseco had to borrow $20 million on 01/01/10. The loan carried interest at 10%. It was repaid on 30/06/11 after a successful six months of operation.

Calculate the total amount that can be capitalised as cost for property, plant and equipment in respect of this development for the year ending 31/12/10.

Solution

The total amount that can be capitalised in property, plant and equipment at 31/12/10 is:

	$
Building and lease	25,000,000
Fixtures and fittings	9,000,000
Legal costs	1,000,000
Interest capitalised ($20,000,000 x 10% x 9/12)	1,500,000
	36,500,000

5 IAS 38 Intangible Assets

Definition

An intangible asset is an identifiable non-monetary asset without physical substance. An asset is identifiable if:

- it is separate;

- arrives from contractual or other legal rights.

Recognition

An intangible asset should be recognised only if:

- it is probable that the future economic benefits that are attributable to the asset will flow to the enterprise; and

- the cost of the asset can be measured reliably.

An intangible asset should initially be measured at cost.

The cost should include the purchase price plus any directly attributable costs of preparing the asset for its intended use.

Recognition and measurement

An intangible asset purchased separately from a business should be capitalised at cost.

Where an intangible asset is acquired when a business is bought, it should be capitalised separately from purchased goodwill, provided that it can be measured reliably on initial recognition. Cost being the fair value of the asset.

If the fair value of an intangible asset purchased as a part of the acquisition of a business cannot be measured reliably, it should not be recognised and will be included within goodwill.

The cost of an intangible asset is measured in the same way as a tangible non-current asset. The cost of an intangible asset comprises:

- its purchase price, including import duties and non-refundable purchase taxes, after deducting trade discounts and rebates;

- any directly attributable cost of preparing the asset for its intended use.

Examples of directly attributable costs are:

- costs of employee benefits arising directly from bringing the asset to its working condition;
- professional fees.

Examples of costs that are not a cost of an intangible asset are:

- costs of introducing a new product or service (including costs of advertising and promotional activities);
- costs of conducting business in a new location or with a new class of customer (including costs of staff training);
- administration and other general overhead costs.

Previously, we considered the 'Framework' and its definition of an asset: 'an asset is a resource controlled by the entity as a result of past events and from which future economic benefits are expected to flow to the entity'. To be recognised as an intangible asset, expenditure must give access to future economic benefits.

The management of the entity must consider the economic conditions that exist and are likely to exist over the useful life of the asset, and then assess the probability of future economic benefits. The assessment should be management's best estimate using all the evidence available, giving greater weight to external evidence. The asset should be measured initially at cost and amortised over its useful life.

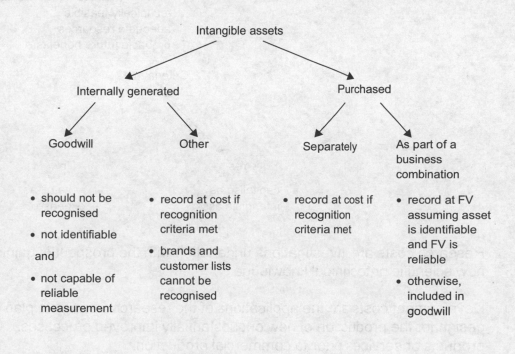

Intangible assets

Internally generated

Purchased

Goodwill

- should not be recognised
- not identifiable

and

- not capable of reliable measurement

Other

- record at cost if recognition criteria met
- brands and customer lists cannot be recognised

Separately

- record at cost if recognition criteria met

As part of a business combination

- record at FV assuming asset is identifiable and FV is reliable
- otherwise, included in goodwill

Internally-generated intangibles

The following internally-generated intangibles may never be recognised:

- goodwill
- brands
- publishing titles
- customer lists

Purchased intangibles

Recognition of intangibles at cost, which could be cash or the fair value of shares given in exchange

Research and development

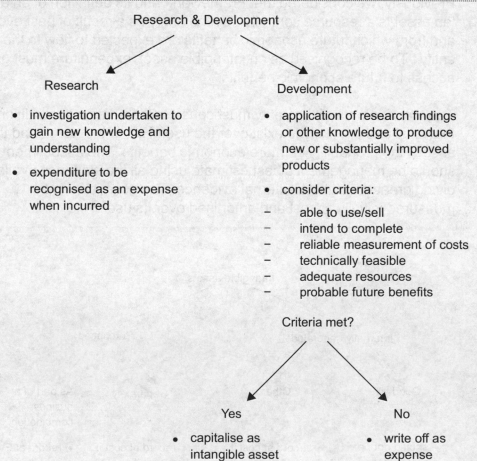

Research & Development

Research

- investigation undertaken to gain new knowledge and understanding
- expenditure to be recognised as an expense when incurred

Development

- application of research findings or other knowledge to produce new or substantially improved products
- consider criteria:
  - able to use/sell
  - intend to complete
  - reliable measurement of costs
  - technically feasible
  - adequate resources
  - probable future benefits

Criteria met?

Yes
- capitalise as intangible asset

No
- write off as expense

Research costs are investigations undertaken with the prospect of gaining new scientific or technical knowledge.

Development costs are the applications of the research findings to plan or design for the production of new or substantially improved processes, products or services prior to commercial production.

Amortisation

Intangible assets with a finite life should be amortised over that life.

Amortisation should begin when the asset is available for use.

Intangible assets are regarded as having an indefinite life if there is no foreseeable limit to the period over which the asset is expected to generate net cash inflows for the entity.

An intangible asset with an indefinite life is not amortised but instead is subject to annual impairment reviews.

Amortisation

The depreciable amount of an intangible asset should be allocated on a systematic basis over the best estimate of its useful life. Amortisation should start from the date the asset is available for use.

As with tangible assets, the most difficult decision for management is determining the useful life of the asset. The useful life of an intangible asset should take account of such things as:

- the expected usage of the asset;

- possible obsolescence and expected actions by competitors;

- the stability of the industry;

- market demand for the products and services that the asset is generating.

The method of amortising the asset should reflect the pattern in which the assets' economic benefits are expected to be consumed by the entity. If that proves difficult to determine, then the straight-line method is acceptable. The residual value of the intangible should be assumed to be zero unless there is a commitment from a third party to purchase the asset or the entity intends to sell the asset and a readily available active market exists. The annual amortisation amount will be charged to profit or loss as an expense.

The useful life and method of amortisation should be reviewed at least at each financial year-end. Changes to useful life or method of amortisation should be effective as soon as they are identified and should be accounted for as changes in accounting estimates (IAS 8), by adjusting the amortisation charge for the current and future periods.

Revaluations

Intangible assets may be revalued to their fair value. The fair value should be determined by an active market.

An active market exists where all of the following conditions are met:

- items traded in the market are homogenous;
- willing buyers and sellers can be found at any time;
- prices are available to the public.

IAS 38 states it is 'uncommon' for an active market to exist for intangible assets.

Disclosure

IAS 38 requires the following disclosure requirements:

For each class of intangible assets:

- The useful lives or amortisation rates used;
- The amortisation methods used;
- The gross carrying amount and accumulated amortisation at the beginning and end of the period;
- The amount of amortisation charged for the period to the comprehensive income statement;
- A reconciliation between the beginning and end of the year balances, i.e. additions, disposals, changes due to impairments or revaluations, amortisation during the period.

Illustration 7 : Research and development

CD is a manufacturing entity that runs a number of operations including a bottling plant that bottles carbonated soft drinks. CD has been developing a new bottling process that will allow the bottles to be filled and sealed more efficiently.

The new process took a year to develop. At the start of development, CD estimated that the new process would increase output by 15% with no additional cost (other than the extra bottles and their contents). Development work commenced on 1 May 2010 and was completed on 20 April 2011. Testing at the end of the development confirmed CD's original estimates.

CD incurred an expenditure of $180,000 on the above development in 2010/11.

CD plans to install the new process in its bottling plant and start operating the new process from 1 May 2011.

The end of CD's reporting period is 30 April.

Required:

(a) Explain the requirements of IAS 38 Intangible Assets for the treatment of development costs.

(b) Explain how CD should treat its development costs in its financial statements for the year ended 30 April 2011.

Solution

(a) Development expenditure can only be regarded as an intangible if it meets the criteria of IAS 38. If the criteria is not met the cost must be written off as an expense to the statement of comprehensive income. The criteria the standard requires to be met to captialise the cost is as follows:

- the technical feasibility of completing the intangible asset so that it can be used or sold;

- the intention to complete the asset to use it or sell it;

- the ability to use or sell the asset;

- that the asset will in fact generate probable future economic benefit – does a market exist for the asset if it is to be sold, or can the asset's usefulness be proven if the asset is to be used internally;

- that it has the technical, financial and other resources to complete the project to make and use or sell the asset;

- that it can measure the expenditure on the development of the asset reliably in order to incorporate the amount in the financial statements.

(b) All of the above criteria seem to have been met by CD's new process:

- it is technically feasible, it has been tested and is about to be implemented;

- it has been completed and CD intends to use it;

- the new process is estimated to increase output by 15% with no additional costs other than direct material costs;

- the expenditure can be measured as the figures have been given.

CD will treat the $180,000 development cost as an intangible non-current asset in its statement of financial position at 30 April 2011. Amortisation will start from 1 May 2011 when the new process starts operation.

Test your understanding 5 : Research and development

An company has incurred the following expenditure during the current year:

(a) $100,000 spent on the design of a new product – it is anticipated that this design will be taken forward over the next two year period to be developed and tested with a view to production in three years time.

(b) $500,000 spent on the testing of a new production system which has been designed internally and which will be in operation during the following accounting year. This new system should reduce the cost of production by 20%.

How should these costs be treated in the financial statements of the company?

6 IAS 36 Impairment Of Assets

An impairment loss is the amount by which the carrying value of an asset exceeds its recoverable amount.

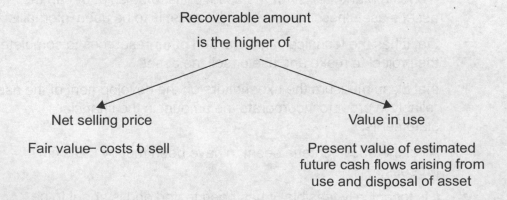

Recoverable amount
is the higher of

Net selling price

Fair value– costs b sell

Value in use

Present value of estimated future cash flows arising from use and disposal of asset

An enterprise should assess at each reporting date whether there is any indication that an asset may be impaired. If such indications exist, the recoverable amount should be estimated, i.e. an impairment review should be carried out. If no such indications exist, it is not necessary to carry out an impairment review.

The following situations may indicate that an asset has been impaired:

- decline in market value;
- technological, legal or economic changes;
- physical damage;
- plans to dispose of asset.

Proceedures to check for impairment

At the end of each reporting period an entity should assess whether there are internal or external indications that the value of any asset is impaired.

In assessing whether there is any indication that an asset may be impaired, an entity shall consider, as a minimum, the following indications:

External sources of information:

- during the period, an asset's market value has declined significantly more than would be expected as a result of the passage of time or normal use;
- significant changes with an adverse effect on the entity have taken place during the period, or will take place in the near future, in the technological, market, economic or legal environment in which the entity operates or in the market to which an asset is dedicated;
- market interest rates or other market rates of return on investments have increased during the period, and those increases are likely to affect the discount rate used in calculating an asset's value in use and decrease the asset's recoverable amount materially;
- the carrying amount of the net assets of the reporting entity is more than its market capitalisation.

Internal sources of information:

- evidence is available of obsolescence or physical damage of an asset;
- significant changes with an adverse effect on the entity have taken place during the period, or are expected to take place in the near future, in the extent to which, or manner in which, an asset is used or is expected to be used. These changes include the asset becoming idle, plans to discontinue or restructure the operation to which an asset belongs, and plans to dispose of an asset before the previously expected date;

> • evidence is available from internal reporting that indicates that the economic performance of an asset is, or will be, worse than expected.

Recognition and measurement of an impairment loss

When the recoverable amount of an asset is below its carrying value, the difference is an impairment loss and must be recorded.

An impairment loss should be recorded as an expense in the income statement, unless the asset has previously been revalued, in which case the impairment can be offset against the revaluation surplus.

Disclosure

For each class of assets, the financial statements should disclose:

• The amount of impairment losses recognised in the statement of comprehensive income during the period and the line item(s) of the statement of comprehensive income in which those impairment losses are included;

• The amount of reversals of impairment losses recognised in the statement of comprehensive income during the period and the line item (s) of the statement of comprehensive income in which those impairment losses are reversed;

• The amount of impairment losses recognised in other comprehensive income during the period;

• The amount of reversals of impairment losses recognised in other comprehensive income during the period.

Illustration 8 : Impairment

The following information relates to three assets held by a company:

	A	B	C
Carrying Value	200	200	200
Net Selling Price	220	125	140
Value in use	160	150	190

Calculate the impairment losses, if any, in respect of the three assets.

Solution

	A	B	C
Recoverable amount (higher of net selling price and value in use)	220	150	190
Carrying value	200	200	200
Impairment	No	(50)	(10)

Test your understanding 6 : Impairment

The following information relates to three assets held by a company:

	A	B	C
Carrying Value	200	200	200
Net Selling Price	250	175	160
Value in use	180	150	180

Calculate the impairment losses, if any, in respect of the three assets.

Disclosure

IAS 36 requires the following disclosure requirements:

For each class of property, plant and equipment:

- The amount of impairment losses recognised in the income statement during the period and where it has been included, i.e. which expense category:

- The amount of reversals for impairment losses recognised in the income statement during the period and where it has been included;

- The amount of impairment losses recognised directly in equity during the period;

- The amount of reversals of impairment losses recognised directly in equity during the period.

Test your understanding 7 : Objective test questions

(1) Cowper plc have spent $20,000 researching new cleaning chemicals in the year ended 31 December 2010. They have also spent $40,000 developing a new cleaning product which will not go into commercial production until next year. The development project meets the criteria laid down in IAS 38 Intangible Assets.

How should these costs be treated in the financial statements of Cowper plc for the year ended 31 December 2010?

A $60,000 should be capitalised as an intangible asset on the SOFP.

B $40,000 should be capitalised as an intangible asset and should be amortised; $20,000 should be written off to the income statement

C $40,000 should be capitalised as an intangible asset and should not be amortised; $20,000 should be written off to the income statement

D $60,000 should be written off to the income statement

(2) A company purchased a property 15 years ago at a cost of $100,000 and have been depreciating it at a rate of 2% per annum, on the straight line basis. The company have had the property professionally revalued at $500,000.

What is the revaluation surplus that will be recorded in the financial statements in respect of this property?

A $400,000

B $500,000

C $530,000

D $430,000

(3) A company owns two buildings, A and B, which are currently recorded in the books at carrying values of $170,000 and $330,000 respectively. Both buildings have recently been valued as follows:

Building A $400,000

Building B $250,000

The company currently has a balance on the revaluation reserve of $50,000 which arose when building A was revalued several years ago. Building B has never been revalued in the past.

What double entry will need to be made to record the revaluations of buildings A and B?

A	Dr	Non-current assets	$150,000
	Dr	Income statement	$80,000
	Cr	Revaluation reserve	$230,000
B	Dr	Non-current assets	$150,000
	Dr	Income statement	$30,000
	Cr	Revaluation reserve	$180,000
C	Dr	Non-current assets	$150,000
	Cr	Revaluation reserve	$150,000
D	Dr	Non-current assets	$150,000
	Dr	Income statement	$50,000
	Cr	Revaluation reserve	$200,000

(4) The following information relates to three assets held by a company:

	Asset A	Asset B	Asset C
	$	$	$
Carrying value	100	50	40
Value in use	80	60	35
Fair value less cost to sell	90	65	30

What is the total impairment loss?

A $15

B $30

C $Nil

D $1

(5) On 1 April 2010 Slow and Steady Ltd showed non-current assets that had cost $312,000 and accumulated depreciation of $66,000. During the year ended 31 March 2011, Slow and Steady Ltd disposed of non-current assets which had cost originally $28,000 and had a carrying value of $11,200.

The company policy is to charge depreciation of 40% on the reducing balance basis, with no depreciation in the year of disposal of an asset.

What is the company charge to the income statement for the year ended 31 March 2011?

A $113,600

B $98,400

C $93,920

D $87,200

(6) A building contractor decides to build an office building, to be occupied by his own staff. Tangible non-current assets are initially measured at cost. **Which of the following expenses incurred by the building contractor cannot be included as a part of the cost of the office building?**

A   Interest incurred on a specific loan taken out to pay for the construction of the new offices

B   Direct building labour costs

C   A proportion of the contractor's general administration costs

D   Hire of plant and machinery for use on the office building site

(7) **The purpose of depreciation is to:**

A   Allocate the cost less residual value on a systematic basis over the asset's useful economic life

B   Write the asset down to its market value each period

C   Charge profits for the use of the asset

D   Recognise that assets lose value over time

(8) **Which of the following tangible non-current assets are NOT usually depreciated:**

A   Machinery purchased through a finance lease

B   Land

C   Buildings with a life in excess of 30 years

D   Vehicles

(9) Plant and machinery, costing $50,000, was purchased on 1 April 2008. This was depreciated for 2 years at 20 per cent using the reducing balance method. On 1 April 2010, the machinery (original cost $25,000) was sold for $12,000. Replacement machines were acquired on the same date for $34,000. **What was the carrying value of plant and machinery at March 2011?**

(10) Roming purchased property costing $440,000 on 1 January 2007. The property is being depreciated over 50 years on a straight-line basis. The property was revalued on 1 January 2011 at $520,000. The useful life was also reviewed at that date and is estimated to be a further 40 years.

Prepare the accounting entries to record the revaluation and calculate the depreciation charge that will apply from 1 January 2011.

7 Summary diagram

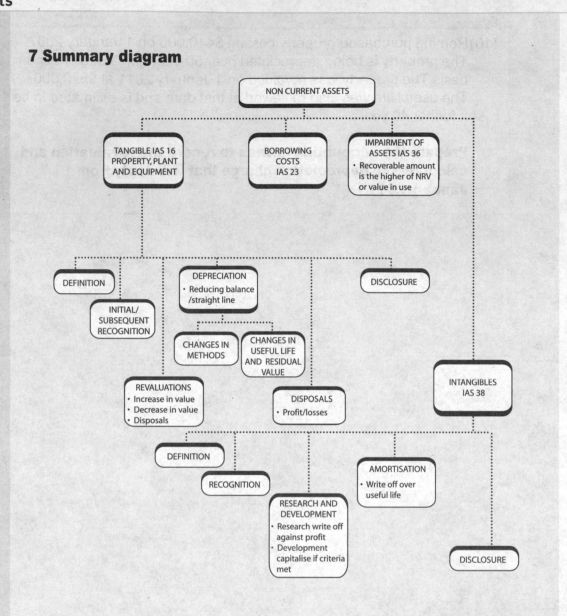

Test your understanding answers

Test your understanding 1 : Changes in depreciation methods

New method: Straight line basis

$$\frac{\text{NBV less RV}}{\text{Remaining UEL}} \quad \frac{\$64,000 - \$10,700}{10 - 2\text{years}} = \$6,662.50 \text{ p.a.}$$

The original depreciation was:

Year 1 = Cost $150,000 x 25% = $37,500

Year 2 = CV $112,500($150,000 – $37,500) x 25% = $28,125

The asset has been depreciated for 2 years when the change of depreciation method occurs and therefore CV would be:

Cost $150,000 – ($37,500 + $28,125) = $84,375

The CV at the date of the change is the carrying value on the statement of financial position for the asset and must therefore be used to recalculate the new depreciation charge.

$$\frac{\text{CV} - \text{residual value}}{\text{Remaining useful economic life}} = \frac{\$84,375 - \$8,500}{8} = \$9,484 \text{ pa}$$

Test your understanding 2 : Changes in useful life of an asset

Revised UEL

$$\frac{\text{NBV less RV}}{\text{New UEL}} \quad \frac{\$35,000^* - \$5,000}{10} = \$3,000 \text{ p.a.}$$

*NBV ($75,000 less four years of dep'n @ $10,000 pa).

Test your understanding 3 : Revaluations

Asset A

Depreciation is $1,000 pa ($50,000/50)

After 4 years (31/12/06) the CV will be $46,000 ($50,000 – $4,000)

This asset increases in value from $46,000 to $69,000. The increase is credited to the revaluation reserve.

Dr Asset	$23,000
Cr Revaluation Reserve	$23,000

The depreciation must now be recalculated on the revalued amount for the remaining life of 46 years.

Depreciation is $1,500 pa ($69,000/46)

After 4 years (31/12/10) the CV will be $63,000 ($69,000 – $6,000)

This asset increases in value from $63,000 to $84,000. The increase is credited to the revaluation reserve.

Dr Asset	$21,000
Cr Revaluation Reserve	$21,000

The depreciation must now be recalculated on the revalued amount for the remaining life of 42 years.

Depreciation is $2,000 pa ($84,000/42)

The carrying value at 31/12/11 will be:

$84,000 – $2,000 = $82,000

Asset B

Depreciation is $2,500 pa ($100,000/40)

After 4 years (31/12/06) the CV will be $90,000 ($100,000 – $10,000)

This asset increases in value from $90,000 to $108,000. The increase is credited to the revaluation reserve.

Dr Asset	$18,000
Cr Revaluation Reserve	$18,000

The depreciation must now be recalculated on the revalued amount for the remaining life of 36 years.

Depreciation is $3,000 pa ($108,000/36)

After 4 years (31/12/10) the CV will be $96,000 ($108,000 – $12,000)

This asset decreases in value from $96,000 to $64,000. The decrease is charged to the revaluation reserve to reduce it to nil and the balance is charged against profits.

Dr Revaluation Reserve	$18,000
Dr Income Statement	$14,000
Cr Asset	$32,000

Note: The revaluation reserve for building A cannot be used for the reduction in value of building B.

The depreciation must now be recalculated on the revalued amount for the remaining life of 32 years.

Depreciation is $2,000 pa ($64,000/32)

The carrying value at 31/12/11 will be:

$64,000 – $2,000 = $62,000

	(a)	(b)
Non-current asset note	$	$
Cost/Valuation		
At 1 July 2010	200	200
Revaluation	550	550
At 30 June 2011	750	750
Acc Dep'n		
At 1 July 2010 (200-132)	68	68
Charge for year	23	4
Revaluation	(68)	(72)
At 30 June 2011	23	0
Carrying amount		
At 1 July 2010	132	132
At 30 June 2011	727	750
Revaluation surplus	618	622
	(750 – 132)	(750 –128)

If the revaluation takes place at the beginning of the year, the current years depreciation charge should be based on the revalued amount. The depreciation charge was based on 2% of cost, ie. $4,000 pa. If the carrying value b/fwd is $132,000, it must mean we have already utilised the asset for 17 years ($4,000 x 17 = $68,000 depreciation to date). When the asset is revalued we must now depreciate the revalued amount over the remaining life of 33 years (50 - 17). This will result in the current years depreciation charge of $22,727 ($750,000/33), rounded to $23.

If the revaluation takes place at the end of the year, the current years depreciation should be based on the original amount, ie. $200,000 x 2%. The total depreciation to date will then be removed from the books and transferred to the revaluation reserve, ie. $68,000 + $4,000.

Test your understanding 5 : Research and development

(a) These costs are research costs and must be written off to the IS for the period.

(b) These appear to be development costs that meet the capitalisation criteria, i.e. expect to complete, will produce economic benefits, etc. Therefore these costs should be capitalised as an intangible asset on the SOFP. Amortisation will not begin until production starts.

Test your understanding 6 : Impairment

	A	B	C
Recoverable amount	250	175	180
Carrying value	200	200	200
Impairment	No	(25)	(20)

NB: Recoverable amount is the higher of the net selling price and value in use.

Test your understanding 7 : Objective test questions

(1) C

(2) D

Current value	500,000
CV at date of revaluation (100,000 – (100,000 × 2% × 15yrs))	(70,000)
Revaluation gain	430,000

(3) A

	Building A	Building B
Current value	400,000	250,000
CV	(170,000)	(330,000)
Revaluation gain/loss	230,000	(80,000)

The gain on Building A will be credited to the revaluation reserve.

The loss on Building B will be debited to the income statement expenses because we do not have a balance on the revaluation reserve in respect of building B to net the loss off against.

We make an overall Dr to fixed assets is $230,000 – $80,000 = $150,000

(4) A

	Asset A $	Asset B $	Asset C $
Carrying value	100	50	40
Value in use	80	60	35
Fair value less cost to sell	90	65	30
Valued at higher of value in use/fair value	90	65	35
Impairment	10	Nil	5

Total Impairment = $15

(5) C

Carrying value at 1 April 2010 ($312,000 – $66,000)	$246,000
Carrying value of disposal	($11,200)
Carrying value at 31 March 2011	$234,800
Depreciation at 40%	$93,920

(6) C

Direct costs relating to the asset can be included such as labour costs, interest on loans to acquire the asset and hire costs. The administration cost is not a direct cost.

(7) A

(8) B

(9) The answer is $ 40,000

	$
Cost 1 April 2008	50,000
20% depreciation	(10,000)
Carrying value 31 March 2009	40,000
20% depreciation	(8,000)
Carrying value 31 March 2010	32,000
Disposal book value ($25,000 x 80% x 80%)	(16,000)
(Cost $25,000 - depreciation for 2 years $9,000)	
Carrying value after disposal	16,000
Purchase	34,000
	50,000
20% depreciation	(10,000)
Carrying value at 31 March 2011	40,000

(10) The annual charge for depreciation was $440,000/50 years 5 $8,800.

The asset had been used and depreciated for 4 years (2007 to 2010).

The carrying value of the asset at the date of valuation was therefore $404,800 (cost of $440,000 – accumulated depreciation of $35,200).

The revaluation surplus is calculated as the valuation amount of $520,000 less the carrying value of the asset of $404,800. The surplus is therefore $115,200.

The revaluation at 1 January 2011 will be recorded as:

		$	$
Debit	Accumulated depreciation	35,200	
Debit	Cost ($520,000 - $440,000)	80,000	
Credit	Revaluation reserve		115,200

The depreciation charge for 2011 and beyond will be based on the asset's valuation over the remaining useful life of the property. The useful life has also been revised to 40 years, so the depreciation will now be $13,000, being value of $520,000 over 40 years.

IFRS 5 Non-Current Assets Held for Sale and Discontinued Operations

Chapter learning objectives

- Explain and apply the accounting rules contained in IASs dealing with reporting financial performance;

- Identify and value an asset held for sale;

- Present discontinued operations correctly using minimum and maximum disclosures.

1 Session content

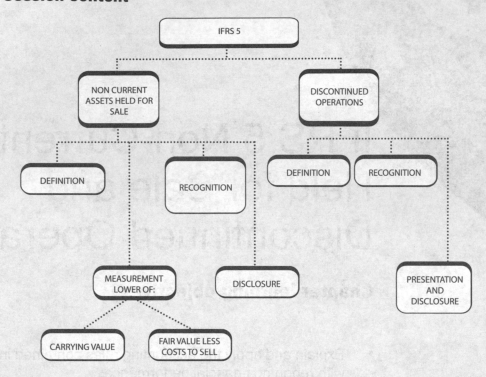

2 Introduction

The objective of IFRS 5 is to establish principles for reporting information about discontinued operations so that users are able to better assess the future performance and cash flows of the entity.

Definition

A discontinued operation is a component of an enterprise that either has been disposed of or is classified as held for sale, and:

- that represents a separate major line of business or geographical area of operations;
- that is a subsidiary acquired exclusively with a view to resale.

A disposal, in the context of IFRS 5, will therefore cover a component that has either been sold or closed with the plan to sell.

Recognition

The requirements of IFRS 5 come into effect at either:

The date the operation has actually been disposed of

When the operation meets the criteria as 'held for sale'

- available for immediate sale in its present condition
- a sale is highly probable
- a reasonable price has been set and
- the sale is expected to be completed within a year

All criteria must be met if the non-current asset is to be held for sale.

For example, for the sale to be highly probable the management must be committed to selling the asset and they must have an active programme to locate a buyer. The asset must also be available to sell immediately in its present condition, i.e. no major repairs are requirement on a buidling before it could be put on the market to sell.

Measurement of assets

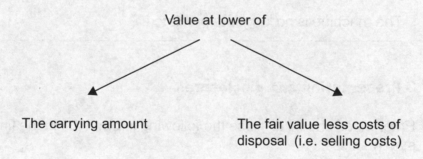

Value at lower of

The carrying amount

The fair value less costs of disposal (i.e. selling costs)

 * Non-current assets 'held for sale' are not depreciated.

If the value of the asset held for sale is less than the carrying value on the statement of financial position it should be written down and the impairment charged against profit.

Illustration 1 : Assets held for sale

On 1 January 2009 Mickey and Minetta Ltd purchases a machine for $20,000. It has an expected useful life of 10 years and nil residual value. The company uses the straight line method of depreciation.

On 31 December 2010 the company decides to sell the machine. Its current market value is $15,000 and the company is confident they will find a buyer very quickly due the short supply in the market for this type of machinery. It will cost the company $500 to dismantle the machine.

At what value should the machine in Mickey and Minetta's statement of financial position at 31 December 2010?

Solution

Current carrying value = 8/10 x $20,000 = $16,000 (we have had the machine for two years, hence charged two year's worth of depreciation against the asset).

Fair value less costs to sell = $15,000 – 500 = $14,500

The machine qualifies as an "asset held for sale" at 31 December 2010 so should be valued at the lower of carrying value or fair value less costs to sell, i.e. $14,500.

The carrying value must be written down from $16,000 to $14,500. The impairment will be charged against profit for the year in the income statement.

The machine is no longer depreciated.

3 Presentation and disclosure

Enterprises should disclose the following information in the financial statements:

Non-current assets 'held for resale'

- Separate disclosure of assets just below the current asset section.

Discontinuing operations

Statement of comprehensive income – there should be a single figure on the face of the statement for the total of:

- Profit after tax

- Gain or loss on disposal of assets

- Gain or loss arising from the adjustment in value from carrying value to fair value

Statement of comprehensive income or note – the single figure should be analysed into:

- Revenues, expenses, profit/loss before tax and income tax expense of the discontinuing operation
- The related tax expense
- Gain or loss arising from the adjustment in value from carrying value to fair value
- Gain or loss on disposal of assets

Statement of Cash flows – there should be a disclosure of net cash flows for the discontinued operations for:

- Net cash flows from operating, investing and financing activities

Additional

- A description of the discontinuing operation/ non-current asset
- A description of the facts and circumstances of the sale
- Expected manner and timing of the disposal (held for sale only)

Presentation

	$
Continued operations	
Revenue	X
Cost of Sales	(X)
Gross profit	X
Distribution costs	(X)
Administrative expenses	(X)
Profit from operations	X
Investment income	X
Finance cost	(X)
Profit before tax	X
Income tax expense	(X)
Profit for the period from continuing operations	X

Discontinued operations

Profit for the period from discontinued operations (see note*)	X
	—
Profit for the period	X
	—

***Note:** Additional disclosure would be provided in the note to the accounts.

Presentation and disclosure

If presented in the statement of comprehensive income or the separate income statement, it must be presented in a section identified as relating to discontinued operations, and be kept separate from continuing operations.

An entity shall disclose on the statement of cash flows or in the notes, net cash flows attributable to the operating, investing and financing activities of discontinued operations.

Comparative information for prior periods should be restated based on the classifications established in the current reporting period. For example, if the retail division is classified as a discontinued operation in 20X2 and its results are disclosed as such separately in the financial statements, then the comparative information for 20X1 should be restated (from continuing operations where it was included last year) and included as a direct comparison within discontinued operations.

Illustration 2 : Discontinued operations

Echo is a company that operates with three divisions A, B and C. During the year ended 31 March 2011 division B closed.

Extracts from the trial balance of Echo plc as at 31 March 2011 areshown below.

	Dr	Cr
	$000	$000
Sales revenue divisions A & C		2,400
Sales revenue division B		650
Operating expenses divisions A & C	1,650	
Operating expenses divisions B	525	
Finance costs (all relating to continuing activities)	70	
Income tax	225	

The income tax charge for the year is made up of a charge of $200,000 on continuing activities and $25,000 for discontinuing activities.

A loss of $50,000 was also incurred on the disposal of assets belonging to division B and $80,000 was spent on restructuring divisions A and C following the termination of division B.

Required:

Prepare the statement of comprehensive income for the year ended 31 March 2011 complying with IAS 1 (revised) *Presentation of Financial Statements* and IFRS 5 *Discontinued Operations.*

Solution

Statement of comprehensive income for Echo Ltd for the year ended 31 March 2011

	$'000
Continued operations	
Revenue	2,400
Operating expenses	(1,650)
Profit from operations	750
Restructuring costs (see note*)	(80)
	670
Finance cost	(70)
Profit before tax	600
Income tax expense	(200)
Profit for the period from continuing operations	400
Discontinued operations	
Profit for the period from discontinued operations (see note**)	50
Profit for the period from total operations	450

Note* for restructuring costs

Restructuring costs have been treated as a material item due to their nature, i.e. unusual item not expected to occur on a regular basis and their size. This means they will be shown as a seperate item on the income statement, rather than be part of other operating expenses. They are not a regular operating expense of the business.

Note** for discontinued operations

Revenue	650
Operating expenses	(525)
Profit from operations	125
Loss on asset disposal	(50)
Tax expense	75
Profit for the period	(25)
	50

Extract from notes to the financial statements:

During the year ended 31 March 2011, Echo closed down Division B, for which the results are separately disclosed. As a result of the discontinued operation, losses on the disposal of assets were incurred of $50,000.

As a consequence of the discontinuance of Division B, restructuring costs were incurred of $80,000 in order to rationalise the remaining divisions.

Test your understanding 1 : Discontinued operations

St Valentine Ltd produces cards and sells roses. However, half way through the year ended 31 March 2011, the rose business was closed and the assets sold off, incurring losses on disposal of non-current assets of $76,000 and redundancy costs of $37,000. The directors reorganised the continuing business at a cost of $98,000.

Trading results are summarised as follows for the year:

	Cards	Roses
	$000	$000
Revenue	650	320
Cost of sales	320	150
Administration expenses	120	110
Distribution costs	60	90

Other trading information (all relating to continuing activities) is as follows:

	Total
	$000
Finance costs	17
Tax expense	31

Required:

Draft the statement of comprehensive income for the year ended 31 March 2011 complying with IAS 1 (revised) *Presentation of Financial Statements* and IFRS 5 *Discontinued Operations*.

Test your understanding 2 : Discontinued operations

Dodgem Ltd is a diversified company which has operated in four main areas for many years. Each of these activities has usually contributed approximately one-quarter of the company's annual operating profit. During the year ended 31 December 2010, the company disposed of its glass-making division.

The company's chief accountant has prepared the following summary of revenues and expenses:

	Glass-making	Other divisions
	$000	$000
Turnover	150	820
Operating expenses	98	470
Losses on disposal of non-current assets	205	61

The company also incurred finance costs of $37,000 during the year, all of which relates to continuing operations. The income tax charge for the year has been estimated at $24,000, made up of a $50,000 charge on the continuing activities and a $26,000 refund for discontinued operations. A dividend of $30,000 was paid during the year.

The company made an issue of 100,000 $1 shares at a premium of 80c per share during the year. Equity at the beginning of the year were made up as follows:

	$000
Share capital	250
Share premium	150
Revaluation reserve	160
Retained earnings	670
	1,230

The balance on the revaluation reserve arose when the company valued the land occupied by the properties used in its retail division. In view of recent developments, it has been decided that this reserve should be reduced to $90,000 to reflect the reduced value of the properties.

Required:

(a) Explain how the analysis required by IFRS 5 Discontinuing Operations assists in assessing a business's future results and cash flows.

(b) Prepare an outline income statement for the year ended 31 December 2010 for Dodgem Ltd in a form suitable for publication, complying with the requirements of IFRS 5.

(c) Prepare a statement of changes in equity for Dodgem Ltd in accordance with the requirements of IAS 1 (revised).

Test your understanding 3 : Single company accounts

The following shows an extract from Archy Ltd's nominal ledger at 30 April 2011:

	$
Administration expenses	950,000
Distribution costs	531,000
Purchases	2,875,000
Finance costs	9,000
Investment income	5,700
Revenue	5,350,000
Ordinary share capital $1	1,000,000
Receivables	55,700
Inventory at 1 May 2010	1,670,000
Cash and cash equivalents	242,000

Land and buildings	
Cost at 1 May 2010	900,000
Accumulated depreciation at 1 May 2010	36,000
Plant and equipment	
Cost at 1 May 2010	102,800
Accumulated depreciation at 1 May 2010	36,400
Intangible asset - carrying value at 1 May 2010	68,000
Retained earnings at 1 May 2010	813,300
Bank loan (repayable on 1 June 2020)	100,000
Payables	62,100

The following additional information is available:

(1) The tax charge for the year is estimated at $227,000.

(2) During the year a piece of plant costing $56,000 and accumulated depreciation of $21,000, met the criteria of *IFRS 5 Non- current Assets Held for Sale and Discontinued Operations.* The plant is available for sale at the price of $32,000 and costs of $1,000 will be incurred in order to complete the sale.

(3) Plant and machinery should be depreciated at 20% on cost and charged to cost of sales.

(4) The land and buildings were originally acquired on 1 May 2007 for $900,000 of which $300,000 related to land. Depreciation is calculated on a straight line basis over a 50 year life and charged to administration expenses.

(5) At the beginning of the year Archy revalued their land and buildings to $1,400,000 of which $460,000 related to land. The remaining life remains unchanged. This has not been accounted for.

(6) Closing inventory was valued at $1,820,000 before any adjustments for damaged items. At the year-end inventory count it was discovered that one line of goods in the warehouse had been damaged. The count shows that 1,250 items were damaged. The inventory was recorded at cost of $150 per item, however, following the damage the items have a scrap value of $40 each.

(7) The intangible asset is a brand which was acquired for $68,000. The useful life of the brand is considered to be indefinite and therefore Archy carries out an annual impairment review to identify the recoverable amount. An expert has estimated the brand's fair value less costs to sell to be $60,000 and the financial controller has estimated the value in use to be $62,000.

Required:

Prepare a statement of comprehensive income and statement of financial position for the year ended 30 April 2011.

Test your understanding 4 : Objective test questions

(1) **According to IFRS 5** *Non-current Assets Held for Sale and Discontinued Operations* **which of the following relate to the criteria for an asset held for sale?**

   (i)   Available for immediate sale in its present condition

   (ii) Sales is highly probable

   (iii) The sale is expected to be completed within the next month

   (iv) A reasonable price has been set

   A   All of the above

   B   i, ii and iii

   C   i, ii and iv

   D   ii, iii and iv

(2) **According to IFRS 5** *Non-current Assets Held for Sale and Discontinued Operations* **which of the following amounts in respect of a discontinued operation must be shown on the face of the income statement?**

   (i)   Revenues

   (ii) Gross profit

   (iii) Profit after tax

   (iv) Operating profit

   A   All of the above

   B   iii only

   C   iii and iv

   D   iv only

(3) **According to IFRS 5** *Non-current Assets Held for Sale and Discontinued Operations* **how should non-current assets held for sale be valued?**

   A   Lower of the carrying value or the fair value

   B   Lower of the carrying value or the fair value less costs of disposal

   C   Higher of the carrying value or the fair value

   D   Higher of the carrying value or the fair value less costs of disposal

(3) **At the reporting date an asset is identified as an asset held for sale after meeting the criteria according to IFRS 5** *Non-current Assets Held for Sale and Discontinued Operations* **. At the reporting date the carrying value of the asset was $150,000 (original cost $200,000 two years ago). The asset has a 10 year life and the company has a policy to depreciate assets using the straight-line method. What should the depreciation be for the year?**

A $20,000

B $15,000

C   None

D $25,000

(4) **At the reporting date an asset is identified as an asset held for sale after meeting the criteria according to IFRS 5** *Non-current Assets Held for Sale and Discontinued Operations* **. Where should the asset appear on the statement of financial position?**

A   Part of the property, plant and equipment under non-current assets

B   It is not shown on the statement of financial position

C   Separately below non-current assets

D   Separately below current assets

4 Summary diagram

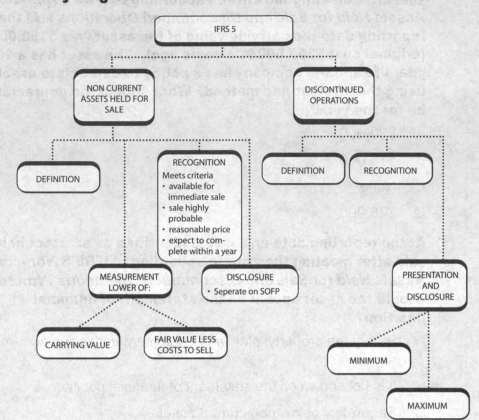

Test your understanding answers

Test your understanding 1 : Discontinued operations

Statement of comprehensive income for St Valentine Ltd for the year ended 31 March 2011

	$
Continued operations	
Revenue	650
Cost of Sales	(320)
Gross profit	330
Distribution costs	(60)
Administrative expenses	(120)
Profit from operations	150
Reorganisation costs	(98)
	52
Finance cost	(17)
Profit before tax	35
Income tax expense	(31)
Profit for the period from continuing operations	4
Discontinued operations	
Loss for the period from discontinued operations (see note*)	(143)
Loss for the period from total operations	(139)

Note for discontinued operations *

Revenue	320
Cost of Sales	(150)
Gross profit	170
Distribution costs	(90)
Administrative expenses	(110)
Loss from operations	(30)
Loss on disposal	(76)
Redundancy costs	(37)
	(143)

Test your understanding 2 : Discontinued operations

(a) The information provided in the financial statements, although historic, is often used by readers of accounts to evaluate future performance. Any additional information about what makes up profits and cash flows can help in the assessment of what is likely to be generated in future periods.

IFRS 5 requires that the financial information be analysed between results from continuing operations and those from discontinuing operations. Discontinuing operations can be an entire part of the business being sold or terminated. It follows then that a discontinuing operation will not generate results in future periods and so should not be included in the users' assessment of future performance. The results of continuing operations are likely to recur in future periods and users can then focus on these results when evaluating what the enterprise is likely to generate in the future.

The analysis of continuing operations and discontinuing operations is required for financial performance, assets and liabilities and cash flows. The standard also requires that the enterprise discloses when the discontinuance will be completed, so that the user can estimate how much that the operation is likely to affect next year's performance.

Statement of comprehensive income for Dodgem Ltd for the year ended 31 December 2010

	$'000
Continued operations	
Revenue	820
Operating expenses	(470)
Profit from operations	350
Loss on disposal of non-current asset	(61)
	289
Finance cost	(37)
Profit before tax	252
Income tax expense	(50)
Profit for the period from continuing operations	202
Discontinued operations	
Loss for the period from discontinued operations (see note*)	(127)
Profit for the period from total operations	75
Other comprehensive income:	
Revaluation reduction	(70)
Total comprehensive income for the period	5

Note for discontinued operations

Revenue	150
Operating expenses	(98)
Operating profit	52
Loss on disposal of non-current assets	(205)
Income tax expense	26
	(127)

(c) **Dodgem Ltd Statement of Changes in Equity for the year ended 31 December 2010**

	Share capital	Share premium	Revaluation reserve	Retained earnings	Total
Balance at 31 December 2009	250	150	160	670	1,230
Revaluation adjustment			(70)		(70)
Profit for the period				75	75
Dividends paid				(30)	(30)
Issue of share capital	100	80			180
Balance at 31 December 2010	350	230	90	715	1,385

Note: share capital issue = 100,000 x $1 = $100,000 and share premium issue = 100,000 x 80c = $80,000

Test your understanding 3 : Single company accounts

Archy statement of comprehensive income for the year ended 30 April 2011

	$
Revenue	5,350,000
Cost of Sales (W1)	(2,881,860)
Gross profit	2,468,140
Distribution costs	(531,000)
Administration expenses (W1)	(970,000)
Profit from operations	967,140
Income from investments	5,700
Finance cost	(9,000)
Profit before tax	963,840
Income tax expense	(227,000)
Profit for year	736,840
Other comprehensive income:	
Revaluation gain (W4)	536,000
Total comprehensive income	1,272,840

Archy statement of financial position as at 30 April 2011

	$	$
Non-current assets		
Property, plant and equipment (W4)		1402,040
Intangible (W3)		62,000
Current assets		
Inventories (W5)	1,682,500	
Trade receivables	55,700	
Cash and cash equivalents	242,000	
		1,980,200
Non-current asset held for sale (W2)		31,000
Total assets		3,475,240

Equity and liabilities
Capital and reserves

Share capital $1	1,000,000	
Revaluation reserve	536,000	
Retained earnings (W6)	1,550,140	
		3,086,140

Non-current liabilities

Bank loan	100,000	
		100,000

Current liabilities

Trade payables	62,100	
Income tax	227,000	
		289,100
		3,475,240

Workings

(W1)

Cost of sales	$
Purchases	2,875,000
Opening inventory	1,670,000
Closing inventory (W5)	(1,682,500)
Depreciation on plant	9,360
Impairment on asset held for sale	4,000
Impairment on intangible asset	6,000
	2,881,860

Administration expenses	$
As per TB	950,000
Depreciation on building	20,000
	970,000

(W2)

Non-current asset held for sale - valued at the lower of:

Carrying value ($56,000 - $21,000) = $35,000 or

Net selling price ($32,000 - $1,000) = $31,000

Value at $31,000

Impairment charged to cost of sales ($35,000 - $31,000) = $4,000

The carrying value of this asset must be removed from the PPE total and shown as an individual line on the SOFP

(W3)

Intangible asset

Compare carrying value with the recoverable amount.

Recoverable amount is the higher of:

Net selling price $60,000

Value in use $62,000

Therefore, recoverable amount is $62,000

The carrying value is $68,000

Impairment charged to cost of sales ($68,000 - $62,000) = $6,000

(W4)

	Property	Plant & Equipment	Total
	$	$	$
Cost/Valuation			
At 1 May 2010	900,000	102,800	1,002,800
Additions	-	-	-
Disposals		-	-
Revaluation	500,000		536,000
Asset held for sale	-	(56,000)	(56,000)
At 30 April 2011	1,400,000	46,800	1,446,800
Accumulated depreciation:			
At 1 May 2010	36,000	36,400	72,400
Revaluation	(36,000)	-	(36,000)
Charged during the year *	20,000	9,360	29,360
Asset held for sale	-	(21,000)	(21,000)
At 30 April 2011	20,000	24,760	44,760
Carrying value			
At 30 April 2011	1,380,000	22,040	1,402,040
At 30 April 2010	864,000	66,400	930,400

* The depreciation on the property on the TB represents 3 years ($900,000 - $300,000)/50 = $12,000 pa. The revaluation happens at the beginning of the year, hence, current year charge should be based on the revalued amount over the remaining life of 47 years = ($1,400,000 - $460,000)/47 = $20,000

The depreciation on the plant and equipment is calculated on the closing cost of $46,800 x 20% = $9,360

We do not depreciate assets held for sale.

(W5)

Inventory	$
Closing inventory at cost	1,820,000
Damaged stock at cost (1,250 x $150)	(187,500)
Damaged stock at NRV (1,250 x $40)	50,000
	1,682,500

Inventory is valued at the lower of cost or NRV

(W6)

Retained earnings	$
Balance at 1 May 2010	813,300
Profit for the period	736,840
	1,550,140

Test your understanding 4 : Objective test questions

(1) C

(2) B

(3) B

(4) C – We do not depreciate assets held for sale

(5) D

IASs 10 and 37

Chapter learning objectives

- Explain the principles of the accounting rules contained in IASs dealing with:
    - events after the reporting period;
    - provisions and
    - contingencies.

1 Session content

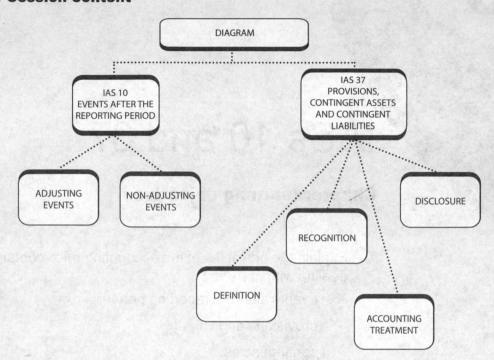

2 IAS 10 Events After The Reporting Period

The purpose of IAS 10 is to define to what extent events that occur after the reporting period should be recognised in the financial statements.

It is a fundamental principle of accounting that regard must be had to all available information when preparing financial statements. This must include relevant events occurring after the reporting period, up to the date on which the financial statements are authorised for issue. The objective of IAS 10 is to:

- define the extent to which different types of events after the reporting period are to be reflected in financial statements;

- define when an entity should adjust its financial statements for events after the reporting period;
  set out the disclosures that the entity should provide about the date the statement of financial position was authorised;

- specify disclosures required about events arising after the end of the reporting period.

IAS 10 defines an event after the end of the reporting period as 'events after the end of the reporting period are those events, favourable and unfavourable, that occur between the end of the reporting period and the date when the financial statements are authorised for issue.'

IAS 10 identifies two main types of events after the reporting period: adjusting events and non-adjusting events.

Adjusting events	Non-adjusting events
'Those events which provide evidence of conditions that existed at the reporting date'	'Those that are indivative of conditions that arose after the reporting date'
FS should be adjusted to reflect the adjusting event	FS should not be adjusted to reflect non-adjusting events
	Non-adjusting events should be disclosed if they affect users' understanding of the FS

Dividends

Equity dividends declared after the reporting period should not be recognised as a liability at the reporting date.

If the dividends are declared before the FS are authorised for issue, they should be disclosed by note.

Going concern

If an event after the reporting date indicates that the entity is no longer a going concern, the financial statements for the current period should not be prepared on the going concern basis.

Disclosure

- Events after the end of the reporting period requiring changes to the financial statements. A material adjusting event after the end of the reporting period requires changes to the financial statements.

- Events after the end of the reporting period requiring disclosure by note. A material event after the end of the reporting period should be disclosed (by note) where it is a non-adjusting event of such importance that its non-disclosure would affect the ability of users of financial statements to reach a proper understanding of the financial position.

  The note should disclose the nature of the event and an estimate of the financial effect, or a statement that it is not practicable to make such an estimate. The estimate should be made before taking account of taxation, with an explanation of the taxation implications where necessary for a proper understanding of the financial position.

- Date directors approve financial statements. The date on which the financial statements are authorised for issue should be disclosed.

Examples of adjusting and non-adjusting events

The key is to look at whether the event gives evidence of conditions that existed at the reporting date. If this is so, and the financial statements have not yet been approved by the directors, then an adjustment will be required.

Examples of adjusting events would be:

- Evidence that inventory is incorrectly valued, i.e. CV is less than cost.

- Evidence that a customer has gone into liquidation.

- Evidence of fraud or error.

- Completion of a court case entered into at the reporting date.

- Completion of an insurance claim.

- Determination after year end, of the sale or purchase price of assets sold or purchased before year end.

- Evidence of a **permanent** diminution in the value of long term investments.

If the evidence shows conditions that have arisen since the reporting date, then no adjustment would be made.

Examples of non-adjusting events would be:

- Acquisition or disposal of a subsidiary after the year end.

- Announcements of a plan to discontinue an operation.

- Destruction of an asset by a fire or flood after the reporting date.

- Announcements of a plan to restructure.

- Share capital transactions after the reporting date.

- Changes in taxation or exchange rates after the reporting date.

- Strikes or other labour disputes

However, if the event is material a note would be required in the accounts.

This would show:

(1) the nature of the event; and

(2) an estimate of its financial effect, or a statement that such an estimate cannot be made.

Illustration 1 : Events after the reporting period

Shortly after the reporting date, 31/12/10, a major credit customer of a company went into liquidation and it is expected that little or none of $12,000 debt will be recoverable. $10,000 of the debt relates to sales made before the year end.

In the 2010 financial statements the whole of the debt has been written off but one of the directors has pointed out that, as the liquidation is an event after the reporting date, the debt should not have been written off but disclosure made by a note.

Advise whether the director is correct.

Solution

The liquidation of the customer is treated as an adjusting event. Only $10,000 debt existed at the reporting date.

Under IAS 10 only the existing debt should be written off in the 2010 financial statements. The remaining $2,000 did not exist at the reporting date and should be written off in the 2011 financial statements.

Test your understanding 1 : Events after the reporting period

Classify each of the following events after the reporting period as adjusting or non-adjusting.

	Adjusting event	Non-adjusting event
Insolvency of a major customer		
Decline in market value of investments		
Loss of non-current assets/inventory due to fire or flood		
Discovery of fraud/error showing that the FS were incorrect		
Announcement of plan to discontinue certain operations		
Evidence concerning the net realisable value of inventory being less than cost		
Resolution of a court case after the reporting date		

3 IAS 37 Provisions, Contingent Liabilities And Assets

Definition

A provision is a liability of uncertain timing or amount.

Background to IAS 37

It is possible to manipulate the results shown in a set of financial statements by recording provisions and later reversing them – a procedure known as profit-smoothing. IAS 37 therefore provides strict guidelines as to when a provision can be recognised to help prevent this form of creative accounting.

Provisions are also a very subjective area of accounting. As a result, inconsistencies can arise in how entities treat such liabilities. IAS 37 seeks to standardise accounting treatment in this area and therefore reduce inconsistency and so improve the comparability of financial statements.

Recognition of provisions

A provision should be recognised in the financial statements when, and only when, the following criteria are met:

- an enterprise has a present obligation (legal or constructive) as a result of a past event;

- it is probable that an outflow of economic benefits will be required to settle the obligation;

- a reliable estimate can be made of the amount of the obligation.

The provision is recognised by making the following double entry:

Dr   Income statement expense
Cr   Provision (SOFP liability)

Legal obligation

An obligation arising from a contract or legislation, e.g. Health and safety act requires certain things to be done.

Constructive obligation

An obligation that arises by an established pattern of past practice, published policies or a current statement that has indicated to other parties that is will accept certain responsibilities and has created a valid expectation that it will meet those responsibilities, e.g. a retail store has a policy to refund dissatisfied customers.

Present obligation

If it is not clear whether there is a present obligation, a present obligation is deemed to exist if 'it is more likely than not that there is a present obligation' at the reporting date.

Past event

A past event gives rise to a present obligation if the entity has no realistic alternative to settling the obligation.

Probable (i.e. more likely than not) that an outflow of resources embodying economic benefits will be required to settle the obligation:

* A transfer of economic benefits is regarded as probable if it is more likely than not to occur.

* Where there are a number of similar obligations the probability that a transfer will be required is determined by considering the class of obligations as a whole, for example, warranties.

A reliable estimate

A reliable estimate can be made of the amount:

* If it is not possible to make a reliable estimate, a provision cannot be made. The item must be disclosed as a contingent liability. IAS 37 notes that it is only in extremely rare cases that a reliable estimate will not be possible.

A reimbursement from a third party, to pay for part or all of the expenditure provided as a provision should only be recognised if it is reasonably certain that it will be received. If it is recognised, it should be treated as a separate asset, rather than set off against the provision.

Measurement of provisions

The provision should be the best estimate of the expenditure required to settle the present obliglation at the end of the reporting period.

The estimates will be based on judgement and likely to be the most likely outcome.

The expected value approach is often used where each outcome is weighted based on the probability of it happening.

For example, an entity provides a one year warranty on its goods to be repaired. If all goods need repairing it would cost $20 million and from past experience only 40% of goods sold will need repairs. The provision would be calculated by: $20 x 40% = $8 million.

Provisions for decommissioning costs

When a facility such as an oil well or a mine is authorised by the government, the licence normally includes a legal obligation for the entity to decommission the facility at the end of its useful life. IAS 37 requires a provision for decommissioning costs to be recognised immediately after operations commence.

Accounting entries:

Dr Asset
Cr Provisions

This means it becomes part of the cost of the asset and would be capitalised as part of PPE on the SOFP. It would then be depreciated accordingly.

Where the provision occurs several years later, the provision should be discounted. This should be recalculated each year. The unwinding of the discount is charged to the income statement under the heading of finance costs and credited to the provision. This is done to ensure the provision is shown at the present value of the expenditure required to settle the obliglation.

For example, if we acquire a mine costing $5 million and we will have it for 20 years, at which time it will be closed down, the present value of dismantling and removing has been estimated at $1 million. The discount rate is 10%.

To account for the purchase we would:

| Dr | Cost NCA | $5 million |
| Cr | Bank/payables | $5 million |

To account for the provision we would:

| Dr | Cost NCA | $1 million |
| Cr | Provisions (SOFP) | $1 million |

We would depreciate the total cost of $6 million (5 + 1) over 20 years = $0.3 million pa

We would then apply the discount rate to the provision at 10%:

Dr Finance costs (IS) ($1 million x 10%) $0.1 million
Cr Provisions (SOFP) $0.1 million

At the end of the year the SOFP would show a NCA carrying value of $5.7 million (6 - 0.3) and a provision of $1.1 million. Depreciation of $0.3 and finance costs of $0.1 would be shown in the IS.

It is unlikely you will have to calculate the discount in the exam.

Provisions for warranties

If an entity sells goods and provides a warranty against faults occurring after the sale, a provision must be created for any future claims that may be made. This normally involves the use of expected values, i.e. the likelihood of something happening.

e.g. An entity estimates the cost of major repair on all goods would be $60,000 and the cost of a minor repair on all goods would be $10,000. The probability of goods needing a major repair is 5%, minor repair 10% and no repairs 85%.

The provision would be calculated as follows:

($60,000 x 5%) + ($10,000 x 10%) = $4,000

Restructuring provisions

A restructuring provision is a programme that is planned and controlled by management, and materially changes either:

- the scope of a business undertaken by an entity; or
- the manner in which that business is conducted.

A provision can only be made if:

- a detailed, formal and approved plan exists; and
- the plan has been announced to those affected.

Definition

A contingent liability is:

- a possible obligation that arises from past events and whose existence will be confirmed only by the occurrence or non-occurrence of one or more uncertain future events not wholly within the control of the enterprise; or

- a present obligation that arises from past events but is not recognised because:
  - it is not probable that an outflow of economic benefits will be required to settle the obligation; or
  - the amount of the obligation cannot be measured with sufficient reliability.

Recognition of contingent liabilities

- Contingent liabilities should not be recognised in the financial statements, but they should be disclosed;

- Except if the possibility of an outflow is remote, in which case the matter is ignored.

A contingent asset is:

Definition

A contingent asset is a possible asset that arises from past events and whose existence will be confirmed only by the occurrence or non-occurrence of one or more uncertain future events not wholly within the control of the enterprise.

Recognition of contingent assets

Contingent assets should not be recognised in the financial statements.

If an inflow of economic benefits is probable, the contingent asset may be disclosed.

Problems with contingencies

It is often very difficult to predict the likelihood of something happening and requires a level of judgement. As assistance, the following probabilities can be used:

Likelihood of occurrence	Level of probability
Remote	Less than 5%
Possible	5–50%
Probable	50–95%
Virtually certain	More than 95%

Summary of the accounting treatment for contingent assets and liabilities

Likelihood of occurrence	Contingent asset	Contingent liability
Remote	No disclosure required	No disclosure required
Possible	No disclosure required	Disclose by note
Probable	Disclose by note	Provide
Virtually certain	Provide	Provide

When disclosure is made by note, the following information should be given:

(1) The nature of the contingency;

(2) The elements of uncertainty;

(3) The estimate of the financial effect.

Disclosure

Under IAS 37 the following disclosures should be made:

- Opening and closing balances;

- Additional provisions made in the period;

- Amounts used (charged against provisions);

- Details of the nature of the provision;

- Details of elements of uncertainty .

Illustration 2 : Provisions and contingencies

For each of the following situations, state the appropriate accounting treatment in accordance with IAS 37.

(1) Onerous contracts

An onerous contract is a contract in which the unavoidable costs of meeting the obligations under the contract exceed the economic benefits expected to be received under it.

An enterprise operates profitably from a factory that it has leased under an operating lease. During December 2010, the enterprise relocates its operations to a new factory. The lease on the old factory continues for the next four years; it cannot be cancelled and the factory cannot be re-let to another user..

(2) Restructuring costs

On 12 December 2010, the board of an enterprise decided to close down a division. Before the reporting date (31 December 2010), the decision was not communicated to any of those affected and no other steps were taken to implement the decision.

(3) Restructuring costs

On 12 December 2010, the board of an enterprise decided to close down a division. On 20 December 2010, a detailed plan for closing down the division was agreed by the board, letters were sent to customers warning them to seek an alternative source of supply and redundancy notices were sent to the staff of the division.

(4) Warranties

A manufacturer gives warranties at the time of sale to purchases of its product. Under the terms of the contract for sale, the manufacturer undertakes to make good manufacturing defects that become apparent within three years from the date of sale. On past experience, it is probable that there will be some claims under the warranties

(5) **Contaminated land**

An enterprise in the oil industry causes contamination and operates in a country where there is no environmental legislation. However, the enterprise has a widely published environmental policy in which it undertakes to clean up all contamination that it causes. The enterprise has a record of honouring this published policy.

(6) **Legal requirement to fit smoke filters**

Under new legislation, an enterprise is required to fit smoke filters to its factories by 30 June 2010. The enterprise has not fitted the smoke filters.

- (i)   Reporting date is 31 December 2009
- (ii)   Reporting date is 31 December 2010

(7) **Repairs and maintenance**

An airline is required by law to overhaul its aircraft once every three years

---

 Solution

(1) **Onerous contracts**

Obligating event = signing of the lease, giving rise to a legal obligation.

There is a probable outflow of resources.

Therefore a provision should be recognised for the best estimate of unavoidable lease payments.

(2) **Restructuring costs**

Does not meet recognition criteria – there is no obligation as the plan has not been communicated, so there is no valid expectation of a payment.

(3) **Restructuring costs**

Obligating event = plan being communicated to those affected, creating a constructive and likely a legal obligation (statutory redundancy payments)

There is a probable outflow of benefits. Therefore a provision should be recognised for the best estimate of costs of closure.

(4) Warranties

Obligating event = sale of the product carrying a warranty.

There is a probable outflow of benefit for warranties as a whole. Therefore a provision should be recognised for the best estimate of costs of making good warranty claims on items sold before the year end.

(5) Contaminated land

Obligating event = contamination of the land, giving rise to a constructive obligation. The company has created a valid expectation that it will honour its published policy.

There is a probable outflow of economic benefit. A provision should be recognised for the best estimate of costs of cleaning up the contaminated land.

(6) Legal requirement to fit smoke filters

(i) 31 December 2009

There is no obligation at the reporting date.

(i) 31 December 2010

There is not an obligating event in that the company has not fitted the smoke filters. However, there is likely to be an obligation to pay fines or penalties as a result of breaching the legislation.

It is difficult to say whether there will be an outflow of resources – the company would have to assess how probable it is that it will be fined for non-compliance with the legislation.

No provision is needed for the costs of fitting the smoke filters. However, if it is probable that the company faces fines or penalties, then these should be provided.

(7) Repairs and maintenance

No provision is recognised as the costs of the overhaul should be capitalised per IAS 16 and depreciated over a three-year useful life.

Test your understanding 2 : Provisions and contingencies

Your company is currently involved in four legal cases, all of them unrelated.

- In Case A, the company is suing a supplier for $100,000.

- In Case B, the company is suing a professional adviser for $200,000.

- In Case C, the company is being sued by a customer for $300,000.

- In Case D, the company is being sued by an investor for $400,000.

The company has been advised by its lawyers that the probabilities of success in each case are as follows:

Case	Likelihood of your company winning the case
A	10%
B	90%
C	98%
D	60%

State the accounting treatment for each of the four cases.

Test your understanding 3 : Objective test questions

(1) Jackson Ltd's year end is 31 December 2010. In February 2011 a major customer went into liquidation and the directors' believe that they will not be able to recover the $450,000 owed to them.

How should this item be treated in the financial statements of Jackson Ltd for the year ended 31 December 2010?

A   The bad debt should be disclosed by note

B   The financial statements are not affected

C   The debt should be provided against

D   The financial statements should be adjusted to reflect the irrecoverable debt

(2) A former employee is claiming compensation of $50,000 from Harriot Ltd for wrongful dismissal. The company's solicitors have stated that they believe that the claim is unlikely to succeed. The legal costs relating to the claim are likely to be in the region of $5,000 and will be incurred regardless of whether or not the claim is successful.

How should these items be treated in the financial statements of Harriot Ltd?

A   Provision should be made for $55,000

B   Provision should be made for $50,000 and the legal costs should be disclosed by note

C   Provision should be made for $5,000 and the compensation of $50,000 should be disclosed by note

D   No provisions should be made but both items should be disclosed by note

(3) Blacksmith Ltd have claimed compensation of $30,000 from another company for breach of copyright. The solicitors of Blacksmith Ltd have advised the directors that their claim is likely to succeed.

How should this item be treated in the financial statements of Blacksmith Ltd?

A   The item should not be included in the financial statements

B   The item should be disclosed by note in the financial statements

C   The financial statements should show an asset of $30,000

D   The financial statements should show an asset of $30,000 and a note should be included explaining the item

(4) **Which of the following items are non-adjusting items per IAS 10 *Events after the Reporting Period*?**

(i)   Changes in the rates of foreign exchange

(ii) Destruction of machinery by fire

(iii) Information regarding the value of inventory

(iv) Mergers and acquisitions

(v)   Insolvency of a customer

A   i, ii and iv

B   iii and v

C   i, iii and v

D   ii, iii and v

(5) **Which of the following could be classified as an adjusting event occurring after the end of the reporting period:**

A   A serious fire, occurring 1 month after the year-end, that damaged the sole production facility, causing production to cease for 3 months.

B   One month after the year-end, a notification was received advising that a large receivables balance would not be paid as the customer was being wound up. No payments are expected from the customer.

C   A large quantity of parts for a discontinued production line was discovered at the back of the warehouse during the year-end inventory count. The parts have no value except a nominal scrap value and need to be written off.

D   The entity took delivery of a new machine from the USA in the last week of the financial year. It was discovered almost immediately afterwards that the entity supplying the machine had filed for bankruptcy and would not be able to honour the warranties and repair contract on the new machine. Because the machine was so advanced, it was unlikely that any local entity could provide maintenance cover.

(6) X is currently defending two legal actions:

* An employee, who suffered severe acid burns as a result of an accident in X's factory, is suing for $20,000, claiming that the directors failed to provide adequate safety equipment. X's lawyers are contesting the claim, but have advised the directors that they will probably lose.

* A customer is suing for $50,000, claiming that X's hair-care products damaged her hair. X's lawyers are contesting this claim, and have advised that the claim is unlikely to succeed.

How much should X provide for these legal claims in its financial statements?

A $0

B $20,000

C $50,000

D $70,000

(7) Which ONE of the following would require a provision to be created by BW at the end of it's reporting period, 31 October 2011:

A   The government introduced new laws on data protection which come into force on 1 January 2012. BW's directors have agreed that this will require a large number of staff to be retrained. At 31 October 2011, the directors were waiting on a report they had commissioned that would identify the actual training requirements.

B   At the end of the reporting period, BW is negotiating with its insurance provider about the amount of an insurance claim that it had filed. On 20 November 2011, the insurance provider agreed to pay $200,000.

C   BW makes refunds to customers for any goods returned within 30 days of sale, and has done so for many years.

D   A customer is suing BW for damages alleged to have been caused by BW's product. BW is contesting the claim and, at 31 October 2011, the directors have been advised by BW's legal advisers it is unlikely to lose the case.

(8) DH has the following two legal claims outstanding:

－   A legal action against DH claiming compensation of $700,000, filed in February 2011. DH has been advised that it is probable that the liability will materialise.

－   A legal action taken by DH against another entity, claiming damages of $300,000, started in March 2008. DH has been advised that it is probable that it will win the case.

How should DH report these legal actions in its financial statements for the year ended 30 April 2011?

	Legal action against DH	**Legal action taken by DH**
A	Disclose by a note to the accounts	No disclosure
B	Make a provision	No disclosure
C	Make a provision	Disclose as a note
D	Make a provision	Accrue the income

4 Summary diagram

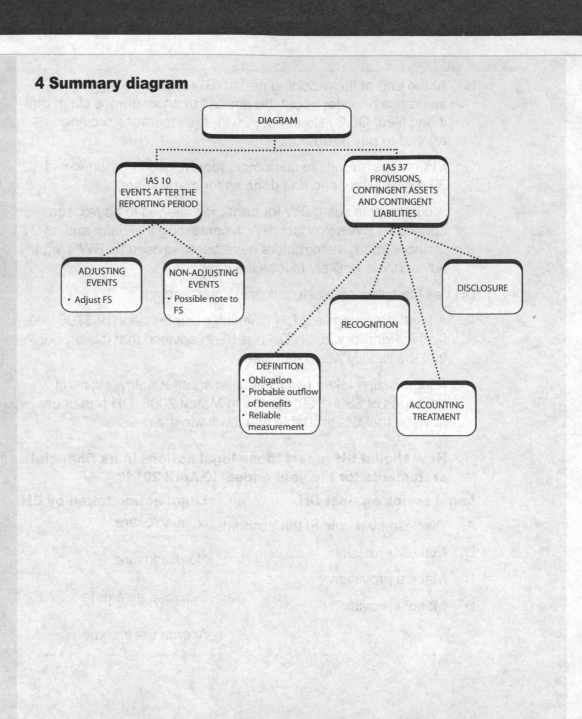

Test your understanding answers

Test your understanding 1 : Events after the reporting period

Insolvency of a major customer	Adjusting event
Decline in market value of investments	Non-adjusting event
Loss of non-current assets / inventories due to fire / flood	Non-adjusting event
Discovery of fraud / error showing that the FS were incorrect	Adjusting event
Announcement of a plan to discontinue operations	Non-adjusting event
Evidence concerning the NRV of inventories	Adjusting event
Resolution of a court case	Adjusting event

Test your understanding 2 : Provisions and contingencies

Case	**Comment**	**Accounting treatment**
A	Contingent gain which is possible	Not recognised
B	Contingent gain which is probable	Disclose as a note
C	Contingent liability which is remote (we are virtually certain we will win)	Not recognised
D	Contingent liability which is possible (we are probable we will win)	Disclose as a note

Disclosure of a note would state the nature of the contingency, elements of uncertainty and the financial effect of the case if the gain/loss should arise.

Test your understanding 3 : Objective test questions

(1) D

(2) C

(3) B

(4) A

(5) B

(6) B

(7) C

(8) C

IAS 12 Income Taxes

Chapter learning objectives

- Explain and apply the accounting rules contained in IAS 12 for current and deferred taxation;

- Identify and account for under and over provisions;

- Calculate deferred taxation;

- Prepare extracts to the financial statements for current and deferred taxation.

1 Session content

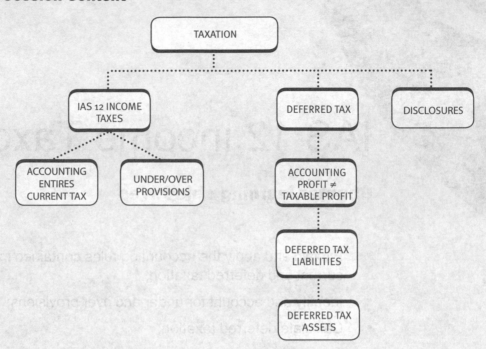

2 IAS 12 Income Taxes

IAS 12 covers the general principles of accounting for tax although tax systems may vary from country to country.

Tax consists of three elements:

- current tax expense;
- over or under provisions in relation to the tax charges of the previous period;
- deferred tax.

3 Current tax

Definitions

Current tax is the estimated amount of tax payable on the taxable profits of the enterprise for the period.

Taxable profits are the profits on which tax is payable, calculated in accordance with the rules of local tax authorities.

At the end of every accounting period, the entity will estimate the amount of tax payable in respect of the period. This estimate is normally recorded as a period end adjustment by making the following double entry:

Dr   Income tax expense (IS)

Cr   Income tax liability (SOFP)

4 Under and over provisions

Definitions

In the following accounting period, the income tax will be paid. At this point, it will normally be discovered that the estimate was over or under the actual amount paid. Any over or under provision will then be recorded in this following accounting period as an adjustment to the income tax expense in the income statement.

Illustration 1 : Under and over provisions

The following information is available for Happy Ltd:

	$
Income tax provision at 31 May 2010	316,000 → opening liability.
Income tax paid on 28 February 2011	263,000
Income tax estimate for the year ended 31 May 2011	383,500

Required:

Show the entries in the income tax account and the extracts from the financial statements for the year ended 31 May 2011.

Solution

At 31 May 2010 we had an opening liability for tax of $316,000. When we made the payment of £263,000, this resulted in an over-provision for 2010 of $53,000 because we had provided for more tax than we needed to pay.

This credit balance would be shown on the trial balance before the adjustments were made for the current year's estimated taxation.

Tax

Bank	263,000	Bal b/d	316,000
Bal c/d	53,000		
	316,000		316,000
		Bal b/d	53,000

At 31 May 2011 the current year tax is estimated at $383,500. This is the amount that **must** be shown on the current year statement of financial position as a liability. It is **not** the charge to the income statement. The income statement charge will be made up of this year's estimated tax liability but will have credit for the over-provision made in 2010 financial statements.

Tax

		Bal b/d	53,000
Bal c/d	383,500	IS (ß)	330,500
	383,500		383,500
		Bal b/d	383,500

Income statement for the year ended 31 May 2011 (extract)

	$
Income tax expense (W1)	330,500

Statement of financial position as at 31 May 2011 (extract)

Current liabilities	
Income tax payable	383,500

(W1)

Income tax expense	
Current tax	383,500
Over-provision	(53,000)
	330,500

Test your understanding 1 : Under and over provisions

The following information is available for Sad Ltd:

	$
Income tax provision at 31 December 2009	56,000
Income tax paid on 28 September 2010	59,900
Income tax estimate for the year ended 31 December 2010	70,000

Required:

Show the entries in the income tax account and the extracts from the financial statements for the year ended 31 December 2010.

Summary

When we look at the trial balance the following applies:

Debit = Under-provision

Credit = Over-provision

When we are preparing the financial statements:

Income statement = current estimate + under-provision – over-provision

Statement of financial position = current estimate

5 Deferred tax

Definitions

Deferred tax is:

- the estimated future tax consequences of transactions and events recognised in the financial statements of the current and previous periods.

Deferred tax is an accounting measurement and does not represent the tax payable to the tax authorities.

Deferred tax is a basis of allocating tax charges to particular accounting periods. The key to deferred tax lies in the two quite different concepts of profit:

- the **accounting profit**, which is the profit before tax, reported to shareholders in the published accounts;

- the **taxable profit**, which is the figure of profit on which the taxation authorities base their tax calculations.

Temporary differences are

Temporary differences are differences between the carrying amount of an asset or liability in the statement of financial position and its tax base (the amount attributed to that asset or liability for tax purposes).

Examples of temporary differences include:

- certain types of income and expenditure that are taxed on a cash, rather than on an accruals basis, e.g. certain provisions;

- the difference between the depreciation charged on a non-current asset that qualifies for tax allowances and the actual allowances (tax depreciation) given (the most common practical example of a temporary difference).

Temporary differences can be:

- taxable temporary differences, i.e. the accounting depreciation is less than the tax depreciation, therefore, we are creating a deferred tax provision for a future tax liability;

- deductable temporary differences results in a deduction from taxable profits when sold and recognised as a deferred tax asset.

Tax base

The tax base of an asset is the written down value of the asset, i.e. cost less accumulated tax depreciation.

For your examination non-current assets are the important examples of temporary differences. They are the major source of temporary differences.

The accounting problem

One important reason why deferred tax should be recognised is that profit for tax purposes may differ from the profit shown by the financial statements. Such a difference may be caused by permanent or temporary factors. For example, if expenses in the income statement are not allowed for tax purposes, a **permanent difference** arises. Nothing can be done about that, and the increased tax charge just has to be accepted.

A **temporary difference** arises when an expense is allowed for both tax and accounting purposes, but the timing of the allowance differs. For example, if relief for capital expenditure is given at a faster rate for tax purposes than the depreciation in the financial statements, the tax charge will be lower in the first years than it would have been based on the accounting profit, but in subsequent years the tax charge will be higher.

For example, an item of plant and machinery is purchased by U in 20X0 for $300,000. The asset's estimated useful life is 6 years, following which it will have no residual value. Plant and machinery is depreciated on a straight-line basis.

Tax depreciation for this item is given at 25% on the straight-line basis for the first 4 years.

Let us first calculate the figures that would appear in the financial statements over the six-year life of the asset:

Financial statements	20X0	20X1	20X2	20X3	20X4	20X5
	$'000	$'000	$'000	$'000	$'000	$'000
Opening carrying value	300	250	200	150	100	50
Accounting depreciation charge	50	50	50	50	50	50
Closing carrying value	250	200	150	100	50	0

Depreciation is charged at $50,000 per annum ($300,000/6 years). Now let us look at how this asset would be treated for tax purposes:

Tax computation	20X0	20X1	20X2	20X3	20X4	20X5
	$'000	$'000	$'000	$'000	$'000	$'000
Opening carrying value	300	225	150	75	0	0
Tax depreciation	75	75	75	75	-	-
Tax written down value	225	150	75	0	0	0

We can see from comparing the above two tables that the carrying value of the asset per accounts differs from the Tax written down value. The annual reduction in the carrying value applied by the entity (that is accounting depreciation) differs from the reduction applied in the tax computation. By the end of the asset's useful life, the two have caught up, as they both show the asset with a carrying value of 0, but the different treatment over 6 years creates the accounting problem that is known as deferred tax.

6 Calculating deferred tax

Deferred tax is calculated by:

Cumulative temporary differences between accounting carrying value and the tax base X tax rate

The provision must be set up for this amount by:

Dr   Income tax expense (IS)
Cr   Deferred tax provision(SOFP)

When a provision increases during a year the **movement** is accounted for by:

Dr   Income tax expense (IS)
Cr   Deferred tax provision(SOFP)

When a provision decreases during a year the **movement** is accounted for by:

Dr   Deferred tax provision(SOFP)
Cr   Income tax expense (IS)

 The cumulative provision is shown on the statement of financial position at each year end.

The movement is shown as an adjustment to the income tax expense on the income statement.

Deferred tax liabilities and assets

Deferred tax liabilities are the amounts of tax payable in future periods in represent of taxable temporary differences, e.g. the carrying value in the accounts of an asset is $10,000 and the tax base is $6,000. Tax is charged at 25%. This would result in a deferred tax liability of ($10,000 - $6,000) x 25% = $1,000.

Deferred tax assets are the amounts of tax recoverable in future periods in respect of deductable temporary differences, the carry forward of unused tax losses and the carry forward of unused tax credits, e.g. a trading loss is carried forward of $20,000. Tax is charged at 25%. This would result in a deferred tax asset of $20,000 x 25% = $5,000.

Dr Deferred tax asset (SOFP) ($20,000 x 25%)	$6,000
Cr Income tax expense (IS)	$6,000

If the loss is used against the profits of the following year of $24,000, the following entries would be made:

Dr Income tax expense (IS) ($24,000 x 25%) $6,000
Cr Deferred tax asset (SOFP) ($20,000 x 25%) $5,000
Cr Income tax liability (SOFP) ($4,000 x 25%) $1,000

The income statement reflects the charge on this year's profit, i.e.
$24,000, however the liability represents the actual amount due to the
tax authorities, i.e. $24,000 - loss b/f $20,000 = $4,000 x 25%.

Illustration 2 : Deferred tax

Messy Ltd does not have a deferred tax account and wishes to create
one for an asset it has recently purchased. The cost of the asset is $300
and will be depreciated over three years on a straight line basis.

The tax depreciation (capital allowances) for the three years will be
$140, $110 and $50 in years 1, 2 and 3.

Required:

Prepare the extracts for the financial statements for all three years,
clearly showing the double entry in the deferred tax account. You should
assume the current tax rate is 30%.

Solution

Year	Accounting carrying value	Tax written down value	Temporary difference	Difference x 30%
1	200	160	40	12
2	100	50	50	15
3	-	-	-	-

The difference at 30% represents the total deferred tax provision
required in the statement of financial position.

The movement in the difference at 30% represents the increase/
(decrease) in the deferred tax provision required for the year. These are
the entries to be made to the income statement.

Income statement		Year 1	Year 2	Year 3
Income tax expense		12	3	

Statement of financial position

Non-current liabilities

		Year 1	Year 2	Year 3
Deferred tax		12	15	0

Deferred Tax

		Bal b/d	0
Bal c/d	12	Year 1 – IS	12
	—		—
	12		12
	—		—
		Bal b/d	12
Bal c/d	15	Year 2 – IS	3
	—		—
	15		15
	—		—
Year 3 – IS	15	Bal b/d	15
Bal c/d	0		
	—		—
	15		15
	—		—

Disclosures

IAS 12 requires the following disclosures to be made in the notes to the financial statements regarding taxation:

- A breakdown of the components of the income tax expense

	$000
Current tax	X
(Over)/under provision in prior periods	(X)/X
Deferred tax	X/(X)
	——
	X
	——

Test your understanding 2 : Deferred tax

Aquarius Ltd's financial statements for the year ended 31 December 2009 show a profit before tax of $145,000. Cumulative temporary differences at the year end amounted to $40,000, i.e. the difference between the accounting carrying value and the tax base. Current tax for the year at 30% has been estimated at $30,000. There is currently no provision for deferred tax.

For the year ended 31 December 2010 the financial statements show a profit before tax of $170,000. Cumulative temporary differences at the year end amounted to $50,000 and current tax for the year at 30% has been estimated at $33,000.

Required:

Prepare relevant extracts from the financial statements to record the above transactions. You should assume the amounts paid for current tax are equal to the estimates made.

Test your understanding 3 : Exam standard question

Parker Ltd's financial statements show the following profit before tax figures:

Y.E. 30.6.2008	$450,000
Y.E. 30.6.2009	$550,000
Y.E. 30.6.2010	$300,000

Income tax which has been calculated based on taxable profits is as follows:

Y.E. 30.6.2008	$96,000
Y.E. 30.6.2009	$108,000
Y.E. 30.6.2010	$59,000

Payments of tax were made nine months following each year-end as follows:

Y.E. 30.6.2008	$90,000
Y.E. 30.6.2009	$118,000
Y.E. 30.6.2010	$55,000

Cumulative temporary differences at the year-ends are as follows:

Y.E. 30.6.2008	$100,000
Y.E. 30.6.2009	$210,000
Y.E. 30.6.2010	$70,000

Assume an income tax rate of 30%.

Required:

Prepare the relevant extracts from the financial statements for each of the three years in respect of income tax.

Test your understanding 4 : Single company accounts

The following trial balance relates to Molly at 31 December 2010:

	Dr	Cr
	$	$
Revenue		50,000
Purchases	20,000	
Distribution costs	10,400	
Administration expenses	15,550	
Loan interest paid	400	
Non-current assets CV	35,000	
Income tax		500
Deferred tax at 1 January 2010		8,000
Interim dividend paid	1,600	
Trade receivables and payables	10,450	29,000
Inventory as at 1 January 2010	8,000	
Cash and cash equivalents	8,100	
Ordinary shares $0.50		8,000
Share premium		3,000
10% Loan notes		8,000
Retained earnings at 1 January 2010		3,000
	109,500	109,500

The following is to be taken into account:

(1) Land that cost $5,000 is to be revalued to $11,000.

(2) A final ordinary dividend of 10c per share is declared before the year-end.

(3) The balance on the income tax account represents an over-provision of tax for the previous year.

(4) The income tax for the current year is estimated at $3,000. The deferred tax provision is to be increased to $8,600.

(5) Closing inventory is valued at $16,000 at cost for the year. Included in this amount is inventory that cost $8,000 but during the inventory count it was identified that these goods had become damaged and as result the selling price was reduced. The goods are now believed to have a selling price of $4,500 and will incur rectification costs of $500.

Required:

Prepare a statement of comprehensive income, statement of financial position and statement of changes in equity for the year-ended 31 December 2010.

Test your understanding 5 : Objective test questions

(1) The following information has been extracted from the accounting records of Clara Ltd:

Estimated income tax for the year ended 30 September 2010	$75,000
Income tax paid for the year ended 30 September 2010	$80,000
Estimated income tax for the year ended 30 September 2011	$83,000

What figures will be shown in the income statement for the year ended 30 September 2011 and the statement of financial position as at that date in respect of income tax?

	Income statement	SOFP
A	$83,000	$83,000
B	$88,000	$83,000
C	$83,000	$88,000
D	$88,000	$88,000

(2) Tamsin plc's accounting records shown the following:

Income tax payable for the year	$60,000
Over provision in relation to the previous year	$4,500
Opening provision for deferred tax	$2,600
Closing provision for deferred tax	$3,200

What is the income tax expense that will be shown in the income statement for the year?

A $58,700

B $63,900

C $65,100

D $56,100

The following information relates to questions **3** and **4**:

At 1 January 2010 Pegasus plc acquired motor vehicles at a cost of $100,000. Depreciation is charged at the rate of 20% per annum on the straight line basis. For tax purposes, tax depreciation will be claimed at the rate of 25% per annum, on the reducing balance basis. The income tax rate is 30%.

(3) **What is the provision for deferred tax that is required as at 31 December 2010?**

A $5,000

B $1,500

C $2,000

D $3,000

(4) **What is the provision for deferred tax that is required as at 31 December 2011?**

A $3,750

B $6,250

C $1,125

D $375

(5) A piece of machinery cost $500. Tax depreciation to date has amounted to $220 and depreciation charged in the financial statements to date is $100. The rate of income tax is 30%.

Which of the following statements is incorrect according to IAS 12 Income Taxes?

    A   The provision for deferred tax in relation to the asset is $36

    B   The tax base of the asset is $280

    C   There is a deductible temporary difference of $120

    D   There is a taxable temporary difference of $120

(6) An asset cost $200,000 and had an estimated useful life of 10 years, with no residual value. Accounting depreciation was calculated on the straight-line basis. Tax depreciation was given at 25% on a reducing balance basis. Assume corporate income tax at 30%. At the end of the second year of operation, the deferred tax provision on the statement of financial position should be:

    A $9,000

    B $14,250

    C $18,000

    D $47,500

(7) WS prepares its financial statements to 30 June. The following profits were recorded from 20X1 to 20X3:

20X1 $100,000
20X2 $120,000
20X3 $110,000

The entity provides for tax at a rate of 30% and incorporates this figure in the year-end accounts. The actual amounts of tax paid in respect of 20X1 and 20X2 were $28,900 and $37,200.

Required:

Prepare extracts from the statement of comprehensive income and statement of financial position of WS for each of the 3 years, showing the tax charge and tax liability.

7 Summary diagram

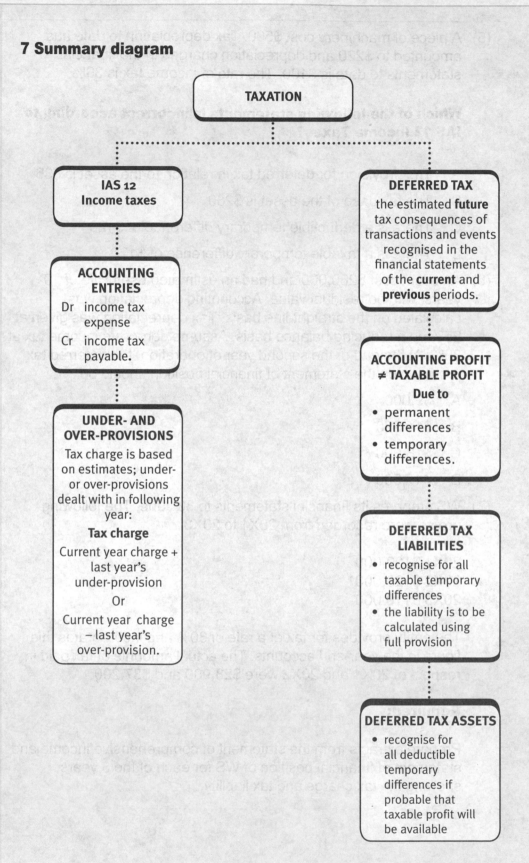

TAXATION

**IAS 12
Income taxes**

DEFERRED TAX
the estimated **future** tax consequences of transactions and events recognised in the financial statements of the **current** and **previous** periods.

ACCOUNTING ENTRIES

Dr   income tax expense

Cr   income tax payable.

ACCOUNTING PROFIT ≠ TAXABLE PROFIT
Due to

• permanent differences
• temporary differences.

UNDER- AND OVER-PROVISIONS

Tax charge is based on estimates; under- or over-provisions dealt with in following year:

Tax charge

Current year charge + last year's under-provision

Or

Current year charge – last year's over-provision.

DEFERRED TAX LIABILITIES

• recognise for all taxable temporary differences
• the liability is to be calculated using full provision

DEFERRED TAX ASSETS

• recognise for all deductible temporary differences if probable that taxable profit will be available

Test your understanding answers

Test your understanding 1 : Under and over provisions

At 31 December 2009 we had an opening liability for tax of $56,000. When we made the payment of £59,900, this resulted in an under-provision for 2009 of $3,900 because we had provided for less tax than we needed to pay.

This debit balance would be shown on the trial balance before the adjustments were made for the current years taxation.

Tax

Bank	59,900	Bal b/d	56,000
		Bal c/d	3,900
	———		———
	59,900		56,000
	———		———
Bal b/d	3,900		

At 31 December 2010 the current year tax is estimated at $70,000. This is the amount that **must** be shown on the current year statement of financial position as a liability. It is **not** the charge to the income statement. The income statement charge will be made up of this years estimated tax liability but will have to be increased for the under-provision made in 2009 financial statements.

Tax

Bal b/d	3,900		
Bal c/d	70,000	IS (ß)	73,900
	———		———
	73,900		73,900
	———		
		Bal b/d	70,000

Income statement for the year ended 31 December 2010 (extract)

	$
Income tax expense (W1)	73,900

Statement of financial position as at 31 December 2010 (extract)

Current liabilities	
Income tax payable	70,000

(W1)

Income tax expense	
Current tax	70,000
Under-provision	3,900
	73,900

Test your understanding 2 : Deferred tax

Income statement (extract)

	2009	2010
	$	$
Profit before tax	145,000	170,000
Income tax expense (W1)	(42,000)	(36,000)
Profit for the year	103,000	134,000

Statement of financial position (extract)

	2009	2010
	$	$
Non-current liabilities:		
Deferred tax provision (W1)	12,000	15,000
Current liabilities:		
Income tax payable (W1)	30,000	33,000

(W1)

Income tax expense	31/12/09	31/12/10
Current tax	30,000	33,000
Deferred tax ($40,000 x 30%)	12,000	
Deferred tax ($50,000 x 30%) less 2009 provision		3,000
	42,000	36,000

Deferred tax provision: YE 31/12/09

Dr Income tax expense (IS)		12,000
Cr Deferred tax liability (SOFP)		12,000

Current tax provision: YE 31/12/09

Dr Income tax expense (IS)		30,000
Cr Current tax liability (SOFP)		30,000

Deferred tax provision: YE 31/12/10

Increase in provision = $50,000 x 30% = 15,000 – 12,000 b/fwd = 3,000

Dr Income tax expense (IS)		3,000
Cr Deferred tax liability (SOFP)		3,000

Current tax provision: YE 31/12/10

Dr Income tax expense (IS)		33,000
Cr Current tax liability (SOFP)		33,000

Test your understanding 3 : Exam standard question

Income statement (extract)

	2008	2009	2010
	$	$	$
Profit before taxation	450,000	550,000	300,000
Income tax expense (W1)	(126,000)	(135,000)	(27,000)
Profit for the period	324,000	415,000	273,000

Statements of financial position (extract)

	2008	2009	2010
	$	$	$
Non-current liabilities			
Deferred tax provision (W2)	30,000	63,000	21,000
Current liabilities			
Income tax payable	96,000	108,000	59,000

(W1) Income tax expense

	2008	2009	2010
	$	$	$
Current tax estimate	96,000	108,000	59,000
Over/under provision (W3)	0	(6,000)	10,000
Deferred tax (W2)	30,000	33,000	(42,000)
	126,000	135,000	27,000

(W2) **Deferred tax provision**

	2008	2009	2010
	$	$	$
Cumulative provision (SOFP) see *	30,000	63,000	21,000
Provision b/fwd	0	30,000	63,000
Movement in provision (IS)	30,000	33,000	(42,000)

* Cumulative temporary differences X 30%

(W3) **Under/over provisions**

	2008	2009	2010
	$	$	$
Current tax estimate	96,000	108,000	59,000
Amount paid	90,000	118,000	55,000
Under/(over) provision	(6,000)	10,000	(3,000)

Remember these under/(over) provisions will not have an effect on the current year accounts but the following year accounts due to the timing of payments.

Test your understanding 4 : Single company accounts

Molly statement of comprehensive income for the year ended 31 December 2010

	$
Revenue	50,000
Cost of Sales (W1)	(16,000)
Gross profit	34,000
Distribution costs	(10,400)
Administration expenses	(15,550)
Profit from operations	8,050
Income from investments	–
Finance cost (W2)	(800)
Profit before tax	7,250
Income tax expense (W3)	(3,100)
Profit for year	4,150
Other comprehensive income:	
Revaluation gain (W4)	6,000
Total comprehensive income	10,150

Molly statement of financial position as at 31 December 2010

	$	$
Non-current assets		
Property, plant and equipment (W4)		41,000
Current assets		
Inventories (W5)	12,000	
Trade receivables	10,450	
Cash and cash equivalents	8,100	
		30,550
Total assets		71,550

Equity and liabilities
Capital and reserves

Share capital $0.50	8,000
Share premium	3,000
Revaluation reserve	6,000
Retained earnings	3,950
	20,950

Non-current liabilities

10% Loan	8,000
Deferred taxation	8,600
	16,600

Current liabilities

Trade payables	29,000
Loan interest payable (W2)	400
Dividends proposed (W6)	1,600
Income tax	3,000
	34,000
	71,550

Molly statement of changes in equity for the year ended 31 December 2010

	Share capital	Share premium	Reval'tion reserve	Retained earnings	Total
	$	$	$	$	$
Balance at 1 January 2010	8,000	3,000	0	3,000	14,000
Net profit for the year (IS)				4,150	4,150
Dividends paid				(1,600)	(1,600)
Dividends declared (W6)				(1,600)	(1,600)
Revaluation of land (W4)			6,000	–	6,000
Balance at 31 December 2010	8,000	3,000	6,000	3,950	20,950

Workings

(W1)

Cost of sales	$
Purchases	20,000
Opening inventory	8,000
Closing inventory (W5)	(12,000)
	16,000

(W2)

Loan interest due (10% x $8,000) = $800 (IS)

Amount paid (TB) $400, therefore accrual required for $400

(W3)

Income tax	$
TB over-provision	(500)
Current year estimate	3,000
Increase in deferred tax provision	600
	3,100

(W4)

PPE	$
TB carrying value	35,000
Increase in valuation of land ($5,000 to $11,000)	6,000
	41,000

(W5)

Inventory	$
Closing inventory at cost	16,000
Damaged inventory at cost	(8,000)
Damaged inventory at NRV ($4,500 - $500)	4,000
	12,000

Inventory is valued at the lower of cost or NRV

(W6)

Dividends 0.10 x 16,000 shares ($8,000/0.50) = $1,600 declared before year-end, therefore provide.

Test your understanding 5 : Objective test questions

(1) B

Income statement (extract)

Current tax y.e. 30.9.11	83,000
Underprovision for y.e. 30.9.10 (80,000 – 75,000)	5,000
	88,000

Statement of financial position (extract)

Income tax payable	83,000

(2) D

Income statement (extract)

Current tax	60,000
Overprovision	(4,500)
Deferred tax (3,200 – 2,600)	600
	56,100

(3) B

Accounting basis	$	Tax basis	$
Cost	100,000	Cost	100,000
Depreciation	(20,000)	Tax depreciation	(25,000)
Carrying value 31/12/10	80,000	Tax base 31/12/10	75,000

Provision for deferred tax = 30% × (80,000 – 75,000) = $1,500

(4) C

Accounting basis	**$**	**Tax basis**	**$**
Cost	100,000	Cost	100,000
Depreciation	(20,000)	Tax depreciation	(25,000)
	80,000		75,000
Depreciation	(20,000)	Tax depreciation	(18,750)
Carrying value 31/12/11	60,000	Tax base 31/12/11	56,250

Provision for deferred tax = 30% × (60,000 – 56,250) = $1,125

(5) C

(6) B

Accounting basis	**$**	**Tax basis**	**$**
Cost	200,000	Cost	200,000
Depreciation (200/10)	(20,000)	Tax depreciation	(50,000)
	180,000		150,000
Depreciation	(20,000)	Tax depreciation	(37,500)
Carrying value end of year 2	160,000	Tax base end of year 2	112,500

Provision for deferred tax = 30% × (160,000 – 112,500) = $14,250

(7) **Income statement (extract)**

	20X1	20X2	20X3
	$	$	$
Profit before taxation	100,000	120,000	110,000
Income tax expense (W1)	(30,000)	(34,900)	(34,200)
Profit for the period	70,000	85,100	75,800

Statements of financial position (extract)

	20X1 $	20X2 $	20X3
Current liabilities			
Income tax payable (profits x 30%)	30,000	36,000	33,000

(W1) Income tax expense

	20X1 $	20X2 $	20X3 $
Current tax estimate	30,000	36,000	33,000
Over/under provision (W2)	0	(1,100)	1,200
	30,000	34,900	34,200

(W2) Under/over provisions

	20X1 $	20X2 $	20X3 $
Current tax estimate	30,000	36,000	33,000
Amount paid	28,900	37,200	?
Under/(over) provision	(1,100)	1,200	?

Remember these under/(over) provisions will not have an effect on the current year accounts but the following year accounts due to the timing of payments.

IAS 17 Leases and IAS 32 Financial Instruments

Chapter learning objectives

- Explain the principles of the accounting rules contained in IASs dealing with leases (lessee only);

- Identify the different accounting treatments for operating and finance leases;

- Calculate the allocation of interest charges to the income statement using the actuarial and the sum of the digits methods;

- Prepare extracts from the statement of financial position and income statement;

- Explain the accounting rules contained in IASs governing share capital transactions;

- Identify the treatment of share issue and redemption costs;

- Account for the issue and redemption of shares;

- Account for the maintenance of capital arising from the purchase by a company of its own shares.

1 Session content

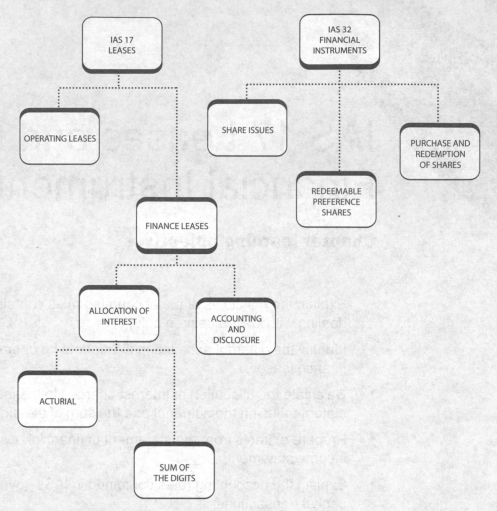

 ## 2 IAS 17 Leases

Definition

IAS 17 defines a lease as an agreement whereby the lessor conveys to the lessee, in return for a payment or series of payments, the right to use an asset for an agreed period of time.

Finance leases and operating leases

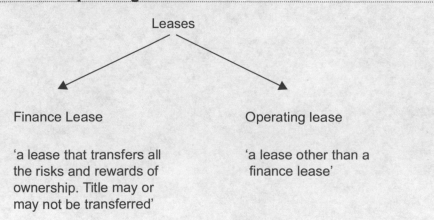

Leases

Finance Lease

'a lease that transfers all the risks and rewards of ownership. Title may or may not be transferred'

Operating lease

'a lease other than a finance lease'

Indications of a finance lease

- Legal title is transferred to the lessee at the end of the lease.

- The lease term is for the majority of the asset's useful economic life.

- The lessee has the option to purchase the asset for a price substantially below the fair value of the asset.

- The lessee bears losses arising from cancelling the lease.

- Lessee has ability to continue the lease for a secondary period at a rate below market rent.

- Present value of the lease payments is at least the majority of the fair value of the asset.

3 Operating leases

Under an operating lease the risks and rewards of ownership lie with the lessor, not the lessee. Therefore, by applying substance it can be concluded that the lessee should not record the item being leased as an asset.

Instead lease payments should be recognised as an expense in the income statement on a systematic basis (using straight line) over the term of the lease. The expense will be included under the appropriate operating expense heading. Any difference between the amounts charged to the income statement and amounts paid will be treated as prepayments and accruals on the statement of financial position.

Disclosure for operating leases

The lease expense will be disclosed in the profit from operations note and should include a general description of the entity's significant lease arrangements.

A note should also be prepared detailing the charges that will be incurred under non-cancellable operating leases for each of the following periods:

- not later than one year;

- later than one year and not later than five years;

- later than five years.

> **Illustration 1 : Operating leases**
>
> Zoo Ltd entered into a four year operating lease on 1 January 2011 for a machine. The initial deposit is $1,000 on 1 January 2011 followed by four annual payments in arrears of $1,000 in arrears on 31 December each year. Payment begin on 31 December 2011.

> What is the charge to the income statement and what amount would appear on the statement of financial position at the end of the first year of the lease?

Solution

Total payments = $5,000 (deposit plus 4 x $1,000 payments)

Income statement (extract)

	$
Operating lease expense ($5,000/4)	1,250

Statement of financial position (extract)

	$
Current assets	
Prepayments (paid $2,000 – $1,250 to the IS)	750

Test your understanding 1 : Operating leases

A company hires a machine under an operating lease for three years with payments to be made as follows:

Year 1	$5,000
Year 2	$10,000
Year 3	$6,000

Prepare extracts from the income statement and the statement of financial position for each of the three years.

4 Finance leases

Under a finance lease the risk and rewards of ownership lie with the lessee. Therefore, by applying substance over form the lessee should recognise the item being leased as an asset in their statement of financial position.

A liability is also recognised for the amounts payable under the terms of the lease.

The accounting treatment for a finance lease can by summarised as follows:

Record NCA and Liability

Dr NCA	Use lower of fair value of asset and
Cr Finance lease payable	present value of minimum lease payments

Depreciate asset

Dr Income statement	Depreciate over the shorter of the lease
Cr Acc Dep'n	term and its useful life
	Except:
	If asset will be owned by lessee at end of lease, then depreciate over useful life

Allocate finance charges

Dr Finance costs	Allocated using an appropriate method as per IAS 17
Cr Finance lease payable	

Record lease payments

Dr Finance lease payable	
Cr Bank	

Disclosure for finance leases

Finance lease payable:

- Split between non-current liabilities and current liabilities.

Non-current assets:

- For each class of asset, the net carrying amount of leased assets as at the reporting date.

Obligations under finance lease note:

	$
Not later than one year	X
Later than one year and not later than five years	X
Later than five years	X
	X
Finance charges allocated to future periods	(X)
	X
Present value of lease payments	X

Allocation of interest

A finance lease is effectively a form of borrowing money to finance the purchase of an asset. Interest charges will therefore be built into the lease payments. These need to be allocated over the length of the lease on a sensible basis.

There are two main methods of allocating the finance charge over the lease period:

- actuarial method;
- sum of the digits method.

Illustration 2 : Allocation of interest charges

A nightclub hires a revolving dance floor for all its useful life. The dance floor was worth $94,000 on the first day of use, 1 January. The contract tells you that there are four payments of $30,000 to be made on the 31 December of each year and that the annual rate of interest is 10.538%.

Required:

(a) Calculate the interest allocation on a sum of digit basis.

(b) Calculate the interest allocation on an actuarial basis.

Solution

	$
Total payments (4 x $30,000)	120,000
Value of asset	(94,000)
Total interest	26,000

(a) **Sum of digit basis**

N = No. of years borrowing = 4

Sum of the digits = n x (n+1)/2

4 x 5/2 = 10

Year 1	4/10	×	26,000	=	$10,400
Year 2	3/10	×	26,000	=	$7,800
Year 3	2/10	×	26,000	=	$5,200
Year 4	1/10	×	26,000	=	$2,600
					$26,000

(b) **Actuarial basis**

	Opening	Interest @ 10.538%	Total	Payment	Closing
1	94,000	9,906	103,906	(30,000)	73,906
2	73,906	7,788	81,694	(30,000)	51,694
3	51,694	5,447	57,141	(30,000)	27,141
4	27,141	2,859	30,000	(30,000)	–

Test your understanding 2 : Sum of the digits

A company cannot afford to buy a necessary piece of machinery so they arrange a finance lease. They will lease the machine over the next five years (after which time it will be scrapped) by payments of $1,200,000 on 31 December of each accounting year. The lease contract commences on 1 January 2010. It is estimated that the machine's open market value is $4,950,000. Interest is to be allocated on the sum of digits basis.

Required:

Prepare relevant extracts from the income statement and statement of financial position as at 31 December 2010. Show how your answer would change if payments were made on 1 January each year instead of 31 December.

Calculate your answer to the nearest $000.

Illustration 3 : Actuarial

A machine is delivered on the first day of the accounting year valued at $2 million. The lease contract requires the annual payment of $600,000 for four years and the machine has a useful economic life of five years. The interest implicit in the deal is given below.

Required:

Prepare extracts from the income statement and statement of financial position for year one and the obligations under finance leases note, assuming that instalments are paid in:

(a) arrears (implicit rate of interest 7.71%);
(b) advance (implicit rate of interest 13.71%).

Solution

	(a) Arrears $000	(b) Advance $000
Income statement (extract)		
Depreciation ($2,000/4)	500	500
Finance charge	154	192
Statement of financial position (extract)		
Non-current asset		
Cost	2,000	2,000
Acc dep'n	(500)	(500)
Carrying value	1,500	1,500
Non-current liabilities (see note below)	1,074	992
Current liabilities (see note below)	480	600

Note for split of current and non-current liabilities:

Obligations under finance leases - part a (payments in arrears)

	$000
Current liability (balancing amount)	480
Non-current liability (amount owing at the end of year 2 in workings below)	1,074
Total liability (end of year 1 in workings below)	1,554

Workings

Arrears:

Year	Opening	Interest 7.71%	Total	Payment	Closing
1	2000	154	2154	(600)	1554
2	1554	120	1674	(600)	1074
3	1074	83	1157	(600)	557
4	557	43	600	(600)	0

Total liability at the end of year 1 = $1,544

Non-current liability at the end of year 1 = $1,074 (amount owing at end of year 2)

Current liability at the end of year 1 = $1,554 – $1,074 = $480

Note for split of current and non-current liabilities:

Obligations under finance leases - part b (payments in arrears)

	$000
Current liability (next payment)	600
Non-current liability (balancing amount)	992
Total liability (end of year 1 in workings below)	1,592

Advance:

Year	Opening	Payment	Total	Interest 13.71%	Closing
1	2000	(600)	1400	192	1592
2	1592	(600)	992	136	1128
3	1128	(600)	528	72	600
4	600	(600)	0	0	0

Total liability at the end of year 1 = $1,592

Current liability at the end of year 1 = $600 (amount due to be paid in year 2)

Non-current liability at the end of year 1 = $1,592 – $600 = $992

NB. Depreciation is calculated on the lower of the lease period or the useful life of the asset. In this scenario the lease period is 4 years and the life of the asset is 5 years. Therefore, depreciate over 4 years.

Test your understanding 3 : Actuarial

A machine is delivered on the first day of the accounting year valued at $1,700,000. The lease contract requires the annual payment of $400,000 for six years and the machine has a useful economic life of seven years. The lease agreement transfers legal title to the company at the end of the lease agreement. The interest implicit in the deal is given below;

Required:

Prepare extracts from the income statement and statement of financial position for year one assuming that instalments are paid in:

(a) arrears (implicit rate of interest 10.84%);

(b) advance (implicit rate of interest 16.32%).

Test your understanding 4 : Exam standard question

Cuthbert Ltd is leasing a machine and the lease has been classified as a finance lease. The present value of the minimum lease payments is $462,600 and the fair value of the machine is $515,000. Under the terms of the lease five annual instalments of $120,000 are payable at the start of each year.

Required:

Prepare extracts from the income statement and statement of financial position, assuming that:

(a) interest is allocated on the sum of digits basis;

(b) interest is allocated on an actuarial basis, and the rate of interest implicit in the lease is 15%.

5 IAS 32 Financial Instruments

Financial instruments, i.e. shares and loans for the purpose of the F1 syllabus, must be recorded in the statement of financial position so as to reflect their true nature. As a result, financial instruments need to be distinguished between liabilities and equity according to their substance (rather than legal form).

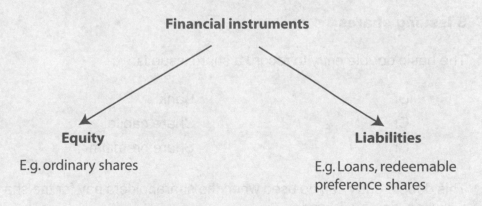

Financial instruments

Equity

E.g. ordinary shares

Liabilities

E.g. Loans, redeemable preference shares

Definitions

Financial instruments

Any contract that gives rise to both a financial asset or one entity and a financial liability or equity instrument of another entity.

Financial asset

Any asset that is:

(a) Cash;

(b) an equity instrument of another entity;

(c) a contractual right to receive cash or another financial asset from another entity; or to exchange financial instruments with another entity under conditions that are potentially favourable to the entity.

Examples of financial assets could be trade receivables or shares when used as an investment.

Financial liability

Any liability that is a contractual obliglation:

(a) to deliver cash or another financial asset to another entity; or

(b) to exchange financial instruments with another entity under conditions that are potentially unfavourable.

Examples of financial liabilities could be trade payables, loans or redeemable preference shares.

Equity instrument

Any contract that evidences a residual interest in the assets of an entity after deducting all of its liabilities.

6 Issuing shares

The basic double entry to record a share issue is:

Dr	Bank
Cr	Share capital
Cr	Share premium

This double entry can be used when the shareholders pay for the shares in full when they are issued.

Share issue costs are required to be accounted for within equity rather than being charged as an expense to the income statement. Such costs are normally charged against share premium:

Dr	Share premium
Cr	Bank

If the issue costs exceed the balance on the share premium account, they should be charged against retained earnings.

If the shares are paid for in instalments many sets of double entries have to be recorded.

Illustration 4 : Issue of shares

Bubble and Squeak Ltd decide to issue 500,000 $1 ordinary shares for $1.60.

Required:

Prepare the double entry for this transaction.

Solution

Transaction value

500,000 × $1.60 = $800,000

Double entry

Dr Cash	$800,000
Cr Share capital (500,000 x $1)	$500,000
Cr Share premium (500,000 x 0.60)	$300,000

Bonus issue of shares

A bonus issue is an issue of shares to existing shareholders for free.

The double entry to record a bonus issue is:

Dr	Share premium
Cr	Share capital

If the entity does not have a share premium account, or if the share premium account is not large enough for the bonus issue, reduce the premium account to nil and then debit the balance to other reserves.

Illustration 5 : Bonus issue

Magic Plc has 8,000,000 $1 ordinary shares in issue.

On 1 April 2009 a bonus issue is made of 1 share for every 4 shares in issue at 31 March 2009. The current market price is $2.15.

Required:

Prepare the double entry for this transaction.

Solution

Number of shares issued

8,000,000 / 4 = 2,000,000

Transaction value – nil

Double entry

Dr Share premium	$2,000,000
Cr Share capital (2,000,000 x $1)	$2,000,000

Rights issue

A rights issue is an issue of shares below the full market value to existing shareholders.

Illustration 6 : Rights issue

Patience Plc has 8,000,000 $1 ordinary shares in issue.

On 1 April 2009 a rights issue is made of 1 share for every 4 shares in issue at 31 March 2009 at a price of $1.40. The current market price is $2.15.

Required:

Prepare the double entry for this transaction.

Solution

Number of shares issued

8,000,000 / 4 = 2,000,000

Transaction value

2,000,000 × $1.40 = $2,800,000

Double entry

Dr Cash	$2,800,000
Cr Share capital (2,000,000 x $1)	$2,000,000
Cr Share premium	$800,000

Test your understanding 5 : Share issues

Giraffe and Rhino Ltd has 50,000 $0.50 shares in issue at 1 January 2010 and no balance b/fwd on the share premium account.

During the year the following share transactions took place as follows:

1 March 2010	Share issue of 100,000 shares at $1.10
1 May 2010	Bonus issue of 1 for 3 shares held at that date
1 September 2010	Rights issue of 1 for 4 shares held at that date for $0.90

Required:

Prepare the double entries for these transactions. Clearly show the total balances at the end of the year on the share capital and share premium accounts.

IAS 1 requirements

Interests of shareholders

The notes to an entity's financial statements contain a detailed note about the entity's share capital. This is hardly surprising given that the shareholders are regarded as the primary audience for the published accounts. They are the owners of the entity and need to be able to see how their ownership interests are reflected in the statement of financial position. They need to know how their interests might be affected by the issue of new shares.

A new issue will raise funds which will increase the value of their existing shares if the proceeds are invested wisely. This will, however, dilute their control. They also need to know about the interests of the other shareholders. In particular, they need to know how the existence of different classes of shares might affect their interests.

Disclosure

We studied the requirements of IAS 1 Presentation of Financial Statements in detail in Chapter 7. The following disclosures are required by the standard in respect of share capital.

IAS 1 requires that, issued capital and reserves attributable to owners must be shown in the statement of financial position. In addition, IAS 1 requires that, in the statement of financial position or in the notes, equity capital and reserves are analysed showing separately the various classes of paid-in capital, share premium and reserves.

IAS 1 also requires that the following information on share capital and reserves be made available either in the statement of financial position or in the notes:

(a) for each class of share capital:

• the number of shares authorised;

• the number of shares issued and fully paid, and issued but not fully paid;

• par value per share, or that the shares have no par value;

• a reconciliation of the number of shares outstanding at the beginning and at the end of the year;

• the rights, preferences and restrictions attaching to that class including restrictions on the distribution of dividends and the repayment of capital;

• shares in the entity held by the entity itself; and

• shares reserved for issuance under options and sales contracts, including the terms and amounts.

(b) a description of the nature and purpose of each reserve within equity.

IAS 1 requires the following to be disclosed in the notes:

- the amount of dividends proposed or declared before the financial statements were authorised for issue, but not recognised as a distribution to owners during the period, and the related amount per share;
- the amount of any cumulative preference dividends not recognised.

Different classes of shares

There are several different dimensions that can be used to describe and classify share capital. These include:

- authorised versus issued;
- nominal value versus issue price;
- specific classes of shares, as described in the entity's internal regulations;
- equity versus non-equity.

The precise rights attached to each class of shares is a matter for the entity's internal regulations. The usual differences can be summed up as follows:

	Ordinary shares	**Preference shares**
Voting rights	Ordinary shareholders almost always have the right to vote at general meetings, although some entities issue both voting and non-voting ordinary shares.	Preference shareholders would not normally have any voting rights.

Rewards	The ordinary dividend is decided by the directors. The ordinary shareholders are entitled to all of the profits after all other claims have been met. Any profits which are not distributed as a dividend will increase the ordinary shareholders' equity.	The preference dividend is usually fixed (e.g. 7.0 per cent of nominal value). The directors may, however, be able to suspend the preference dividend if the entity could not afford to pay it. In this case, the directors will probably be required to suspend the ordinary dividend. If the preference shares are 'cumulative', then any unpaid preference dividend will be paid once the entity's circumstances permit, before the ordinary shareholders can receive any dividend.
Risks	The ordinary shareholders are the last to be paid if the entity fails. In practice, this means that they may lose everything they have invested.	The preference shareholders will not be paid until after all of the entity's debts have been repaid.

Preference shares have become unpopular. From the shareholder's point of view, they carry a higher risk than making a loan and they do not have the potential for unlimited dividends offered by ordinary shares. This means that they have to carry a high rate of dividend to make them attractive.

From the entity's point of view, preference dividends cannot be charged as expenses for tax purposes and so they are a very expensive source of finance. There was, however, a brief period when unusual types of preference and other shares became popular as a result of a surge of interest in 'new financial instruments'. These were a means of raising finance which could be treated as share capital in the statement of financial position (thereby reducing the gearing ratio) but which gave the buyer the same rights as debt (thereby making them a cheap source of funds). Now IAS 32 and IAS 39 require these types of shares to be treated as debt in the financial statements (see below).

Entities are required to disclose the authorised share capital and the numbers and nominal value of each class of share which has been allotted. The effects of any allotment which took place during the year should be stated. The entity also has to disclose any options which have been granted to subscribers, stating the numbers of shares involved, the period during which this right can be exercised and the price to be paid. Details also have to be given of any redeemable shares, including the terms on which redemption will take place and the dates when this may occur.

Issue of shares

The bookkeeping entries in respect of the issue of shares are not complicated. The exact legal requirements may vary from one country to another and there may be additional requirements specified for entities quoted on the local stock exchange. In general, the procedures required to issue a share will follow a similar sequence of events. The accounting entries will follow the chronology of the share issue itself, for example:

(1) The entity announces the availability of the shares and their selling price, usually in a formal document.

(2) Applicants for shares submit formal requests for part of the issue. These applications will be accompanied by a proportion of the asking price, as requested by the entity in its announcement.

(3) If the issue is oversubscribed, then the entity has to decide how the shares should be allocated to the applicants. Any unsuccessful applicants will have their application money returned.

(4) The entity will 'allot' or formally issue the shares. The new shareholders will be asked to pay for a further proportion of the total asking price or the full balance outstanding.

(5) The entity will make further 'calls' of cash until the shares have been paid for in full. The timing of these calls will be determined by the entity's needs for long-term finance.

The selling price of the shares will be set so as to make the offer attractive to potential investors, but not so attractive that the shares are significantly underpriced. If the shares are sold too cheaply, then the existing shareholders will have their investment diluted. The price is, therefore, likely to be set just below the current market price. If this exceeds the nominal value of the shares, then the difference is called the 'share premium'.

Entities usually take precautions to ensure that the issue is fully sold. If there is a risk that some shares will be left over, then the entity can pay a financial institution to underwrite the offer. In return for a premium, the underwriter will agree to buy any unpaid shares left at the closing date of the offer.

If a shareholder does not pay the amounts due on the allotment or calls, then there will usually be provisions included in the issue documents that specify that the shares will be forfeited if payment is not made when due. The entity will be entitled to sell the forfeited shares for any amount that it can get, provided the total amount paid by the original shareholder and the new owner exceeds the nominal value of the shares.

Accounting for the issue of shares

The simplest way to organise the bookkeeping in respect of share capital is to have one account for the nominal value of the shares which have been issued and another for the premium, if any, created when those shares were issued. The balance on these accounts increases as soon as any allotment is made or any call is requested.

The cash received on application is recorded in an 'application and allotment' account. This is like a suspense account with the balance representing the amount paid to the entity in anticipation of either the receipt of some shares or the return of the payment. Once the shares have been allotted, the cash paid on application becomes the property of the entity and the shares transferred to the new shareholders discharge the entity's commitment to them. The entries on application are:

1. Debit   Bank
   Credit   Application and allotment account
   Being monies received on application of new shares
2. Debit   Application and allotment account
   Credit   Bank
   Being return of monies to unsuccessful applicants
3. Debit   Application and allotment account
   Credit   Share capital
   Credit   Share premium
   Being transfer of monies to share capital and premium accounts on allotment of shares

If the shares have not been paid for in full upon application a similar process will follow, i.e. transfer monies to application and allotment account and then transfer the share capital and premium accordingly.

4. Debit   Application and allotment account
   Credit   Share capital
   Credit   Share premium
   Being amounts due on allotment of shares
5. Debit   Bank
   Credit   Application and allotment account
   Being monies received on allotment of shares
6. Debit   Investment in own shares
   Credit   Application and allotment account
   Being transfer of balance on allotment monies due but not received

If further calls are required, a similar set of entries will be made. The amount requested will be debited to a call account and credited to share capital. Cash will be credited to the call account as it is received. If there is any balance left on the allotment or call accounts once the final deadline for receipt of payments has passed, then the shares will be forfeited. The balance on the account will be transferred to an 'investment in own shares' account. These shares will normally be reissued. Any amount received in excess of the original shareholder's default will be credited to share premium. The entries are:

7. Debit   Bank
    Credit   Investment in own shares account
    Being monies received on forfeited shares
8. Debit   Investment in own shares account
    Credit   Share premium
    Being transfer of balance to share premium

Example:

Randall had a balance on its share capital account of $2 million and a balance on share premium of $600,000. The directors decided to issue a further 500,000 $1 shares for $1.40 each.

The issue was announced and all applicants were asked to send a cheque for 10¢ for every share applied for. A total of 1,100,000 shares were applied for on the due date.

The directors decided to reject the smaller applications and returned application monies for a total of 100,000 shares. The remaining applicants were allotted one share for every two applied for, and were deemed to have paid 20¢ per share.

Applicants were asked to pay a further 90¢ per share, this being deemed to include the share premium associated with the issue. All allotment monies were received by the due date.

A final call of 30¢ per share was made. Payments were received in respect of 495,000 shares. The holder of 5,000 shares defaulted on this call and his shares were forfeited.

The forfeited shares were reissued for 50¢ each.

The accounting entries would be:

1. Debit   Bank (110,000 x 10c)   110,000
    Credit Application and allotment account   110,000
    Being monies received on application of new shares

2. Debit   Application and allotment account   10,000
    Credit Bank (100,000 x 10c)   10,000
    Being return of monies to unsuccessful applicants

3   Debit   Application and allotment account   100,000
    Credit Share capital   100,000
    Being transfer of monies to share capital on allotment of shares

   NB. All monies are transferred to the capital account as less than the nominal value has been received

4. Debit   Bank (500,000 x 90c)   450,000
    Credit Application and allotment account   450,000
    Being monies received on allotment of shares

5. Debit   Application and allotment account   450,000
    Credit Share capital (balance)   250,000
    Credit Share premium (500,000 x 40c)   200,000

6. Debit   Call account (500,000 x 30c)   150,000
    Credit Share capital   150,000
    Being amounts due on call

7. Debit   Bank (495,000 x 30c)   148,500
    Credit Call account   148,500
    Being payments made on call

8   Debit   Investment in own shares (5,000 x 30c) 1,500
    Credit Call account   1,500
    Being amounts due but not received on call

9   Debit   Bank (5,000 x 50c)   2,500
    Credit Investment in own shares   2,500
    Being amounts received on re-issue of shares

10 Debit   Investment in own shares   1,000
    Credit Share premium   1,000
    Being premium on re-issued shares (2,500 - 1,500)

7 Redeemable preference shares

IAS 32 classifies a redeemable preference share as a **liability,** not an equity instrument.

When a company issues redeemable shares, over the period between the issue and redemption of the shares, there is a finance cost to the company. The finance cost consists of two elements:

- The dividend paid;
- The difference between the eventual cost of redemption and the original amount raised from the share issue (after deducting issue costs).

The finance charge should be allocated to each year over the life of the shares so as to give a constant rate of interest.

Measurement of financial instruments

Financial instruments are initially measured at:

- fair value of the consideration (issue price less issue costs).

Accounting for finance charges

The finance charge is calculated in a similar way to finance leases:

- issue costs;
- dividends due over the issue period;
- redemption costs.

The total finance cost is spread over the issue period using the actuarial method.

Illustration 7 : Redeemable preference shares

A company issues $40 million of 8% preference shares at par. Issue costs are $2 million, and the shares are redeemable at par after four years. (Ignore redemption costs). The rate of interest required to provide a constant annual rate of interest is about 9.6%.

Required:

Calculate the finance charge for the preference shares in each of the four years, and the outstanding financial liability at the end of each year. Make your calculations to the nearest $100,000.

Solution

	$m
Money raised from share issue less issue costs (40 – 2)	38.0
Redemption cost	(40.0)
Dividends paid (4 years × $40m × 8%)	(12.8)
	———
Total finance charge	(14.8)
	———

Year	Opening balance ($m)	Finance cost @9.6% ($m)	Dividend Paid ($m)	Redemption ($m)	Closing balance ($m)
1	38	3.6	(3.2)		38.4
2	38.4	3.7	(3.2)		38.9
3	38.9	3.7	(3.2)		39.4
4	39.4	3.8	(3.2)	(40)	–

The opening balance in year 1 = net proceeds ($40m – $2m issue costs)

The finance cost is calculated by multiplying the opening balance by the rate of interest, i.e. year 1 = $38m x 9.6% = $3.6m. This finance cost is the charge to the income statement for the year under the heading of finance costs.

The dividend paid = $40m x 8% = $3.2m pa.

The closing balance shows the liability for the statement of financial position.

Note: Dividends paid will debit liability account and credit cash. They **will not** be shown as a distribution of profit in the statement of changes in equity.

Test your understanding 6 : Redeemable preference shares

Orange Ltd issues $20 million of 5% preference shares at par. Issue costs are $2 million, and the shares are redeemable at par after four years. (Ignore redemption costs). The rate of interest required to provide a constant annual rate of interest is about 8%.

Required:

Calculate the finance charge for the preference shares in each of the four years, and the outstanding financial liability at the end of each year. Make your calculations to the nearest $000.

8 Purchase and redemption of shares

Treasury shares

When a company has purchased its own equity shares, but has not cancelled them by the reporting date, the shares will be reclassified as treasury shares and shown as a deduction in equity.

The double entry is.

Dr	Treasury shares or distributable reserve	amount paid to repurchase shares
Cr	Bank	amount paid to repurchase shares

The transaction will be disclosed in the statement of changes in equity.

These shares can be re-issued at a later date

Treasury shares

International rules for accounting do not state **exactly** where the debit entry should be made (unlike UK GAAP). It is down to the individual country to state where this should be made. Hence, in an examination unless the examiner states the rules of the country, you can use either of these reserves for the debit entry.

Suppose that a company has the following statement of financial position:

	$000
Total Assets	4,000
Ordinary share capital, $1	2,000
Share premium	500
Retained earnings	1,500
	4,000

The company has decided to purchase 100,000 shares for $180,000 but has not cancelled them at the end of the reporting period.

Required:

Prepare the statement of financial position, as it would appear after the above transaction.

Solution

	$000
Total assets ($4,000 – $180)	3,820
Ordinary share capital, $1	2,000
Share premium	500
Treasury shares	(180)
Retained earnings	1,500
	3,820

Workings

Dr treasury shares 180,000

Cr bank 180,000

When a company decides to buy back their own shares and cancel them, the double entry would be as follows:

Dr Share capital account	Nominal value
Dr Share premium account	Premium value
Cr Bank	

Note: We cannot deduct more from the premium account than has previously been recorded for those shares. If the purchase premium exceeds the premium on original issue, the excess will be deducted from retained earnings.

This has created a reduction in capital, a reduction in the "permanent" value owed to shareholders. This permanent value is reinstated with a transfer from "distributable reserves", i.e. retained earnings. This transfer should be the nominal value of the shares purchased and cancelled.

Dr Distributable reserve (usually retained earnings)	Nominal value
Cr Capital reserve	Nominal value

Illustration 9 : Purchase of shares

Suppose that a company has the following statement of financial position:

	$000
Total Assets	4,000
Ordinary share capital, $1	2,000
Share premium	500
Retained earnings	1,500
	4,000

The company has decided to purchase and cancel 100,000 shares for $180,000. These shares had been originally issued at $1.50.

Required:

Show the double entries to record the transaction.

Prepare the statement of financial position, as it would appear after the above transaction.

Solution

Purchase

Dr share capital (100,000 x $1)	$100,000
Dr share premium (100,000 x $0.50)	$50,000
Dr retained earnings	$30,000
Cr cash	$180,000

Transfer from distributable reserve

Dr Retained earnings	$100,000
Cr Capital reserve	$100,000

	$000s
Total assets ($4,000 – $180)	3,820
Ordinary share capital, $1 ($2,000 – $100)	1,900
Share premium ($500 – $50)	450
Capital reserve	100
Retained earnings ($1,500 – $130)	1,370
	3,820

chapter 17

Test your understanding 7 : Single company accounts

The following trial balance relates to Fryatt at 31 May 2011:

	Dr	Cr
	$	$
Revenue		630,000
Cost of sales	324,000	
Distribution costs	19,800	
Administration expenses	15,600	
Loan interest paid	6,800	
Land and Buildings		
Cost at 1 June 2010	240,000	
Accumulated depreciation at 1 June 2010		40,000
Plant and equipment		
Cost at 1 June 2010	140,000	
Accumulated depreciation at 1 June 2010		48,600
Trade receivables and payables	51,200	35,200
Inventory as at 31 May 2011	19,600	
Cash and cash equivalents	4,300	
Ordinary shares $1		25,000
Share premium		7,000
Bank loan (repayable 31 December 2014)		20,000
Retained earnings at 1 June 2010		15,500
	_____	_____
	821,300	821,300

The following notes are relevant:

(1) Plant and equipment is to be depreciated on the reducing balance basis at the rate of 20% per annum. The property cost includes land at a cost of $60,000. The building is depreciated over 30 years on a straight line basis. All depreciation is charged to cost of sales.

(2) On 1 June 2010 Fryatt commenced using an item of plant and machinery under a lease agreement, making three annual payments of £29,000. The first payment was made on 31 May 2011 and has been charged to cost of sales. The present value of the minimum lease payments is $72,000 and fair value $78,000. Legal title will pass at the end of the lease period. The plant has an estimated useful life of 6 years and the rate of interest implicit in the lease is 10%.

(3) The directors have estimated the provision for income tax for the year to 31 May 2011 at $7,200.

Required:

Prepare, in a form suitable for publication, the statement of financial position and an income statement for the year ended 31 May 2011.

Test your understanding 8 : Objective test questions

(1) A company leases a machine under a finance lease agreement for four years. The value of the machine is $500,000 and the contract requires an annual payment of $150,000 with instalments to be paid at the start of each of the four years.

Assuming interest is to be allocated on the sum of digits basis, how will the interest be allocated over the four years of the agreement?

	Year 1	Year 2	Year 3	Year 4
A	40,000	30,000	20,000	10,000
B	50,000	33,333	16,667	–
C	25,000	25,000	25,000	25,000
D	50,000	30,000	15,000	5,000

(2) A company leases a machine under a finance lease agreement for four years. The value of the machine is $200,000 and the contract requires an annual payment of $70,000 with instalments to be paid at the end of each of the four years.

Assuming interest is to be allocated on the sum of digits basis, how will the interest be allocated over the four years of the agreement?

	Year 1	Year 2	Year 3	Year 4
A	32,000	24,000	16,000	8,000
B	40,000	26,667	13,333	–
C	20,000	20,000	20,000	20,000
D	40,000	30,000	8,000	2,000

(3) A company purchases a computer under a lease agreement with legal title of the asset passing after two years. The company usually depreciates computers over three years. The company also leases a machine under a finance lease agreement for seven years. Legal title does not pass to the lessee at the end of the agreement. The company usually depreciates machinery over ten years.

Over what period of time should the computer and machine be depreciated?

	Computer	Machine
A	2 years	7 years
B	2 years	10 years
C	3 years	7 years
D	3 years	10 years

(4) A company leases a motor vehicle under a finance lease. The present value of minimum lease payments is $27,355 and the fair value of the vehicle is $29,000. The interest rate implicit in the lease is 10%. The terms of the lease require three annual instalments to be paid of $10,000 each at the start of each year.

At the end of the first year of the lease what amount will be shown in the company's statement of financial position under the headings of non-current liabilities under finance lease and current liabilities under finance lease?

	Current liabilities	Non-current liabilities
A	$9,091	$10,000
B	$10,000	$10,900
C	$10,900	$10,000
D	$10,000	$9,091

(5) A company leases some furniture under a five year operating lease. The agreement states that $9,000 is payable for four years commencing in the second year of the agreement. The furniture has an estimated useful life of ten years.

How much will be charged to the income statement in year one in respect of this lease?

A $nil

B $3,600

C $7,200

D $9,000

(6) A finance lease runs for 5 years, with annual payments in arrears of $25,000. The fair value of the asset was $90,000. **Using the sum-of-digits method, what would the outstanding lease creditor be at the end of year 2?**

A $47,000

B $61,000

C $64,500

D $40,000

(7) L leases a delivery vehicle to D on an operating lease. The terms of the lease are:

- term 3 years

- special introductory discount in year one, rental reduced to $2,000

- annual rentals of $5,000 per year for years two and three.

How much should D recognise as an expense in its profit or loss for the first year of the lease?

A $2,000

B $4,000

C $5,000

D $12,000

(8) An item of machinery leased under a five-year finance lease on 1 October 2009 had a fair value of $51,900 at date of purchase. The lease payments were $12,000 per year, payable in arrears.

If the sum-of-digits method is used to apportion interest to accounting periods, calculate the finance cost for the year ended 30 September 2011.

(9) **Data for Questions 9 and 10**

CS acquired a machine, using a finance lease, on 1 January 2009. The machine had an expected useful life of 12,000 operating hours, after which it would have no residual value.

The finance lease was for a five-year term with rentals of $20,000 per year payable in arrears. The cost price of the machine was $80,000 and the implied interest rate is 7.93% per year. CS used the machine for 2,600 hours in 2009 and 2,350 hours in 2010.

Using the actuarial method, calculate the non-current liability and current liability figures required by IAS 17 Leases to be shown in CS's Statement of financial position at 31 December 2010.

(10) **Calculate the non-current asset – property, plant and equipment carrying value that would be shown in CS's Statement of financial position at 31 December 2010. Calculate the depreciation charge using the machine hours method.**

Test your understanding 9 : Objective test questions 2

(1) **Which of the following statements are true in respect of a bonus issue?**

(i)   No finance is directly raised from a bonus issue.

(ii) Bonus issues are often at a price below market value.

(iii) Only capital reserves can be used to finance a bonus issue.

A   i and iii

B   i only

C   ii and iii

D   i and ii

(2) A company makes a bonus issue of 10,000 50c ordinary shares. Before the bonus issue, the company has a balance of $4,000 on its share premium reserve and $26,000 on its retained earnings.

Which of the following double entries can be made to record this bonus issue?

A	Dr	Share Premium	$5,000
	Cr	Share Capital	$5,000
B	Dr	Share Premium	$10,000
	Cr	Share Capital	$10,000
C	Dr	Share Premium	$4,000
	Dr	Retained earnings	$1,000
	Cr	Share Capital	$5,000
D	Dr	Share Premium	$4,000
	Dr	Retained earnings	$6,000
	Cr	Share Capital	$10,000

(3) A company purchases 5,000 of its own $1 ordinary shares at a price of $1.20 per share.

What balance will be shown for treasury shares on the statement of financial position?

A $6000

B $5,000

C $1,000

D $11,000

(4) During the year, a company issues 400,000 50c shares at a price of $1.30. Costs amounting to $35,000 were incurred in relation to the share issue. There was no opening balance on the share premium account.

What will be the balance on the share premium account following the above share issue?

A $120,000

B $85,000

C $320,000

D $285,000

(5) Treasury shares are defined as:

A equity shares sold by an entity in the period

B equity shares repurchased by the issuing entity, not cancelled before the period end

C non-equity shares sold by an entity in the period

D equity shares repurchased by the issuing entity and cancelled before the period end

9 Summary diagram

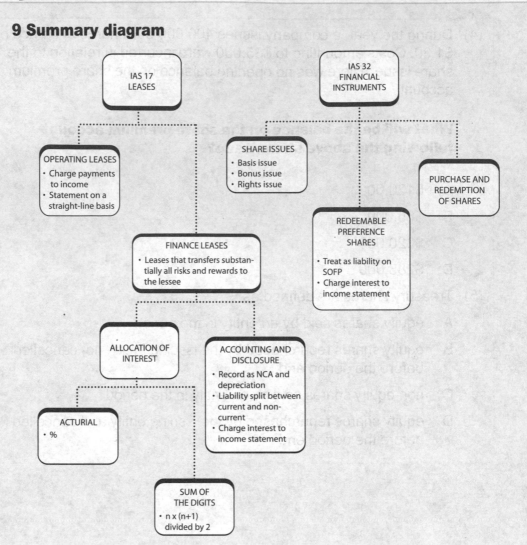

Test your understanding answers

Test your understanding 1 : Operating leases

Total lease payments = $5,000 + $10,000 + $6,000 = $21,000.

Length of lease = three years

Annual charge to income statement = $21,000/3 = $7,000

Income statement (extract)

	1	2	3
Operating lease expense	7,000	7,000	7,000

Statement of financial position (extract)

	1	2	3
Prepayments		1,000	nil
Accruals	2,000		

Workings

By the end of year one, a total of $7,000 has been charged to the IS but only $5,000 has been paid and so an accrued expense is required in the statement of financial position of $2,000.

By the end of year two, a total of $14,000 has been charged to the IS and $15,000 has been paid and so a prepayment is required in the statement of financial position of $1,000.

Test your understanding 2 : Sum of the digits

If payments were made in arrears, i.e. at the end of the year:

	$000
Income statement (extract)	
Depreciation ($4,950/5)	990
Finance charge	350

Statement of financial position (extract)

Non-current asset	
Cost	4,950
Acc Dep'n ($4,950/5)	(990)
Carrying value	3,960
Non-current obligation under finance lease	3,180
Current obligation under finance lease	920

Workings

	$000
Total payments (5 x $1,200)	6,000
Value of asset	(4,950)
Total interest	1,050

Sum of digits = N = 5 years

n x (n+1)/2 = (5 x 6)/2 = 15

Year 1	5/15	×	1,050	=	$350
Year 2	4/15	×	1,050	=	$280
Year 3	3/15	×	1,050	=	$210
Year 4	2/15	×	1,050	=	$140
Year 5	1/15	×	1,050	=	$70

Year	Opening	Interest	Total	Payment	Closing
1	4,950	350	5,300	(1,200)	4,100
2	4,100	280	4,380	(1,200)	3,180

Total liability at the end of year 1 = $4,100

Non-current liability at the end of year 1 = $3,180 (amount owing at end of year 2)

Current liability at the end of year 1 = $4,100 – $3,180 = $920

If payments were made in advance, i.e. at the beginning of the year:

Income statement (extract)	$000
Depreciation ($4,950/5)	990
Finance charge	420

Statement of financial position (extract)

Non-current asset	
Cost	4,950
Acc Dep'n ($4,950/5)	(990)
Carrying value	3,960
Non-current obligation under finance lease	2,970
Current obligation under finance lease	1,200

Workings

	$000
Total payments (5 x $1,200)	6,000
Value of asset	(4,950)
Total interest	1,050

Sum of digits = N = 4 years

n x (n+1)/2 = (4 x 5)/2 = 10

Year 1	4/10	×	1,050	=	$420
Year 2	3/10	×	1,050	=	$315
Year 3	2/10	×	1,050	=	$210
Year 4	1/10	×	1,050	=	$105

Year	Opening	Payment	Total	Interest	Closing
1	4,950	(1,200)	3,750	420	4,170
2	4,170	(1,200)	2,970	315	3,285

Total liability at the end of year 1 = $4,170

Non-current liability at the end of year 1 = $2,970 (total liability - current liability)

Current liability at the end of year 1 = $1,200 (payment)

487

Test your understanding 3 : Actuarial

	(a) Arrears	(b) Advance
	$000	$000
Income statement (extract)		
Depreciation (1,700/7)	243	243
Finance cost	184	212
Statement of financial position (extract)		
Non-current asset		
Cost	1,700	1,700
Acc dep'n	(243)	(243)
Carrying value	1,457	1,457
Non-current liabilities	1,245	1,112
Current liabilities	239	400

Workings

Arrears:

Year	Opening	Interest 10.84%	Total	Payment	Closing
1	1700	184	1884	(400)	1484
2	1484	161	1645	(400)	1245
3	1245	135	1380	(400)	980
4	980	106	1086	(400)	686
5	686	74	760	(400)	360
6	360	40	400	(400)	0

Total liability at the end of year 1 = $1,484

Non-current liability at the end of year 1 = $1,245 (amount owing at end of year 2)

Current liability at the end of year 1 = $1,484 – $1,245 = $239

Advance:

Year	Opening	Payment	Total	Interest 16.32%	Closing
1	1700	(400)	1300	212	1512
2	1512	(400)	1112	181	1293
3	1293	(400)	893	146	1039
4	1039	(400)	640	104	743
5	743	(400)	343	57	400
6	400	(400)	0	0	0

Total liability at the end of year 1 = $1,512

Current liability at the end of year 1 = $400 (amount due to be paid in year 2)

Non-current liability at the end of year 1 = $1,512 – $400 = $1,112

NB. Depreciation is calculated on the lower of the lease period or the useful life of the asset. In this scenario the lease period is 6 years and the life of the asset is 7 years. However, as legal title passes at the end of the lease period the higher can be used, ie. 7 years, as the company will continue to use the asst in the year.

Test your understanding 4 : Exam standard question

	(a) Sum of digits $	(b) Actuarial $
Income statement (extract)		
Depreciation ($462,600/5)	92,520	92,520
Interest	54,960	51,390
Statement of financial position (extract)		
Non-current asset		
Cost	462,600	462,600
Acc dep'n	(92,520)	(92,520)
Carring value	370,080	370,080
Non-current liabilities (Total liability – current liability)	277,560	273,990
Current liabilities (payment due as in advance)	120,000	120,000

Workings

Sum of digits:

n = 4, n x (n+1)/2

4 x 5/2 = 10

(payments are made in advance and so only borrowing money for four years)

	$
Total payments (5 x $120,000)	600,000
Value of asset (lower of MLP and fair value)	(462,600)
Total Interest	137,400

Year 1	4/10	×	137,400	=	$54,960
Year 2	3/10	×	137,400	=	$41,220
Year 3	2/10	×	137,400	=	$27,480
Year 4	1/10	×	137,400	=	$13,740

$137,400

Year	Opening	Payment	Total	Interest	Closing
1	462,600	(120,000)	342,600	54,960	397,560
2	397,560	(120,000)	277,560	41,220	318,780
3	318,780	(120,000)	198,780	27,480	226,260
4	226,260	(120,000)	106,260	13,740	120,000
5	120,000	(120,000)	nil	nil	nil

Actuarial:

Year	Opening	Payment	Total	Interest 15%	Closing
1	462,600	(120,000)	342,600	51,390	393,990
2	393,990	(120,000)	273,990	41,099	315,089
3	315,089	(120,000)	195,089	29,263	224,352
4	224,352	(120,000)	104,352	15,648	120,000
5	120,000	(120,000)	nil	nil	nil

Test your understanding 5 : Share issues

(1) Opening balance

Share capital = 50,000 x 0.50 = $25,000

(2) 1 March 2010

Number of shares issued

100,000

Transaction value

100,000 × $1.10 = $110,000

Double entry

Dr Cash	$110,000
Cr Share capital (100,000 x 0.50 nominal)	$50,000
Cr Share premium (balance)	$60,000

(3) 1 May 2010

Number of shares issued

(50,000 + 100,000)/3 = 50,000

Transaction value

nil

Double entry

Dr Share premium	$25,000
Cr Share capital (50,000 x 0.50 nominal)	$25,000

(4) 1 September 2010

Number of shares issued

(50,000 + 100,000 + 50,000)/4 = 50,000

Transaction value

50,000 × $0.90 = $45,000

Double entry

Dr Cash	$45,000
Cr Share capital (50,000 x 0.50 nominal)	$25,000
Cr Share premium (balance)	$20,000

Total share capital = 25,000 + 50,000 + 25,000 + 25,000 = $125,000

Total share premium = 60,000 – 25,000 + 20,000 = $55,000

Test your understanding 6 : Redeemable preference shares

	$m
Excess of redemption cost over money raised (20 – 18)	2.0
Dividends paid (4 years × $20m × 5%)	4.0
	——
Total finance charge	6.0
	——

Year	Opening balance ($m)	Finance cost @ 8% ($m)	Dividend Paid ($m)	Redemption ($m)	Closing balance ($m)
1	18	1.4	(1.0)		18.4
2	18.4	1.5	(1.0)		18.9
3	18.9	1.5	(1.0)		19.4
4	19.4	1.6	(1.0)	(20)	–

The opening balance in year 1 = net proceeds ($20m – $2m issue costs)

The finance cost is calculated by multiplying the opening balance by the rate of interest, i.e. year 1 = $18m x 8% = $1.4m. This finance cost is the charge to the income statement for the year under the heading of finance costs.

The dividend paid = $20m x 5% = $1m pa.

The closing balance shows the liability for the statement of financial position.

Note: Dividends paid will debit liability account and credit cash. They **will not** be shown as a distribution of profit in the statement of changes in equity.

Test your understanding 7 : Single company accounts

Fryatt income statement for the year ended 31 May 2011

	$
Revenue	630,000
Cost of sales (W1)	(331,280)
Gross profit	298,720
Distribution costs	(19,800)
Administration expenses	(15,600)
Profit from operations	263,320
Finance cost (W4)	(14,000)
Profit before tax	249,320
Income tax expense	(7,200)
Profit for year	242,120

Fryatt statement of financial position as at 31 May 2011

	$	$
Non-current assets		
Property, plant and equipment (W2)		327,120
Current assets		
Inventories	19,600	
Trade and other receivables	51,200	
Cash and cash equivalents	4,300	
		75,100
Total assets		402,220

Equity and liabilities

Capital and reserves

Issued ordinary share capital	25,000	
Share premium	7,000	
Retained earnings (W4)	257,620	
		289,620

Non-current liabilities

Bank loan	20,000	
Finance lease payable (W3)	26,220	
		46,220

Current liabilities

Trade payables	35,200	
Finance lease payable (W3)	23,980	
Income tax	7,200	
		66,380

Total equity and liabilities	402,220

Workings

(W1)

	COS
	$
Per TB	324,000
Depreciation plant and equipment	18,280
Depreciation building	6,000
Depreciation lease	12,000
Remove lease payment	(29,000)
	331,280

(W2)

	Property	Plant & equipment	Lease	Total
	$	$	$	$
Cost/Valuation				
At 1 June 2010	240,000	140,000	-	380,000
Additions	-	-	72,000	72,000
Disposals	-	-	-	-
At 31 May 2011	240,000	140,000	72,000	452,000
Accumulated depreciation:				
At 1 June 2010	40,000	48,600	-	88,600
Charged during the year *	6,000	18,280	12,000	36,280
Disposals	-	-	-	-
At 31 May 2011	46,000	66,880	12,000	124,880
Net book value				
At 31 May 2011	194,000	72,120	60,000	327,120
At 31 May 2010	200,000	91,400	-	291,400

* Property depreciation ($ 240,000 - $60,000)/30 = $6,000

Lease depreciation $72,000/6 = $12,000

Plant and equipment depreciation = ($140,000 - $48,600) x 20% = $18,280

(W3)

	Opening	Interest 10%	Sub	Payment	Closing
31/05/11	72,000	7,200	79,200	(29,000)	50,200
31/05/12	50,200	5,020	55,220	(29,000)	26,220

Total liability at 31/05/11 = $50,200

NCL = $26,220 (amount owing at 31/05/12)

CL = $23,980 (balance)

(W4)

Finance cost

	$
As per TB	6,800
Finance lease	7,200
	14,000

(W5)

Retained earnings

	$
As per TB	15,500
Profit for the period (IS)	242,120
	257,620

Test your understanding 8 : Objective test questions

(1) B

Sum of digits:

N=3 (because payments are in advance)

N(N+1)/2 = 3 × 4/2 = 6

Total payments (4 × 150,000)	600,000
Value of asset	(500,000)
Total Interest	100,000

Year 1	Year 2	Year 3	Year 4
3/6 × 100,000	2/6 × 100,000	1/6 × 100,000	–
50,000	33,333	16,667	0

(2) A

Sum of digits:

N=4 (because payments are in arrears)

N(N+1)/2 = 4 × 5/2 = 10

Total payments (4 × 70,000)	280,000
Value of asset	(200,000)
Total Interest	80,000

Year 1	Year 2	Year 3	Year 4
4/10 × 80,000	3/10 × 80,000	2/10 × 80,000	1/10 × 80,000
32,000	24,000	16,000	8,000

(3) C

(4) D

	Opening	Payment	Sub-total	Interest 10%	Closing
1	27,355	(10,000)	17,355	1,736	19,091
2	19,091	(10,000)	9,091	909	10,000

(5) C

(9,000 × 4)/5 yrs = $7,200

(6) B

Sum of digits:

N=5 (because payments are in arrears)

N(N+1)/2 = 5 × 6/2 = 15

Total payments (5 × 25,000)	125,000
Value of asset	(90,000)
Total Interest	35,000

Year 1	**Year 2**
5/15 × 35,000	4/15 × 35,000
= 11,667	= 9,333

Year 1 = 90,000 + 11,667 - 25,000 = $76,667

Year 2 = 76,667 + 9,333 - 25,000 = $61,000

(7) B
Total expense = 2,000 + 5,000 + 5,000 = $12,000
Total years 3
Expense to IS $12,000/3 = $4,000pa

(8) Sum of digits:

N=5 (because payments are in arrears)

N(N+1)/2 = 5 × 6/2 = 15

30 September 2011 = year 2 of the lease - 4/15

4/15 x $8,100 = $2,160

Finance cost = total payments (5 x $12,000) less fair value $51,900
= $8,100

(9) The total liability at the end of 2010 = $51,605

The non-current liability = $35,697 (amount still owing in one year's time)

The current liability = $15,908 ($51,605 - $35,697)

Year	Opening	Interest 7.93%	Payment	Closing
2009	80,000	6,344	(20,000)	66,344
2010	66,344	5,261	(20,000)	51,605
2011	51,605	4,092	(20,000)	35,697
2012	35,697	2,831	(20,000)	18,528
2013	18,528	1,472	(20,000)	0

(10) Depreciation = $80,000/12,000 X (2,600 + 2,350) = $33,000

Carrying value = $80,000 - $33,000 = $47,000

Test your understanding 9 : Objective test questions 2

(1) B

(2) C

(3) A

5,000 shares × $1.20 = $6,000

(4) D

400,000 shares × ($1.30 – 0.50) =	320,000
Issue costs	(35,000)
	285,000

(5) B

IAS 11 Construction Contracts

Chapter learning objectives

- Explain and apply the accounting rules contained in IASs dealing with construction contracts;

- Calculate the stage of completion of a contract using the cost basis and the work certified basis;

- Prepare income statement and statement of financial position extract for profitable and loss making contracts;

- Identify disclosure requirements.

1 Session content

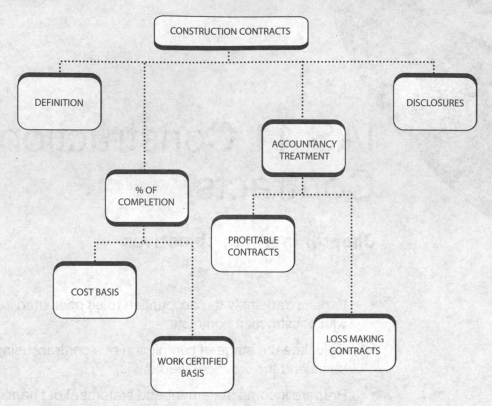

2 Introduction

Definition

A construction contract is defined as being a contract specifically negotiated for the construction of an asset or a combination of assets that are related. A construction contract is a contract to a substantial asset, such as a bridge, a building, a ship or a tunnel.

The nature of construction contracts is such that the dates when the activity is started and is completed often fall into different accounting periods. The accounting issue is therefore when the revenue and costs associated with the contract should be recognised.

There are two alternative views on the situation as follows:

Recognise results on completion	Recognise results as contract progresses
Complies with prudence since it will not be certain that the contract is profitable until completion	Complies with the matching concept as results will match work performed during the accounting period
Reliable since revenue, costs and profits will be known with certainty on completion	Less reliable since calculations will involve estimates regarding the future.

Not relevant since reported results will not reflect activities of the entity in the period	Achieves relevance since reported results will reflect the activities of the entity
Is likely to cause reported results to be distorted and so incomparable	Will enable financial statements to be more comparable with other entities

Therefore, we have a conflict between the prudence concept and the accruals concept. However, IAS 11 aims satisfy these requirements by ensuring we match related revenue to related expenditure, however, still maintaining the concept of prudence.

Accounting treatment of construction contracts

IAS 11 states that when the outcome of a construction contract can be estimated reliably, contract revenue and contract costs should be recognised in the income statement by reference to the stage of completion of the contract activity at the reporting date.

Consequently:

Revenue	Revenue of work completed in period
Cost of sales	Costs of work completed in period
Gross profit	Sub-total

The stage of completion may be calculated in various ways, e.g. cost basis, work certified basis.

The cost basis is calculated as follows:

$$\frac{\text{Costs incurred to date}}{\text{Total cost for the contract}} = \% \text{ of completion}$$

The work certified basis is calculated as follows:

$$\frac{\text{Work certified to date}}{\text{Total revenue for the contract}} = \% \text{ of completion}$$

When the overall outcome (profit or loss) cannot be estimated reliably IAS 11 requires revenue to be recognised equal to costs incurred in period (assuming the revenue will probably be recovered). Therefore, nil profit will be recognised.

Profitable contracts

Workings:

- Calculate overall expected profit on the contract.
- Calculate percentage completion of contract as at the reporting date.

Income statement

- Revenue for period = (% × total revenue) – revenues previously recognised in prior periods
- Cost of sales = (% × total costs) – costs previously recognised in prior periods
- Gross profit = Revenue – Cost of Sales

Statement of financial position

- IAS 11 requires the 'gross amount due from/to customers' to be disclosed in the statement of financial position as either an asset or a liability. This represents any contract costs incurred but not yet transferred to cost of sales.

	$
Costs incurred	X
Recognised profits	X
Recognised losses	(X)
Amounts billed/invoiced/progress billings	(X)
'From'/('To')	X/(X)

This figure represents costs that have been spent but that relate to future activity on the contract (work in progress costs) and revenue of work that has been completed but not yet billed to the client.

- Amounts due from customers = asset (positive figure)
- Amounts due to customers = liability (negative figure)

Contract revenue and costs

Contract revenue

Contract revenue is the amount of revenue the contract has been agreed for, i.e. contract price.

Contract costs

Contract costs comprise of costs that directly relate to the contract, i.e. site labour costs, materials, costs of depreciation for equipment used in the contract, costs of hiring/moving equipment for the contract, etc.

Gross amounts due from customers

This represents the total cost incurred plus any recognised profits (in the income statement) less amounts invoiced to customers. This amount is shown as an asset because it represents money that has been spent on the project but customers have not yet been invoiced because it relates to a future activity (no work done yet).

Gross amounts due to customers

This represents the total costs incurred plus any recognised profits (in the income statement) less amounts invoiced to customers. This amount is shown as a liability because the amounts invoiced to customers exceeds the amount spent on the project so far, therefore strictly this money is owed to customers (although wouldn't actually be repaid).

Accounting treatment

We incur costs on a contract:

Dr   Contract costs
Cr   Bank/payables

We raise an invoice:

Dr   Receivables
Cr   Progress payments

We receive payment from the customer:

Dr   Bank
Cr   Receivables

We record a sales value (based on stage of completion):

Dr   Progress payments
Cr   Revenue

We match related costs (based on stage of completion):

Dr   Cost of sales
Cr   Contract costs

The income statement profit is calculated by looking at the sales account less cost of sales account.

The statement of financial position is calculated by netting off the contract and the progress payments accounts.

Illustration 1 : Cost basis contract

Softfloor House Ltd build bars. The project generally takes a number of months to complete. The company has three contracts in progress at the year ended April 2011.

	A	B	C
	$000	$000	$000
Costs incurred to date	200	90	600
Estimated costs to complete	200	110	100
Contract price	600	300	750
Progress billings	40	70	630

Softfloor calculates the percentage of completion by using the cost basis.

Required:

Calculate the effects of the above contract upon the financial statements.

Solution

Overall contract profit

	A	B	C
	$000	$000	$000
Contract price	600	300	750
Costs incurred to date	(200)	(90)	(600)
Estimated costs to complete	(200)	(110)	(100)
Gross profit	200	100	50

% of completion on cost basis

A 200/400 =   50%
B 90/200 =   45%
C 600/700 =   86% (rounded)

Income statement (extract)

	A	B	C
	$000	$000	$000
Revenue (% x contract price)	300	135	645
Costs (% x total cost)	(200)	(90)	(600)
Gross profit	100	45	45

Statement of financial position (extract)

	A	B	C
	$000	$000	$000
Costs incurred	200	90	600
Profit recognised	100	45	45
Less: progress billings	(40)	(70)	(630)
Amounts due from customers (asset)	260	65	15

Illustration 2 : Work certified basis contract

Hardfloor House Ltd fits out nightclubs. The project generally takes a number of months to complete. The company has three contracts in progress at the year ended April 2011.

	A	B	C
	$000	$000	$000
Costs incurred to date	320	540	260
Estimated costs to complete	40	90	120
Contract price	416	684	400
Work certified to date	312	456	200
Progress billings	250	350	230

Hardfloor calculates the percentage of completion by using the work certified basis.

Required:

Calculate the effects of the above contract upon the financial statements.

Solution

Overall contract profit

	A	B	C
	$000	$000	$000
Contract price	416	684	400
Costs incurred to date	(320)	(540)	(260)
Estimated costs to complete	(40)	(90)	(120)
Gross profit	56	54	20

% of completion on work certified basis

A 312/416 =   75%
B 456/684 =   67% (rounded)
C 200/400 =   50%

Income statement (extract)

	A	B	C
	$000	$000	$000
Revenue (% x contract price)	312	456	200
Costs (% x total cost)	(270)	(422)	(190)
Gross profit	42	34	10

Statement of financial position (extract)

	A	B	C
	$000	$000	$000
Costs incurred	320	540	260
Profit recognised	42	34	10
Less: progress billings	(250)	(350)	(230)
Amounts due from customers (asset)	112	224	40

Illustration 3 : Contracts over a number of years

Continuing with the previous illustration, all three contracts complete the following year with the following cumulative results:

	A	B	C
	$000	$000	$000
Total costs incurred to date	370	640	380
Contract price	416	684	400
Progress billings	410	670	390

Required:

Calculate the effects of the above contract upon the financial statements.

Solution

Income statement (extract)

	A	B	C
	$000	$000	$000
Revenue (100% x contract price) - amounts recognised	104	228	200
Costs (100% x total cost) - amounts recognised	(100)	(218)	(190)
Gross profit	4	10	10

Statement of financial position (extract)

	A	B	C
	$000	$000	$000
Costs incurred (cumulative)	370	640	380
Profit recognised (cumulative)	46	44	20
Less: progress billings (cumulative)	(410)	(670)	(390)
Amounts due from customers (asset)	6	14	10

Explanatory note:

Contract A :

Revenue $416 - $312 already recognised = $104 this year
Cost $370 - $270 already recognised = $100 this year

Overall profit = $416 - $370 = $46

Test your understanding 1 : Contracts over a three year period

An airport terminal project started in 2009 and will be completed in 2011. The total income of $9 million may be anticipated with reasonable certainty at the year-end 31 December 2009.

The following information is relevant:

	At 31.12.09	At 31.12.10	At 31.12.11
	$000	$000	$000
Costs to date	2,800	4,800	7,500
Estimated costs to complete	4,200	2,700	–
Work certified	2,700	6,300	9,000

Required:

Calculate the effects of the above contract upon the income statement on the work certified basis and costs basis for all three year ends.

Test your understanding 2 : Profit making contracts

Reeve Ltd have undertaken four long-term contracts in the year. The following information has been obtained at the end of the year in relation to each project:

	A	B	C	D
	$000	$000	$000	$000
Contract price	500	1,000	2,000	3,000
Work certified to date	150	200	500	1,300
Costs incurred to date	200	220	600	700
Estimated costs to complete	200	unknown	1,100	1,100
Amounts billed	140	160	700	1,200

Required:

Prepare extracts from the financial statements for each of the four projects, assuming that % completion is calculated on the work certified basis.

3 Loss making contracts

IAS 11 requires that an expected loss on a construction contract should be recognised as an expense immediately.

Revenue will be calculated as before, but the whole loss will then be recorded on the gross line and cost of sales will be calculated as a balancing figure.

Illustration 4 : Loss making contracts

The following figures relate to a contract:

	$000
Contract price	900
Work certified	495
Costs incurred to date	525
Estimated costs to complete	435
Amounts invoiced to customers	475

Required:

Prepare extracts from the financial statements. The percentage completion should be calculated on the work certified basis.

Solution

Overall contract

	$000
Contract price	900
Costs to date	(525)
Costs to complete	(435)
Total loss	(60)

% completion on work certified basis

495/900 = 55%

Income statement (extract)

Revenue (55% x 900)	495
Cost of sales (balancing figure)	(555)
Gross loss	(60)

As this is a loss making contract, the whole of the loss must be recognised immediately (prudence).

Statement of financial position (extract)

Gross amounts due to customers

Costs incurred	525
Losses recognised	(60)
Progress billings	(475)
Amounts due to customers (liability)	(10)

Test your understanding 3 : Exam standard question

Hindhead build specialist equipment for use in the building industry. Each piece of equipment takes between one and two years to build and so the company is required to account for construction contracts.

The company has four contracts in process at the year end 30 April 2011:

	A	B	C	D
	$000	$000	$000	$000
Contract price	500	890	420	750
Work certified to date	375	534	280	–
Costs incurred to date	384	700	468	20
Estimated costs to complete	48	115	168	650
Progress billings	360	520	224	–

Required:

Prepare extracts from the financial statements for each of the four projects, assuming that revenues and profits are recognised on the work certified basis.

4 Disclosures

An entity should disclose the following for construction contracts:

- contract revenue recognised;
- methods used to identify contract revenue recognised;
- methods used to identify the stage of completion;
- for work-in-progress (SOFP figure) calculation.

Test your understanding 4 : Exam standard question

Details from DV's long-term contract, which commenced on 1 May 2010, at 30 April 2011 were:

	$'000
Total contract value	3,000
Invoiced to client work done	2,000
Costs to date - attributable to work completed	1,500
Costs to date - inventory purchased but not yet used	250
Estimated costs to complete	400
Progress payments received from client	900

DV uses the percentage of costs incurred to total costs to calculate attributable profit.

Calculate the amount that DV should recognise in its statement of comprehensive income for the year ended 30 April 2011 for revenue, cost of sales and attributable profits on this contract according to IAS 11 Construction Contracts.

Test your understanding 5 : Objective test questions

(1) The following information relates to a construction contract:

	$
Contract price	5 million
Work certified to date	2 million
Costs to date	1.8 million
Estimated costs to complete	2.2 million

What is the revenue, cost of sales and gross profit that can be recognised in accordance with IAS 11, assuming that the company's policy is to calculate attributable profit on the work certified basis?

	Revenue	Cost of sales	Gross profit
A	$2 million	$1.8 million	$200,000
B	$2 million	$1.6 million	$400,000
C	$2 million	$1.55 million	$450,000
D	$2.25 million	$1.8 million	$450,000

(2) The following information relates to a construction contract:

	$
Contract price	300,000
Work certified to date	120,000
Costs to date	100,000
Estimated costs to complete	250,000

What is the revenue, cost of sales and gross profit that can be recognised in accordance with IAS 11, assuming that the company's policy is to calculate attributable profit on the work certified basis?

	Revenue	**Cost of sales**	**Gross profit**
A	$120,000	$170,000	$50,000 loss
B	$120,000	$100,000	$20,000
C	$120,000	$140,000	$20,000 loss
D	$120,000	$70,000	$50,000

(3) A company is currently accounting for a construction contract. The work certified at the year end is $240,000 and cost of sales has been calculated as $180,000. Cost incurred to date amount to $200,000 and $250,000 has been invoiced to the customer.

What is the amount due to/from customers that should be recorded in the statement of financial position in relation to this construction contract?

A $10,000

B $20,000

C $40,000

D $50,000

(4) A company is currently accounting for a construction contract. The contract price is $2 million and work certified at the year-end is $1.3 million. Costs incurred to date amount to $1.4 million and it is estimated that a further $1 million will be incurred in completing this project. $1.3 million has been invoiced to the customer.

What is the amount due to/from customers that should be recorded in the statement of financial position in relation to this construction contract?

A $100,000

B $300,000

C $400,000

D $1.1 million

(5) Using the information in question 4 how would your answer appear on the statement of financial position?

A   Gross amounts due to customer – current asset

B   Gross amounts due to customer – current liability

C   Gross amounts due from customer – current asset

D   Gross amounts due from customer – current liability

(6) The following information relates to a construction contract:

	$'000
Contract price	370
Work certified to date	320
Costs to date - attributable to work completed	360
Estimated costs to complete	50

What is the revenue and cost of sales that can be recognised in accordance with IAS 11, assuming that the company's policy is to calculate attributable profit on the work certified basis?

	Revenue $'000	Cost of sales $'000
A	320	360
B	320	400
C	370	360
D	370	410

(7) The following information relates to a construction contract:

	$
Contract price	40 million
Percentage complete	45%
Costs to date	16
Estimated costs to complete	18

How much revenue and gross profit can be recognised in accordance with IAS 11?

(8) **Data for questions 8 and 9:**

CN started a three-year contract to build a new university campus on 1 April 2009. The contract had a fixed price of $90 million.

CN incurred costs to 31 March 2011 of $77 million and estimated that a further $33 million would need to be spent to complete the contract.

CN uses the percentage of cost incurred to date to total cost method to calculate stage of completion of the contract.

Calculate revenue earned on the contract to 31 March 2011, according to IAS 11 Construction Contracts.

(9) **State how much gross profit/loss CN should recognise in its statement of comprehensive income for the year ended 31 March 2010, according to IAS 11 Construction Contracts.**

5 Summary diagram

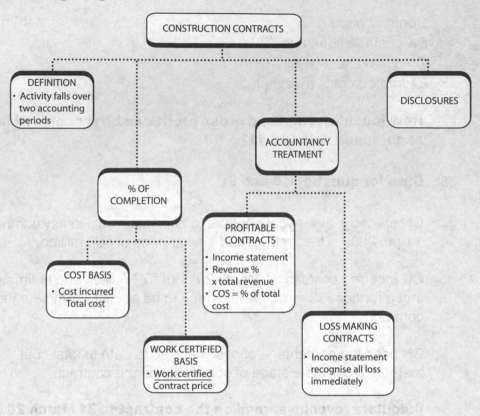

Test your understanding answers

Test your understanding 1 : Contracts over a three year period

Overall contract profit

	Ye 31/12/09	Ye 31/12/10	Ye 31/12/11
	$000	$000	$000
Contract price	9,000	9,000	9,000
Costs incurred to date	(2,800)	(4,800)	(7,500)
Estimated costs to complete	(4,200)	(2,700)	–
Gross profit	2,000	1,500	1,500

% of completion on cost basis

Ye 31/12/07   2800/7000 =   40%
Ye 31/12/08   4800/7500 =   64%
Ye 31/12/09   7500/7500 =   100%

Income statement (extract)

	Ye 31/12/09	Ye 31/12/10	Ye 31/12/11
	$000	$000	$000
Revenue (% x contract price)	3,600	2,160	3,240
Costs (% x total cost)	(2,800)	(2,000)	(2,700)
Gross profit	800	160	540

Workings

	31.12.09	31.12.10	31.12.11
% completion	40%	64%	100%
Revenue	40% × 9,000 = 3,600	64% x 9000 – 3,600 = 2,160	9,000 – 3,600 – 2,160 = 3,240
Cost of sales	40% × (2,800 + 4,200) = 2,800	64% × (4,800 + 2,700) – 2,800 = 2,000	100% × 7,500 – 2,800 – 2,000 = 2,700

% of completion on work certified basis

Ye 31/12/09   2700/9000 =   30%
Ye 31/12/10   6300/9000 =   70%
Ye 31/12/11   9000/9000 =   100%

Income statement (extract)

	Ye 31/12/09	Ye 31/12/10	Ye 31/12/11
	$0009	$000	$000
Revenue	2,700	3,600	2,700
Cost of Sales	(2,100)	(3,150)	(2,250)
Gross profit	600	450	450

Workings

	31.12.09	31.12.10	31.12.11
% completion	30%	70%	100%
Revenue	30% × 9,000 = 2,700	6,300 − 2,700 = 3,600	9,000 − 2,700 − 3,600 = 2,700
Cost of sales	30% × (2,800 + 4,200) = 2,100	70% × (4,800 + 2,700) − 2,100 = 3,150	100% × 7,500 − 2,100 − 3,150 = 2,250

Test your understanding 2 : Profit making contracts

Overall contract profit

	A	B	C	D
	$000	$000	$000	$000
Contract price	500	1,000	2,000	3,000
Costs incurred to date	(200)	(220)	(600)	(700)
Estimated costs to complete	(200)	Unknown	(1,100)	(1,100)
Gross profit	100	?	300	1,200

% of completion on work certified basis

A 150/500 =   30%
B 200/1000 =   20%
C 500/2000 =   25%
D 1300/3000   43% (rounded)

Income statement (extract)

	A	B	C	D
	$000	$000	$000	$000
Revenue (% x contract price)	150	220	500	1,300
Costs (% x total cost)	(120)	(220)	(425)	(780)
Gross profit	30	nil	75	520

NB. Project B has a unknown cost to complete and is therefore neither profitable or a loss making contract. Therefore, costs incurred become cost of sales and the revenue will be the same amount to show a nil profit on this contract.

Statement of financial position (extract)

	A	B	C	D
	$000	$000	$000	$000
Costs incurred	200	220	600	700
Profit recognised	30	–	75	520
Less: progress billings	(140)	(160)	(700)	(1,200)
Amounts due (to)/from customers	90	60	(25)	20

Test your understanding 3 : Exam standard question

Overall profit/loss on contract

	A	B	C	D
Contract price	500	890	420	750
Costs to date	(384)	(700)	(468)	(20)
Costs to complete	(48)	(115)	(168)	(650)
Total estimated profit	68	75	(216)	80

% completion on work certified basis

A 375/500 = 75%
B 534/890 = 60%
C 280/420 = 67% (rounded)
D 0/750 = 0%

Income statement (extract)

	A	B	C	D
Revenue (% x contract price)	375	534	280	20
Cost of Sales (% x total cost)	(324)	(489)	(496)	(20)
Gross profit/loss	51	45	(216)	–

Statement of financial position (extract)

	A	B	C	D
Costs incurred	384	700	468	20
Profits/losses recognised	51	45	(216)	–
Progress billings	(360)	(520)	(224)	–
Amounts due (to)/from customers	75	225	28	20

Project D

Although work has been done on this project no work has yet been certified, hence we cannot recognise a profit in the income statement. However, we cannot ignore that costs have been incurred, hence they become the cost of sales and the revenue becomes the same amount to recognise a nil profit.

Test your understanding 4 : Exam standard question

The contract makes an overall profit of $850 ($3,000 - $2,150)

Stage of completion = 70% (1,500/2,150)

	$'000
Costs to date - attributable to work completed	1,500
Costs to date - inventory purchased but not yet used	250
Estimated costs to complete	400
Total cost	2,150

	$'000
Statement of comprehensive income figures:	
Revenue (3,000 x 70%)	2,100
Cost of sales (2,150 x 70%)	(1,500)
Profit	600

Test your understanding 5 : Objective test questions

(1) B

	$m
Total revenue	5
Costs to date	(1.8)
Costs to complete	(2.2)
Total profit	1

% completion = 2 million/5 million = 40%

	$m
Revenue (40% × 5)	2
Cost of sales (40% × 4)	(1.6)
Gross profit	0.4

(2) A

	$
Total revenue	300,000
Costs to date	(100,000)
Costs to complete	(250,000)
Total loss	(50,000)

	$m
Revenue	120,000
Cost of sales (ß)	(170,000)
Gross loss	(50,000)

(3) A

Costs to date	200,000
Recognised profits (240,000 – 180,000)	60,000
Invoiced	(250,000)
Amount due from	10,000

(4) B

Total revenue	2
Costs to date	(1.4)
Costs to complete	(1)
Total loss	(0.4)
Costs to date	1.4
Recognised loss	(0.4)
Progress billings	(1.3)
Amount due to	(0.3)

(5) B

(6) A

	$'000
Total revenue	370
Costs to date	(360)
Costs to complete	(50)
Total loss	(40)
	$'000
Revenue (work certified)	320
Cost of sales (balancing item)	(360)
Total loss	(40)

We must recognise the whole of the loss in order to be prudent - hence COS will be the balancing item.

(7) The overall contract makes a profit of $6 million ($40 - $16 - $18)

The revenue to be recognised will be 45% x total revenue of $40 = $18 million and the profit to be recognised will be 45% of total profit of $6 = $2.7 million

(8) The overall contract makes a loss of $20 million ($90 - $77 - $33)

The percentage of cost incurred to date to total cost = 70% (77/110)

The revenue to be recognised will be 70% x total revenue of $90 = $63 million

(9) The contract makes an overall loss of $20 which must be recognised immediately in order to be prudent.

IAS 7 Statement of Cash Flows

Chapter learning objectives

- Prepare a statement of cash flows in a form suitable for publication;
- Identify the importance of the statement of cash flows;
- Identify the difference between the indirect and direct method of calculating cash generated from operations.

1 Session content

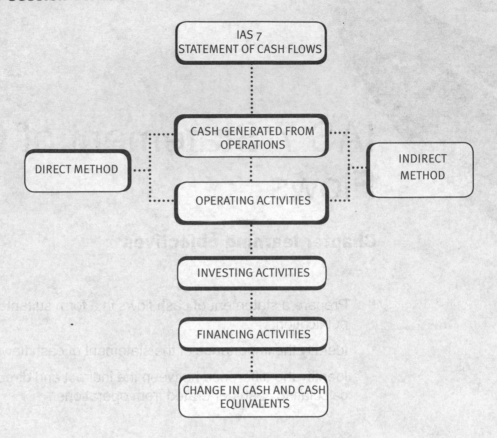

2 The importance of statements of cash flows

The statement of cash flows is an important part of the financial statements because:

- It helps users to assess liquidity and solvency – an adequate cash position is essential in the short term both to ensure the survival of the business and to enable debts and dividends to be paid.

- It helps users to assess financial adaptability – will the company be able to take effective action to alter its cash flows in response to any unexpected events?

- It helps the users assess future cash flows – an adequate cash position in the longer term is essential to enable asset replacement, repayment of debt and to fund further expansion. Users will use current cash flow information to help them assess future cash flows.

- Cash flow means survival – a company may be profitable, but if they do not have an adequate cash position, they may not be able to survive.

- It helps to highlight where cash is being generated – the cash flow statement will clearly detail cash that is being generated from the core activities of the business and other non-operating activities.

- Cash flows are objective – a cash flow is a matter of fact whereas the calculation of profit is subjective.

- It can help to indicate problems early on.

3 Definitions In IAS 7

Cash

Cash 'comprises cash on hand and at bank (including overdrafts) and demand deposits'.

Cash equivalents

Cash equivalents are short-term, highly liquid investments that are readily convertible to known amounts of cash and which are subject to an insignificant risk of changes in value, e.g. short-dated treasury bill.

Operating activities

Operating activities are the principal revenue-producing activities of the enterprise and other activities that are not investing or financing activities.

Investing activities

Investing activities are the acquisition and disposal of long-term assets and other investments not included in cash equivalents.

Financing activities

Financing activities are activities that result in changes in the size and comprise of the equity share capital and borrowings of the enterprise.

Statement of cash flows the year ended 31 December 2009

	$	$
Cash flows from operating activities		
Net profit before taxation	X	
Adjustments for:		
Depreciation/amortisation	X	
Provision increases /decrease	X/(X)	
(Profit)/loss on disposal	(X)/X	
Interest receivable/investment income	(X)	
Finance costs	X	
	———	
Operating profit before working capital changes	X	
(Increase)/decrease in inventories	(X)/X	
(Increase)/decrease in trade and other receivables	(X)/X	
Increase/(decrease) in trade and other payables	X/(X)	
	———	
Cash generated from operations	X	
Interest paid	(X)	
Tax paid	(X)	
	———	
Net cash from operating activities		X
Cash flows from investing activities		
Purchase of property, plant and equipment	(X)	
Purchase of intangibles	(X)	
Purchase of investments	(X)	
Proceeds from sale of property, plant and equipment	X	
Proceeds from sale of intangibles	X	
Proceeds from sale of investments	X	
Interest received	X	
Dividends received	X	
	———	
Net cash from investing activities		(X)
Cash flows from financing activities		
Proceeds from issue of ordinary shares	X	
Proceeds from issue of preference shares	X	
Proceeds from long-term borrowings	X	
Redemption of long-term borrowings	(X)	
Dividends paid	(X)	
	———	
Net cash from financing activities		(X)
Net increase in cash and cash equivalents		X
Cash and cash equivalents at beginning of period		X
		———
Cash and cash equivalents at end of period		X/(X)
		———

4 Cash flows from operating activities

The first main heading in the standard statement of cash flows proforma per IAS 7 is 'cash generated from operations'.

There are two ways in which this figure can be calculated.

Indirect method

This method (shown in the above proforma), involves taking the profit before taxation per the income statement, adjusting it for non-cash items and converting the income and expenses figure from the accruals basis to the cash basis, so that just the cash flows from operating activities remain.

Cash flows from operating activities	$
Profit before taxation	X
Adjustments for:	
Depreciation/amortisation	X
Provision increases/decreases	X/(X)
(Profit)/loss on disposal	(X)/X
Interest receivable/investment income	(X)
Finance costs	X
Operating profit before working capital changes	X
(Increase)/decrease in inventories	(X)/X
(Increase)/decrease in trade and other receivables	(X)/X
Increase/(decrease) in trade and other payables	X/(X)
Cash generated from operations	X

Adjustments using the indirect method

Depreciation/amortisation

Depreciation is not a cash flow.

- Capital expenditure purchases/disposals will be recorded under "investing activities" at the time of the cash outflow/inflow.

- Depreciation is the writing off of the capital expenditure over its useful life and simply an "accounting entry". It should be added back to profit because it was a non-cash expense deducted from the profit.

Profit/loss on disposal

When a non-current asset is disposed of:

- the cash inflow from the sale (the proceeds) is recorded under "investing activities";

- a profit/loss on disposal is an "accounting entry" recorded by comparing carrying value and proceeds;

- a loss on disposal should be added back because it was a non-cash expense deducted from the profit;

- a profit on disposal should be deducted because it was a non-cash reduction to expenses added to the profit.

Provisions

Provisions are not a cash flow, they are an "accounting entry". They are required to ensure profits reflect the due amounts, rather than the amounts paid/received, hence applying the accruals concept. Therefore, an adjustment must be made for them when preparing the statement of cash flows.

When a provision is made:

- an increase should be added to profit because it was an expense from profit, which is not a cash item;

- a decrease should be deducted from profit because it was a reduction in an expense from profit, which is not a cash item.

Interest receivable/investment income

The amount from the income statement should be deducted from the profit because this is not necessarily the amount that has been received (income statement is prepared on the accruals basis). The actual cash amount received will appear under "investing activities".

Interest payable

The expense from the income statement should be added to the profit because this is not necessarily the amount that has been paid. The actual cash amount will appear after cash generated from operations.

Change in receivables

- An increase in receivables is a reduction to cash (the more the customers owe, the less cash in the bank);

- a decrease in receivable is an increase to cash.

Change in inventory

- An increase in inventory is a reduction to cash (the more inventory we buy, the less cash in the bank);

- a decrease in inventory is an increase to cash.

Change in payables

- An increase in payables is an increase to cash (the more the suppliers are owed, the more cash we have in the bank);

- a decrease in payables is a reduction to cash.

Direct method

This method involves simply adding cash inflow and deducting cash outflows in respect of operating activities.

	$
Cash receipts from customers	X
Cash payments to suppliers	(X)
Cash payments to employees	(X)
Cash payments for expenses	(X)
Cash generated from operations	X

Comparison of the methods

IAS 7 encourages, but does not require, the use of the direct method.

- Indirect method
  - The reconciliation highlights the fact that profit and cash are not equal.
  - Does not show significant elements of trading cash flows.
  - Low cost in preparing the information.

- Direct method
  - Discloses information not shown elsewhere in the financial statements.
  - Shows the cash flows from trading.
  - Gives the users more information in estimating future cash flows

Illustration 1 : Indirect method

The following information is available for Splatter Ltd for the year ended 30 September 2011:

Income statement

	$000
Sales revenue	444
Cost of sales	(269)
Gross profit	175
Distribution costs	(35)
Administrative expenses	(8)
Profit from operations	132
Finance costs	(18)
Profit before tax	114
Income tax expense	(42)
Profit for the year	72

The expenses can be analysed as follows:

	$000
Wages	72
Auditors' remuneration	12
Depreciation	84
Cost of materials used	222
Profit on disposal of non-current assets	(60)
Rental income	(18)
	312

The following information is also available:

	30/09/11	30/09/10
	$000	$000
Inventories	42	24
Receivables	48	42
Payables	(30)	(18)

Required:

Prepare the section of the cash flow statement for cash generated from operations using the indirect method for the year ended 30 September 2011 in compliance with IAS 7 *Statement of Cash Flows*.

Solution

Splatter Ltd Statement of cash flows for the year ended 30 September 2011

	$000
Cash flows from operating activities	
Profit before tax	114
Depreciation	84
Profit on disposal of non-current assets	(60)
Finance costs	18
Operating profit before working capital changes	156
Increase in inventories (42 – 24)	(18)
Increase in trade receivables (48 – 42)	(6)
Increase in trade payables (30 – 18)	12
Cash generated from operations	144

Illustration 2 : Direct method

Required:

Using the information for Splatter Ltd in the previous illustration, prepare the section of the cash flow for cash generated from operations using the direct method for the year ended 30 September 2011 in compliance with IAS 7 *Statement of Cash Flows*.

Solution

Splatter Ltd Statement of cash flows for the year ended 30 September 2011

	$000
Cash flows from operating activities	
Cash receipts from customers (W1)	438
Rental income	18
Cash payments to suppliers (W2)	(228)
Cash payments to employees	(72)
Cash payments for expenses	(12)
	——
Cash generated from operations	144

(W1)

Cash receipts from customers

	$000
Opening receivables	42
Sales revenue	444
Closing receivables	(48)
	——
Cash received from customers	438

(W2)

Cash payments to suppliers

	$000
Opening inventories	24
Purchases (ß)	240
Closing	(42)
	——
Cost of materials used	222

	$000
Opening payables	18
Purchases (above)	240
Closing payables	(30)
	——
Payments to suppliers	228

Illustration 3 : Statement of cash flows

Below are extracts from the financial statements of Pincer Ltd:

Statement of comprehensive income for the year ended 31 March 2011

	$m
Sales revenue	1,162
Cost of sales	(866)
Gross profit	296
Distribution costs	(47)
Administrative expenses	(110)
Profit from operations	139
Interest receivable	79
Finance costs	(55)
Profit before tax	163
Income tax expense	(24)
Profit for the year	139
Other comprehensive income	
Gain on revaluation	251
Total comprehensive income for the year	390

Statements of financial position:

	31 March 2011		31 March 2010	
	$m	$m	$m	$m
Assets				
Non-current assets				
Property, plant and equipment	1,023		600	
Intangible assets	277		234	
Investments	69		68	
		1,369		902

Current assets

Inventories	246	128
Trade and other receivables	460	373
Cash	250	124
	956	625
Total Assets	2,325	1,527

Equity and liabilities
Capital and reserves

Issued share capital	29	24
Share premium	447	377
Revaluation reserve	251	–
Accumulated reserves	116	26
	843	427

Non-current liabilities

Loan	755	555
Deferred taxation	4	2
	759	557

Current liabilities

Trade and other payables	244	311
Overdrafts	437	207
Taxation	42	25
	723	543
Total equity and liabilities	2,325	1,527

Additional information:

- Profit from operations is after charging depreciation on the property, plant and equipment of $22 million and amortisation on the intangible fixed assets of $7 million. The revaluation reserve relates wholly to property, plant and equipment.

- During the year ended 31 March 2011, plant and machinery costing $1,464 million, which had a carrying value of $424 million, was sold for $250 million.

- During the year ended 31 March 2011 25 million 20c shares were issued at a premium of $2.80.

- Dividends paid during the year were $49 million.

Solution

Pincer Ltd Statement of cash flows for the year ended 31 March 2011

	$m	$m
Cash flows from operating activities		
Profit before tax		163
Depreciation		22
Amortisation		7
Loss on disposal of non-current assets (250 – 424)		174
Interest receivable		(79)
Finance costs		55
		___
Operating profit before working capital changes		342
Increase in inventories (246 – 128)		(118)
Increase in trade receivables (460 – 373)		(87)
Decrease in trade payables (311 – 244)		(67)
		___
Cash generated from operations		70
Interest paid		(55)
Income tax paid (W1)		(5)
		___
Net cash from operating activities		10
Cash flows from investing activities		
Purchases of property, plant and equipment (W3)	(618)	
Purchase of intangibles (W2)	(50)	
Purchase of investments (69 – 68)	(1)	
Proceeds of property, plant and equipment	250	
Interest received	79	
	___	
Net cash from investing activities		(340)
Cash flow from financing activities		
Proceeds from issue of shares (W4)	75	
Proceeds from long-term borrowing (755 – 555)	200	
Dividends paid	(49)	
	___	

Net cash from financing activities	226

Net increase in cash and cash equivalents	(104)
Cash and cash equivalents at beginning of period (124 – 207)	(83)

Cash and cash equivalents at end of period (250 – 437)	(187)

Workings

(W1)

Tax

Bank (ß)	5	Bal b/d (current)	25
Bal c/d (current)	42	Bal b/d (deferred)	2
Bal c/d (deferred)	4	IS	24
	51		51
		Bal b/d (current)	42
		Bal b/d (deferred)	4

Note: Current and deferred tax have been included in the same account for speed, as we only need to find the cash amount for the answer. Remember. deferred tax is simply a provision and any movement will go to the income statement. We do not pay deferred tax.

(W2)

Intangible non-current assets

Bal b/d	234	Amortisation	7
Bank (ß)	50	Bal c/d	277
	284		284
Bal b/d	277		

(W3)

Property, plant and equipment

Bal b/d	600	Dep'n	22
Reval'n	251	Disposal	424
Bank (ß)	618	Bal c/d	1,023
	___		___
	1,469		1,469
	___		___
Bal b/d	1,023		

(W4)

25 million x $3 = $75 million

Test your understanding 1 : Simple statement of cash flows

Yog Ltd's income statement for the year ended 31 December 2010 and statements of financial position as at 31 December 2009 and 31 December 2010 were as follows:

Income statement for the year ended 31 December 2010

	$000	$000
Sales		360
Raw materials consumed	35	
Staff costs	47	
Depreciation	59	
Loss on disposal	9	
	___	
		(150)
		___
Profit from operations		210
Finance costs		(14)
		___
Profit before tax		196
Income tax expense		(62)
		___
Profit for the period		134

Statements of financial position as at 31 December

	31 Dec 2010		31 Dec 2009	
	$000	$000	$000	$000
Assets				
Non-current assets				
Cost		798		780
Depreciation		(159)		(112)
		639		668
Current assets				
Inventories	12		10	
Trade receivables	34		26	
Cash and cash equivalents	24		28	
		70		64
Total assets		709		732
Equity and liabilities				
Capital reserves				
Share capital		180		170
Share premium		18		12
Retained earnings		343		245
		541		427
Non-current liabilities				
Long-term loans		100		250
Current liabilities				
Trade payables	21		15	
Income tax	47		40	
		68		55
Total equity and liabilities		709		732

During the year, the company paid $45,000 for a new piece of equipment and a dividend was paid amounting to $36,000.

Required:

Prepare a statement of cash flows for the year ended 31 December 2010 for Yog Ltd in accordance with the requirements of IAS 7 using the indirect method.

Test your understanding 2 : Exam standard question

Below are extracts from the financial statements of Poochie Ltd:

Income Statement for the year ended 31 March 2011

	$
Sales revenue	30,650
Cost of sales	(26,000)
Gross profit	4,650
Distribution costs	(900)
Administrative expenses	(500)
Profit from operations	3,250
Investment income	680
Finance costs	(400)
Profit before tax	3,530
Income tax expense	(300)
Profit for the period	3,230

Statements of financial position:

	31 March 2011		31 March 2010	
	$	$	$	$
Assets				
Non-current assets				
Property, plant and equipment	2,280		850	
Investments	2,500		2,500	
		4,780		3,350
Current assets				
Inventories	1,000		1,950	
Trade and other receivables	1,900		1,200	
Cash and cash equivalents	410		160	
		3,310		3,310
Total Assets		8,090		6,660

Equity and liabilities
Capital and reserves

Share capital	1,000	900
Share premium	500	350
Retained earnings	3,410	1,380
	4,910	2,630

Non-current liabilities

Long term borrowings (inc. finance leases)	2,300	1,040
	2,300	1,040

Current liabilities

Trade and other payables	250	1,890
Interest payable	230	100
Taxation	400	1,000
	880	2,990
Total equity and liabilities	8,090	6,660

Additional information:

- Profit from operations is after charging depreciation on the property, plant and equipment of $450.

- During the year ended 31 March 2011, plant and machinery costing $80 and with accumulated depreciation of $60, was sold for $20.

- During the year ended 31 March 2011, the company acquired property, plant and equipment costing $1,900, of which was $900 was acquired by means of finance leases. Cash payments of $1,000 were made to purchase property, plant and equipment.

- $90 was paid under finance leases.

- The receivables at the end of 2011 includes $100 of interest receivable. There was no balance at the beginning of the year.

- Investment income of $680 is made up of $300 interest receivable and $380 dividends received.

- Dividends paid during the year were $1,200.

Required:

Prepare a statement of cash flows for Poochie Ltd for the year ended 31 March 2011 in compliance with IAS 7 Statement of Cash Flows using the indirect method.

Test your understanding 3 : Exam standard question

Below are extracts from the financial statements of Yam Yam Ltd:

Statement of comprehensive income for the year ended 30 September 2011

	$000
Sales revenue	2,900
Cost of sales	(1,734)
Gross profit	1,166
Distribution costs	(520)
Administrative expenses	(342)
Profit from operations	304
Investment income	5
Finance costs	(19)
Profit before tax	290
Income tax expense	(104)
Profit for the period	186
Other comprehensive income	
Gain on revaluation	50
Total comprehensive income for the year	236

Statements of financial position:

	30 September 2011		30 September 2010	
	$000	$000	$000	$000
Assets				
Non-current assets				
Property, plant and equipment	634		510	
		634		510
Current assets				
Inventories	420		460	
Trade receivables	390		320	
Interest receivable	4		9	
Investments	50		0	
Cash at bank	75		0	
Cash at hand	7		5	
		946		794
Total Assets		1,580		1,304
Equity and liabilities				
Capital and reserves				
Share capital $0.50 each	363		300	
Share premium	89		92	
Revaluation reserve	50		0	
Retained earnings	63		(70)	
		565		322
Non-current liabilities				
10% Loan notes	0		40	
5% Loan notes	329		349	
		329		389
Current liabilities				
Trade and other payables	550		400	
Bank overdraft	0		70	
Accruals	36		33	
Taxation	100		90	
		686		593
Total equity and liabilities		1,580		1,304

Additional information:

- On 1 October 2010, Yam Yam Ltd issued 60,000 $0.50 shares at a premium of 100%. The proceeds were used to finance the purchase and cancellation of all of its 10% loan notes and some of its 5% loan notes, both at par. A bonus issue of one for ten shares held was made at 1 November 2010; all shares in issue qualified for the bonus.

- The current asset investment was a 30 day government bond.

- Non-current assets included certain properties that were revalued during the year.

- Non-current assets disposed of during the year had a carrying value of $75,000; cash received on disposal was $98,000.

- Depreciation charged for the year was $87,000.

- The accruals balance includes interest payable of $33,000 at 30 September 2010 and $6,000 at 30 September 2011.

- Interim dividends paid during the year were $53,000.

Required:

Prepare a statement of cash flows for Yam Yam Ltd for the year ended 30 September 2010 in compliance with IAS 7 *Statement of Cash Flows* using the indirect method.

Test your understanding 4 : Objective test questions

(1) Barlow Ltd uses the 'indirect method' for the purpose of calculating net cash flow from operating activities in the statement of cash flows.

The following information is provided for the year ended 31 December 2010:

	$
Profit before tax	5,600
Depreciation	956
Profit on sale of equipment	62
Increase in inventories	268
Increase in receivables	101
Increase in payables	322

What is the net cash flow from operating activities?

A $6,571

B $6,541

C $6,447

D $5,803

(2)   Evans plc had the following balances in its' statement of financial position as at 30 June 2010 and 2011:

	2010	2011
10% Debentures	$150,000	$130,000
Share Capital	$100,000	$120,000
Share Premium	$35,000	$45,000

How much will appear in the statement of cash flows for the year ended 30 June 2011 under the heading 'cash flows from financing activities'?

A $nil

B $10,000 inflow

C $30,000 inflow

D $40,000 inflow

(3)   At 1 January 2010 Casey Ltd had property, plant and equipment with a carrying value of $250,000. In the year ended 31 December 2010 the company disposed of assets with a carrying value of $45,000 for $50,000. The company revalued a building from $75,000 to $100,000 and charged depreciation for the year of $20,000. At the end of the year, the carrying value of property, plant and equipment was $270,000.

How much will be reported in the statement of cash flows for the year ended 31 December 2010 under the heading 'cash flows from investing activities'?

A $10,000 outflow

B $10,000 inflow

C $35,000 outflow

D $50,000 inflow

The following information relates to questions **4** and **5**:

IAS 7 requires cash flows to be analysed under three headings – cash flows from operating activities, investing activities and financing activities. Several items that may appear in a cash flow statement are listed below:

(4) (i) Cash paid for the purchase of non-current assets

(ii) Dividends received

(iii) Interest paid

(iv) Repayment of borrowings

(v) Tax paid

(5) **Which of the above items would appear under the heading 'cash flows from investing activities'?**

A   i only

B   i and ii

C   i, ii, iii and iv

D   ii, iii and 4

(6) **Which of the above items would appear under the heading 'cash flows from operating activities'?**

A   i only

B   iii and v

C   iii, iv and v

D   ii, iii and v

(6) How much interest was paid in the year?

	$'000
Interest accrued b/fwd	600
Interest charged to the statement of comprehensive income	700
Interest accrued c/fwd	500

A $600,000

B $700,000

C $800,000

D $1,300,000

(8) At 1 October 2010, BK had the following balance:

Accrued interest payable $12,000 credit

During the year ended 30 September 2011, BK charged interest payable of $41,000 to its statement of comprehensive income. The closing balance on accrued interest payable account at 30 September 2011 was $15,000 credit.

How much interest paid should BK show on its statement of cash flows for the year ended 30 September 2011?

A $38,000

B $41,000

C $44,000

D $53,000

(9) Accrued income tax payable, balance at 31 March 2010 $920,000.

Accrued income tax payable, balance at 31 March 2011 $890,000.

Taxation charge to the statement of comprehensive income for the year to 31 March 2011 $850,000.

Deferred tax balance at 31 March 2010 $200,000.

Deferred tax balance at 31 March 2011 $250,000

.

How much should be included in the statement of cash flows for income tax paid in the year?

A $800,000

B $830,000

C $850,000

D $880,000

5 Summary diagram

**IAS 7
STATEMENT OF CASH FLOWS**

CASH GENERATED FROM OPERATIONS

= Cash from day-to-day trading.

DIRECT METHOD

- Cash received from customers

Less:

- cash paid to suppliers
- cash paid for expenses
- cash paid for wages and salaries.

INDIRECT METHOD

Adjust net profit before tax for finance charges, investment income and non-cash items.

OPERATING ACTIVITIES

- Interest paid
- Taxes paid.

INVESTING ACTIVITIES

- PPE purchases and sales
- Interest received
- Dividends received.

FINANCING ACTIVITIES

- Share issues
- Loan note transactions
- Finance lease payments
- Dividends paid.

CHANGE IN CASH AND CASH EQUIVALENTS

Cash: cash on hand (including overdrafts and on demand deposits)

Cash equivalents: short-term, highly-liquid investments that are readily convertible into known amounts of cash and are subject to an insignificant risk of changes in value.

Test your understanding answers

Test your understanding 1 : Simple statement of cash flows

Yog Ltd statement of cash flows for the year ended 31 December 2010

	$000	$000
Cash flows from operating activities		
Profit before taxation	196	
Adjustments for:		
Depreciation	59	
Loss on disposal	9	
Finance costs	14	
	───	
Operating profit before working capital changes	278	
Increase in inventories (12 – 10)	(2)	
Increase in trade receivables (34 – 26)	(8)	
Increase in trade payables (21 – 15)	6	
	───	
Cash generated from operations	274	
Interest paid	(14)	
Income tax paid (W1)	(55)	
	───	
Net cash from operating activities		205
Cash flows from investing activities		
Purchase of non-current assets	(45)	
Proceeds from sale of non-current assets (W2)	6	
	───	
Net cash from investing activities		(39)
Cash flows from financing activities		
Proceeds from issues of ordinary shares (W3)	16	
Repayment of loans (250 – 100)	(150)	
Dividends paid	(36)	
	───	
Net cash from financing activities		(170)
Net decrease in cash and cash equivalents		(4)
Cash and cash equivalents at beginning of period		28
		───
Cash and cash equivalents at end of period		24
		───

Workings

(W1)

Tax payable

Bank (ß)	55	Bal b/d	40
Bal c/d	47	Income statement	62
	—		—
	102		102
	—		—
		Bal b/d	47

(W2)

Non-current assets – cost

Bal b/d	780	Disposal (ß)	27
Additions	45	Bal c/d	798
	—		—
	825		825
	—		—
Bal b/d	798		

Accumulated depreciation

Disposal (ß)	12	Bal b/d	112
Bal c/d	159	Income statement	59
	—		—
	171		171
	—		—
		Bal b/d	159

NBV of disposal = 27 – 12 = $15

Loss on disposal = $9

$\Rightarrow$ proceeds = $15 – $9 = $6 (asset sold $9 less than NBV)

(W3)

Share issue = (180 + 18) - (170 + 12) = 16

Test your understanding 2 : Exam standard question

Poochie Ltd Statement of cash flows for the year ended 31 March 2011

	$	$
Cash flows from operating activities		
Profit before tax	3,530	
Depreciation	450	
Investment income	(680)	
Finance costs	400	
	———	
Operating profit before working capital changes	3,700	
Decrease in inventories (1,950 – 1,000)	950	
Increase in trade receivables (W4)	(600)	
Decrease in trade payables (1,890 – 250)	(1640)	
	———	
Cash generated from operations	2,410	
Interest paid (W2)	(270)	
Income tax paid (W1)	(900)	
	———	
Net cash from operating activities		1240
Cash flows from investing activities		
Purchase of property, plant and equipment (W3)	(1,000)	
Proceeds from sale of property, plant and equipment	20	
Interest received (W4)	200	
Dividends received	380	
	———	
Net cash from investing activities		(400)
Cash flow from financing activities		
Proceeds from issue of shares (W5)	250	
Proceeds from long-term borrowing (W6)	450	
Payment of finance leases	(90)	
Dividends paid	(1,200)	
	———	
Net cash from financing activities		(590)
		———
Net increase in cash and cash equivalents		250
Cash and cash equivalents at beginning of period		160
		———
Cash and cash equivalents at end of period		410
		———

Workings

(W1)

Tax

Bank (ß)	900	Bal b/d	1,000
Bal c/d	400	IS	300
	1,300		1,300
		Bal b/d	400

(W2)

Interest payable

Bank (ß)	270	Bal b/d	100
Bal c/d	230	IS	400
	500		500
		Bal b/d	230

(W3)

Property, plant and equipment

Bal b/d	850	Dep'n	450
Finance lease	900	Disposal (80 – 60)	20
Bank (ß)	1,000	Bal c/d	2,280
	2,750		2,750
Bal b/d	2,280		

(W4)

Interest receivable

Bal b/d	0	Bank (ß)	200
IS	300	Bal c/d	100
	___		___
	300		300
	___		___
Bal b/d	100		

Receivable B/d = $1,200

Receivables C/d = $1,800 ($1,900 – $100 interest receivable)

Increase in receivables = $600

(W5)

Share issue = ($1,000 + $500) – ($900 + $350) = $250

(W6)

Long-Term Borrowings

Bank repayment	90	Bal b/d	1,040
of finance lease		Bank (ß)	450
Bal c/d	2,300	Finance leases	900
	_____		_____
	2,390		2,390
	_____		_____
		Bal b/d	2,300

Test your understanding 3 : Exam standard question

Yam Yam Ltd Statement of cash flows for the year ended 30 September 2011

	$000	$000
Cash flows from operating activities		
Profit before tax	290	
Depreciation	87	
Profit on disposal of non-current asset (98 – 75)	(23)	
Investment income	(5)	
Finance costs	19	
	‒‒‒	
Operating profit before working capital changes	368	
Decrease in inventories (460 – 420)	40	
Increase in trade receivables (390 – 320)	(70)	
Increase in trade payables (550 – 400)	150	
Increase in sundry accruals (W5)	30	
	‒‒‒	
Cash generated from operations	518	
Interest paid (W2)	(46)	
Income tax paid (W1)	(94)	
	‒‒‒	
Net cash from operating activities		378
Cash flows from investing activities		
Purchase of property, plant and equipment (W3)	(236)	
Proceeds from sale of property, plant and equipment	98	
Interest received (W4)	10	
	‒‒‒	
Net cash from investing activities		(128)
Cash flow from financing activities		
Proceeds from issue of shares (60 x $1)	60	
Redemption of 10% loan notes (40 – 0)	(40)	
Redemption of 5% loan notes (349 – 329)	(20)	
Dividends paid	(53)	
	‒‒‒	
Net cash from financing activities		(53)
		‒‒‒
Net increase in cash and cash equivalents		197
Cash and cash equivalents at beginning of period (5 – 70)		(65)
		‒‒‒
Cash and cash equivalents at end of period (50 + 75 + 7 + 0)		132
		‒‒‒

Workings

(W1)

Tax

Bank (ß)	94	Bal b/d	90
Bal c/d	100	IS	104
	——		——
	194		194
	——		——
		Bal b/d	100

(W2)

Interest payable

Bank (ß)	46	Bal b/d	33
Bal c/d	6	IS	19
	——		——
	52		52
	——		——
		Bal b/d	6

(W3)

Property, plant and equipment

Bal b/d	510	Dep'n	87
Revaluation	50	Disposal	75
Bank (ß)	236	Bal c/d	634
	——		——
	796		796
	——		——
Bal b/d	634		

(W4)

Interest Receivable

Bal b/d	9	Bank (ß)	10
IS	5	Bal c/d	4
	14		14
Bal b/d	4		

(W5)

Accruals b/d (excluding interest) = \$33 − 33 = 0

Accruals c/d (excluding interest) = \$36 − 6 = 30

Increase in accruals = 30

Test your understanding 4 : Objective test questions

(1) C

Cash flows from operating activities	\$
Profit before tax	5,600
Adjustments for:	
Depreciation	956
(Profit)/loss on disposal	(62)
(Increase)/decrease in inventories	(268)
(Increase)/decrease in trade and other receivables	(101)
(Decrease)/increase in trade and other payables	322
Cash inflow from operations	6,447

(2) B

Repayment of debentures (150,000 – 130,000)   (20,000)
Issue of shares ((120,000 – 100,000) + (45,000 – 35,000))   30,000
                                                        _____
Net inflow   10,000
                                                        _____

(3) A

Property, plant and equipment

Bal b/d	250,000	Disposals	45,000
Revaluation	25,000	Depreciation	20,000
Additions (ß)	60,000		
		Bal c/d	270,000
	335,000		335,000
Bal b/d	270,000		

Purchase of property, plant and equipment   (60,000)
Proceeds from sale of property, plant and equipment   50,000
                                                        _____
Net outflow   (10,000)
                                                        _____

(4) B

(5) B

(6) C (600 + 700 - 500)

(7) A (12 + 41 - 15)

(8) B (920 + 800 - 890)
Movement on deferred tax = $50,000
Income statement charge $850,000 - $50,000 = $800,000 relates to current tax

Pillar F

F1 – Financial Operations

Specimen Examination Paper

Instructions to candidates

You are allowed three hours to answer this question paper.
You are allowed 20 minutes reading time **before the examination begins** during which you should read the question paper and, if you wish, highlight and/or make notes on the question paper. However, you will **not** be allowed, **under any circumstances**, to open the answer book and start writing or use your calculator during this reading time.
You are strongly advised to carefully read ALL the question requirements before attempting the question concerned (that is all parts and/or sub-questions). The requirements for questions 2, 3 and 4 are contained in a dotted box.
ALL answers must be written in the answer book. Answers or notes written on the question paper will **not** be submitted for marking.
Answer the ONE compulsory question in Section A. This has ten sub-questions on pages 3 to 6.
Answer the SIX compulsory sub-questions in Section B on pages 7 to 10.
Answer the TWO compulsory questions in Section C on pages 11 to 14.
The country 'Tax Regime' for the paper is provided on page 2. Maths Tables are provided on pages 15 and 16
The list of verbs as published in the syllabus is given for reference on the inside back cover of this question paper.
Write your candidate number, the paper number and examination subject title in the spaces provided on the front of the answer book. Also write your contact ID and name in the space provided in the right hand margin and seal to close.
Tick the appropriate boxes on the front of the answer book to indicate the questions you have answered.

F1 – Financial Operations

Note: Information on relevant tax rules will be published on the CIMA website at least 6 weeks prior to the date of the examination and be reproduced within the examination paper.

COUNTRY X - TAX REGIME FOR USE THROUGHOUT THE EXAMINATION PAPER

Relevant Tax Rules for Years Ended 30 April 2007 to 2010

Corporate Profits

Unless otherwise specified, only the following rules for taxation of corporate profits will be relevant, other taxes can be ignored:

(a) Accounting rules on recognition and measurement are followed for tax purposes.

(b) All expenses other than depreciation, amortisation, entertaining, taxes paid to other public bodies and donations to political parties are tax deductible

(c) Tax depreciation is deductible as follows: 50% of additions to Property, Plant and Equipment in the accounting period in which they are recorded; 25% per year of the written-down value (i.e. cost minus previous allowances) in subsequent accounting periods except that in which the asset is disposed of. No tax depreciation is allowed on land.

(d) The corporate tax on profits is at a rate of 25%.

(e) Tax losses can be carried forward to offset against future taxable profits from the same business.

Value Added Tax

Country X has a VAT system which allows entities to reclaim input tax paid.

In country X the VAT rates are:

    Zero rated   0%

    Standard rated 15%

SECTION A – 20 MARKS

[Note: The indicative time for answering this section is 36 minutes]

ANSWER *ALL* TEN SUB-QUESTION IN THIS SECTION

Instructions for answering Section A:

The answers to the ten sub-questions in Section A should ALL be written in your answer book.

Your answers should be clearly numbered with the sub-question number and ruled off, so that the markers know which sub-question you are answering. **For multiple choice questions, you need only write the sub-question number and the letter of the answer option you have chosen.** You do not need to start a new page for each sub-question.

Question One

1.1 Which of the following statements is correct?

A   Tax evasion is legally arranging affairs so as to minimise the tax liability.
Tax avoidance is the illegal manipulation of the tax system to avoid paying taxes due.

B   Tax evasion is legally arranging affairs so as to evade paying tax.
Tax avoidance is tax planning, legally arranging affairs so as to minimise the tax liability.

C   Tax evasion is using loop holes in legislation to evade paying tax.
Tax avoidance is the illegal manipulation of the tax system to avoid paying taxes due.

D   Tax evasion is the illegal manipulation of the tax system to avoid paying taxes due.
Tax avoidance is tax planning, legally arranging affairs so as to minimise the tax liability.

(2 marks)

TURN OVER

1.2   A has been trading for a number of years. The tax written down value of A's property, plant and equipment was $40,000 at 31 March 2009. A did not purchase any property, plant and equipment between 1 April 2009 and 31 March 2010.

A's Income statement for the year ended 31 March 2010 is as follows:

	$
Gross profit	270,000
Administrative expenses	(120,000)
Depreciation - property, plant and equipment	(12,000)
Distribution costs	(55,000)
	83,000
Finance cost	(11,000)
Profit before tax	72,000

Administration expenses include entertaining of $15,000.

What is A's income tax due for the year ended 31 March 2010?

A   8,750

B   13,750

C   15,500

D   22,250

(2 marks)

1.3   B buys goods from a wholesaler, paying the price of the goods plus VAT. B sells goods in its shop to customers. The customers pay the price of the goods plus VAT.

From the perspective of B, the VAT would have

A   Effective incidence

B   Formal incidence

C   Ineffective incidence

D   Informal incidence

(2 marks)

1.4   CT has taxable profits of $100,000 and pays 50% as dividends.
The total tax due is calculated as:

CT's corporate income tax ($100,000 x 25%)	$25,000
CT's shareholder's personal income tax on dividends received ($50,000 x 20%)	$10,000
Total tax due	$35,000

The tax system in use here would be classified as a:

A   Imputation tax system

B   Partial imputation tax system

C   Classical tax system

D   Split rate tax system

(2 marks)

1.5 The International Accounting Standards Board's *Framework for the Presentation and Preparation of Financial Statements* sets out four qualitative characteristics, relevance and reliability are two, list the other two.

(2 marks)

1.6 The CIMA Code of Ethics for Professional Accountants sets out four principles that a professional accountant is required to comply with. Two principles are objectivity and professional competence/due care, list the other two.

(2 marks)

1.7 The purpose of an external audit is to:

A check the accounts are correct and to approve them.

B enable the auditor to express an opinion as to whether the financial statements give a true and fair view of the entity's affairs.

C search for any fraud taking place in the entity.

D check that all regulations have been followed in preparing the financial statements and to authorise the financial statements.

(2 marks)

1.8 Goodwill arising on acquisition is accounted for according to IFRS 3 *Business combinations.*

Goodwill arising on acquisition is:

A carried at cost, with an annual impairment review.

B written off against reserves on acquisition.

C amortised over its useful life.

D revalued to fair value at each year end.

(2 marks)

1.9 IT has 300 items of product ABC2 in inventory at 31 March 2010. The items were found to be damaged by a water leak. The items can be repaired and repackaged for a cost of $1.50 per item. Once repackaged, the items can be sold at the normal price of $3.50 each.
The original cost of the items was $2.20 each. The replacement cost at 31 March 2010 is $2.75 each.

What value should IT put on the inventory of ABC2 in its statement of financial position at 31 March 2010?

A $600

B $660

C $810

D $825

(2 marks)

1.10 (i) CD is Z's main customer.

(ii) FE is a supplier of Z.

(iii) ST is Z's chairman of the board and a major shareholder of Z.

(iv) K is Z's banker and has provided an overdraft facility and a $1,000,000 loan.

(v) JT is the owner of a building entity that has just been awarded a large building contract by Z. JT is also the son of ST.

Which 2 of the above can be regarded as a related party of Z?

A (i) and (iii)

B (ii) and (iv)

C (iii) and (v)

D (iv) and (v)

(2 marks)

(Total for Question One = 20 marks)

Reminder

All answers to Section A must be written in your answer book.

Answers or notes to Section A written on the question paper will **not** be submitted for marking.

End of Section A

Section B starts on the opposite page

SECTION B – 30 MARKS

[Note: The indicative time for answering this section is 90 minutes]

ANSWER *ALL* SIX SUB-QUESTIONS IN THIS SECTION – 5 MARKS EACH

Question Two

(a)   ATOZ operates in several countries as follows:

- ATOZ was incorporated in country BCD many years ago. It has curtailed operations in BCD but still has its registered office in country BCD and carries out a small proportion (less than 10%) of its trade there.

- ATOZ buys most of its products and raw materials from country FGH.

- ATOZ generates most of its revenue in country NOP and all its senior management live there and hold all the management board meetings there.

Required:

(i)   Explain why determining corporate residence is important for corporate income tax.

(2 marks)

(ii)   Explain which country ATOZ will be deemed to be resident in for tax purposes.

(3 marks)

(Total for sub-question (a) = 5 marks)

(b)   WX operates a retail business in country X and is registered for VAT purposes.

During the last VAT period WX had the following transactions:

Purchases of materials and services, all at standard VAT rate, $130,000 excluding VAT.

Purchase of new machinery, $345,000, inclusive of VAT.

Sales of goods in the period, all inclusive of VAT where applicable, were:

Sales of goods subject to VAT at standard rate $230,000
Sales of goods subject to VAT at zero rate $115,000

TURN OVER

Assume you are WX's trainee management accountant and you have been asked to prepare the VAT return and calculate the net VAT due to/from the tax authorities at the end of the period.

Assume WX has no other transactions subject to VAT and that all VAT paid can be recovered.

Required:

(i)　Explain the difference between a single stage sales tax and VAT.

(2 marks)

(ii)　Calculate the net VAT due to/from WX at the end of the period.

(3 marks)

(Total for sub-question (b) = 5 marks)

(c)　Country K uses prescriptive accounting standards. Country K's standard on intangible assets has a list of intangible assets covered by the standard and an extensive list of items that are not allowed to be recognised as assets. RS has incurred expenditure on a new product that does not appear to be specifically listed as "not allowed" by the standard. RS's management want to classify the expenditure as an intangible non-current asset in RS's statement of financial position. They argue that the type of expenditure incurred is not listed in the accounting standard as being "not allowed" therefore it is allowed to be capitalised.

RS's auditors have pointed out that the expenditure is not listed as being "allowed" and therefore should not be capitalised.

Required:

Explain the possible advantages of having accounting standards based on principles rather than being prescriptive. Use the scenario above to illustrate your answer.

(Total for sub-question (c) = 5 marks)

(d)　BD is a well established double glazing business, manufacturing building extensions, doors and windows in its own manufacturing facility and installing them at customer properties.

BD's financial statements for the year ended 31 March 2009 showed the manufacturing facility and installation division as separate reportable segments.

On 1 March 2010, BD's management decided to sell its manufacturing facility and concentrate on the more profitable selling and installation side of the business.

At BD's accounting year end, 31 March 2010, BD had not found a buyer for its manufacturing facility and was continuing to run it as a going concern. The facility was available for immediate sale; the management were committed to the sale and were actively seeking a buyer. They were quite sure that the facility would be sold before 31 March 2011.

The manufacturing facility's fair value at 31st March 2010 was $2.8 million, comprising total assets with a fair value of $3.6 million and liabilities with a fair value of $0.8 million. BD's management accountant calculated that the manufacturing facility had incurred a loss for the year of $0.5 million before tax and the estimated cost of selling the manufacturing facility was $0.2 million.

Required:

Explain, with reasons, how BD should treat the manufacturing facility in its financial statements for the year ended 31 March 2010.

(Total for sub-question (d) = 5 marks)

(e)   L leases office space and a range of office furniture and equipment to businesses. On 1 April 2009 C acquired a lease for a fully furnished office space (office space plus office furniture and equipment) and a separate lease for a computer system from L.

The office space was a lease of part of a large building and the building had an expected life of 50 years. The lease was for 5 years with rental payable monthly. The first year was rent free. The $1,000 per month rental commenced on 1 April 2010.

The computer system lease was for 3 years, the expected useful life of the system was 3 years. The $15,000 per year lease rental was due annually in arrears commencing with 31 March 2010. The interest rate implicit in the lease is 12.5% and the cost of the leased asset at 1 April 2009 was $35,720. C depreciates all equipment on the straight line basis.

Under the terms of the computer system lease agreement C is responsible for insuring, servicing and repairing the computers.   However, L is responsible for insurance, maintenance and repair of the office.

C allocates the finance charge for finance leases using the actuarial method.

Required:

Explain the accounting treatment, required by international financial reporting standards, in the financial statements of C in respect of the two leases for the year ended 31 March 2010.

(Total for sub-question (e) = 5 marks)

TURN OVER

(f) PS issued 1,000,000 $1 cumulative, redeemable preferred shares on 1 April 2009. The shares were issued at a premium of 25% and pay a dividend of 4% per year.

The issue costs incurred were $60,000. The shares are redeemable for cash of $1.50 on 31 March 2019. The effective interest rate is 5.18%. Ignore all tax implications.

The management accountant of PS has extracted the following amounts from the preferred shares ledger account, for the year ended 31 March 2010:

Account - Non-current liability – Preferred shares

Net amount received on issue	$1,190,000
Finance cost @5.18%	$61,642
Less dividend paid	($40,000)
Balance at 31 March 2010	$1,211,642

Required:

(i) Explain the IAS 32 *Financial instruments – presentation* and IAS 39 *Financial instruments – recognition and measurement* requirements for the presentation and measurement of an issue of preferred shares.

(3 marks)

(ii) Using the information provided above, explain the amounts that PS should include for the preferred shares in its statement of comprehensive income and statement of financial position for the year ended 31 March 2010.

(2 marks)

(Total for sub-question (f) = 5 marks)

End of Section B

SECTION C – 50 MARKS

[Note: The indicative time for this section is 90 minutes]

ANSWER *BOTH* QUESTIONS IN THIS SECTION – 25 MARKS EACH

Question Three

XY's trial balance at 31 March 2010 is shown below:

	Notes	$000	$000
Administrative expenses		303	
Available for sale investments	(ii)	564	
Cash and cash equivalents		21	
Cash received on disposal of land			48
Cost of goods sold		908	
Distribution costs		176	
Equity dividend paid	(ix)	50	
Income tax	(iii)	12	
Inventory at 31 March 2010		76	
Land at cost – 31 March 2009	(v)	782	
Long term borrowings	(viii)		280
Ordinary Shares $1 each, fully paid at 31 March 2010	(vii)		500
Property, plant and equipment – at cost 31 March 2009	(vi)	630	
Provision for deferred tax at 31 March 2009	(iv)		19
Provision for property, plant and equipment depreciation at 31 March 2009	(vi)		378
Retained earnings at 31 March 2009			321
Revaluation reserve at 31 March 2009			160
Revenue			1,770
Share premium at 31 March 2010			200
Trade payables			56
Trade receivables		210	
		3,732	3,732

Additional information provided:

(i)   XY trades in country X.

(ii)   Available for sale investments are carried in the financial statements at market value. The market value of the available for sale investments at 31 March 2010 was $608,000. There were no purchases or sales of available for sale investments during the year.

(iii)   The income tax balance in the trial balance is a result of the underprovision of tax for the year ended 31 March 2009.

(iv)   The taxation due for the year ended 31 March 2010 is estimated at $96,000. The tax depreciation cumulative allowances at 31 March 2009 for property, plant and equipment were $453,000.

(v)   Land sold during the year had a book value of $39,000. The fair value of the remaining land at 31 March 2010 was $729,000.

(vi)   Property, plant and equipment is depreciated at 20% per annum straight line. Depreciation of property, plant and equipment is considered to be part of cost of sales. XY's policy is to charge a full year's depreciation in the year of acquisition and no depreciation in the year of disposal.

(vii)   XY issued 100,000 equity shares on 31 October 2009 at a premium of 50%. The cash received was correctly entered into the financial records and is included in the trial balance.

(viii) Long term borrowings consist of a loan taken out on 1 April 2009 at 5% interest per year. No loan interest has been paid at 31 March 2010.

(ix)   XY paid a final dividend of $50,000 for the year ended 31 March 2009.

Required:

(a)   Calculate the deferred tax amounts relating to property, plant and equipment, that are required to be included in XY's statement of comprehensive income for the year ended 31 March 2010 and its statement of financial position at that date. Ignore all other deferred tax implications.

(5 marks)

(b)   Prepare XY's statement of comprehensive income and statement of changes in equity for the year to 31 March 2010 and a statement of financial position at that date, in a form suitable for presentation to the shareholders and in accordance with the requirements of International Financial Reporting Standards.

(20 marks)

Notes to the financial statements are not required, but all workings must be clearly shown. Do not prepare a statement of accounting policies.

(Total for Question Three = 25 marks)

Question Four

The draft summarised Statements of Financial Position at 31 March 2010 for three entities, P, S and A are given below:

	P $000	P $000	S $000	S $000	A $000	A $000
Non-current Assets						
Property, plant and equipment		40,000		48,000		34,940
Investments:						
40,000 Ordinary shares in S at cost		60,000				
Loan to S		10,000				
8,000 Ordinary shares in A at cost		13,000				
		123,000		48,000		34,940
Current Assets						
Inventory	8,000		12,000		8,693	
Current a/c with S	8,000		0		0	
Trade receivables	17,000		11,000		10,106	
Cash and cash equivalents	1,000		3,000		3,033	
		34,000		26,000		21,832
Total Assets		157,000		74,000		56,772
Equity and Liabilities						
Equity shares of $1 each		100,000		40,000		20,000
Retained earnings		21,000		13,000		7,800
		121,000		53,000		27,800
Non-current liabilities						
Borrowings		26,000		10,000		10,000
Current liabilities						
Trade payables	10,000		5,000		18,972	
Current a/c with P	0		6,000		0	
		10,000		11,000		18,972
Total Equity and Liabilities		157,000		74,000		56,772

Additional information:

(i)   P's acquired all of S's equity shares on 1 April 2009 for $60,000,000 when S's retained earnings were $6,400,000. P also advanced S a ten year loan of $10,000,000 on 1 April 2009.

(ii)   The fair value of S's property, plant and equipment on 1 April 2009 exceeded its book value by $1,000,000. The excess of fair value over book value was attributed to buildings owned by S. At the date of acquisition these buildings had a remaining useful life of 20 years. P's accounting policy is to depreciate buildings using the straight line basis.

(iii)   At 31 March 2010 $250,000 loan interest was due and had not been paid. Both P and S had accrued this amount at the year end.

(iv)   P purchased 8,000,000 of A's equity shares on 1 April 2009 for $13,000,000 when A's retained earnings were $21,000,000. P exercises significant influence over all aspects of A's strategic and operational decisions.

(v)   S posted a cheque to P for $2,000,000 on 30 March 2010 which did not arrive until 7 April 2010.

(vi)   No dividends are proposed by any of the entities.

(vii)   P occasionally trades with S. In March 2010 P sold S goods for $4,000,000.
         P uses a mark up of one third on cost. On 31 March 2010 all the goods were
         included in S's closing inventory and the invoice for the goods was still
         outstanding.

(viii)   P's directors do not want to consolidate A. They argue that they do not
         control A, therefore it does not need to be consolidated. They insist that A
         should appear in the consolidated statement of financial position at cost of
         $13,000,000.

Required:

(a)   Draft a response that explains to P's directors the correct treatment of A in
       the consolidated financial statements. Include comments on any ethical
       issues involved.

                                                                          (5 marks)

(b)   Prepare a Consolidated Statement of Financial Position for the P Group of entities
       as at 31 March 2010, in accordance with the requirements of International
       Financial Reporting Standards.

                                                                         (20 marks)

Notes to the financial statements are not required but all workings must be shown.

                                                      (Total for Question Four = 25 marks)

End of Question Paper

MATHS TABLES AND FORMULAE

Present value table

Present value of $1, that is $(1 + r)^{-n}$ where r = interest rate; n = number of periods until payment or receipt.

Periods (n)	Interest rates (r)									
	1%	2%	3%	4%	5%	6%	7%	8%	9%	10%
1	0.990	0.980	0.971	0.962	0.952	0.943	0.935	0.926	0.917	0.909
2	0.980	0.961	0.943	0.925	0.907	0.890	0.873	0.857	0.842	0.826
3	0.971	0.942	0.915	0.889	0.864	0.840	0.816	0.794	0.772	0.751
4	0.961	0.924	0.888	0.855	0.823	0.792	0.763	0.735	0.708	0.683
5	0.951	0.906	0.863	0.822	0.784	0.747	0.713	0.681	0.650	0.621
6	0.942	0.888	0.837	0.790	0.746	0.705	0.666	0.630	0.596	0.564
7	0.933	0.871	0.813	0.760	0.711	0.665	0.623	0.583	0.547	0.513
8	0.923	0.853	0.789	0.731	0.677	0.627	0.582	0.540	0.502	0.467
9	0.914	0.837	0.766	0.703	0.645	0.592	0.544	0.500	0.460	0.424
10	0.905	0.820	0.744	0.676	0.614	0.558	0.508	0.463	0.422	0.386
11	0.896	0.804	0.722	0.650	0.585	0.527	0.475	0.429	0.388	0.350
12	0.887	0.788	0.701	0.625	0.557	0.497	0.444	0.397	0.356	0.319
13	0.879	0.773	0.681	0.601	0.530	0.469	0.415	0.368	0.326	0.290
14	0.870	0.758	0.661	0.577	0.505	0.442	0.388	0.340	0.299	0.263
15	0.861	0.743	0.642	0.555	0.481	0.417	0.362	0.315	0.275	0.239
16	0.853	0.728	0.623	0.534	0.458	0.394	0.339	0.292	0.252	0.218
17	0.844	0.714	0.605	0.513	0.436	0.371	0.317	0.270	0.231	0.198
18	0.836	0.700	0.587	0.494	0.416	0.350	0.296	0.250	0.212	0.180
19	0.828	0.686	0.570	0.475	0.396	0.331	0.277	0.232	0.194	0.164
20	0.820	0.673	0.554	0.456	0.377	0.312	0.258	0.215	0.178	0.149

Periods (n)	Interest rates (r)									
	11%	12%	13%	14%	15%	16%	17%	18%	19%	20%
1	0.901	0.893	0.885	0.877	0.870	0.862	0.855	0.847	0.840	0.833
2	0.812	0.797	0.783	0.769	0.756	0.743	0.731	0.718	0.706	0.694
3	0.731	0.712	0.693	0.675	0.658	0.641	0.624	0.609	0.593	0.579
4	0.659	0.636	0.613	0.592	0.572	0.552	0.534	0.516	0.499	0.482
5	0.593	0.567	0.543	0.519	0.497	0.476	0.456	0.437	0.419	0.402
6	0.535	0.507	0.480	0.456	0.432	0.410	0.390	0.370	0.352	0.335
7	0.482	0.452	0.425	0.400	0.376	0.354	0.333	0.314	0.296	0.279
8	0.434	0.404	0.376	0.351	0.327	0.305	0.285	0.266	0.249	0.233
9	0.391	0.361	0.333	0.308	0.284	0.263	0.243	0.225	0.209	0.194
10	0.352	0.322	0.295	0.270	0.247	0.227	0.208	0.191	0.176	0.162
11	0.317	0.287	0.261	0.237	0.215	0.195	0.178	0.162	0.148	0.135
12	0.286	0.257	0.231	0.208	0.187	0.168	0.152	0.137	0.124	0.112
13	0.258	0.229	0.204	0.182	0.163	0.145	0.130	0.116	0.104	0.093
14	0.232	0.205	0.181	0.160	0.141	0.125	0.111	0.099	0.088	0.078
15	0.209	0.183	0.160	0.140	0.123	0.108	0.095	0.084	0.079	0.065
16	0.188	0.163	0.141	0.123	0.107	0.093	0.081	0.071	0.062	0.054
17	0.170	0.146	0.125	0.108	0.093	0.080	0.069	0.060	0.052	0.045
18	0.153	0.130	0.111	0.095	0.081	0.069	0.059	0.051	0.044	0.038
19	0.138	0.116	0.098	0.083	0.070	0.060	0.051	0.043	0.037	0.031
20	0.124	0.104	0.087	0.073	0.061	0.051	0.043	0.037	0.031	0.026

Cumulative present value of $1 per annum, Receivable or Payable at the end of each year for

n years $\quad \frac{1-(1+r)^{-n}}{r}$

Periods	Interest rates (r)									
(n)	1%	2%	3%	4%	5%	6%	7%	8%	9%	10%
1	0.990	0.980	0.971	0.962	0.952	0.943	0.935	0.926	0.917	0.909
2	1.970	1.942	1.913	1.886	1.859	1.833	1.808	1.783	1.759	1.736
3	2.941	2.884	2.829	2.775	2.723	2.673	2.624	2.577	2.531	2.487
4	3.902	3.808	3.717	3.630	3.546	3.465	3.387	3.312	3.240	3.170
5	4.853	4.713	4.580	4.452	4.329	4.212	4.100	3.993	3.890	3.791
6	5.795	5.601	5.417	5.242	5.076	4.917	4.767	4.623	4.486	4.355
7	6.728	6.472	6.230	6.002	5.786	5.582	5.389	5.206	5.033	4.868
8	7.652	7.325	7.020	6.733	6.463	6.210	5.971	5.747	5.535	5.335
9	8.566	8.162	7.786	7.435	7.108	6.802	6.515	6.247	5.995	5.759
10	9.471	8.983	8.530	8.111	7.722	7.360	7.024	6.710	6.418	6.145
11	10.368	9.787	9.253	8.760	8.306	7.887	7.499	7.139	6.805	6.495
12	11.255	10.575	9.954	9.385	8.863	8.384	7.943	7.536	7.161	6.814
13	12.134	11.348	10.635	9.986	9.394	8.853	8.358	7.904	7.487	7.103
14	13.004	12.106	11.296	10.563	9.899	9.295	8.745	8.244	7.786	7.367
15	13.865	12.849	11.938	11.118	10.380	9.712	9.108	8.559	8.061	7.606
16	14.718	13.578	12.561	11.652	10.838	10.106	9.447	8.851	8.313	7.824
17	15.562	14.292	13.166	12.166	11.274	10.477	9.763	9.122	8.544	8.022
18	16.398	14.992	13.754	12.659	11.690	10.828	10.059	9.372	8.756	8.201
19	17.226	15.679	14.324	13.134	12.085	11.158	10.336	9.604	8.950	8.365
20	18.046	16.351	14.878	13.590	12.462	11.470	10.594	9.818	9.129	8.514

Periods	Interest rates (r)									
(n)	11%	12%	13%	14%	15%	16%	17%	18%	19%	20%
1	0.901	0.893	0.885	0.877	0.870	0.862	0.855	0.847	0.840	0.833
2	1.713	1.690	1.668	1.647	1.626	1.605	1.585	1.566	1.547	1.528
3	2.444	2.402	2.361	2.322	2.283	2.246	2.210	2.174	2.140	2.106
4	3.102	3.037	2.974	2.914	2.855	2.798	2.743	2.690	2.639	2.589
5	3.696	3.605	3.517	3.433	3.352	3.274	3.199	3.127	3.058	2.991
6	4.231	4.111	3.998	3.889	3.784	3.685	3.589	3.498	3.410	3.326
7	4.712	4.564	4.423	4.288	4.160	4.039	3.922	3.812	3.706	3.605
8	5.146	4.968	4.799	4.639	4.487	4.344	4.207	4.078	3.954	3.837
9	5.537	5.328	5.132	4.946	4.772	4.607	4.451	4.303	4.163	4.031
10	5.889	5.650	5.426	5.216	5.019	4.833	4.659	4.494	4.339	4.192
11	6.207	5.938	5.687	5.453	5.234	5.029	4.836	4.656	4.486	4.327
12	6.492	6.194	5.918	5.660	5.421	5.197	4.988	7.793	4.611	4.439
13	6.750	6.424	6.122	5.842	5.583	5.342	5.118	4.910	4.715	4.533
14	6.982	6.628	6.302	6.002	5.724	5.468	5.229	5.008	4.802	4.611
15	7.191	6.811	6.462	6.142	5.847	5.575	5.324	5.092	4.876	4.675
16	7.379	6.974	6.604	6.265	5.954	5.668	5.405	5.162	4.938	4.730
17	7.549	7.120	6.729	6.373	6.047	5.749	5.475	5.222	4.990	4.775
18	7.702	7.250	6.840	6.467	6.128	5.818	5.534	5.273	5.033	4.812
19	7.839	7.366	6.938	6.550	6.198	5.877	5.584	5.316	5.070	4.843
20	7.963	7.469	7.025	6.623	6.259	5.929	5.628	5.353	5.101	4.870

Formulae

Annuity

Present value of an annuity of $1 per annum, receivable or payable for n years, commencing in one year, discounted at r% per annum:

$$PV = \frac{1}{r}\left[1 - \frac{1}{[1+r]^n}\right]$$

Perpetuity

Present value of $1 per annum, payable or receivable in perpetuity, commencing in one year, discounted at r% per annum:

$$PV = \frac{1}{r}$$

LIST OF VERBS USED IN THE QUESTION REQUIREMENTS

A list of the learning objectives and verbs that appear in the syllabus and in the question requirements for each question in this paper.

It is important that you answer the question according to the definition of the verb.

LEARNING OBJECTIVE	VERBS USED	DEFINITION
Level 1 - KNOWLEDGE What you are expected to know.	List State Define	Make a list of Express, fully or clearly, the details/facts of Give the exact meaning of
Level 2 - COMPREHENSION What you are expected to understand.	Describe Distinguish Explain Identify Illustrate	Communicate the key features Highlight the differences between Make clear or intelligible/State the meaning or purpose of Recognise, establish or select after consideration Use an example to describe or explain something
Level 3 - APPLICATION How you are expected to apply your knowledge.	Apply Calculate/compute Demonstrate Prepare Reconcile Solve Tabulate	Put to practical use Ascertain or reckon mathematically Prove with certainty or to exhibit by practical means Make or get ready for use Make or prove consistent/compatible Find an answer to Arrange in a table
Level 4 - ANALYSIS How are you expected to analyse the detail of what you have learned.	Analyse Categorise Compare and contrast Construct Discuss Interpret Prioritise Produce	Examine in detail the structure of Place into a defined class or division Show the similarities and/or differences between Build up or compile Examine in detail by argument Translate into intelligible or familiar terms Place in order of priority or sequence for action Create or bring into existence
Level 5 - EVALUATION How are you expected to use your learning to evaluate, make decisions or recommendations.	Advise Evaluate Recommend	Counsel, inform or notify Appraise or assess the value of Propose a course of action

Financial Pillar

Operational Level Paper

F1 – Financial Operations

Specimen Paper

Thursday Morning Session

The Examiner's Answers – Specimen Paper

F1 - Financial Operations

SECTION A

Answers to Question One

1.1   D

1.2

	$
Accounting profit	72,000
Add accounting depreciation	12,000
Add entertaining costs	15,000
Less tax depreciation	(10,000)*
	89,000
Taxed at 25%	22,250

Answer therefore   **D**

*$40,000 x 25% = $10,000

1.3   B

1.4   C

1.5   Comparability and understandability

1.6   Integrity and confidentiality

1.7   B

1.8   A

1.9   Cost $2.20
        Selling price $3.50
        Repair costs $1.50
        Net realisable value $2.00

Use lower of cost and net realisable value = $2.00 x 300 units = $600
Therefore answer is   A

1.10   C

SECTION B

Answer to Question Two

Requirement (a)

(i)   It is important to determine corporate residence as corporate income tax is usually a residence-based tax. Whether corporate income tax will be charged depends on the residence, for tax purposes, of any particular entity.

(ii)   The OECD model tax convention provides that an entities status shall be determined as follows:

   a) it shall be deemed to be a resident only of the State in which its place of effective management is situated;

   b) if the State in which its place of effective management is situated cannot be determined or if its place of effective management is in neither State, it shall be deemed to be a resident only of the State with which its economic relations are closer;

   c) if the State with which its economic relations are closer cannot be determined, it shall be deemed to be a resident of the State from the laws of which it derives its legal status.

ATOZ will be deemed to be resident in country NOP as that is where its place of effective management is.

Requirement (b)

(i)   Single-stage sales taxes apply at one level of the production/distribution chain only; they can be applied to any one of the following levels:

   • the manufacturing level;

   • the wholesale level;

   • the retail level.

Tax paid by entities is not recoverable.

VAT charges tax at every level, but tax paid at one level can usually be recovered by deducting it from tax collected at the next level. The ultimate consumer bears all the tax.

(ii)

Outputs:	Sale excluding VAT	VAT
	$	$
Standard rate	200,000	30,000
Zero rate	115,000	0
Total		30,000
Inputs		
Materials and services	130,000	19,500
New machinery	300,000	45,000
		64,500
Amount due to be refunded by tax authority		34,500

Requirement (c)

The possible advantages of having accounting standards based on principles rather than being prescriptive include:

- It will be harder to construct ways of avoiding the requirements of individual standards, for example, in country K the prescriptive standard sets out definitions of what is allowed and what is not allowed, this causes problems if some items are not specified, such as in RS's case. Whereas if the standard sets out general principles, it is much harder to avoid the standard's requirements as what is included will be defined by applying the principle.

- If a prescriptive standard lists items or specifies quantities they may go out of date fairly quickly and need to be regularly updated. This may be the problem with RS, the expenditure incurred may not have been required when the standard was agreed. If principles based standards are used they do not go out of date unless a principle is changed.

- If an actual value is specified in a standard, it may be possible for some entities to construct various means of avoiding the application of that requirement. If a general principle is specified it will apply no matter what value is put on it

- With principle based standards the requirements in certain situations will need to be applied using professional judgement, which can help ensure that the correct application is used. Whereas a prescriptive standard would require a certain treatment to be used, regardless of the situation, which could lead to similar items being treated the same way even if the circumstances are different.

- Principles-based GAAP should ensure that the spirit of the regulations are adhered to, whereas the prescriptive system is more likely to lead to the letter of the law being followed rather than the spirit.

Requirement (d)

The manufacturing facility has been shown as a separate reportable operating segment according to IFRS 8. This means that it must be a separate operating unit whose operating results are regularly reviewed by BD's chief operating decision maker. This implies that there is discrete financial information available for the manufacturing facility's operations. It will therefore meet the IFRS 5 definition of a discontinued operation, a component of an entity classified as held for sale and is part of a single plan to dispose of a separate major line of business.

The manufacturing facility loss of $0.5 million will be shown as one amount as a discontinued operation on the statement of comprehensive income, at the end of the income statement section, after profit from continuing activities and before other comprehensive income. The detailed breakdown of the loss will be given in the notes to the statement of comprehensive income.

The manufacturing facility has not been disposed of by the year end, so it will be classified as a "non-current asset held for sale". Non-current assets held for sale are valued in the statement of financial position at fair value less the cost to sell. The assets and liabilities have to be shown separately, so the assets of $3.4 million (assets $3.6 million less cost to sell $0.2 million) will be shown after current assets, with the heading non-current assets held for sale. The liabilities of $0.8 million will be shown under current liabilities and headed "liabilities directly associated with non-current assets classified as held for sale".

Requirement (e)

Office Space - *Operating lease*
Rentals due: Total payments 4 years at $1,000x12 = £48,000
Spread over 5 years = $48,000/5 = $9,600 p.a.

Income statement for year to 31 March 2010 (extract)
Administrative expenses - Office rentals $9,600

Statement of financial position as at 31 March 2010 (extract)
Current liability - Accrued rentals $9,600

Computer System
Finance Charge: Allocate finance charge using actuarial method at 12.5% interest paid in arrears.

Depreciate asset using normal accounting policy.

Payment date	Opening bal	Income statement Finance charge	Paid	Balance at year end
31.03.10	35720	4465	-15000	25185
31.03.11	25185	3148	-15000	13333
31.03.12	13333	1667	-15000	0

Summary of accounting entries:
Income statement for year ended 31.03.10 (extract)

	£
Finance charges	4,465
Depreciation	11,907

Depreciation 35720/3 = 11,907

Statement of Financial Position (extract)
Non-current assets

Leased equipment under finance leases at cost	35,720
Accounting depreciation	11,907
NBV	23,813
Non-current liabilities	
Obligations under finance leases	13,333
Current liabilities	
Obligations under finance leases	11,852

Requirement (f)

(i) IAS 32 requires the particular rights attaching to a preference share to be analysed to determine whether it exhibits the fundamental characteristic of a financial liability. There are a number of characteristics that will indicate that there is an obligation to transfer financial assets to the holder of the share, in each case the preferred share will need to be classified as debt rather than equity.

If the terms of issue provide for mandatory redemption for cash the preferred shares will be treated as liabilities.
If the preference shares are non-redeemable, the appropriate classification is based on an assessment of the substance of the contractual arrangements and the definitions of a financial liability and equity instrument. For example if the preferred shares are cumulative it means that a dividend will always eventually have to be paid and is therefore not discretionary. Therefore the preferred shares are classified as debt.

(ii) PS's shares provide for a cash redemption and are therefore classified as debt. In the statement of financial position the preferred shares will be shown under non-current liabilities. The dividend paid on the preferred shares will be treated as finance cost in the income statement.

PS Extracts from financial statements:

PS Statement of comprehensive income for year ended 31 March 2010 (extract)
Finance expense $61,642

PS Statement of financial position as at 31 March 2010 (extract)
Non-current liabilities
Preferred shares $1,211,642

SECTION C

Question Three

Requirement (a)

	Balance at 31 March 2009 $000		Balance at 31 March 2010 $000		Difference = Change in Year $000
	$000		$000		
Property, plant and equipment					
Accounting book value					
Cost	630		630		
Depreciation	378		504		
Net book value		252		126	
Tax written down value					
Cost	630		630		
Tax depreciation	453		497		
		177		133	
Cumulative difference		75		(7)	(82)
Deferred tax @ 25%		18.75		(1.75)	(20.50)
Rounded		19		(2)	(21)

Financial statements

Statement of comprehensive income (extract)

	$000
Income tax expense – deferred tax	(21)

Statement of financial position (extract)

Current assets – deferred tax	2

Requirement (b)

XY - Statement of comprehensive income for the year ended 31 March 2010

Continuing Operations		$000
Revenue		1,770
Cost of sales		(1,025)
Gross Profit		745
Administrative expenses	(317)	
Distribution costs	(176)	(493)
Profit from operations		252
Finance cost		(14)
Profit before tax		238
Income tax expense (W5)		(87)
Profit for the period from continuing operations		151
Other Comprehensive Income		
Gain on fair value adjustment of available for sale investments		44
Profit for the year		195

XY Statement of Financial Position at 31 March 2010

$000

Non-current assets *(Net book value)*

Land	729	
Property, plant and equipment	126	
Available for sale investments	608	1,463

Current assets

Inventory	76	
Trade receivables	210	
Deferred tax asset	2	
Cash and cash equivalents	21	309
Total assets		1,772

Equity and liabilities

Equity

Share capital		500
Share premium	200	
Revaluation reserve	204	404
Accumulated profits		422
Total equity		1,326

Non-current liabilities

Long term borrowings	280	
Total non-current liabilities		280

Current liabilities

Trade payables	56	
Tax payable	96	
Interest payable	14	
Total current liabilities		166
Total equity and liabilities		1,772

XY – Statement of changes in equity for the year ended 31 March 2010

	Equity shares $000	Share premium	Revaluation Reserve $000	Accumulated profits $000	Total $000
Balance at 1 April 2009	400	150	160	321	1,031
New share issue	100	50			150
Statement of comprehensive income			44	151	195
Dividend paid				(50)	
					(50)
Balance at 31 March 2010	500	200	204	422	1,326

Workings (All figures in $000)

(W1) Land Impairment

Land

Balance b/fwd	782
Disposal	(39)
	743
Fair value c/f	729
Impairment	(14)

(W2) Depreciation

Property, plant and equipment

Depreciation = 630 x 20% = 126

(W3) Gain on disposal

Cost	39
Cash received	48
Gain on disposal	9

(W4) Cost of sales

Trial balance	908
Gain on disposal (W3)	(9)
Depreciation – property, plant and equipment (W2)	126
	1,025

(W5) Administrative Expenses

Per trail balance	303
Land - impairment	14
	317

(W6) Taxation expense

Year	96
Last year under-estimate	12
Reduction in deferred tax (see part (a))	(21)
	87

(W7) Interest due

Accrued interest = 280 x 5% = 14

Question Four

Requirement (a)

Draft

To   P's Directors

From   Management Accountant

Treatment of A in the P Group Consolidated Financial Statements

Entities should be consolidated according to the requirements of International Financial Reporting Standards and not according to whether the entity makes a profit or loss during the year.

P owns 40% of the equity shares in A and exercises significant influence over all aspects of A's strategic and operational decisions.

P does not control A as it only holds 40% of the shares/votes. P would need >50% of the equity shares to be able to exercise control over A. The argument that A does not need to be consolidated is partially correct, A cannot be consolidated as a subsidiary. Instead A will need to be consolidated as an associated entity using the equity method, as P exercises significant influence over all aspects of A's strategic and operational decisions.

Equity accounting recognises the post acquisition profits and losses of the associated entity and includes the group share instead of simply recording dividends received from the associated entity.

To treat A as a simple investment at cost could be construed as unethical as it would not follow the requirements of international financial reporting standards. The CIMA Code of Ethics for Professional Accountants requires an accountant to have integrity. Integrity implies fair dealing and truthfulness. A professional accountant should not be associated with financial reports that they believe omits or obscures information required to be included where such omission or obscurity would be misleading. Treating A as an investment would obscure the full extent of P's commitment to its associate and could therefore be unethical. We cannot therefore allow A to be treated as an investment.

Requirement (b)

Group holdings:
P in S
40,000,000/40,000,000 = 100% Treat as wholly owned subsidiary

P in A
8,000,000/20,000,000 = 40% Treat as an associate

(i) Fair value of net assets of S at acquisition

	$000
Equity Shares	40,000
Retained earnings	6,400
Fair value adjustment	1,000
	47,400

The property has a useful life of 20 years, excess depreciation is therefore $1,000,000/20 = $50,000.

	Dr. $000	Cr. $000
Consolidated retained profits	50	
Consolidated property, plant and equipment		50

(ii) Goodwill - S

	$000
Cost	60,000
Fair value of net assets acquired (100%)	47,400
Goodwill	12,600

(iii) Investment in associate -A

	$000
Cost	13,000
Add group share of post acquisition losses (7,800 – 21,000) x 40%=	(5,280)
Investment at 31 March 2010	7,720

(iv) Current accounts

	Dr. $000	Cr. $000
P receives a cheque from S		
Cash and bank	2,000	
Current account with S		2,000
Cancel current accounts on consolidation		
Current account with P	6,000	
Current account with S		6,000

(v) Intra-group trading

Mark up on cost 33⅓% = 25% margin on selling price.
Selling price $4,000,000; unrealised profit = $4,000,000 x 25% = $1,000,000

	Dr. $000	Cr. $000
Consolidated retained profits	1,000	
Consolidated current assets – inventory		1,000

(vi) Cancellation of loan to S

	Dr. $000	Cr. $000
Loan to S		10,000
Non-current liabilities – Borrowings	10,000	
Loan interest		
Trade payables	250	
Trade receivables		250

(vii) Consolidated Retained Earnings

	$000
Balance P	21,000
S – group share of post acquisition profits (13,000 – 6,400)	6,600
Associate – A, group share of post acquisition profits (iii)	(5,280)
Excess depreciation on fair value increase of property	(50)
Cancel unrealised profit in inventory (v)	(1,000)
	21,270

P Group - Consolidated Statement of Financial Position as at 31 March 2010

		$000
Non-Current Assets		
Goodwill		12,600
Property, plant and equipment		
(40,000+48,000+1,000-50)		88,950
Investment in associate (iii)		7,720
		109,270
Current Assets		
Inventory (8,000+12,000-1,000)		19,000
Trade receivables (17,000+11,000-250)		27,750
Cash and bank (1,000+3,000+2,000)	6,000	
		162,020
Equity and Reserves		
Ordinary Shares		100,000
Retained Earnings (vii)		21,270
		121,270
Non-current liabilities		
Borrowings (26,000+10,000-10,000)	26,000	
Current Liabilities		
Trade payables (10,000+5,000-250)	14,750	
		162,020

© The Chartered Institute of Management Accountants 2009

Index

Index

Index